T0305282

Hedge Fund Analysis

Founded in 1807, John Wiley & Sons is the oldest independent publishing company in the United States. With offices in North America, Europe, Australia, and Asia, Wiley is globally committed to developing and marketing print and electronic products and services for our customers' professional and personal knowledge and understanding.

The Wiley Finance series contains books written specifically for finance and investment professionals as well as sophisticated individual investors and their financial advisors. Book topics range from portfolio management to e-commerce, risk management, financial engineering, valuation and financial instrument analysis, as well as much more.

For a list of available titles, visit our Web site at www.WileyFinance.com.

Hedge Fund Analysis

*An In-Depth Guide to Evaluating Return
Potential and Assessing Risks*

FRANK J. TRAVERS, CFA

WILEY

John Wiley & Sons, Inc.

Published by John Wiley & Sons, Inc., Hoboken, New Jersey.
Published simultaneously in Canada.

For general information on our other products and services or for technical support, please contact our Customer Care Department within the United States at (800) 762-2974, outside the United States at (317) 572-3993, or fax (317) 572-4002.

Wiley also publishes its books in a variety of electronic formats. Some content that appears in print may not be available in electronic books. For more information about Wiley products, visit our Web site at www.wiley.com.

Library of Congress Cataloging-in-Publication Data:

Travers, Frank J.
  Hedge fund analysis : an in-depth guide to evaluating return potential and assessing risks / Frank J. Travers. – 1st ed.
      p. cm. – (Wiley finance ; 778)
   Includes index.
    ISBN 978-1-118-17546-0; ISBN 978-1-118-22710-7 (ebk); ISBN 978-1-118-23756-4 (ebk); ISBN 978-1-118-26474-4 (ebk)
   1. Hedge funds. 2. Risk management. I. Title.
   HG4530.T695 2012
   332.64'524 –dc23   2012010597

10 9 8 7 6 5 4 3 2 1

I dedicate this book to my wife Tara and my children, Brendan, Sean, and Lauren.
My writing skills are insufficient to properly describe how much I love and am inspired by each of you. Thank you for bringing such joy to my life.

Contents

Introduction   xi

PART ONE

Background

CHAPTER 1
Hedge Fund History   3

    So Who Invented the Hedge Fund?   4
    The Samurai   4
    The Academic   5
    The Legend   14
    The Innovator   17

CHAPTER 2
Hedge Fund Asset Class   29

    Definition   29
    Hedge Fund Structure   31
    Hedge Fund Strategies   32
    Advantages of Allocating to Hedge Funds   43
    Hedge Fund Size and Age Impacts Performance   52

PART TWO

Hedge Fund Due Diligence

CHAPTER 3
Due Diligence Process   57

    Key Areas of Focus within Each Component of Due Diligence   57
    The Due Diligence Process Highlighted in This Book   60

Putting It All Together   67
Some Initial Thoughts   70

CHAPTER 4
Initial Data Collection   **77**

Data Collection   78
Due Diligence Questionnaire (DDQ)   80
Fictional Capital Management   80
Other Materials   106
Further Analysis   108
13F Analysis   116
Hedge Fund Journal   119

CHAPTER 5
Initial Interview   **121**

Initial Call or Meeting   121
Phone Interviews   122
Meeting Notes   139

CHAPTER 6
Quantitative Analysis   **145**

Performance Measures   146
Absolute Return Measures   146
Absolute Risk Measures   154
Regression-Based Statistics   164
Peer Group Analysis   168

CHAPTER 7
Portfolio Analysis   **173**

Attribution Analysis   174
Fundamental Analysis   189
Evaluating Portfolio Data   193

CHAPTER 8
Onsite Interviews   **217**

Onsite Meeting Strategies   219
One-on-One Meetings   219
Meeting with More Than One Person   222

Different Perspectives 223
Meeting Notes 224
Onsite Interviews at Fictional Capital Management (FCM) 228

CHAPTER 9
Operational Due Diligence 259

Case Study: Bayou Fund 259
Definition 261
Importance of Operational Due Diligence 263
Categorization of Operational Due Diligence 267
Interview with FCM Operational Staff 301

CHAPTER 10
Risk Due Diligence 309

Graphical Depiction of Hedge Fund Risks 312
Risk Due Diligence 314
Factor Decomposition Analysis 330
Interview with FCM Risk Manager 333

CHAPTER 11
Reference and Background Checks 339

Onlist and Offlist References 340
Internet and Social Media 341
Contacting References 343
Problematic References 346
Whose References Should You Check? 349
How Many Reference Calls Are Enough? 350
Background Checks 352
Summary of Reference Calls for FCM 353

CHAPTER 12
Hedge Fund Scoring Model and Decision Making 357

Hedge Fund Scoring Model 358
Putting It All Together 374

About the Author 379

Index 381

Introduction

"An investment in knowledge pays the best interest."

Benjamin Franklin

It is estimated that there are somewhere between 8,000 and 10,000 hedge funds in existence today. This leads to a number of questions.

- How can we screen through this list to come up with a more manageable universe?
- Why do we hire certain hedge fund managers and not others?
- What factors go into hiring and firing decisions?
- How do we evaluate and assess a portfolio manager's or team's investment edge?
- What are the best questions to ask hedge fund managers in order to get a true sense of their skill set and how they may relate to other investments in your portfolio?
- How can we accurately evaluate hedge fund risk and what kind of information do we need from the funds we hire to effectively monitor changes?
- What are the biggest mistakes often made when analyzing hedge funds and, more importantly, how can we avoid them?

Effective hedge fund analysis requires that we answer these and hundreds of other questions covering all aspects of the hedge fund business including the underlying investment strategy, back office, administration, legal, operations, financial, marketing, client service, transparency, reporting, and so forth.

However, the process is dynamic and involves a combination of art and science to efficiently navigate the shifting waters. Have a look at Figure I.1.

This three-dimensional image is known as a "Necker's cube." It is named after Swiss crystallographer Louis Alber Necker, who discovered it in 1832.

Necker's Cube

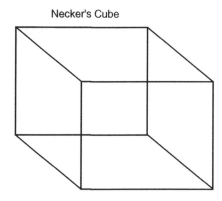

FIGURE I.1   Necker's Cube

It is often used as a means of illustrating shifting perspectives. If you look at the image for a few seconds, you will quickly notice that it is a perfectly orthogonal cube that allows for two opposing interpretations of three-dimensionality. The images in Figure I.2 illustrate the two opposing views.

The illusion created by the Necker's cube is somewhat analogous to how we can interpret information gleaned in the due diligence process in many different ways ... with each being correct.

Hedge fund analysis can be conducted in many different ways and can employ a myriad of models and techniques, but the basic elements of the

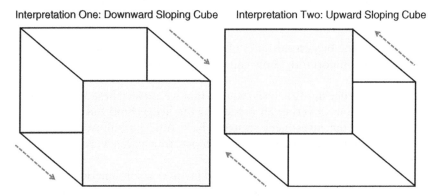

FIGURE I.2   Interpretation One: Downward Sloping Cube vs. Interpretation Two: Upward Sloping Cube

process are always the same. This book will lay out a specific method of analyzing hedge funds.

MY OBJECTIVE IN WRITING THIS BOOK

When I graduated from college in late 1989, I thought I had acquired a fair amount of knowledge about the financial world and the investment business in particular. I started my first job all bright-eyed and bushy-tailed and expected to blaze a quick path to greatness. I expected to apply all the economic and financial theory I had mastered in school to my position as an analyst at a fund of funds company.

Needless to say, I was shocked at just how little I knew. So I did what came naturally...I went to the library and bookstores to find books that would provide some instruction on manager due diligence techniques. Surprise number two—there were none. I had to learn things the hard way.

A decade later, I had moved up through the ranks and had become a portfolio manager at a fund of funds organization, and one of my junior analysts asked me if I knew of any books that they could read on the topic of manager due diligence. I was sure that several books had been written since I had last looked, but a few Internet searches later concluded that there were still none. I decided then and there that I would try my hand at writing and planned a two-book series. The first would focus on the analytical techniques used to review traditional (long-only and long-biased) managers and the second would focus on alternative investments.

I was fortunate to find a great publisher in Wiley & Sons and published the first book, titled *Investment Manager Analysis*, in 2004. I planned on writing the follow-up immediately but life kind of got in the way. The market collapse in 2008 was a slap to the face of the hedge fund industry. Many hedge fund managers strayed from their stated strategies, and Madoff's colossal fraud brought the topic of hedge fund due diligence to the forefront.

While a great many books have been written about hedge funds and about analytical techniques, I felt that none detailed a start-to-finish process that incorporated all aspects of the process, including the following:

Components of Hedge Fund Due Diligence

- Operational
- Risk management
- Investment
- Accounting/financial
- Legal

THE STRUCTURE OF THE BOOK

This book is divided into two parts. The first part provides background information, including the history of the asset class, a discussion of its pros and cons, and finally how hedge funds fit in diversified institutional portfolios. The second part details a template for hedge fund due diligence with chapters dedicated to each aspect of the process.

Part One: Background

- Hedge fund history
- Growth of the industry
- Pros and cons
- How hedge funds can fit in diversified portfolios

Part Two: Hedge Fund Due Diligence

- Process template
- Hedge fund universe and filtering
- Initial information request
- The initial interview
- Performance analysis
- Investment & portfolio analysis
- Risk analysis
- Operational analysis
- Accounting/financial analysis
- Legal analysis
- Detailed face-to-face interviews
- Primer on interviewing skills
- Quantitative due diligence modelling
- Putting it all together

Part Two details a methodical process which the reader can use to analyze hedge fund managers. To illustrate how each step in the process works, I have created a fictional manager (Fictional Capital Management or "FCM") and take the reader through each step in the process, peeling back the onion one layer at a time so that we can ultimately make an informed and intelligent investment decision.

Since I am writing this book for the practitioner and for anyone else looking to evaluate and understand how hedge funds work, my writing style will lean more toward the practical than the academic. There are a great many books and scholarly papers that explain the nitty-gritty of the investment world and I will defer to them as source material for understanding how a swap works or how to employ Beysian methods in quantitative risk management. This book will assume a level of comfort with global investing, financial instruments, and how the markets work. It is my goal to create a book that will point out what is important in hedge fund analysis and how to take the massive amounts of information that we are bombarded with daily to make sound investment decisions.

CONTACT

If you have any comments or questions, please feel free to contact me at frank.travers@hfanalysis.com. I encourage readers to contact me with any questions that they may have and to ask for clarification of any of the material presented in this book.

Hedge Fund Analysis

One

Background

CHAPTER 1

Hedge Fund History

"History doesn't repeat itself, but it does rhyme."

Mark Twain

I recently read an article printed in the financial press that questioned the viability of hedge funds as an asset class. Following the bear market decline and the corresponding volatile market environment, the article suggested that investors had begun to question whether or not hedge funds actually hedge and whether or not the asset class was doomed. Managers responded that it had become too hard to find profitable shorts, as all the best shorts quickly become crowded trades—which can lead to short squeezes.

The author of the article suggested that many hedge fund managers had become overconfident going into the market decline and had begun to invest outside of their core mandates and, even worse, did not do a good job of matching the liquidity of their fund's underlying investments with that of their underlying investors. As a result, some hedge fund investors are still waiting to receive redemption proceeds.

Additionally, the article highlighted that the SEC is tracking hedge funds more closely and that they are currently determining how to best regulate them.

What is most striking about the article (titled "Hard Times Come to the Hedge Funds") is that it was written by Carol Loomis and was published by *Fortune* magazine in June 1970.[1] The bear market referred to in the article occurred the previous year and had a disastrous impact on the hedge fund industry. Many hedge funds shut down and the asset class went into a dark period that lasted nearly two decades. I suggest that readers interested in hedge fund history read this article in its entirety because it provides perspective on hedge fund history and clearly shows that no matter how much things change and progress, history is likely to repeat itself (or at least rhyme).

SO WHO INVENTED THE HEDGE FUND?

The hedge fund industry is generally linked historically to Alfred Winslow Jones, who created the basic format for the hedge fund—which still exists to this day. However, a number of other early pioneers had invested with an absolute return methodology long before Jones entered the investment business.

THE SAMURAI

It has been suggested[2] that the world's first commodity trading advisor (CTA) or macro fund was created and managed to great success in the mid- to late 1700s in Japan. During the Tokugawa shogunate (1615 to 1867) Japan changed from many separate provinces to a single unified country. This had a positive impact on commerce and the nation's official marketplace for rice, which effectively was the currency in Japan, formed in Osaka due to its favorable location near the sea. The Dojima Rice Exchange was officially set up in the late 1600s and initially dealt only in the physical purchase and sale of rice. However, as rice became big business, more and more rice farmers and merchants began to sell "coupons" against the future delivery of rice. These coupons became actively traded because they provided buyers and sellers the ability to effectively go *long* or *short* various grades of rice at different delivery dates in the future. This market is generally considered to be the world's first futures exchange.

Munehisa Honma was born in 1724 into a wealthy merchant family in Sakata. He took over the family business in 1750, and his talent and skill as a trader has since become the stuff of legend. His first innovation was to study years' worth of price, weather, and crop data (it is rumored that he analyzed hundreds of years' worth of data) and to make forecasts of rice production and quality based on changes in weather and other seasonal effects. By reviewing the historical price movements and plotting them against other factors, he was able to anticipate when rice harvests would be strong and when they would be weak—and trade using that information. This combination of historical technical data combined with fundamental information gave him a genuine edge over his trading competition. This is a concept that we now take for granted, but back then no one else had thought to do it.

In addition, he devised a system of early price discovery. As most rice trading was done in Osaka and he was situated in Sakata (a considerable distance away), he developed an ingenious signaling system by positioning people on rooftops at regular intervals across the distance between the two cities. Once the official price was determined in Osaka, the first team member would signal the next team member using flags. This person would then signal the next in line until the message was received back home; not quite real-time quotes, but this innovation allowed for quicker price discovery. With this information in hand long before other traders in Sakata had access to it, Honma was able to gain a significant advantage over his peers (what we would today refer to as "low latency" trading).

Honma did not run a hedge fund as we define them today, but he certainly embraced the spirit of absolute return investing. He looked to make money by investing both long and short and developed ingenious methods that gave him a clear edge over his competition.

He was so successful as a trader he eventually became a financial consultant to the Japanese government and later was given the honorary title of samurai. He authored a book colorfully titled *Fountain of Gold: The Three Monkey Record of Money*.[3] This work is credited with being one of the first investment books that focused on market and investor psychology. In his book, Honma posited that there was a clear link between supply and demand (in rice markets) but determined that investor perception and sentiment could cause temporary dislocations that an astute trader could take advantage of. He is also credited with developing many of the principles of what we now refer to as contrarian investing and reversion to the mean. In his book, he suggests that when markets are oversold there may exist a buying opportunity and vice versa. He also employed a more philosophical approach to investing, describing the rotation of the markets as yin (a bear market) and yang (a bull market).

Many of his technical and charting techniques became the basis for what is now referred to as Japanese candlestick charting, which is still used to this day (largely in Japan).

Monehisa Honma's Innovations:

Using past price history to develop expectations for the future

Employing charts and graphs to quickly and efficiently see potential opportunities—the precursor to candlestick charting techniques

Realizing a method of early price discovery (flag communication system)

Early work relating to behavioral finance

THE ACADEMIC

In 1931, Karl Karsten published a significant but largely unheralded work titled *Scientific Forecasting*.[4] While most people have never heard of this book, it contains some of the most important early work on absolute return investing ever documented.[5] The book details eight years of statistical analysis that his firm, the Karsten Statistical Laboratory, performed to develop an automated system designed to gauge the state of the economy and stock market. Their objective was to determine if they could develop a systematic method of beating the market using publicly available information.

Karsten and his team reviewed a variety of "economic conditions," or what we would now refer to as economic/market indicators, to determine which data series had a statistically significant impact on the subsequent return of the equity market. He ultimately determined that thirteen indicators passed their tests. He broke the indicators into two main categories: (1) broad market and (2) industry specific.

Economic/Broad Market Indicators	Industry-Specific Indicators
The wholesale commodity price level	The building trades industry
The bond market	The automobile industry
The stock market	The petroleum industry
The short-term money rate	The iron and steel industry
The long-term money rate	The railroads
General business activity	The public utilities
	The chain stores

Not being financial experts themselves, Karsten and his team started the analytical process by holding conferences with experts in each field specified in the thirteen indicators and then tested a number of data series to determine their relative importance and the degree of influence that they had during the period studied. They looked at each time series over their respective histories but also recognized that recent history might be more relevant, so they reran the statistical work to look at the impact from recent periods as well as the overall time frame.

Some of the thirteen indicators were measured by a single factor or data series while others represented a combination of several. The complete list of underlying factors used to determine and track the indicators follows.

Data Series Used to Determine Barometers

Bank debits in New York City	Commercial paper rates
Bank debits outside of New York City	Bond price average
Gold movement	Stock price index
Freight car surplus or shortage	Wholesale price index
Unfilled steel orders	Farm products price index
Electrical power sales	Railroad gross earnings
Building contracts rewarded	Shares traded
Pig iron furnaces in blast	Gasoline consumption
Automobile production	Lubricating oil production
Call-loan interest rates	

Karsten divided these factors into three main categories:

1. Financial conditions
2. Speculative conditions
3. Business conditions

Some of these factors were thought to be leading and lagging indicators so they created various statistical combinations with different time leads and lags.

The results of their labor (remember that all of the regressions and correlation analyses were computed by hand) was the development of six "barometers" that Karsten believed would help to forecast stock price movements.

Karsten's Six Barometers:

1. Volume of trade
2. Building activity
3. Interest rates
4. Bond price level
5. Wholesale price level
6. Stock of leading industries (railroads, public utilities, steel, oil, automotive, and store stocks)

Karsten then tested his work by creating a paper portfolio. In creating the model for this portfolio, he foreshadowed several methods, techniques, and concepts that would not become commonplace on Wall Street for several decades. Among them, he wrote that diversification is the key to successful investing.

> *It would seem the part of caution to divide the risks as much as possible, not to stake everything upon any single operation or bet.*[6]

In addition, he also seemed to recognize that some stocks and groups of stocks exhibited greater returns than the market as a whole and, as such, it would be fruitful to buy the most attractive candidates and sell short an equal dollar amount of the stocks in the market (meaning go short the market index), as this would provide an opportunity to profit regardless of market gyrations and isolate the effectiveness of the underlying signals. He essentially formed the basis for market or dollar-neutral investing and the concept of alpha investing or absolute returns.

Ultimately, Karsten created a strategy that divided the equity market into six sectors (rails, utilities, steels, motors, stores, and oils) and applied each of the six barometers to each sector to create a single ranking for each sector from most attractive to least attractive. After a great deal of testing, they determined that buying a fixed dollar amount of the two most attractive sectors and simultaneously selling short an equal dollar amount of the least attractive two sectors would allow them to profit regardless of the direction of the market.

Their statistical work indicated that they did not have to buy all the stocks in each group; concluding that a basket of the largest stocks in each sector would effectively provide the same return as a basket consisting of all the underlying names in that group in the marketplace. The selected names were weighted according to their market capitalization. The holdings within each group are highlighted as follows:

Rails (basket represented 54 percent of the total market cap within the sector):

Company Name	% Held in Basket
Pennsylvania	24
New York Central	20
Atch. Top. & S. Fe	13
Union Pacific	12
Southern Pacific	10
Baltimore & Ohio	7
Chesapeake & Ohio	7
Norfolk & Western	7

Utilities (basket represented 70 percent of the sector's total market cap within the sector):

Company Name	% Held in Basket
Amer. Tel. & Tel.	37
Consolidated Gas	15
Columbia Gas & Electric	10
Electric Bond & Sh.	10
United Gas & Imp.	10
North American	8
Pacific Gas & Electric	5
United Corp.	5

Steels (basket represented 76 percent of the sector's total market cap within the sector):

Company Name	% Held in Basket
U.S. Steel	74
Bethlehem Steel	14
Amer. Roll. Mills	4
Inland Steel	4
Republic	4

Motors (basket represented 80 percent of the sector's total market cap within the sector):

Company Name	% Held in Basket
General Motors	81
Packard	9
Chrysler	6
Nash	4

Stores (basket represented 54 percent of the sector's total market cap within the sector):

Company Name	% Held in Basket
Woolworth	34
Sears Roebuck	19
Macy	10
Montgomery Ward	10
Kresge, S. S.	9
Penney, J. C.	8
First National Stores	5
Kroger Groc. & Bak. Co.	5

Oils (basket represented 85 percent of the sector's total market cap within the sector):

Company Name	% Held in Basket
Standard Oil of N. J.	29
Standard Oil of Ind.	16
Standard Oil of Cal.	15
Standard Oil of N.Y.	11
Gulf of Pa.	10
Texas Corp.	10
Vacuum Oil	9

The monthly results of the theoretical (paper) portfolio are shown in Tables 1.1 and 1.2. The cumulative performance is illustrated in Figure 1.1. According to his book, Karsten applied leverage equal to four times the actual value of the securities—200 percent gross exposure for the long book and 200 percent gross exposure for the short book to achieve these results.

TABLE 1.1   Karsten Paper Portfolio—Monthly Performance

	Monthly Return Paper Portfolio	Monthly Return DJIA	Out/Under Performance
3/1/1928	20.1%	8.7%	11.4%
4/1/1928	3.2%	2.8%	0.4%
5/1/1928	5.2%	0.9%	4.3%
6/1/1928	1.2%	−3.6%	4.8%
7/1/1928	1.6%	1.9%	−0.3%
8/1/1928	−2.9%	12.0%	−14.9%
9/1/1928	5.9%	−0.8%	6.7%
10/1/1928	8.0%	5.8%	2.2%
11/1/1928	2.2%	6.7%	−4.5%
12/1/1928	13.7%	12.9%	0.8%
1/1/1929	4.9%	0.0%	4.9%
2/1/1929	13.5%	2.6%	10.9%
3/1/1929	0.7%	−4.5%	5.2%
4/1/1929	−1.0%	8.7%	−9.7%
5/1/1929	23.6%	−6.7%	30.3%
6/1/1929	−0.9%	12.5%	−13.4%
7/1/1929	24.9%	7.6%	17.3%
8/1/1929	15.8%	3.5%	12.3%
9/1/1929	5.2%	−13.4%	18.6%
10/1/1929	16.1%	−21.8%	37.9%
11/1/1929	12.2%	−3.1%	15.3%
12/1/1929	10.6%	−1.2%	11.8%
1/1/1930	5.0%	8.1%	−3.1%
2/1/1930	15.9%	1.5%	14.4%
3/1/1930	4.5%	5.5%	−1.0%
4/1/1930	0.7%	−9.8%	10.5%
5/1/1930	0.7%	5.0%	−4.3%
6/1/1930	−0.6%	−18.1%	17.5%
7/1/1930	9.7%	7.2%	2.5%
8/1/1930	−4.4%	0.0%	−4.4%
9/1/1930	−2.0%	−10.1%	8.1%
10/1/1930	−3.9%	−13.6%	9.7%
11/1/1930	0.5%	−0.5%	1.0%
12/1/1930	16.8%	−6.5%	23.3%

TABLE 1.2   Karsten Paper Portfolio—Annual Performance

	Monthly Return Paper Portfolio	Monthly Return DJIA	Out/Under Performance
1928	73.0%	56.9%	16.1%
1929	218.7%	−19.3%	238.0%
1930	48.6%	−30.4%	79.0%

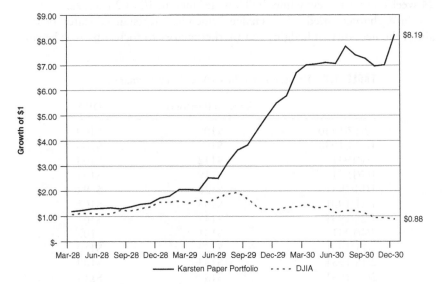

FIGURE 1.1   Karsten Paper Portfolio (Cumulative Performance from Mar-28 to Dec-30)

The paper portfolio declined in value in only seven of the 34 months under review while the Dow declined in 14 months over the same period. The two return streams had a low correlation to each other (0.06 over the period), and the end result of investing $100 in each on March 1, 1928, would have resulted in a gain of $719 for the paper portfolio against a loss of $12 for the Dow Jones Index.

While concluding that the paper portfolio was a clear success, Karsten recognized that a theoretical analysis would not be enough to convince the Wall Street crowd of his system's effectiveness. As a result, he determined that it would be necessary to manage real money in an actual broker-age account and record the results. So on December 17, 1930, his firm established an account with a New York brokerage house and managed a "fund" using the aforementioned barometers and according to the specified guidelines. The results are presented in Table 1.3 and reflect the growth of a $100 investment made on December 17, 1930.

The performance data highlighted in Table 1.3 and Figure 1.2 indicate that Karsten's dollar neutral portfolio significantly outperformed the Dow Jones Industrial Average over the review period. Karsten's portfolio experienced a cumulative return of 78 percent while the Dow Jones fell 21 percent over the period. The Karsten portfolio declined in value in only four of the 24 weeks under review while the Dow declined in 10 of 24 weeks.

In a chapter titled "The Hedge Principle," Karsten educates readers about the necessity of hedging out market factors to focus on what he calls

TABLE 1.3 Karsten Portfolio—Weekly Performance

	Karsten Portfolio	DJIA
12/17/1930	$100	$100
12/24/1930	$105	$100
1/1/1931	$112	$103
1/7/1931	$119	$104
1/14/1931	$128	$ 98
1/21/1931	$133	$102
1/28/1931	$143	$101
2/4/1931	$131	$103
2/11/1931	$133	$110
2/18/1931	$133	$109
2/25/1931	$133	$115
3/4/1931	$138	$109
3/11/1931	$140	$110
3/18/1931	$143	$111
3/25/1931	$145	$111
4/1/1931	$140	$103
4/8/1931	$143	$102
4/15/1931	$152	$ 99
4/22/1931	$148	$ 99
4/29/1931	$152	$ 87
5/6/1931	$169	$ 90
5/13/1931	$186	$ 90
5/20/1931	$171	$ 83
5/27/1931	$171	$ 79
6/3/1931	$178	$ 79

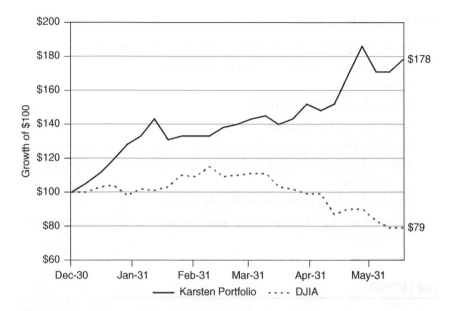

FIGURE 1.2 Karsten Portfolio (Cumulative Performance)

the sample portfolio's "out of line movement" (the concept of alpha, which had not yet been invented). The following quote summarizes the concept:

> *Our results will depend entirely upon the correctness of our pre-diction of the out of line movement. Stock market gyrations which affect all stocks, and which were not predicted in our forecast, would have no effect upon the results of our gamble. The specula-tion would be limited to the thing predicted.*[7]

Contrary to popular opinion, it was Karsten who first coined the term *hedge fund* (Chapter 12 in Karten's book is titled "The Hedge Funds on Paper"). In addition, in a rather mysterious passage in his book, Karsten states that while they were testing their strategy at the New York brokerage they were aware of another investment account being managed there that seemed to apply the same types of principles. The names of the brokerage house and the other investor are not mentioned in the book. Perhaps he could have been referring to the legendary investor highlighted in the following section.

Karl Karsten's Innovations:

Created model for what we now call dollar neutral investing

Quantitative (model driven) asset management

Focus on alpha

Coined the term "hedge fund"

Emphasized diversification

Use of baskets to represent investment opportunities (sector baskets)

Weighted baskets by market capitalization (not a common practice at that time)

Used lead and lag indicators in statistical models

Predicted the use of mathematics and quantitative techniques in money management

THE LEGEND

Benjamin Graham is widely considered to be the father of value investing and one of the true innovators in the investment world. He is the co-author of the seminal book *Security Analysis*,[8] which is considered required reading by anyone in the investment business, as well as *The Intelligent Investor*, another classic tome. Over several decades of teaching at Columbia University, he motivated many other now legendary investors, including Warren Buffett (who also worked for Graham before branching off on his own and eventually creating what is now known as Berkshire Hathaway).

What is not well known in the investment community is that Graham may well be the first hedge fund manager as we have come to define them today. After all, he employed many of the concepts and strategies now embraced within the hedge fund community. He managed a market-neutral account, invested in distressed and other event-driven strategies, put on hedged merger trades, and employed a variety of other instruments and strategies to "hedge" portfolio risk and to take advantage of unique "arbitrage" opportunities. In addition, he also collected a base fee and an incentive fee. Sounds very much like a hedge fund to me.

Benjamin Graham started his career on Wall Street as an assistant in the bond department at Newberger, Henderson and Loab just prior to the start of World War I. In 1915, he made the first of many arbitrage trades when he determined that the breakup value of the Guggenheim Exploration Company was significantly greater than its actual value traded in the marketplace. When Guggenheim management expressed interest in dissolving as a holding company to distribute the shares of its underlying holdings (which consisted of shares in four publicly traded copper and smelting companies), Graham calculated that the stock market value of the four underlying holding companies exceeded the value of Guggenheim by 10.7 percent (he estimated that the value of the underlying holdings amounted to $76.23 while Guggenheim shares were valued at $68.88). Assuming the simultaneous purchase of Guggenheim shares and the short sale of the four underlying copper/smelting companies, an arbitrage value of $7.35 per share of Guggenheim stock was possible. The obvious risk lay in the possibility that shareholders would not approve of the dissolution. Graham was able to establish this trade, and when the company eventually went through with the dissolution in January 1917, Graham's reputation grew right along with investment performance.

His first role as a portfolio manager came when a friend from Columbia University, Professor Algernon Tassin, gave him $10,000 to manage. The arrangement was for Graham to manage the money using his unique value-oriented methodology and to employ his skills as an arbitrageur. The profits were to be split evenly between the two. After some initial success, Graham made investments in some illiquid stocks that suffered greatly in the liquidity crunch brought on by World War I, and the account suffered margin calls. The account lost much of its value, and it took Graham several years to eventually build it back to its original value (what we would now refer to as a high water mark).

After the war, Graham continued his successful ways and was made partner at his firm. Following several years of successful trading for his clients, many of them began to open personalized accounts for Graham to manage on their behalf to take advantage of his expertise, and they contracted to pay him 25 percent of the resulting profits. He was so successful in this endeavor that a few investors eventually pooled their money and established a $250,000 account to be managed by Graham. For his services, he received a fixed salary ($10,000) and was contracted to keep 20 percent of the profits of the account. Graham created the Grahar Corporation ("Gra" came from his last name and "har" came from the last name of the cornerstone investor, Louis Harris) in 1923. One of Graham's most profitable trades while managing the Grahar Corporation was a trade involving DuPont and General Motors (GM). At that time, DuPont owned a significant number of GM shares and was trading at levels comparable to GM (so an investment in DuPont was akin to buying GM and getting the DuPont business for free). He believed that the market was overvaluing GM and undervaluing DuPont. As a result, he established a relative value trade where he was long DuPont and short GM in the expectation that investors would eventually realize this inefficiency (which did eventually occur).

Graham managed this account until the end of 1925, when he proposed a new fee schedule to Louis Harris (one in which the performance fee would increase as portfolio returns increased). Harris rejected the new fee proposal, and the Grahar Corporation was dissolved.

In 1926 (at the ripe old age of 31), Graham created the Benjamin Graham Joint Account, which was funded with $450,000 at inception and eventually grew to roughly $2.5 million within a few years. The joint account did well from its inception through 1928. In 1929, when the markets started to decline, Graham covered many short positions at nice profits. He did not reestablish new short positions while maintaining his long exposure. He was reluctant to establish new short positions because he believed stocks were trading at such low valuations that they did not make attractive short candidates. This resulted in a more directionally long book at a time of extreme market weakness. The joint account declined −20 percent in 1929 versus a decline of −15 percent for the Dow, and it declined another −50 percent in 1930 versus a decline of −29 percent for the Dow. The joint account also declined in 1931 and 1932, but had significantly outperformed the Dow (falling −16 percent vs. −48 percent in 1931 and −3 percent vs. −17 percent in 1932). The joint account's total return over this four-year period was −70 percent versus −74 percent for the Dow.

Graham and his partner, Jerry Newman, went many years without receiving any profit share, and times were tough financially for Graham. Recognizing that it might take years to recover the account's value, the fee structure was changed from the "upward scaling" model originally agreed upon to a flat 20 percent of profits starting on January 1, 1934. In addition, responding to IRS questions regarding the joint account's status as a partnership or a corporation, Graham formed the Graham-Newman Corporation on January 1, 1936, to manage client assets.

In the Graham-Newman Corporation's annual report dated February 28, 1946, Graham and Newman started by stating their investment policy.

The current Prospectus of the Corporation states that its general investment policy is:

1. To purchase securities at prices less than their intrinsic value as determined by careful analysis, with particular emphasis on purchase of securities at less than their liquidating value.
2. To engage in arbitrage and hedging operations in the securities field.

TABLE 1.4 Strategy Breakout for Graham-Newman Fund

Percentage Distribution of Portfolio by Type of Operations		
Type	1/31/1943	1/31/1946
Cash & Gov't Securities	3	11
Arbitrages, Reorganizations, Guaranteed Issues	17	36
Liquidations	12	12
Hedges & Convertible Issues	—	20
Financial Companies	9	13
General Portfolio	59	8
Total	100%	100%

The annual report goes on to document the account's broad asset allocation and the changes implemented by the portfolio managers between 1943 and 1946 (see Table 1.4).

The decrease in the general portfolio was due to Graham and Newman's assessment that the equity market had become fully valued over the period and reduced exposure to lock in profits and to reduce volatility. They recognized that a significant reduction in their long stock portfolio might cause periods of relative underperformance in bull markets but believed that action was true to their value-oriented roots.

The only real difference between the Graham-Newman Corporation and modern-day hedge funds is in the legal structuring. Modern hedge funds are set up as limited partnerships. The limited partnership structure was created and employed to great success by the investor in the next section.

Benjamin Graham's Innovations:

Distressed investing

Merger arbitrage

Base and performance fee combination

High water mark

Portfolio hedging

Volatility reduction methods

THE INNOVATOR

In 1966, Carol Loomis published an article in *Fortune* magazine titled "The Jones Nobody Keeps Up With,"[9] and the modern hedge fund industry was born.

In this article, Loomis introduced readers to Alfred Winslow Jones and informed us that he managed a "hedged fund" that had outperformed every mutual fund in the country for the previous 10 years by a wide margin. She stated that Jones's fund gained 670 percent for the 10 years ending in May 1965 versus a return of 358 percent for the Dreyfus fund, which was the best-performing mutual fund over the same period.

Figure 1.3 illustrates Jones's performance over the preceding five-year period compared to the best-performing mutual fund, the Fidelity Trend Fund managed by Gerald Tsai, as well as the Dow Jones Industrials Index. As in the 10-year review period, Jones outperformed his mutual fund peer by a considerable amount and more than doubled the return of the Dow.

Needless to say, these exceptional returns caught Wall Street's attention, and within a few years the number of hedged funds grew from a handful to roughly 140 according to some reports.

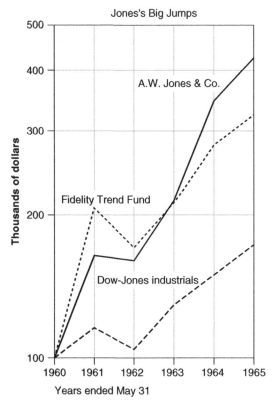

FIGURE 1.3　A. W. Jones's Hedge Fund
Performance (from Loomis's Article)

By many accounts A. W. Jones was the least likely hedge fund manager you would ever encounter. Jones was born in 1900 and didn't begin his fund management career until 1949. He held many positions in fields far removed from Wall Street. He spent a year as a purser on a tramp steamer, worked as a statistician, and eventually joined the U.S. State Department, where he started as a vice commissioner in Germany in 1930.

After his time with the State Department, Jones worked under a pseudonym for the Leninist Organization and attended the Marxist Workers' School in Berlin. In the early 1930s he represented the Leninist Organization in Britain and attempted to persuade the Labour Party to take military action against Adolf Hitler, who was viewed as a burgeoning threat.

After returning to the United States in 1934, Jones pursued a degree in sociology at Columbia University, got married, and honeymooned at the front lines of war-torn Spain. It is rumored he ran with the likes of Dorothy Parker and Ernest Hemingway.

His time in Germany and Spain alerted Jones to the struggles of the working class. After returning home to the United States, he completed his PhD and published a doctoral thesis under the title "Life, Liberty and Property" in 1941. Jones began to write for *Fortune* magazine and in 1948 published an article that likely prompted his career as a hedge fund manager. The article was titled "Fashions in Forecasting,"[10] and it detailed for readers new technical methods of betting on the stock market.

In 1949, Jones along with four friends/partners launched a general partnership that many view as the first hedge fund as we now define them. They pooled their money and launched with $100,000 ($40,000 from Jones). He would remain a significant investor in his funds for the rest of his life. This concept of investing alongside clients is another trait that is indicative of the modern hedge fund. Having skin in the game helps keep the manager's and investor's interests properly aligned.

In 1952, Jones converted the general partnership to a limited partnership, and the rest is history. Jones built upon the techniques employed by Karsten and Graham to create an investment vehicle/strategy that has withstood the test of time.

His first innovation was to create the fund as a private partnership, as opposed to a public fund (like a mutual fund). This allowed him to fly under the Security and Exchange Commission's (SEC) radar screen and gave him the ability to employ leverage and apply short selling to create a specific risk/return profile.

In addition, he determined that the use of cash as a means of diversification and risk dampening was inefficient. Instead, his method relied upon creating a portfolio with two components: a long book and a short book. He asserted that a long book that employs leverage will give the portfolio manager a better chance of capturing gains based on strong stock selection. The short book was used as a means of reducing overall market risk, but could also add value if their stock selection in this book was good.

As an example, Jones details in a 1960 annual letter to shareholders in his fund the following scenario. Two investors are each given $100,000 to invest. Both investors are bullish about the market's future opportunity and are equally skilled at selecting stocks. The first investor decided to invest $80,000 in a basket of stocks and $20,000 in what he determined to be safe bonds (as a means of dampening overall portfolio volatility).

The second investor employs leverage and increases the initial $100,000 to $200,000. He then takes $130,000 and invests it in a basket of securities he believes will outperform the market and takes the remaining $70,000 and sells short a basket of stocks he believes will underperform the market.

The first investor has $80,000 exposed to the market but the second investor only has $60,000 exposed to the market ($130,000 in the long book minus the $70,000 in the short book). In current terminology, we would say that the second investor has a gross (levered) exposure of 2x or 200 percent and a net exposure (the difference between the long and short books) of 60 percent. The first investor would have a gross exposure of 1x or 100 percent (equities plus bonds) and a net equity exposure of 80 percent.

Using two techniques previously attributed to riskier investing (leverage and shorting), Jones was able to build a better mousetrap—a fund with greater ability to make money when the market went up while reducing volatility when the market declined (by virtue of its lower net exposure).

In creating this new methodology, Jones recognized that he had no real stock-picking ability. So he devised another method of portfolio management that still exists today. He developed the multiple manager concept. He asked brokers to create paper portfolios for him with their best long and short ideas, and he used his statistics background to determine which brokers actually added value and which didn't by tracking the broker's "model" portfolios. He would then use this information to construct his portfolio. He also incentivized brokers to call him with their best ideas by paying them based on how well their stock picks performed. As simple as this sounds, it was something that others just hadn't thought to do. This gave him a significant advantage because brokers knew that they would be paid handsomely for providing successful trade ideas to Jones, and this performance incentive led them to call Jones ahead of his competition.

Eventually, Jones would use this model portfolio technique to hire individuals to work as in-house portfolio managers. This was an incredibly effective employment screen, as he was able to view a real history of their ideas and determine if they would add value to his fund as portfolio managers. This hiring practice is still in effect to this day. In fact, there are several hedge funds that use Jones' method of tracking and analyzing sell-side research as a means of adding potential alpha.

A further illustration of just how far ahead of his time Jones was is an innovation he referred to as relative velocity. In Jones's 1961 shareholder report, he makes the following statement:

> *Different stocks habitually move up and down at different rates and hedging $1,000 of a stodgy stock against $1,000 of a fast mover would give no true balance of risk. We must therefore compute the velocity of all our stocks, both long and short, by their past performances, compared with the past performance of a good measure of the market as a whole.*[11]

He goes on to say that he and his team used the S&P 500 as a measure of the overall stock market and then measured the size and amplitude of each of their stocks relative to this index. Because these measures were all calculated manually, they performed the velocity calculations every two years on a universe of roughly 2,000 stocks.

He used two stocks to provide an example. He calculated that the average move in Sears was roughly 80 percent that of the S&P 500 while the average move in General Dynamics was 196 percent compared to the S&P 500. He asserted that it would be foolish to buy $1,000 worth of Sears and hedge it with $1,000 of General Dynamics because the relative velocity of each stock was not aligned. To effectively offset the heightened volatility in General Dynamics, one would need to buy nearly twice as much stock in Sears Roebuck.

Jones used the relative velocity measure to better manage what he perceived to be the true risks and exposures within his fund. Once he determined a desired net exposure for his fund, he would apply the relative velocity calculation to every stock he owned to ensure that he matched the targeted exposure and risk with the actual portfolio exposure and risk. In other words, Jones created the concept of market beta and put it in practice long before it would be formally introduced by William Sharpe in 1964.[12]

In addition, Jones also developed a method of evaluating the performance of his portfolio managers as well as the overall fund. Now that Jones had effectively developed a measure of stock and portfolio beta, he set his sights on determining how much of his fund's performance came from market moves and how much came from the investment decisions that they had made—what we now call alpha versus beta.

Using the earlier example of a $100,000 account levered to $200,000, with $130,000 in long positions and −$70,000 in short positions, we can estimate how much of the account's return comes from superior stock selection versus market influences.

Assume that we are evaluating the account's performance over a one-month period using the following assumptions:

1. S&P 500 return of +1% over the period.
2. Long positions gained $2,500 in value over the period.
3. Short positions lost −$400 in value over the period.

So over the period in question, the account gained $2,100 in value (the sum of the $2,500 gained by the long positions and the −$400 lost by the short positions). This translates to a gain of 2.1 percent for the account based on the original $100,000 invested. To determine the market impact, Jones applied the following steps:

Determine amount gained and return for the long portfolio due to skill:

Step One

    Gain in long portfolio—(market return × amount invested in long portfolio)

    $= \$2,500 - (1\% \times \$130,000)$

    $= \$2,500 - \$1,300$

    $= \$1,200 \quad \$1,200/\$100,000$

    $= 1.2\%$

Step Two

    Using the amount lost, determine return for the short portfolio:

    $= -\$400 - (1\% \times -\$70,000)$

    $= -\$400 - (-\$700)$

    $= \$300$

    $= 0.3\% \quad [\$300/\$100,000]$

Step Three

    Determine amount and return based on the market performance:

    $=$ Portfolio net exposure × market return

    $= \$60,000 \times 1\%$

    $= \$600$

    $= 0.6\% \quad [\$600/\$100,000]$

— Return due to manager skill: 1.5% (1.2% from longs and 0.3% from shorts)

— Return due to market moves: 0.6%

— Total gain for the period: 2.1% (return from manager skill + return from the market)

As the 1960s came to an end, Jones took a less active role in the management of his hedge fund, and the portfolio managers left managing the fund began to question the merits of shorting or hedging the portfolio. After all, markets had been on a multiyear run and shorts were largely unprofitable; they were a drag on performance. As a result, the fund began to hedge less and its net exposure to the market rose significantly. When the market declined in 1969, Jones's hedge fund experienced its worst losses ever. This led Jones to come back to the fund to reinstitute his hedged principle and recoup losses.

As the Loomis article that we highlighted in the beginning of the chapter indicated, many other hedge fund managers had also lost their way. Funds hedged less and owned securities that were less liquid than expected. Hedge funds, which a few years earlier had been poised to take over the asset management industry, found themselves on life support. It would take nearly two decades before hedge funds returned to prominence.

A. W. Jones's Innovations:

LP structure

Invest alongside clients

Multiple portfolio manager structure

Pay brokers for best ideas

Use of leverage (to amplify returns as well as protect the portfolio)

Use of statistics to measure and evaluate portfolio managers

Portfolio attribution (stock selection versus market returns)

Concept of alpha and beta

Creation of an asset class

The hedge fund industry started with a $100,000 investment in A. W. Jones's fund in 1949 and has experienced some bumps along the way, but it has developed into a multitrillion-dollar industry. Figure 1.4 illustrates just how much things have changed over the years. Total assets in the hedge

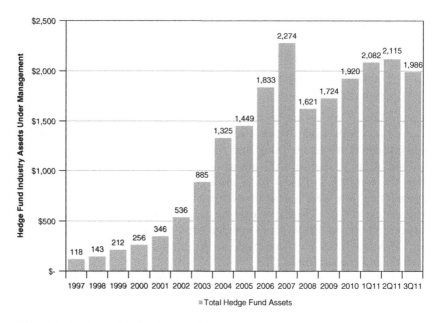

FIGURE 1.4   Growth in Hedge Fund Assets

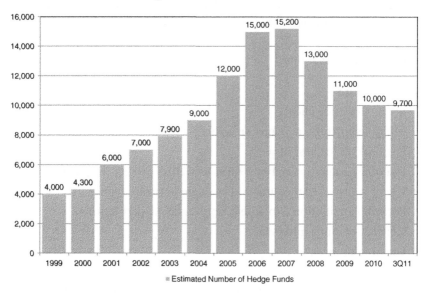

FIGURE 1.5   Growth in the Number of Hedge Funds

TABLE 1.5 Hedge Fund Industry's Life Cycle

Stage Years	Foundation 1925–1948	Birth 1949–1965	Emergence 1965–1969	Death 1970–1985	Reemergence 1985–1999	Explosion 2000–Present
Environment	Pioneers in this period all but forgotten to time but they forged a path for others to follow. Many concepts created would be used later by others.	Jones created a "better mousetrap" and managed money in relative obscurity.	*Fortune* article profiling A. W. Jones brings the "hedged fund" into the limelight and imitators followed.	In the late 1960s, hedge funds stopped hedging and were unprepared for the market decline in 1969. Performance suffered, assets left the industry, and only a few funds emerged.	Returns led by hedge fund titans (Steinhardt, Soros, and Robertson) in combination with a bull equity market reenergized the industry leading to an increase in the number of hedge funds and assets.	Institutions enter the market; bursting of the tech bubble highlights advantages of hedge funds versus traditional asset classes. Financial meltdown in 2008 leads to regulatory changes and heightened scrutiny.
Players	Karl Karsten Benjamin Graham	A. W. Jones	A. W. Jones Fairfield Partners Cerberus Associates	Michael Steinhardt George Soros	Steinhardt Soros Julian Robertson	Winton Renaissance Paulson S.A.C. Tudor Bridgewater Brevan Howard

TABLE 1.6 Hedge Fund Strategy Composition as of 3Q 2011

Hedge Fund Industry Strategy Composition ($Billions)

	2011	1997
CTA	269	23
Multi Strategy	249	42
Emerging Markets	224	7
Fixed Income	193	23
Event Driven	179	12
Equity Long/Short	178	32
Equity Long Bias	164	19
Macro	119	17
Distressed	118	3
Sector Specific	104	9
Convertible Arbitrage	37	6
Equity Market Neutral	32	8
Other	28	6
Merger Arbitrage	16	3
Total Hedge Fund Assets	**$ 1,911**	**$ 210**

fund industry (as calculated by BarclayHedge) grew from $118 billion in 1997 to just under $2 trillion at the end of the third quarter of 2011.

In addition to the growth in assets, the number of hedge funds has grown as well. Using information provided by BarclayHedge, we can see that the number of hedge funds has grown from 4,000 in 1999 to 9,700 at the end of the third quarter of 2011.

The hedge fund industry has gone through several iterations over the last six decades. The industry's life cycle is highlighted in Table 1.5.

In addition to changes in the size and scope of the hedge fund industry over the last few decades, there has also been a dramatic change in the depth within the industry. Table 1.6 illustrates how the strategy composition of the industry has changed between 1997 and 2011. The total level of assets in the hedge fund industry grew 9.1x from $210 billion to $1.9 trillion.

NOTES

1. Carol Loomis, "Hard Times Come to the Hedge Funds," *Fortune*, January 1970.

2. Veryan Allen, "Best Hedge Funds?" hedgefund.blogspot.com, April 2008.
3. Steve Nilson, *Beyond Candlesticks*. New York: Wiley, 1994.
4. Karl Karsten. *Scientific Forecasting: Its Methods and Application to Practical Business and to Stock Market Operations* (New York: Greenberg, 1931).
5. Christopher Dennistoun, "Karsten, Jones and the Origin of Hedge Funds," Eurekahedge.com, March 2004.
6. Karsten, *Scientific Forecasting*, p. 190.
7. Karsten, *Scientific Forecasting*, p. 190.
8. Benjamin Graham, and Dodd, David, *Security Analysis* (New York: McGraw-Hill, 1934).
9. Carol Loomis, "The Jones Nobody Keeps Up With," *Fortune*, April 1966.
10. Alfred Winslow Jones, "Fashions in Forecasting," *Fortune,* March 1949.
11. A. W. Jones and Co., "Basic Report," May 31, 1961.
12. William Sharpe, "Capital Asset Prices—A Theory of Market Equilibrium under Conditions of Risk," *Journal of Finance*, 1964.

CHAPTER 2

Hedge Fund Asset Class

"I playfully suggest that they drop the 'h' and become 'edge funds.'
After all, their claim is they seek an edge on the rest of the market."
Sebastian Mallaby, author of *More Money Than God*

Chapter 1 provided historical context for the hedge fund industry, from its obscure beginnings to its current status as a major influence in global financial markets. This chapter will define the modern hedge fund, highlight the major strategies, and discuss how and why hedge funds fit in the asset allocation picture.

DEFINITION

When I think of a hedge fund, I think of a private investment vehicle in which the underlying investment manager offers some unique "edge" that is embedded within the process, systems, or the investment team. It can be something tangible, such as a quantitative model that interprets data in some unique way, or it can refer to a more qualitative edge, such as the stock-picking ability of the fund's managers.

The term *hedge fund* is a bit of a misnomer, as there are many hedge funds that do not actually hedge at all while others hedge only some of the time.

To be more formal, hedge funds can be defined as an investment structure for managing a private investment pool that can invest in physical securities and derivatives markets. They can employ leverage and have an absolute return mandate. Legally, they can take the form of a limited partnership, corporation, trust, or mutual fund based on where the fund is domiciled.

In any case, there are a number of characteristics that in my view distinguish hedge funds from the more traditional, long-only model.

- **Return objective**—Unlike traditional funds, which are benchmarked to various indexes, hedge funds have an absolute return objective. Hedge fund managers look to achieve positive results over time irrespective of the market's direction.
- **Opportunistic mandates**—Hedge funds tend to have more flexible mandates. Since the objective is to achieve absolute returns, mandates tend to offer wider opportunity sets and often allow the hedge fund manager to adjust portfolio exposures based on his or her views of prospective market opportunities.
- **Leverage**—As discussed in Chapter 1, leverage is not necessarily a dirty word. A talented hedge fund manager can employ leverage and, in conjunction with appropriate risk management, can achieve better risk-adjusted returns than traditional funds.
- **Exposure management/hedging**—Hedge funds can employ both long and short investments and can adjust overall portfolio exposures—some can even go net short (which can be advantageous when the market is declining in value). While not all hedge funds hedge, most do to some degree.
- **Skin in the game**—Hedge fund managers typically have significant amounts of their personal liquid net worth invested alongside investors, which clearly aligns interests between the fund manager and clients.
- **Fees**—Hedge funds typically charge two fees on top of normal operating expenses. The management fee is designed to provide sufficient capital to pay for the "management" of the fund while the performance fee (also referred to as an incentive fee) is designed to provide income based on how well the underlying fund performs.
- **Liquidity provisions**—Hedge funds typically provide for specific redemption frequency (such as monthly, quarterly, annually) and also require a specific notice period (such as 60 or 90 days). In addition, some hedge funds can gate investors (stop redemptions once they exceed a specified percentage of total assets in the fund) or create side pockets for illiquid investments. In fact, most hedge fund operating agreements contain language to the effect that hedge fund managers "may" suspend redemptions if they believe that the redemptions will put the remaining investors in an unfair position. Hedge funds often "lock up" investor capital for a period of time upon initial investment. These locks can be soft (meaning an investor can redeem but must pay a fee to do so) and hard (meaning the investor cannot redeem within the lock period for any reason).
- **Transparency**—This is a hot-button topic. There is no generic statement when it comes to hedge fund transparency. The media often portray

hedge funds as secretive, but this is unfair. Hedge funds tend to be open to investors and potential investors. Hedge funds run the gamut when it comes to transparency, with some providing full position-level transparency and others providing basic exposures and performance reporting.

- **Low correlation**—Hedge funds generally provide a low level of correlation to traditional asset classes and strive to produce low correlation across hedge fund strategies.
- **Service providers**—Hedge funds employ a number of service providers to house securities, trade, perform risk management, audit services, and provide legal work. The list of providers includes prime brokers, audit firms, accountants, administrators, risk aggregators, law offices, third-party marketing firms, and so on.

HEDGE FUND STRUCTURE

While there are a number of ways that hedge funds can be legally organized, the majority of them are set up in what is known as a master-feeder structure. The organizational chart in Figure 2.1 highlights the major features of this structure. This structure allows the investment manager to pool both offshore and onshore client assets to achieve economies of scale and improve upon operational efficiencies, which can lead to lower costs to investors.

The master fund company is typically incorporated in a tax-neutral offshore jurisdiction (such as the Cayman Islands or Bermuda) into which distinct feeder funds invest. By employing this format, the tax implications to U.S. taxable investors and U.S. tax-exempt and non-U.S. investors is

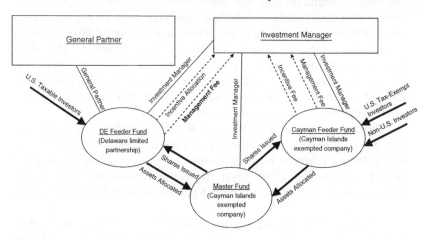

FIGURE 2.1 Typical Hedge Fund Structure

minimized without one class of investors negatively impacting the tax status of another class of investors.

HEDGE FUND STRATEGIES

Hedge funds can be categorized into a number of different strategies and substrategies. The following section defines the major hedge fund strategies and provides historical calendar year performance as well as annualized performance and standard deviation statistics.

Equity-Oriented Strategies

As the name states, equity-oriented strategies primarily employ equity securities and equity-like securities (such as swaps and options) in a variety of ways and can incorporate both generalist and sector-specific mandates.

- Variable Equity Long/Short strategies generally include hedge funds in which the underlying manager believes there is value to be gained from the evaluation and investment in both a long and short portfolio of equity securities due to inherent pricing inefficiencies in the marketplace. In Chapter 1, we referred to this type of fund as employing the "Jones model." Managers can utilize value, growth, or a hybrid methodology to outperform the traditional equity benchmark (such as the S&P 500 for U.S. stocks). These funds can specialize in small-, mid-, or large-cap stocks or can shift among market caps based on prevailing opportunities in the marketplace. They can also focus on specific countries or regions, or they can have a global mandate. A fund's gross and net exposures can vary by mandate and will often move along with the manager's view of the opportunities available or may stay within a predetermined range. The short portfolio can be viewed as either an additional source of potential alpha or as a hedge to the long portfolio. The short book is dependent upon the availability of stock borrow, costs, and the legal/regulatory environment. In some countries, shorting is not allowed, and in others the costs associated with shorting are fairly high (predominantly in emerging markets).

  The calendar year performance history in Figure 2.2 highlights that equity long/short strategies (as represented by the HFRI Equity Hedge Index) achieved positive results in 19 out of 22 years since the index's inception in 1990. Over the entire performance period, the index returned 13.0 percent with 9.3 percent standard deviation on an annualized basis.

- Long Biased strategies tend to carry an overall net exposure greater than 50 percent and may even run above 100 percent (aggressive funds can

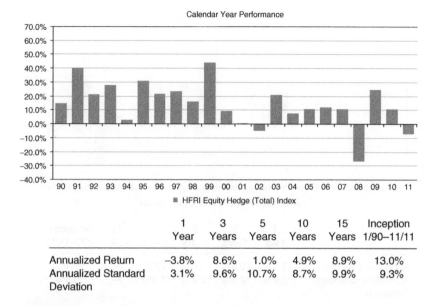

FIGURE 2.2 Historical Performance of HFRI Equity Hedge Index (Jan-90 to Nov-11)

employ leverage to increase exposure to the market without offsetting short exposure). This strategy will often have a higher level of volatility due to the heightened exposure to the market and, as such, will often have a higher beta and correlation to the overall equity market.

The calendar year performance history in Figure 2.3 shows that long biased equity strategies (as represented by the Barclay Equity Long Bias Index) achieved positive results in 12 out of 15 years since the index's inception in 1997. Over the entire performance period, the index returned 10.1 percent with 10.4 percent standard deviation on an annualized basis.

- **Short Biased strategies** are essentially the opposite of long biased strategies. The fund's mandate will typically call for a minimum net exposure of −50 percent (and will often be skewed more toward −100 percent). Allocators typically hire short biased hedge funds to balance out exposures within their portfolios. Over the longer term, managers in this strategy have had a difficult time achieving positive returns because markets have generally risen. However, in times of market volatility and market drawdowns, exposure to this type of fund may help to dampen overall portfolio volatility. Short biased hedge fund managers tend to be highly contrarian (as they are short the market when most other hedge funds are generally long the market) and tend to experience dramatic changes in assets under management, as allocators often invest

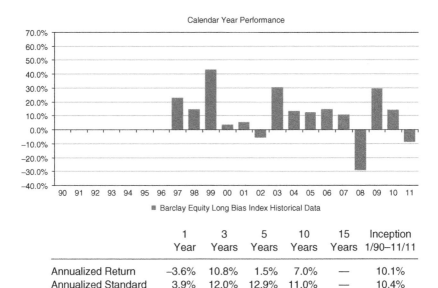

	1 Year	3 Years	5 Years	10 Years	15 Years	Inception 1/90–11/11
Annualized Return	−3.6%	10.8%	1.5%	7.0%	—	10.1%
Annualized Standard Deviation	3.9%	12.0%	12.9%	11.0%	—	10.4%

FIGURE 2.3 Historical Performance of Barclay Equity Long Bias Index (Jan-97 to Nov-11)

when times are tough and redeem when the outlook picks up. Funds in this strategy benefit when broad markets decline and/or when portfolio securities decline in price when the market increases in value. Short biased hedge funds also benefit from the interest received on the cash proceeds from the short sale.

The calendar year performance history in Figure 2.4 highlights that equity short biased strategies (as represented by the HFRI Equity Hedge Short Bias Index) achieved positive results in 11 out of 22 years since the index's inception in 1990. Over the entire performance period, the index returned 0.3 percent with 19.0 percent standard deviation on an annualized basis.

Relative Value

Relative value managers look to exploit a perceived mispricing in a specific investment or combination of investments. These funds typically look to find an arbitrage opportunity and find a way to extract a profit after paying commissions. Typical relative value strategies include convertible arbitrage, fixed income arbitrage, and equity market neutral funds.

- **Convertible bond arbitrage** managers look to profit from perceived pricing discrepancies within convertible bonds and hybrid securities. A

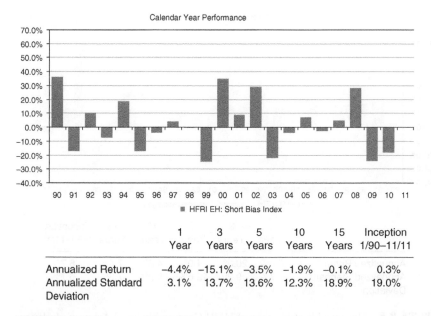

Calendar Year Performance

	1 Year	3 Years	5 Years	10 Years	15 Years	Inception 1/90–11/11
Annualized Return	–4.4%	–15.1%	–3.5%	–1.9%	–0.1%	0.3%
Annualized Standard Deviation	3.1%	13.7%	13.6%	12.3%	18.9%	19.0%

FIGURE 2.4 Historical Performance of HFRI Equity Hedge Short Bias Index (Jan-90 to Nov-11)

convertible bond is best described as a bond with an embedded call option on the underlying company's stock. Convertible bonds therefore can exhibit qualities of both credit and equity and are often referred to as hybrid securities. A typical trade in this strategy would involve buying a convertible bond and shorting the common stock of the underlying company. The conversion feature embedded in a convertible bond allows the bond's price to trade similarly to the price of the underlying stock price. In the example previously cited, if the price of the underlying stock increases in value, the trade will lose value on the short sale but can make money on the bond and vice versa (in the case of the stock declining in price). Price fluctuations create the need to consistently reassess the hedge and adjust as needed. In addition, the manager can consciously under- or overhedge the trade to take on an element of directionality.

The calendar year performance history in Figure 2.5 highlights that convertible bond arbitrage strategies (as represented by the HFRI Convertible Bond Arbitrage Index) achieved positive results in 18 out of 22 years since the index's inception in 1990. Over the entire performance period, the index returned 8.7 percent with 6.7 percent standard deviation on an annualized basis.

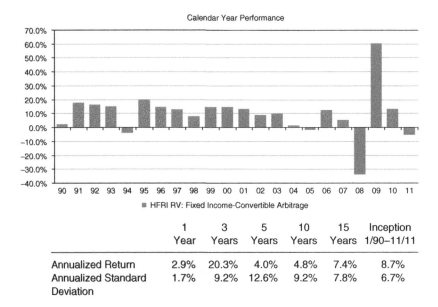

Calendar Year Performance

■ HFRI RV: Fixed Income-Convertible Arbitrage

	1 Year	3 Years	5 Years	10 Years	15 Years	Inception 1/90–11/11
Annualized Return	2.9%	20.3%	4.0%	4.8%	7.4%	8.7%
Annualized Standard Deviation	1.7%	9.2%	12.6%	9.2%	7.8%	6.7%

FIGURE 2.5   Historical Performance of HFRI Convertible Bond Arbitrage Index (Jan-90 to Nov-11)

■ **Fixed income arbitrage** managers attempt to isolate price anomalies between related fixed income securities. Underlying strategies may include interest rate swap arbitrage, U.S. versus non-U.S. government bond arbitrage, and yield curve arbitrage, to name a few. An example would be the purchase of government bonds at the short end of the yield curve and the simultaneous sale of government bonds at the long end of the yield curve. Trades typically focus on single risk factors such as duration, convexity, or steepness of the yield curve.

The calendar year performance history in Figure 2.6 highlights that fixed income arbitrage strategies (as represented by the HFRI Fixed Income Corporate Index) achieved positive results in 18 out of 22 years since the index's inception in 1990. Over the entire performance period, the index returned 7.9% with 6.7% standard deviation on an annualized basis.

■ The **equity market neutral strategy** typically employs both long and short portfolios of equity securities that are dollar neutral (equal dollar amounts of long and shorts), beta neutral (matching the long and short portfolios by adjusting for each stock's beta), and/or factor neutral (achieving neutrality across such factors as style, market cap, geography, sector, industry, etc.). These strategies tend to be quantitatively oriented. The portfolio managed by Karl Karsten mentioned in Chapter 1 would

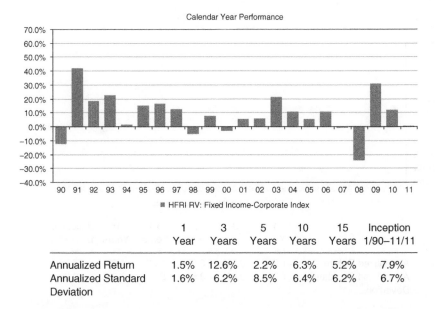

FIGURE 2.6 Historical Performance of HFRI Fixed Income Corporate Index (Jan-90 to Nov-11)

now be referred to as dollar neutral. A.W. Jones did not manage a beta-neutral portfolio, but his method of adjusting for relative velocity was his way of adjusting for stocks with different market sensitivities and was a precursor to beta. Quantitative funds tend to employ sophisticated risk models and optimization techniques to isolate underlying portfolio risks and to construct optimal portfolios.

The calendar year performance history in Figure 2.7 highlights that equity market neutral strategies (as represented by the HFRI Equity Hedge Equity Market Neutral Index) achieved positive results in 20 out of 22 years since the index's inception in 1990. Over the entire performance period, the index returned 7.0 percent with 3.3 percent standard deviation on an annualized basis.

Event Driven

Event-driven strategies are typically dependent upon an impending corporate event, such as a merger, liquidation, bankruptcy, spin-out, recapitalization, and so forth.

- An **activist strategy** is one where the hedge fund manager believes that some kind of corporate change would benefit the company (and

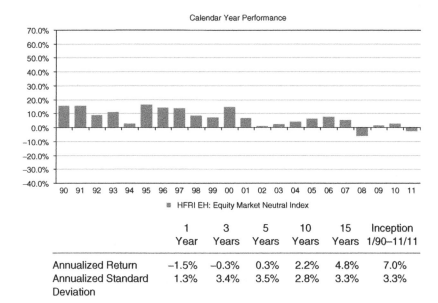

	1 Year	3 Years	5 Years	10 Years	15 Years	Inception 1/90–11/11
Annualized Return	−1.5%	−0.3%	0.3%	2.2%	4.8%	7.0%
Annualized Standard Deviation	1.3%	3.4%	3.5%	2.8%	3.3%	3.3%

FIGURE 2.7   Historical Performance of HFRI Equity Hedge Equity Market Neutral Index (Jan-90 to Nov-11)

ultimately shareholders) and takes either an active or passive role to prompt the company's management to instigate the proposed changes. A hedge fund manager that takes an active role may look to buy enough of a company's outstanding shares so that he or she can take a board seat and personally initiate changes. A manager that employs passive (or soft) activism may write a letter to company management or to the company's board to suggest potential changes.

- **Merger arbitrage** funds look to lock in the "spread" between the current market price of a stock and its value in the case of a merger. A typical transaction in this strategy would include buying shares in a company for which a public announcement of the merger has been published and short the corresponding acquiror. Mergers can be transacted on a cash basis (the acquiror pays cash for shares in the acquiree) or a stock basis (the acquiror pays for the merger by issuing stock in the acquiror's company to the acquiree). In the case of a stock for stock merger, the spread would be the difference in price between the stocks of the two companies past the announcement. In the case of a cash merger, it is harder to hedge the position. Hedge fund managers that

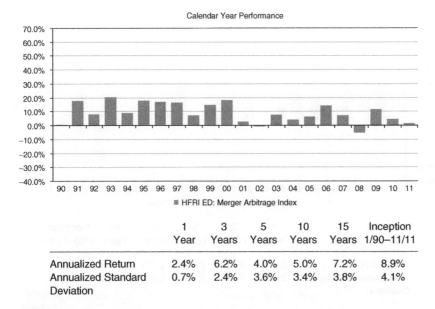

FIGURE 2.8 Historical Performance of HFRI Event-Driven Merger Arbitrage Index (Jan-90 to Nov-11)

establish positions based on expected merger activity and/or rumors in the marketplace are considered to engage in rumor-trage. The risk in a merger arbitrage trade is that the deal does not come to fruition.

The calendar year performance history in Figure 2.8 highlights that merger arbitrage strategies (as represented by the HFRI Merger Arbitrage Index) achieved positive results in 20 out of 22 years since the index's inception in 1990. Over the entire performance period, the index returned 8.9 percent with 4.1 percent standard deviation on an annualized basis.

▪ **Distressed and high-yield strategies** deal with the credit securities of companies with below-investment-grade ratings. High-yield hedge fund managers can purchase below-investment-grade securities for their yield and/or because they ultimately believe that the bonds will be paid down by the company (high-yield bonds trade at a discount to par). Both high-yield and distressed hedge fund managers can invest in securities across a company's capital structure with different maturity dates, seniority, and other terms to find what they believe to be the security with the best risk/reward potential. In the case of bankruptcy, managers may start out holding debt and end up holding equity as part of the restructuring deal.

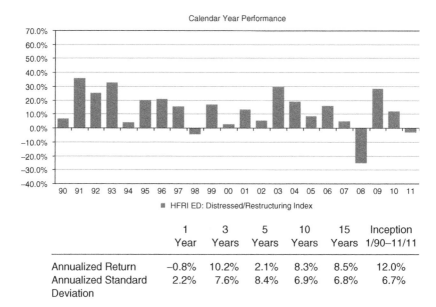

Calendar Year Performance

■ HFRI ED: Distressed/Restructuring Index

	1 Year	3 Years	5 Years	10 Years	15 Years	Inception 1/90–11/11
Annualized Return	−0.8%	10.2%	2.1%	8.3%	8.5%	12.0%
Annualized Standard Deviation	2.2%	7.6%	8.4%	6.9%	6.8%	6.7%

FIGURE 2.9 Historical Performance of HFRI Event-Driven Distressed/Restructuring Index (Jan-90 to Nov-11)

The calendar year performance history in Figure 2.9 highlights that distressed strategies (as represented by the HFRI Event-Driven Distressed/Restructuring Index) achieved positive results in 19 out of 22 years since the index's inception in 1990. Over the entire performance period, the index returned 12.0 percent with 6.7 percent standard deviation on an annualized basis.

Directional Strategies

Directional strategies such as global macro and commodity trading advisor (CTA) can employ either qualitative techniques, quantitative techniques, or a combination of the two in an attempt to adapt to changing market dynamics by taking directional (long or short) positions in equity, credit, currency, or commodity markets based on their perceived risk/reward profiles. Directional funds tend to offer low correlation to traditional strategies and to other hedge fund strategies.

■ A **global macro** manager looks to exploit opportunities in global markets by establishing either long or short positions and often employing

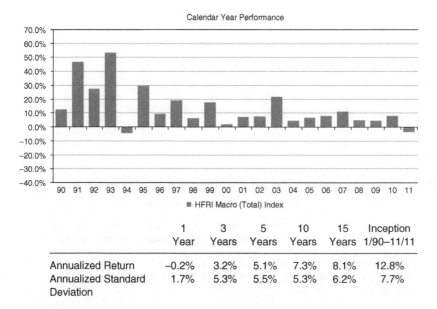

	1 Year	3 Years	5 Years	10 Years	15 Years	Inception 1/90–11/11
Annualized Return	–0.2%	3.2%	5.1%	7.3%	8.1%	12.8%
Annualized Standard Deviation	1.7%	5.3%	5.5%	5.3%	6.2%	7.7%

FIGURE 2.10 Historical Performance of HFRI Macro (Total) Index (Jan-90 to Nov-11)

leverage to enhance the opportunity. A global macro manager may be bullish Asian equity markets in the first quarter due to growth prospects and bearish in the second quarter due to negative sentiment and flow of funds. As a result, the fund manager in this example would likely be long Asia in Q1 and short in Q2, which puts him or her in a position to dynamically shift allocations and potentially profit amid changing market environments. Most hedge fund managers in this space employ top-down economic and market analysis and typically do not invest in securities of specific companies.

The calendar year performance history in Figure 2.10 highlights that macro strategies (as represented by the HFRI Macro Total Index) achieved positive results in 20 out of 22 years since the index's inception in 1990. Over the entire performance period, the index returned 12.8 percent with 7.7 percent standard deviation on an annualized basis.

■ A **commodity trading advisor, or CTA,** typically utilizes quantitative models to determine which securities are over- or undervalued and to construct a portfolio that provides an optimized risk/return profile that takes into account such issues as commissions and slippage (cost due to time decay in trading).

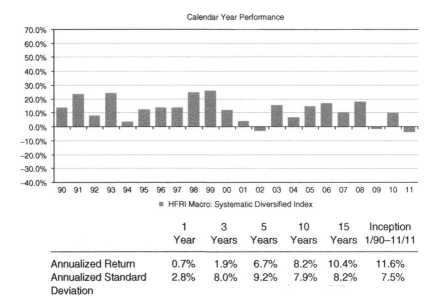

	1 Year	3 Years	5 Years	10 Years	15 Years	Inception 1/90–11/11
Annualized Return	0.7%	1.9%	6.7%	8.2%	10.4%	11.6%
Annualized Standard Deviation	2.8%	8.0%	9.2%	7.9%	8.2%	7.5%

FIGURE 2.11 Historical Performance of HFRI Macro Systematic Diversified Index (Jan-90 to Nov-11)

The calendar year performance history in Figure 2.11 highlights that CTA strategies (as represented by the HFRI Macro Systematic Diversified Index) achieved positive results in 19 out of 22 years since the index's inception in 1990. Over the entire performance period, the index returned 11.6 percent with 7.5 percent standard deviation on an annualized basis.

Multi-Strategy

■ **Multi-strategy** funds typically employ several of the strategies mentioned previously and can offer dedicated allocations across strategies (silo approach). They can opportunistically shift allocations to strategies where there is a perceived risk/return benefit (opportunistic approach).

The calendar year performance history in Figure 2.12 highlights that multi-strategy (as represented by the Hedgefund.net Multi-Strategy Index) achieved positive results in 18 out of 22 years since the index's inception in 1990. Over the entire performance period, the index returned 11.3 percent with 5.9 percent standard deviation on an annualized basis.

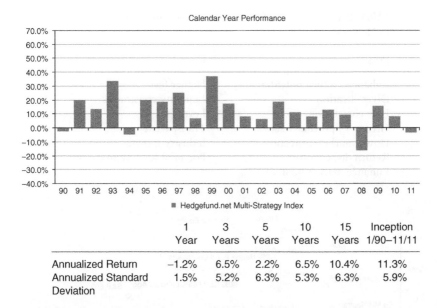

Calendar Year Performance

■ Hedgefund.net Multi-Strategy Index

	1 Year	3 Years	5 Years	10 Years	15 Years	Inception 1/90–11/11
Annualized Return	−1.2%	6.5%	2.2%	6.5%	10.4%	11.3%
Annualized Standard Deviation	1.5%	5.2%	6.3%	5.3%	6.3%	5.9%

FIGURE 2.12 Historical Performance of Hedgefund.net Multi-Strategy Index (Jan-90 to Nov-11)

ADVANTAGES OF ALLOCATING TO HEDGE FUNDS

Now that we have discussed the history of hedge funds and highlighted their growth in recent decades, it is important to also understand why hedge funds are an attractive asset class and how they are used by institutional investors. Table 2.1 lists the pros and cons of investing in hedge funds.

Since the focus of this book is hedge fund analysis, I will assume that the reader has already decided that hedge funds are a viable asset class. As such, the remainder of this chapter will briefly cover the major benefits of investing in hedge funds along with the primary issues surrounding the asset class.

Return Enhancement

Historically, hedge funds have performed better than their long-only peers and indexes—with less volatility. The risk/return chart in Figure 2.13 illustrates the long-term annualized performance and annualized standard deviation for a variety of hedge fund strategies and compares them to

TABLE 2.1 Summary of Pros and Cons of Investing in Hedge Funds

Pros	Cons
Enhanced return potential	Higher fees
Diversification	Liquidity constraints
Low correlation	Leverage
Greater opportunity set	Transparency
Down-market protection	Industry growth
Return dispersion	Potential for systemic risk
Enhance market liquidity	

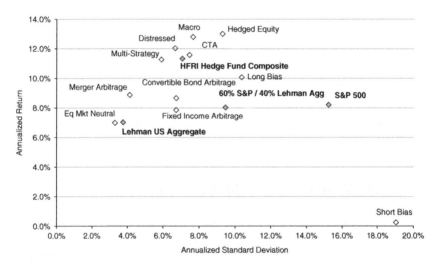

FIGURE 2.13 Risk/Return Graph for Period Jan-90 to Nov-11

traditional benchmarks over the period beginning January 1990 through November 2011.

The HFRI Hedge Fund Composite Index, which represents a composite of all hedge funds tracked by Hedge Fund Research, Inc., returned 11.3 percent annualized over the period with a 7.3 percent annualized standard deviation. This compares quite favorably to the S&P 500 Index (which returned 8.2 percent with a 15.2 percent standard deviation) and the Lehman U.S. Aggregate Index (which returned 7.0 percent with a 3.8 percent standard deviation). A blended benchmark that consists of 60 percent S&P 500 and 40 percent Lehman U.S. Aggregate returned 8.0 percent with 9.5 percent standard deviation.

The graph also illustrates which specific strategies have performed well and which have not. Multi-strategy performed in line with the HFRI Composite with a slightly lower standard deviation while distressed outperformed the composite with lower risk. Macro, CTA, and hedged equity all outperformed the composite but with slightly higher standard deviation. Equity market neutral and merger arbitrage underperformed the composite but did so with significantly lower standard deviation. Convertible bond arbitrage and fixed income arbitrage each performed below the composite and had similar standard deviation statistics.

The two strategies that underperformed the composite and did so with higher levels of standard deviation were long biased and short biased equity. In fact, short biased equity barely eked out a positive return for the period (+0.3 percent) while turning in the highest level of standard deviation (19 percent) over the period.

An examination of the calendar year returns in the first part of this chapter clearly indicates that performance among the hedge fund strategies was higher in the 1990s than in the 2000s. Table 2.2 highlights this by showing the annualized return and standard deviation for each of the hedge fund strategies alongside the S&P 500 and Lehman U.S. Aggregate indexes over these two time periods.

The average annualized return for this group of hedge fund strategies in the 1990s (1/90 to 12/99) was 13.6 percent while the average annualized return in the 2000s (1/00 to 11/11) was 5.9 percent. The variability in returns (standard deviation) was close over the two periods. The biggest drop in performance was in the Equity Hedge strategy, which declined from a return of 23.7 percent in the 1990s to just 4.7 percent subsequently.

However, this coincides with the decline in the performance of the S&P 500, which returned 18.2 percent in the 90s and just 0.5 percent since (along with an increase in standard deviation). It is sobering to consider that the stock market has been quite volatile in the 2000s but an investment in the S&P 500 over that period would have been essentially flat. However, over the same period, the HFRI Equity Hedge Index significantly outperformed the S&P 500, returning 4.7 percent versus 0.5 percent for the S&P.

Diversification/Correlation

Hedge funds have historically been a good diversifier to traditional, long-only portfolios because they have exhibited lower correlation over time. Table 2.3 measures the correlation dynamics among the various hedge fund strategies as well as standard long-only benchmarks.

The average hedge fund strategy correlation relative to the S&P 500 was 0.43; it was 0.08 relative to the Lehman U.S. Aggregate over the period.

TABLE 2.2 Performance Comparison: 1990s (Jan-00 to Dec-99) versus 2000s (Jan-00 to Nov-11)

	1990s		2000s	
	Annualized Return	Annualized Standard Deviation	Annualized Return	Annualized Standard Deviation
HFRI Fund Wgted Composite	18.3%	6.9%	5.8%	6.9%
HFRI Equity Hedge (Total) Index	23.7%	8.7%	4.7%	9.3%
Barclay Equity Long Bias Index	7.2%	9.0%	6.4%	11.5%
HFRI EH: Short Bias Index	−1.6%	19.8%	1.9%	18.4%
HFRI RV: FI-Convert Arb Index	11.5%	3.5%	6.4%	8.5%
HFRI EH: Equity Market Neutral	11.2%	3.1%	3.5%	3.2%
HFRI RV: Fixed Income-Corporate	10.9%	7.3%	5.4%	6.2%
HFRI ED: Merger Arbitrage Index	12.6%	4.6%	5.8%	3.4%
HFRI ED: Distress/Restruct Index	16.6%	6.6%	8.3%	6.6%
HFRI Macro (Total) Index	20.5%	9.2%	6.7%	5.6%
HFRI Macro: Syst Div Index	16.0%	6.7%	8.0%	8.0%
Hedgefund.net Multi-Strategy	15.9%	5.9%	7.5%	5.8%
Average	*13.6%*	*7.6%*	*5.9%*	*7.8%*
S&P 500 Total Return	18.2%	13.4%	0.5%	16.4%
Lehman U.S. Aggregate Total Return	7.7%	3.9%	6.4%	3.7%

The average correlation of the hedge fund strategies to one another was 0.34 over the period.

As we know, the mathematics of modern portfolio theory eloquently informs us that a collection of uncorrelated assets can improve the risk/return profile for a total portfolio. As Table 2.3 shows, hedge funds have historically exhibited lower levels of correlation to the long-only benchmarks as well as among themselves. However, in recent years correlations have increased

TABLE 2.3 Correlation Table for Period Jan-90 to Nov-11

Correlation Table
January 1990 through November 2011

	S&P 500 Total Return	Lehman U.S. Aggregate Total Return	HFRI Equity Hedge (Total) Index	Barclay Equity Long Bias Index	HFRI EH: Short Bias Index	HFRI EH: Equity Market Neutral Index	HFRI Event-Driven (Total) Index	HFRI ED: Merger Arbitrage Index	HFRI ED: Distressed/ Restructuring Index	HFRI Macro (Total) Index	HFRI Macro: Systematic Diversified Index	HFRI RV: Fixed Income-Convertible Arbitrage Index	Hedgefund.net Multi-Strategy Index
S&P 500 Total Return	1.00												
Lehman U.S. Aggregate TR	0.14	1.00											
HFRI Equity Hedge (Total) Index	0.73	0.07	1.00										
Barclay Equity Long Bias Index	0.85	−0.04	0.96	1.00									
HFRI EH: Short Bias Index	−0.71	−0.01	−0.74	−0.83	1.00								
HFRI EH: Equity Market Neutral Ind.	0.25	0.10	0.49	0.46	−0.13	1.00							
HFRI Event-Driven (Total) Index	0.70	0.06	0.84	0.91	−0.62	0.40	1.00						
HFRI ED: Merger Arbitrage Index	0.53	0.10	0.59	0.72	−0.41	0.34	0.75	1.00					
HFRI ED: Distressed/Restructuring Ind.	0.52	0.01	0.70	0.75	−0.48	0.39	0.85	0.57	1.00				
HFRI Macro (Total) Index	0.34	0.29	0.56	0.54	−0.35	0.32	0.51	0.33	0.43	1.00			
HFRI Macro: Systematic Div. Ind.	0.43	0.06	0.53	0.51	−0.51	0.24	0.40	0.29	0.26	0.58	1.00		
HFRI RV: Fixed Income-Convertible Arbitrage Ind.	0.46	0.18	0.58	0.58	−0.32	0.30	0.65	0.48	0.65	0.25	0.07	1.00	
Hedgefund.net Multi-Strategy Ind.	0.60	0.12	0.81	0.85	−0.57	0.43	0.75	0.53	0.67	0.59	0.51	0.58	1.00

Average Hedge Fund correlation to S&P 500   0.43
Average Hedge Fund correlation to Lehman US Agg   0.08
Average correlation among Hedge Fund Strateies   0.34

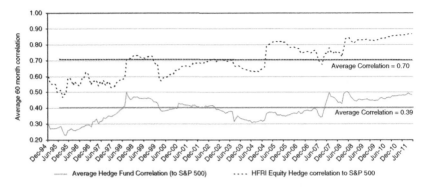

FIGURE 2.14 Rolling 5-Year Correlation

somewhat. Figure 2.14 measures the average rolling 60-month correlation of the hedge fund indexes highlighted in this chapter relative to the S&P 500 (solid line) as well as the correlation of the HFRI Equity Hedge Index relative to the S&P 500 (dotted line).

In each case, the trend has been moving up, and the most recent 60-month correlation statistics are at or near historical highs. In addition, current numbers are significantly higher than their long-term average.

Table 2.4 highlights the most recent five-year correlation statistics for each of the 11 strategies highlighted in this chapter and compares them to their long-term average correlation. All but three strategies have experienced

TABLE 2.4 Recent Hedge Fund Correlation versus Long-Term Average Hedge Fund Correlation

	Latest 5-Year Correlation	Average Correlation Since 1/90
HFRI Equity Hedge (Total) Index	0.87	0.70
Barclay Equity Long Bias Index	0.91	0.84
HFRI EH: Short Bias Index	−0.91	−0.76
HFRI EH: Equity Market Neutral Index	0.47	0.19
HFRI Event-Driven (Total) Index	0.83	0.67
HFRI ED: Merger Arbitrage Index	0.75	0.49
HFRI ED: Distressed/Restructuring Index	0.73	0.49
HFRI Macro (Total) Index	0.20	0.33
HFRI Macro: Systematic Diversified Index	−0.02	0.55
HFRI RV: Fixed Income-Convertible Arbitrage Index	0.67	0.36
Hedgefund.net Multi-Strategy Index	0.82	0.58

an increase in correlations over the last five years. The exceptions are short bias (which has become more negatively correlated), HFRI Systematic Diversified Macro (which actually exhibits slight negative correlation), and the HFRI Macro Index. The Macro systematic index is generally reflective of CTA and other quantitative macro hedge funds. The decrease in correlation in the HFRI Macro Index may be due in large part to the fact that it includes the Systematic (CTA) Index as a subcomponent.

As with all backward-looking performance-related data, the reader should put these statistics in historical perspective. The global market environment is ever changing, and because hedge funds can have fairly open mandates, past performance (and related statistics) should always be used in conjunction with a thorough evaluation of current conditions. The use of scenario analysis is always helpful when trying to get a handle on future possibilities.

Dispersion

Another way to look at the opportunity set within the hedge fund universe is to look at the disparity or dispersion of returns across strategies.

Figure 2.15 graphically depicts the differential between the best- and worst-performing hedge fund strategies on a calendar year basis. This is an important indicator because it shows that good asset allocation can add value over time, but it also highlights the fact that despite increasing

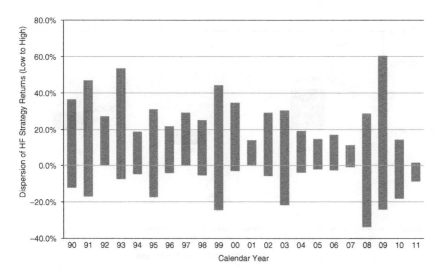

FIGURE 2.15 Calendar Year Dispersion among Hedge Fund Strategies

correlations among hedge fund strategies, different strategies can experience divergent return patterns and, hence, can improve a portfolio's total risk/return profile.

Protection in Down Markets   The year 2008 was a very difficult one, not just for hedge funds, but for investors generally. The HFRI Composite declined −19 percent while the S&P 500 declined −37 percent. There is no denying that hedge funds turned in disappointing results. That disappointment was further compounded by the Madoff scandal, an increase in side pockets due to illiquid investments, investor gates, and excess leverage in the system overall. However, despite the negative performance hedge funds outperformed the rest of the market—and in some cases by a wide margin.

Figure 2.16 represents the cumulative performance of the S&P 500 in months when it had achieved a positive result (up markets) as well as in months in which it had declined in value (down markets). The corresponding returns for the HFRI Hedge Fund Composite Index were used to determine its up and down market performance. This chart illustrates that hedge funds generally underperform in rising markets but have more than made up for that shortfall in declining markets, falling significantly less than the S&P 500. Due to the destructive power of negative compounding, when the full period return is calculated, the annualized hedge fund return of 11.3 percent beats the 8.2 percent for the S&P 500. A comparison of monthly returns for the S&P 500 and HFRI Composite in 2008 appears in Figure 2.17.

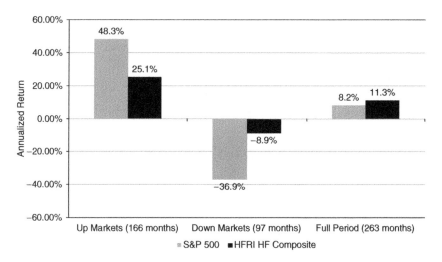

FIGURE 2.16   Up/Down Chart for Period Jan-90 to Nov-11

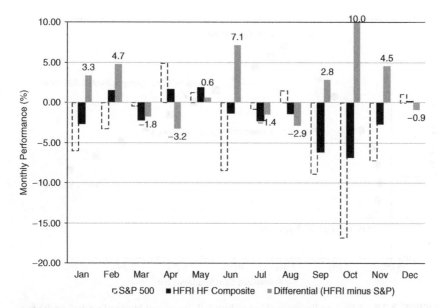

FIGURE 2.17   Monthly Performance Comparison: HFRI Composite versus S&P 500 in 2008

The solid grey bars in this figure represent the relative out-/ under-performance for each month in 2008. The HFRI Composite Index outperformed the S&P 500 Index in seven out of 12 months.

Efficient Use of Capital

The efficient frontier graph in Figure 2.18 shows how an incremental allocation to hedge funds (represented by the HFRI Composite) to a portfolio of equities (S&P 500) and a portfolio of bonds (Lehman U.S. Aggregate) can impact the overall risk/return parameters. The efficient frontier equity graph (depicted in the chart by squares) starts with a 100 percent allocation to the S&P 500 and a 0 percent allocation to the HFRI Composite and adjusts the allocation in 10 percent increments (90 percent/10 percent, 80 percent/20 percent, and so on) until the allocation swings to 0 percent allocation to the S&P 500 and 100 percent allocation to the HFRI Composite. The efficient frontier bond graph (depicted in the chart with circles) uses the same logic applied to a portfolio that consists of the Lehman U.S. Aggregate and the HFRI Composite.

The end result is that a portfolio that includes hedge funds would have added value to a single asset class portfolio in isolation. The equity-efficient

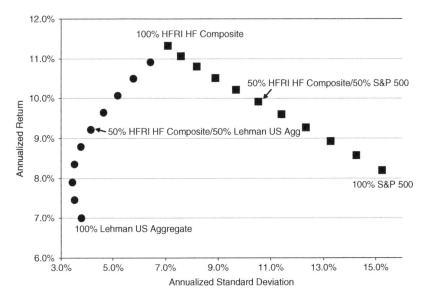

FIGURE 2.18 Efficient Frontier (Hedge Funds/Equity and Hedge Funds/Bonds) for Period Jan-90 to Nov-11

frontier highlights that any allocation to hedge funds would have improved the risk and return while there is more of a curve associated with the bond-efficient frontier (indicating that bonds returned less than hedge funds but did so with less risk).

However, it is important to note that while return and volatility paint a positive picture, the efficient frontier does not take into consideration either skew or kurtosis. Hedge funds tend to exhibit negative skew and positive kurtosis, which must play into an investor's understanding of the asset class and asset allocation plan. Skewness is a measure of how symmetrical a hedge fund's return distribution has been. Kurtosis measures a hedge fund's tendency to exhibit extreme performance (either positive or negative).

HEDGE FUND SIZE AND AGE IMPACTS PERFORMANCE

A number of academic studies have suggested that smaller and younger hedge funds have generally performed better than their peers in the hedge fund industry. One of the aforementioned studies was conducted by Pertrac, a leading hedge funds database firm. The results are highlighted in Table 2.5.

TABLE 2.5 Summary of Results from Pertrac Study on Hedge Fund Performance Due to Size and Age of Fund

Year	Size of Hedge Fund			Age of Hedge Fund		
	Small	Medium	Large	Young	Mid-Age	Mature
1996	24.9%	16.6%	18.6%	29.1%	22.7%	18.3%
1997	20.2%	17.2%	18.1%	24.2%	16.4%	16.9%
1998	8.5%	5.9%	6.7%	11.6%	5.8%	6.6%
1999	32.2%	26.5%	18.5%	34.5%	34.7%	25.3%
2000	16.4%	12.9%	12.4%	20.4%	16.5%	10.8%
2001	12.0%	7.3%	7.7%	14.3%	10.6%	8.7%
2002	5.7%	3.9%	3.7%	8.6%	4.6%	2.8%
2003	24.7%	17.1%	15.5%	22.8%	23.0%	23.3%
2004	12.2%	9.4%	7.3%	12.8%	10.9%	10.4%
2005	12.4%	11.3%	9.0%	14.1%	10.6%	10.9%
2006	14.0%	13.2%	11.6%	15.3%	12.6%	12.7%
2007	11.7%	10.3%	10.2%	15.0%	9.5%	9.5%
2008	−17.0%	−16.0%	−14.1%	−11.3%	−19.5%	−17.9%
2009	21.5%	22.6%	18.7%	25.2%	21.5%	21.0%
2010	13.0%	11.1%	11.0%	13.3%	12.7%	11.8%
Annualized Return	13.6%	10.9%	10.0%	16.2%	12.2%	10.9%
Annualized Standard Deviation	7.0%	5.9%	6.0%	6.4%	7.0%	6.8%
Sharpe (5%)	1.17	0.95	0.82	1.63	0.98	0.85

Methodology

- Merged five hedge fund databases (BarclayHedge, BarclayCTA, Hedgefund.net, Hedge Fund Research, and Morningstar Hedge, formerly Altvest).
- Deleted duplicate entries, fund of funds, and non-U.S. dollar–denominated funds.
- Small funds defined as having < $100 million in assets.
- Medium funds defined as having between $100 million and $500 million in assets.
- Large funds defined as having > $500 million in assets.
- Young funds defined as having less than two years' history.
- Mid-age funds defined as having between two and four years' history.
- Mature funds defined as having greater than four years' history.
- All funds were reclassified monthly to determine which size and age bucket they would be in.

The results of this study are eye-opening. Small hedge funds (defined as funds having less than $100 million in assets) and young hedge funds (defined as having less than a two-year track record) were able to achieve significantly higher returns with a slight pickup in standard deviation for small funds and lower standard deviation for young funds.

There is no definitive (and widely agreed upon) reasoning for this historical outperformance but the following may help to explain it:

- Smaller hedge funds are more nimble.
- Smaller hedge funds have a bigger opportunity set whereas large funds can only invest in bigger investments due to their size.
- Many strategies are capital constrained and have a capacity threshold.
- Portfolio managers of young funds are incentivized to perform well so that they can establish and grow their business. More established funds sometimes avoid taking risk to maintain their business and to protect their reputation.

Hedge Fund Due Diligence

Due Diligence Process

*"Not everything that counts can be counted, and not everything
that can be counted counts."*

Albert Einstein

The process of evaluating and assessing hedge funds combines elements of
both art and science. The successful due diligence analyst will determine
how to straddle this fence to make an informed and intelligent investment
decision.

The illustration in Figure 3.1 highlights the various components that
feed into the decision to hire or fire a hedge fund manager. The circular
design of the illustration can be misleading, though, as the due diligence
process tends to be dynamic. There are number of things that must be
completed before an investment decision can be made, but there is no set
formal procedure that begins with step one and finishes with step 10. I have
found that one of the biggest mistakes that one can make when analyzing a
hedge fund is to apply a "check the box" mentality, which often leads the
analyst to not see the forest for the trees.

KEY AREAS OF FOCUS WITHIN EACH COMPONENT
OF DUE DILIGENCE

There are literally hundreds of areas of discussion when it comes to hedge
fund manager analysis. The bullet points that follow represent some of the
most critical points.

Sourcing and Screening

- Hedge funds can be sourced from a variety of places, including
databases, service providers, and other hedge fund managers.
- They can be screened based on strategy, risk/return parameters, geography, market cap, liquidity, fees, and so on.

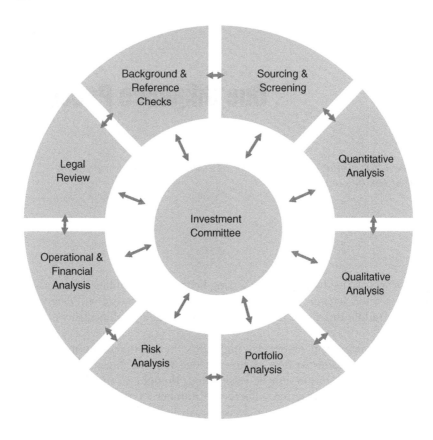

FIGURE 3.1 Elements of the Hedge Fund Due Diligence Process

Quantitative Analysis
    We can screen and analyze funds based on a variety of performance-based statistics:

- Sharpe ratio
- Downside deviation
- Alpha vs. beta
- Correlation

Fund Terms
- Liquidity
- Notice period
- Fees

- Sidepockets
- Gates

Qualitative Analysis

- Investment professional's skill
- Fund's edge
- Team dynamic
- Team pedigrees
- References
- Short alpha

Portfolio Analysis

- Exposure analysis
- Attribution
- Long book vs. short book
- Liquidity analysis
- Style drift

Risk Analysis

- Factor analysis
- Quality of risk metrics
- Skew and kurtosis
- Stress testing
- Scenario analysis

Operational Analysis

- Independent valuation
- Independent administration
- Appropriate service providers
- Multiple signatories to move cash

Financial Analysis

- Review of audited financial statements
- Expense review

Legal Analysis

- Review all firm and fund documents (offering memorandums, subscription forms, articles of incorporation, etc.).
- Check for appropriate compliance procedures.
- Determine effectiveness of chief compliance officer.

References and Background Checks

- Check references with former colleagues and clients.
- Check all historical data and statements.
- Perform background check for all key employees.

Once having established a foundation or core philosophy for performing due diligence, I have found that each hedge fund tends to make its way through the process in its own way and in its own time. As a result, the due diligence process is more akin to a jigsaw puzzle in which we have been given most but not all of the pieces. Some people start the puzzle at the corners and work their way in while other start with a specific puzzle piece and work outward from that point. Different ways of approaching the same problem but the same result in the end.

THE DUE DILIGENCE PROCESS HIGHLIGHTED IN THIS BOOK

Due diligence is a fluid process; however, there are a number of core tenets that all analysts must adhere to. The remainder of this chapter will cover some of the background elements in the process—manager sourcing and screening—ultimately deciding upon a fictitious hedge fund that we will review over the course of the remainder of the book. The goal is to educate the reader about the process in the most detailed and practical way possible. To do so, we will follow the order illustrated in Figure 3.2.

Manager Sourcing

A hedge fund due diligence analyst has a great many tools at his or her disposal that can be used to source hedge fund ideas. They run the gamut from free Internet websites to expensive third-party databases. However, I have found that the most valuable source of hedge fund ideas comes from my personal network in the industry. I have spent more than 20 years analyzing investment managers and can draw upon a vast network of people including prime brokers, auditors, accountants, brokerages, financial services providers, and hedge fund managers themselves.

Databases

There are about a dozen hedge fund database companies that collect data from hedge funds on a monthly basis and package the information in a way that is easy to manipulate and to search for relevant data and for

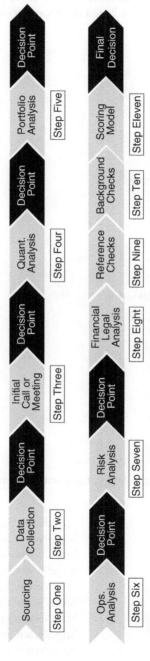

FIGURE 3.2 Stepwise Due Diligence Process Flowchart

Step One — Sourcing
Step Two — Data Collection
Decision Point
Step Three — Initial Call or Meeting
Decision Point
Step Four — Quant. Analysis
Decision Point
Step Five — Portfolio Analysis
Decision Point

Step Six — Ops. Analysis
Decision Point
Step Seven — Risk Analysis
Decision Point
Step Eight — Financial Legal Analysis
Step Nine — Reference Checks
Step Ten — Background Checks
Step Eleven — Scoring Model
Final Decision

comparative purposes. These databases allow the user to search for hedge funds and filter the information based on a variety of factors including the following:

Qualitative Fields
- Firm location
- Fund strategy
- Fund inception date
- Redemption frequency
- Notice period
- Liquidity
- Ability to gate or sidepocket
- Fees
- Lockup
- Onshore/offshore

Performance-Based Fields
- Annualized return
- Annualized standard deviation
- Sharpe ratio
- Drawdown
- Up capture
- Down capture

Regression-Based Fields
- Beta
- Alpha
- Correlation

Some of the predominant hedge fund database and data analysis companies are:

BarclayHedge	http://www.barclayhedge.com
HedgeCo.net	http://www.hedgeco.net
Morningstar	http://corporate.morningstar.com
HFN	http://www.hedgefund.net
Hedge Fund Research	http://www.hedgefundresearch.com
Lipper TASS	http://www.lipperweb.com
Eurekahedge	http://www.eurekahedge.com
Pertrac	http://www.pertrac.com
Fundspire	http://www.fundspire.com
Opalesque	http://www.opalesque.com

FinLab	http://www.finlab.com
HEDGEweb	http://www.hedgeweb.net
Greenwich Alternative	http://www.greenwichai.com
Preqin	http://www.preqin.com
HedgeTracker	http://www.hedgetracker.com
HedgeFundAlert	http://www.hfalert.com/about_launches.php

Many of these websites contain updated news relating to hedge funds, manager interviews/profiles, and links to other areas of interest. I suggest spending some time on each site and visiting them regularly to stay abreast of the most recent news, which will often include information on newly launched funds as well as other funds that have shut down.

While the databases listed are set up differently, most of the information they gather is similar.

Service Providers

Database searches are fairly straightforward. In addition, there are a number of other sources that we can mine for new and interesting hedge fund ideas.

Prime Brokers   We will cover prime brokers in greater detail in the chapter on operational due diligence, but they are worth a mention here because they are a great source of information to the hedge fund due diligence analyst. All hedge funds work with prime brokers to leverage their operational, investment, trading, and risk systems; however, prime brokers also provide what is known as capital introduction services to hedge funds. Specialists in the capital introduction departments at prime brokerage houses provide a much needed bridge between hedge funds and allocators (fund-of-funds, pension plans, foundations, endowments, consultants, and high net worth individuals). Many prime brokers will arrange conferences so that hedge fund managers can connect personally with allocators. These conferences often focus on a specific strategy, geography, theme, or the hedge fund's stage of development (early stage funds, for example). Prime brokers often hold breakfast or lunch meetings to introduce allocators to their hedge fund clients as well.

In addition, the professionals at prime brokerages often reach out to allocators directly to gain information about what trends are developing in the marketplace (such as what strategies are most and least in demand). I typically reach out to my contacts in the prime brokerage community whenever I conduct a specific search so that I can ask them if they have come across any funds that they think could fit the search parameters or to give me an idea of what fund launches are on the horizon (new funds that might be interesting but are still in the formation stage).

Many of the larger prime brokerages collect a great deal of information about the hedge funds they work with and summarize that data in regular reports that highlight interesting and useful information such as current levels of hedge fund leverage, regional allocation shifts, popular hedge fund investment themes, and stocks with a high percentage of hedge fund ownership (there are several indexes and an exchange-traded fund [ETF] that actually track the performance of the most owned names by hedge funds).

Auditors/Accounting Firms   Hedge funds employ accounting and audit firms to conduct fund audits and to manage the general partner's books. For our purposes here, it is important to know that accountants and other professionals at audit and accounting firms have a great deal of exposure to hedge funds here in the United States and abroad. The professionals at these firms can also provide useful sourcing information and can help facilitate introductions. These firms are often good sources for smaller and/or younger hedge funds in particular, as they often need the most help marketing themselves.

Software Vendors/IT Firms   I don't generally obtain many new hedge fund ideas through these kinds of organizations, but I am always on the lookout for contacts within the industry and converse with representatives from these companies to see if they can shed light on the technology side of things (which is important when you have to review the technology and systems utilized by a hedge fund—which we will cover during the operational component of the due diligence process). In addition, many technology firms specialize in hedge funds, so I can leverage from their experiences in the industry.

Media   I don't watch the financial news live on television, but I do spend time each day reviewing their websites to see if there are any interesting or informative articles, interviews, or news clips. Hedge fund managers and other industry experts appear regularly on television. I have found that watching these clips when they are made available to be enlightening. In some cases, I have reached out to a specific hedge fund after viewing a clip by someone in their organization or after hearing industry experts discuss a potential investment theme. For example, after watching a clip a few years ago with several agricultural experts discussing how growth in China and other "emerging" countries would drive protein prices higher for several decades, I was intrigued and conducted a database search for funds that specialize in agriculture (I also contacted several prime brokers to ask if they knew of any funds that could capitalize on this theme).

In addition to television websites, there are a host of other websites that provide a wealth of information about economics, markets, hedge funds, and news. I have provided a list of my favorite sites in Table 3.1. This is

TABLE 3.1 Top Media Sources for Hedge Fund Information

Bloomberg   http://www.bloomberg.com
One of my favorite sites. Great source of real-time news, interviews, and other
    articles. Links to Bloomberg live TV and radio (both free) are provided as well
    as selected clips from the past.

Seeking Alpha   http://seekingalpha.com
Great site that provides real-time news flow and informative articles on investing
    ideas and themes. Discussion of hedge fund manager holdings (provided by
    13F filings).

Deal Book   http://dealbook.nytimes.com
New York Times blog edited by Andrew Ross Sorkin that covers the investment
    world and has a section dedicated to hedge funds.

Deal Breaker   http://dealbreaker.com
As the name implies, this site breaks news relating to the investment industry
    including a section dedicated to hedge funds.

ZeroHedge   http://www.zerohedge.com
Commentary (often stinging) on current markets, personalities, investment
    themes, and global issues of the day.

Business Insider   http://www.businessinsider.com/clusterstock
Website that provides a wealth of information about the industry in general.
    Combines news, interviews, video, and interesting (often humorous)
    slideshows.

FT Alphaville Blog   http://ftalphaville.ft.com/blog
The *Financial Times* blog is always interesting and provides a thorough list of
    other financial blogs. Access to the FT.com website requires a subscription but
    I highly recommend it (I feel it is the best financial paper in the world).

CNBC   http://www.cnbc.com
News and free clips from their live business shows (real-time streaming access is
    provided for a fee—this includes the ability to search their archives for video
    clips).

Abnormal Returns   http://abnormalreturns.com
Great source for quotes from industry professionals. This site pulls all the best
    information from other financial websites and provides links to them.

SEC Info   http://www.secinfo.com
Great source of information regarding filings by hedge fund managers, including
    all published 13F reports.

(continues)

TABLE 3.1 (*Continued*)

Wall Street Journal   http://online.wsj.com
This is a pay-to-view site, but well worth the money. If you don't want to pay
for the WSJ Online, visit its sister site, www.MarketWatch.com.

Opalesque   http://www.opalesque.com
Combination of hedge fund news, interviews, indexes. Includes a TV and radio
channel that provide interviews with leading figures in the hedge fund
industry.

FinViz   http://finviz.com/news.ashx.
Aggregates topical news and articles that appear in financial blogs.

not meant to be an exhaustive list, but I consistently pick up very useful
information from these sites and typically visit them on a regular basis
(some daily, some weekly, the rest on a less regular basis).

Google   I think Google deserves a section all to itself. I use this website
throughout the day to see how the markets are performing and to track
real-time news breaks (Google Finance/Google News), to search for specific
topics or names (Google Search), to search for academic papers (Google
Scholar), and to set up real-time and periodic alerts (Google Alerts). I find
the Google Alerts function particularly useful. I have set up alerts that will
automatically e-mail me when specific words or phrases appear anywhere
on the Web. I have a very extensive list of search words/terms that include:

- The names of key investment personnel at hedge funds that I am invested
  in (as well as the names of the firms and funds).
- The names of key people at hedge funds that I am currently reviewing
  or plan to review in the future.
- Key phrases that are relevant to various aspects of the business (for
  example, I search for the phrase "new hedge fund launch" as one way of
  finding references to websites/articles/news/academic papers that may
  mention if any hedge funds are launching or newly launched).
- A news-only search for the term "hedge fund."

The key to using Google Search is to word the phrases efficiently. For
example, if you want to set up an automated Google Alert for a portfolio
manager whose name is John Smith (and you search for the term "John
Smith"), you will likely receive hundreds of e-mail alerts each day, as this is
a very common name. A more efficient way to search for John Smith would

be to search for a combination of terms. For example, it would be more effective to search for the phrase "John Smith" in combination with the name of his hedge fund, Fictional Capital. You may still receive some alerts that don't apply to "your" John Smith, but the number of irrelevant alerts will be greatly minimized.

Google gives you the flexibility of sending alerts as they occur (an e-mail alert sent out as soon as it is found by the search engine) or at a specific time of the day (set by the user). For example, I receive one daily alert at the end of each day for the search term "hedge fund" (which yields many results). In addition, I limit the alerts only to news stories and blogs (instead of all webpages). Google gives you the additional flexibility of confining your alerts to websites, news, blogs, video, discussions, and books (or across all those categories).

PUTTING IT ALL TOGETHER

Now that we have discussed many of the various methods of sourcing funds, we can apply these techniques to a mock hedge fund manager search (we will use this search in this book as a starting point as we go through all of the various stages in the due diligence process). For the purposes of this book, we will assume that I work at a firm called Hedge Fund Analysis, Inc. and that I am the lead analyst on this search (and the subsequent due diligence analyst). To initiate the process, we will start the hedge fund search by using a third-party database to screen for the following criteria:

Criteria	Description
Strategy	Equity long/short (exclude all closed funds)
Geography	United States, North America
Office Location	United States
Vehicle	Show only offshore funds
Track Record	Minimum of three years
Return	Annualized return in top quartile of the Equity L/S universe
Size	Minimum assets under management of $250 million
Liquidity	No greater than quarterly redemptions

A diagram illustrating how the different search (filter) terms impact the database search is shown in Figure 3.3.

Our database started with roughly 9,000 hedge funds across all strategies. As we applied each of the filters, the number of funds remaining in the universe got smaller until we had a list that was more manageable.

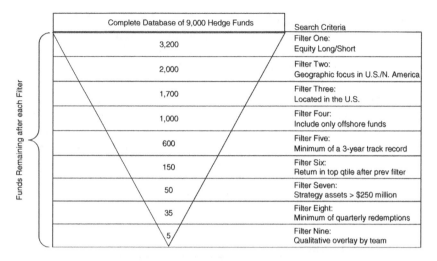

Complete Database of 9,000 Hedge Funds	Search Criteria
3,200	Filter One: Equity Long/Short
2,000	Filter Two: Geographic focus in U.S./N. America
1,700	Filter Three: Located in the U.S.
1,000	Filter Four: Include only offshore funds
600	Filter Five: Minimum of a 3-year track record
150	Filter Six: Return in top qtile after prev filter
50	Filter Seven: Strategy assets > $250 million
35	Filter Eight: Minimum of quarterly redemptions
5	Filter Nine: Qualitative overlay by team

Funds Remaining after each Filter

FIGURE 3.3   Results of the Database Screening Process

You can see that actual number of hedge funds remaining after applying all the filters is 35 (after the eighth filter). However, I added a qualitative overlay to the process that effectively reduced the search results considerably (with just five hedge funds remaining). The qualitative overlay consisted of a review of the 35 remaining hedge fund candidates by the investment team. Funds were eliminated based on the following factors:

- Previous team member experience with the fund managers.
- Funds that had erroneous information in the database (which happens regularly).
- Funds that were listed as being open to new assets but have recently closed or will close before we can complete due diligence.
- Similarity to other hedge funds in which we are currently invested (no need to allocate to two funds that do exactly the same thing).

In addition, two funds were added by the investment team that did not report to any of the published databases.

The resulting five hedge funds in our search were then run through a standard performance database and a summary report was created (Table 3.2) for discussion by the investment team.

The summary sheet highlights several key statistics including performance-based return and risk figures as well as information specific to the operation of the hedge fund (fees, liquidity, etc.).

TABLE 3.2 Summary Information for the Five Hedge Fund Candidates

Summary Statistics for Equity Long/Short Manager Search

	Performance - Periods ending November 2011									Fund/Firm Information						
	2006	2007	2008	2009	2010	2011	Annualized Return	Std Dev	Sharpe Ratio	Base Fee	Performance Fee	Redemption Frequency	Notice Period	Lock	Fund Assets	Firm Assets
Fund 1	1.83	5.41	−32.66	55.55	19.47	−3.97	5.22	17.52	0.10	1.0%	20%	Mo	60 days	1Yr Soft	$1B	$3B
Fund 2	1.76	15.41	−22.19	26.64	7.21	−17.87	0.38	10.95	−0.36	2.0%	20%	Qtr	90 days	None	$700M	$700M
Fund 3	1.26	14.37	3.6	12.5	4.99	0.93	7.42	6.00	0.41	2.0%	20%	Qtr	65 days	None	$350M	$500M
Fund 4	−1.20	19.63	−23.87	14.92	8.11	3.6	2.98	11.21	−0.12	1.5%	20%	Qtr	30 days	1Yr Soft	$500M	$500M
Fund 5	0.41	15.93	8.18	8.00	9.75	−0.54	8.22	7.70	0.43	1.5%/1%	20%	Qtr	90 days	None/1Yr Hard	$275M	$275M
S&P 500	15.79	5.49	−37.00	26.46	15.06	1.08	2.09	17.42	−0.07							

SOME INITIAL THOUGHTS

The summary report provides a starting point for comparing the hedge funds that have made it through the initial filters. While performance should never dictate any final investment decision, it is often a good starting point. It is also very important to understand firm/fund size as well as liquidity terms before making any investment.

Fund One This fund managed to outperform the S&P 500 over the full period (five years ended November 2011) and did so with a level of volatility similar to the S&P 500. As a result, Fund 1's Sharpe ratio is modestly positive while the S&P's is slightly negative. Of the five funds being considered, this one has experienced the highest level of volatility by a considerable margin. Fund 1 declined the most in 2008 relative to the other four but experienced the biggest comeback in 2009 (which appears to be the major driver in its five-year annualized return). This fund has the lowest fees (1 percent management fee and 20 percent performance fee) and best liquidity terms (monthly redemptions with 60 days' notice). The redemption terms include a one-year "soft" lock, which means that an investor can redeem within the first year of investment but will pay a fee (penalty) of 2 percent for doing so. The penalty is paid to the hedge fund, meaning that the investors remaining in the fund will benefit. The firm manages $3 billion in total assets and about one third of that is in this strategy. The remaining $2 billion is invested in a long-only version of the hedge fund.

Fund Two This fund turned in the lowest annualized performance over the five-year period of the funds under review with standard deviation in the middle of the range. As a result, its Sharpe ratio is negative (even more so than the S&P 500). Its return in 2008 was well above that of the S&P 500 and its 2009 return was virtually identical to the S&P. This fund's real outlier performance is in the year-to-date period in 2011, falling nearly −18 percent while the S&P 500 was up 1 percent (the other four managers were also up in 2011). The manager charges a 2 percent/20 percent fee schedule and has fairly standard liquidity terms for an equity long/short manager. This fund is the only product managed by the firm.

Fund Three This fund did not experience any negative years over the time period. Its annualized performance is the second best in the group, and it also experienced the lowest level of annualized standard deviation. As a result, its Sharpe ratio is one of the highest (second only to Fund Five). This is a smaller firm (currently managing $350 million), and its fees are among the highest in the group. Redemption terms are appropriate to its strategy.

Fund Four This fund declined in both 2006 (modestly) and 2008 (in line with Fund Two but well ahead of the S&P 500). Overall, its annualized performance and standard deviation are middle of the pack, and the Sharpe ratio was slightly negative. This fund offers 1.5 percent management fees (which is less than funds Two and Three) but has a one-year soft lock (with a 2 percent penalty for redemptions within one year of initial investment). This fund is the firm's only product.

Fund Five Like Fund Three, this fund did not experience any negative years over the time period under review. Its 8.2 percent performance in 2008 was the best in the group. As a result, this fund's annualized performance was also the best in the group, and its annualized standard deviation was second lowest (and significantly lower than the S&P 500). It has the highest Sharpe ratio, just edging out Fund Three (0.43 vs. 0.41). This fund offers two fee options with adjusting liquidity. Option one calls for a 1.5 percent management fee and a 20 percent performance fee; option two offers a 1 percent management fee and a 20 percent performance fee. For those opting for option two, they will have a one-year soft lock (with a 2 percent penalty). For those investors who don't mind a soft lock, this fund manager offers lower fees. The liquidity is appropriate to the strategy (quarterly redemptions with 90 days' notice). This fund is the smallest of the group ($275 million), and this fund is the firm's only product.

To help review these funds, we have also created several basic graphs and reports (Figures 3.4 through 3.9 and Table 3.3).

The risk/return chart (Figure 3.4) and the growth of a dollar chart (Figure 3.5) show that funds Three and Five have similar return profiles. The correlation table (Table 3.3) highlights that funds One and Two are highly correlated to the S&P 500 and that Fund Three had the lowest correlation to the S&P (followed closely by Fund Five). The rolling correlation graphs (Figures 3.6 and 3.7) show that funds One and Two have consistently exhibited a high level of correlation to the S&P and that Fund Three has a significant rise in its rolling 24-month correlation since the fall of 2009. Fund Five is the only one that exhibited a decline over the period (albeit a very modest one).

Lastly, the up/down chart (Figure 3.8) yields some interesting information. Fund One's up-market return was almost identical to the S&P 500 (but its down-market return was by far the worst of the group). Fund Three had the lowest up-market return but made up for that by turning in the best down-market return of the group (by far). Figure 3.9 takes the data calculated and presented in the up/down performance analysis and creates a ratio of the up-market performance relative to the absolute value of the down-market performance. Over the five-year review period, Fund

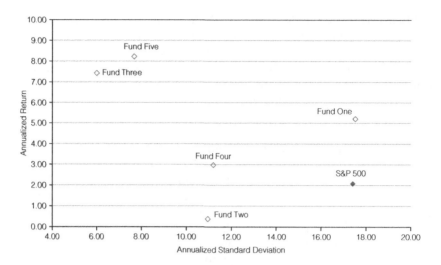

FIGURE 3.4   Risk/Return Chart for Period Dec-05 to Nov-11

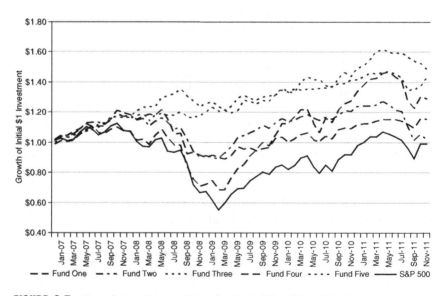

FIGURE 3.5   Cumulative Return Chart for Period Dec-05 to Nov-11

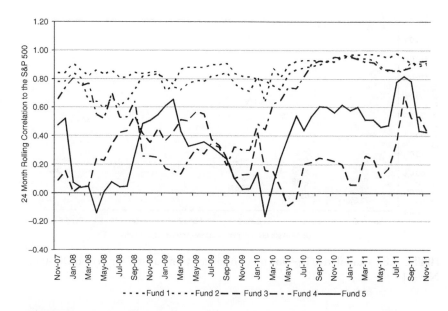

FIGURE 3.6 24-Month Rolling Correlation Chart for Period Dec-05 to Nov-11 (Relative to the S&P 500 Index)

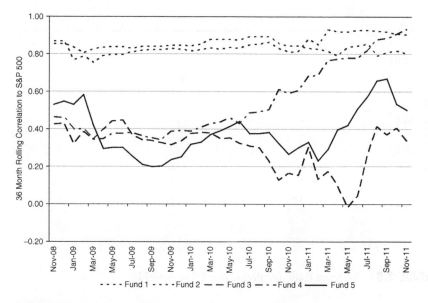

FIGURE 3.7 36-Month Rolling Correlation Chart for Period Dec-05 to Nov-11 (Relative to the S&P 500 Index)

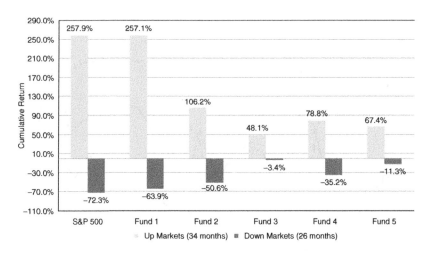

FIGURE 3.8 Cumulative Up/Down Performance Comparison for Period Dec-05 to Nov-11

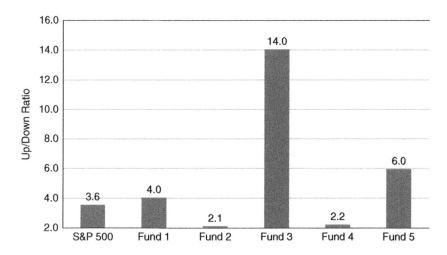

FIGURE 3.9 Up/Down Ratio for Period Dec-05 to Nov-11

TABLE 3.3 Correlation Table for Period Dec-05 to Nov-11

	Fund 1	Fund 2	Fund 3	Fund 4	Fund 5	S&P 500
Fund 1	1.00					
Fund 2	0.83	1.00				
Fund 3	0.48	0.50	1.00			
Fund 4	0.69	0.61	0.39	1.00		
Fund 5	0.42	0.46	0.24	0.39	1.00	
S&P 500	0.85	0.80	0.30	0.57	0.35	1.00

Average Correlation (funds 1–5)	
Fund 1	0.60
Fund 2	0.45
Fund 3	0.40
Fund 4	0.52
Fund 5	0.38

Three had experienced a cumulative up-market return 14 times that of its cumulative down-market return. The fund with the next best ratio is Fund Five, with a six times multiple. The S&P 500 index experienced a 3.6 times multiple.

Based on the results of the summary-level data in conjunction with the basic return and correlation charts, we can prioritize the due diligence process. We will collect data from each of the underlying hedge fund managers but will begin the process by reviewing Fund Five—based on its risk/return profile, up/down capture, and correlation to the S&P 500 and to the other funds under review.

CHAPTER 4

Initial Data Collection

"Experts often possess more data than judgment."

Colin Powell

"The goal is to transform data into information, and information into insight."

Carly Fiorina

In the preceding chapter, we scanned third-party databases to find hedge fund candidates that would fulfill our search criteria. We then reviewed the resulting candidates and discussed which were the most promising. Summary statistics were presented and a series of basic performance and volatility charts were reviewed so that we could prioritize the remaining names on the list.

After careful consideration of the data, I think it is safe to conclude that funds Three and Five exhibited the most attractive risk/return profiles—they were both able to weather the difficult market environment in 2008 (when the S&P 500 declined −37 percent), and each provided the highest annualized returns while doing so with the lowest variation in returns (standard deviation).

PAST PERFORMANCE

It is important not to be overly influenced by performance statistics at this stage. In my view, investment decisions based solely or largely on past performance have been responsible for more bad investment calls (and results) than any other single factor. I have run searches like the one we are using in this book hundreds of times in the past and have often found that the funds that look best on paper (i.e., have the best performance over time or have the most attractive recent performance) are often not the most appropriate investments in real life. As hedge fund due diligence analysts, we should approach each fund with an open mind and not let performance results blind us to other options.

As a result, we will request information from all five of the hedge fund candidates but we will start with Fund Five. When we have completed our analysis of each of the five candidates, we will be in a better position to evaluate which fund is the best fit with our total portfolio of investments.

In this book, we will use Fund Five (which will henceforth be referred to as Fictional Capital Management or FCM) as our case study. We will analyze this hedge fund from start to finish and will include mock interviews with key investment personnel and an operational review, and we will run through each of the other elements of the due diligence process in detail.

DATA COLLECTION

As we take a hedge fund through the due diligence process, we will request a great deal of information along the way; however, we do not need to collect and review all that data in the beginning. My initial request for information typically covers fairly basic items, such as:

- Fund presentation.
- Due diligence questionnaire (DDQ).
- 6–12 months of historical monthly fund letters (and/or quarterly letters).
- Firm/fund organizational chart (which is typically found in the presentation or the DDQ).
- Biographies of key professionals at the firm (again typically found in the presentation or DDQ).

To request this information, I generally e-mail the hedge fund's marketer or investor relations contact and use a format similar to that in Figure 4.1.

From: Frank Travers

To: Bill Hobson

Sent: December 15, 2011

Subject: Initial Information Request – Fictional Capital Management

Bill,

My firm, Hedge Fund Analysis, Inc., is requesting information in order to conduct initial due diligence on your hedge fund and to arrange for an introductory call or meeting after reviewing the materials. Could you please provide the following information on your fund(s) so that we can begin the review process?

Requested Information:

— Fund Presentation

— Due Diligence Questionnaire

— Last 12 monthly fund reports (and/or Quarterly reports)

— Professional Bios/Organizational Chart

Please feel free to include any additional information not requested above if you feel it will shed light on your organization or underlying fund(s). Once we have had a chance to review the materials, we will contact you if there is a potential fit and will set up either a phone call or in-person meeting if possible.

If you would like any additional information about my firm, please go to our website at www.hfanalysis.com or contact me at the phone number or e-mail address listed below.

Regards,

Frank J. Travers, CFA

Hedge Fund Analysis, Inc.
frank.travers@hfanalysis.com

FIGURE 4.1   Sample E-Mail to Request Data from FCM

I send e-mails like the one illustrated in Figure 4.1 all the time. The information is generally "off the shelf," meaning the hedge fund has all or most of the requested items readily available—they simply have to e-mail the information back to me. In our search example, we will send this e-mail template to each of the five funds under review and start to review the information as it becomes available.

DUE DILIGENCE QUESTIONNAIRE (DDQ)

Most hedge funds create DDQs for potential as well as existing investors. These documents generally follow a similar format and include detailed questions and corresponding answers that cover the following broad categories:

- Firm overview
- Strategy overview
- Biographies of key personnel
- Investment process
- Risk management
- Trading
- Fund terms
- Back office and operations
- Legal and compliance

DDQs can range from a dozen pages to several hundred depending on the size of the organization, the number of products managed, or the complexity of the underlying funds. Most firms use similar templates when developing their DDQs, so I have found that it is not necessary to create a specialized one for my own use. Many hedge funds use the DDQ template provided by the Alternative Investment Management Association (AIMA) (www.aima.org). I generally get most of what I need from the DDQs created and distributed by the hedge fund managers. I always have additional questions after reading through the DDQ and associated presentation but have found it best to send an e-mail to the manager with follow-up questions or to schedule a call or meeting to ask the remaining questions personally.

FICTIONAL CAPITAL MANAGEMENT

I have included a comprehensive due diligence questionnaire template in the following section. Most of the questions in the DDQ template are fairly straightforward. However, there are a number of questions that require specialized knowledge and understanding in order to properly evaluate the hedge fund manager's responses. As such, I have included commentary (in italics) under selected questions to:

- Explain what the question means and how to interpret the response, and/or
- Detail certain answers provided by Fictional Capital Management that are relevant to our review in the current and following chapters.

Sample Due Diligence Questionnaire Template (with selected responses from Fictional Capital Management)

1. Firm Overview
Contact Information

    Company name: Fictional Capital Management, LLC (FCM)

    Address:

    Telephone:

    Fax:

    E-mail:

    Name of contact(s): *Bill Hobson*

    Title of contact(s): *Chief Operating Officer*

    Telephone of contact(s):

    E-mail of contact(s):

    Website (include username/password if needed):

Company Information

    Provide a brief company history:

        FCM is a privately owned investment firm based in New York. It was founded in July 2006 by Ted Acoff and Jaime Wernick who had previously worked together at GCH Advisers. The FCM Fund launched in December 2006. The firm manages a long/short equity hedge fund with a focus on small-mid-cap stocks primarily in the United States. The firm employs eight people, including two portfolio managers, two analysts, and a trader.

    Type of company/entity:

        Limited Liability Corporation

    Date and place of incorporation:

        June 2006

    Domicile:

        USA

Subsidiaries, branch offices, or other locations, if any:
None

- Detail the functions performed at these subsidiaries, branches, and locations.
- Which regulatory authority is the company registered with?

FCM is a Registered Investment Advisor with the SEC.

- Date of registration:
- *August 2009*
- Registration number:
- Scope of registered activities:
- Specify reliance on any regulatory exemptions:
- Please specify the date of the most recent regulatory inspection, if any:

List any affiliations, directorships, and memberships of the company and/or its principals:
None

Specify nature of services provided by the company (discretionary investment management or advisory):
Discretionary management of investment portfolios.

Please list the total assets under management by the company:
$275 million

Ownership

Describe the company's and group ownership structure.
100% employee owned.

- List the names of all owners:
  Ted Acoff, Jaime Wernick, Bill Hobson
- Percentage ownership:
  Acoff: 40 percent; Wernick: 40 percent; Hobson: 20 percent.
- Role within the company:
  Acoff: portfolio manager; Wernick: director of research; Hobson: COO.

Organization

How many full-time employees are there?
Eight

Please include below or attach a short background of principals (education, career background, etc.):
Ted Acoff: Started his career as an analyst at Cannon Capital (1992–1998); joined GCH Advisers in 1998 as a senior analyst

and was made co-portfolio manager of the GCH Equity fund in 2003. He co-founded FCM in 2006.

Jaime Wernick: *Started his career as an investment banker at Jenners, Blakely (1995–2000); joined GCH Advisers in 2001 as a senior analyst and was made co-portfolio manager of the GCH Equity fund in 2003. He co-founded FCM in 2006.*

Bill Hobson: *Started his career as controller at Bellman Capital (1997–2002); joined GCH Advisers in 2003 as Chief Operating Officer and co-founded FCM in 2006.*

See attachment for additional personnel bios.

Is there a key-person clause in effect? If so, provide details.

Yes. If Ted Acoff and Jaime Wernick are not able to manage the day-to-day functions of the fund for 90 consecutive days, the fund will fully liquidate all holdings and return capital to investors within a timely manner (refer to the OM for additional details).

Do any of the principles and key professionals have any outside business interests? If so, please provide details and an estimate of how much time they spend on those interests.

No

What are the average years of professional experience in the company, both years as a professional as well as years in the company?

The average number of years' experience for the key investment professionals (Acoff and Wernick) is 17 years.

Please enclose an organization chart depicting the names of senior managers in charge of the following areas and headcount:

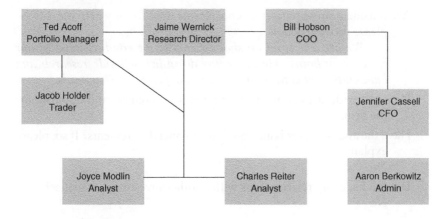

- Trading: *1*
- Reporting:
- Investment research: *4*

- Portfolio management: *1*
- Information technology: *1*
- Administration: *3*
- Risk management: *2*
- COO/operations: *3*
- Legal: *0*
- Compliance: *1*
- Business development: *1*

What has been the turnover rate among the company's personnel? Please list of all employees that have either joined or left the firm since its inception.

Julie Crelle left the firm in March 2008. She was an analyst. Jennifer Cassell (CFO) joined in January 2009. Charles Reiter (analyst) joined in August 2009. Aaron Berkowitz (admin) joined in March 2011.

Where do the primary trading, research, and portfolio management activities take place?

All functions are conducted out of the firm's office in Westchester, New York.

Where do middle and back office functions take place?

All functions are conducted out of the firm's office in Westchester, New York.

Where are the accounts maintained?

In our offices in Westchester, NY. We have backup files stored externally via automatic daily feed with an offsite data storage facility.

Are outside representatives or consultants used for any activities? If so, please provide details.

We are a bottom-up shop; therefore we conduct most of our research in-house. However, we do utilize sell side research and have employed consultants for specific projects when needed.

Please provide details of the appointed legal counsel and auditors for the firm.

Have the auditors ever issued qualified financial statements? If so, please explain.

No

Do you have any relationships with another investment manager?

No

Do you share office space or any other resources with another firm? If so, please give details.
No

Does this create conflicts and, if so, how are those conflicts managed?

References

Please provide at least two references for each of the principals involved in the management of the firm and/or fund.

- Name:
- Profession:
- Company:
- Title:
- Telephone:
- Fax:
- E-mail:
- Description of current and/or past relationship with the company or the principal:

See attachment one for a complete list of references for the principals.

Track Record

Number of portfolios/accounts/products managed by the company:
We manage a single strategy in a master feeder structure (with both an onshore and offshore feeder).

Number of funds managed/advised by the company (include fund name and assets managed by the fund):
We manage a single strategy in a master feeder structure (with both an onshore and offshore feeder).

Total assets managed/advised by the company:
$275 million

Inception date of the fund under review:
December 2006

Has the track record been audited? If yes, by whom?
Yes. By the fund's audit firm.

What is the level of trading activity of the portfolio? Please provide information in terms of coverage of assets/instruments measured and whether numbers are for notional or nominal values. If relevant, please indicate average holding periods for long and short positions.

The portfolio has turned over an average of 2 times per year, with the exception of 2008 when turnover increased to roughly 2.5 times in that year. The firm manages its assets in a bottom-up manner and, as such, holding times will change over time. Generally our long positions can be held from 1 month to 18 months; however, short positions tend to turn over between 1 month and 6 months.

Risk Management

Discuss position concentration (e.g., industries, countries) and stop-loss limits and their management:

Maximum position size for long positions is 10 percent (but few positions have gotten that big historically) with the average long position typically weighted at 4–6 percent. Maximum short position size is 6 percent with the average short position being 2–3 percent. The fund has no formal limits on sector or geographical exposure.

How often are these limits applied?

We have only hit our position limits on a few occasions in the past (all longs) and have quickly pared back the position to conform to the stated maximum position weights.

How do you adjust your risk capital allocation when there is a significant increase in equity due to trading profits?

We set price targets for all of our positions and generally sell or cover when (1) the stock has reached its target or (2) something has subsequently occurred that has forced us to rework the price target or rethink the investment thesis. In addition, we have informal stop-loss provisions in place for long positions. When a long declines by 20 percent or more, we review the investment thesis and adjust the position if necessary. We have a strict stop loss for shorts at a loss of −20 percent.

Has your risk management process changed since inception? If so, please explain how and why.

We introduced the hard stop loss for shorts in mid-2007. Additionally, prior to 2009 Ted Acoff (portfolio manager) was responsible for risk management. Since then, Bill Hobson (COO) has taken over as risk manager.

Do you use an external risk monitor? If so, provide contact details for the external monitor as well as a description of the services they perform.

No. We perform all risk management in-house.

Detail the risk management systems you employ.

- Company name(s): *Prime Broker's risk system, Bloomberg*
- Product name(s):
- Date of implementation: *Since inception*

If risk systems have changed, please state what systems were used before and explain the reasoning for the change.

What is the current minimum liquidity of positions and how do you measure it?

> *We measure liquidity by measuring the estimated number of days to liquidate each position (based on trailing 30-day volume).*

Operational Risk

How does the company define operational risk?

> *The risk that anything non-investment-related can have a material negative impact on any aspect of the fund's or firm's management.*

Does the company have an operational risk management framework? Does the framework consider how the company identifies, assesses, monitors, and controls operational risks?

> *Yes, see the attachment.*

Identify the key operational personnel and provide detail on years in the industry as well as years with the firm.

> *Bill Hobson (COO)—Bill has 20 years' experience as an accountant, hedge fund controller, and COO. Bill holds a CPA designation.*
>
> *Jennifer Cassell (CFO)—Jennifer has 12 years' experience, 10 as an accountant and two as FCM's CFO. Jennifer holds a CPA designation.*
>
> *Aaron Berkowitz (Admin Asst.)—Aaron joined FCM upon graduation from Dartmouth earlier in March 2011. This is Aaron's first job in the industry.*

Does the board of directors approve and regularly review the operational risk management framework?

> *The board of directors meets quarterly telephonically and in person once annually. During the in-person annual meeting, the board reviews the existing operational framework.*

Who is responsible for implementing the operational risk framework? Are there clear lines of responsibility across senior management?

> *Bill Hobson (COO) is responsible for all non-investment-related activities at FCM. He is charged with managing the business,*

marketing to new clients, and servicing existing clients. All other operational functions (accounting, financial, and trade related) are managed daily by Jennifer Cassell (CFO) with assistance from Aaron Berkowitz.

How does the company ensure that employees understand their responsibilities for implementing the operational risk framework?

All operational employees are assigned specific responsibilities and those responsibilities are reviewed (and revised when necessary) on an annual basis. In addition, FCM is a small firm, with three dedicated operational staff, so communication is ongoing and active.

What ongoing assurance does the firm provide to clients over the effectiveness of its operational risk framework? If a SAS70 has been completed, please list any key weaknesses identified.

We believe that FCM employs industry best practices. We have made strides in the last few years to improve our systems and have made additional hires (CFO, admin. assistant) to stay ahead of asset growth.

Operational Risk for Outsourced Functions

What due diligence process does the company perform prior to the appointment of an outsourced service provider? Please specify if this process differs for different service providers, e.g., custodian, administrator, and prime broker.

FCM reviews the proposals from a minimum of three (and typically five) potential service providers. We review all materials and meet with each candidate to discuss services and terms. FCM's three partners then decide which firm best fits our needs. Prior to initiating any new service provider, we review the proposed change with our board of directors, who must approve the change.

Are service-level agreements in place between the company and its outsourced service providers? If so, how does the company monitor services against the prescribed standards?

Yes, we have formal agreements with each service provider. All contracts are reviewed by Bill Hobson (COO) in conjunction with our legal counsel (when needed). All contracts are reviewed by FCM's partners and, ultimately, the board of directors prior to renewals.

Does the company perform periodic reviews of the outsourced service providers?

> *We believe we have top-notch service providers and will review*
> *any relationship should an issue arise or if a better alternative were*
> *to present itself.*

2. **Investment Research**

What outside sources are used?
> *We are a bottom-up shop; therefore we conduct most of our*
> *research in-house. However, we do utilize sell-side research and*
> *have employed consultants for specific projects when needed.*

What proportion of research is generated internally? *100 percent*

Describe the typical flow of an investment idea from inception to a
trading position:
> *The investment team meets formally every Monday morning*
> *to discuss current positions and names in the pipeline. We are*
> *a small firm, so the team members discuss positions informally*
> *daily in real time. Investment ideas tend to be initiated by Jaime*
> *Wernick, the firm's director of research, but we have a collegial*
> *work environment where ideas can come from anyone on the*
> *team. Once an idea is formed, the group will discuss it and it*
> *will be assigned. One of the team members will become the lead*
> *analyst in charge of conducting detailed research (which includes*
> *developing internal financial models) and making an investment*
> *recommendation to the group. The idea will be discussed many*
> *times from inception to conclusion. Once a stock idea is discussed,*
> *Ted Acoff is charged with determining its size in the portfolio.*
> *Specific upside and downside targets are set at the time the position*
> *is established and monitored vigorously.*

If applicable, please describe your back testing of investment ideas:
> *Not applicable*

Have you published or commissioned any research/academic papers?
Do you use the services of any external person and/or entity to
perform research or to make introductions? Please give details.
> *Yes. We have hired specialist researchers and academics on a*
> *few occasions to supplement our own research. An example would*
> *be the hire of Smithson Consulting in 2006 to conduct research on*
> *several specialized medical technology companies.*

3. **Execution and Trading**

Describe members of the trade execution group, their functions, and
their experience:
> *Jacob Holder. He has 10 years' industry experience.*

Who is authorized to place orders on behalf of the fund?
> *Jacob Holder and Ted Acoff.*

Is there a clear separation of functions between front and back office?
> *Yes. Bill Hobson manages all non-investment-related functions and is supported by Jennifer Cassell (CFO) and Aaron Berkowitz (admin. assistant).*

How are executed trades allocated to accounts? Please explain in detail, particularly with respect to split fills:
> *The firm manages one product with onshore and offshore feeders. All trades are allocated in pro rata share to each fund.*

Are any positions allocated as of the end of the trading day or immediately after execution, rather than prior to or at the time of order entry?
> *No*

Does the manager undertake any cross trades or netting and if so, what procedures are utilized?
> *No*

What is the company's policy with respect to trading and system errors? Please explain in detail:

Have there been any major "trade breaks"? If so, please describe the issue and the remedy.

Are trades reconciled to broker confirmations? By whom and how often?
> *Yes, trades are reconciled daily by Jacob Holder (trader) and Aaron Berkowitz. Daily trade reconciliations are further reviewed by Jennifer Cassell (CFO).*

Are cash positions reconciled? By whom and how often?
> *Yes, cash is reconciled daily by Aaron Berkowitz. Daily cash reconciliations are further reviewed by Jennifer Cassell (CFO).*

Does the company make use of "soft dollars"?
> *Yes*

4. Compliance

Who is responsible for compliance in the company?
> *FCM employs the services of a third-party compliance firm, Excel Compliance, Inc.*

Does a dedicated compliance officer/team exist? Does the company maintain a written compliance manual? If yes, please provide details:

> *Yes, FCM has a written compliance manual (see attachment). Bill Hobson had been the firm's compliance officer until 2011, when Excel Compliance, Inc. was hired to fulfill that function.*

When was the manual last updated?

> *The compliance manual was updated in 4Q 2011 following the appointment of Excel Compliance, Inc.*

Please describe any current or potential conflict of interest or any relationships that may affect its trading or trading flexibility, for example, associated broker/dealer.

> *FCM has not had any conflicts previously nor are we aware of any that exist today.*

What are the company's employees' own account-dealing procedures?

> *Employees are not allowed to trade stocks in their personal accounts. FCM believes that is the best way to avoid any conflicts. All employees are encouraged to invest in the firm's hedge fund product (management and performance fees are waived for all internal investments).*

Does the company have regular compliance monitoring programs? If so, please give details:

> *Yes. See the attached compliance manual for details.*

Do any of the company's principals have other business involvement?
No

If yes, describe and quantify how much of their professional time is dedicated to each:

5. **Legal**

Are there or have there in the last 10 years been any criminal, civil, regulatory, or administrative proceedings against (i) the Investment Manager or any of its principals or (ii) the Investment Product or any of its directors, or any similar such matters including reparations, arbitrations, and negotiated settlements? If so, please provide details:
No

Has the company or its principals ever been the subject of any action or warnings from a regulatory body?
No

Has any application to a regulatory body on behalf of the company ever been withdrawn? If so, please give details:
No

6. **Anti–Money Laundering Policy**

   Confirm that the company has established anti–money laundering
   (AML) procedures. Elaborate on the procedure to ensure compliance with AML policies including details of any training provided
   to employees:
   See attached AML policy for details.

   Please advise which jurisdiction's regulations you comply with:

   Please advise who your AML officer is:

   Please provide a summary of your AML procedures:

7. **Insurance**

   What types of insurance do you have in place?
   Commercial general liability coverage
   Workers compensation coverage
   Short-term disability coverage
   Errors and omissions coverage

8. **Business Continuity**

   Does the company have a formal business continuity management plan?
   If so, please describe the basic provisions:
   Yes, see attached BCP manual for all details.

   What contingency plans do you have in terms of:

   - Computer system fault?
   - Incapacitated investment decision makers?
   - Technical failure at prime broker's location?
   - Presence of in-house computer technician?
   - Backup systems?

9. **Fund Information**
Fund Details

   Contact details:
   - Name:
   - Address:
   - Telephone:
   - Fax:

   List share classes and denominations of each share class:

   Date(s) of inception:

   Is the fund regulated? If so, please provide details (including where and
   by whom) and explain any requirements for regulation:

Describe the fund's ownership structure.

Is the fund listed on any exchange(s)? If so, please provide details:

Fees

Management fee:
Class A: 1.5 percent
Class B: 1 percent

Performance fee:
20 percent

Hurdle rate/high water mark:
HWM

Sales fee (if any):
None

Redemption fee:
None

Any other fees:
None

What costs, if any, are recharged to the fund?

Are your fees calculated and charged in terms of equalization structure by:

- Issuing a different series of shares every time shareholders subscribe?
- The equalization share method? *Yes*
- The equalization and depreciation deposit method?
- The equalization-adjustment method?
- Others? (Please describe):

Do you ever share fees with a third party?
No

Have any investors been granted rebates or any other preferential fees/terms?
Yes, early investors in the fund have a discounted fee schedule (class B).

Disclose any soft dollar/soft commission agreement(s):

Ratio of expenses (other than the company's management and incentive fee) to NAV for each of the last three year ends:

Ratio of total expenses to NAV for each of the last three year ends:

Highlight unamortized launch costs (if any):

Liquidity

Minimum initial investment amount:

Minimum subsequent investment:

Subscription frequency:

Redemption frequency:
Quarterly (class B investors have a one-year hard lockup)

Redemption notice period:
90 days

Redemption cash proceeds time line (include details regarding holdbacks and timing of those payments):
90 percent within 30 days; remainder following annual fund audit.

Does the fund have any lockup period or any other liquidity constraints (e.g., suspension of redemptions and gates)?
Class B investors have a one-year hard lockup.

Is there a "gate" and how is that computed (on an aggregate basis or investor by investor basis), and how is the amount in excess of the gate treated?
The fund has no gate.

Have these provisions ever been invoked and under what conditions would these restrictive provisions be invoked in the future?
No.

What is the maximum period that a shareholder would be prevented from having his or her redemption notice accepted and redeemed?
Not applicable

After a shareholder has given the fund administrator the minimum required notice for redemption, please state the maximum number of days it will take to receive the redemption proceeds, including all possible restrictions (e.g., gate provisions, etc.).
90 percent within 30 days; remainder following annual fund audit.

Has the manager undertaken any analysis of costs attached to liquidating the fund over certain time frames; for example, one day, three days, five days, one month, and so on? If so, please enclose.

Does the fund allow for transfer of shares or limited partnership interests between nominees?
Any transfers are at the discretion of the fund manager and upon the approval of the board of directors.

Fund Directors

Please list the number of directors, their names, the degree of relationship with investment manager and service providers, directors' fees paid, and the duration of the company's professional relationship with each director.

Ted Acoff—Portfolio Manager

Jaime Wernick—Director of Research

Bill Hobson—COO

John Mendelsonn—former CFO at GCH Advisors (now retired)

Susan Pearson—macro trader at Lilly Capital (also a day one fund client)

Andrew Dearns—partner at Professional Risk Systems, Inc.

The principals of FCM do not receive any director's fees. The three nonaffiliated board members each receive $15,000 per annum in fees.

How often do the fund directors meet?

Quarterly (via phone)

Annually (in person)

What powers do the fund's directors have?

Have the fund's directors ever disagreed with any firm decision? If so, please provide details.

No

Have there been any changes to the roster of fund directors? If so, provide contact details and an explanation for the change.

Does the fund have D&O insurance?

Yes

Are there provisions in the fund documentation relating to indemnification of directors?

Yes

Fund Administration

Details:

- Name:
- Address:
- General telephone:
- General fax:
- General e-mail:
  - Name of contact:

- Title of contact:
- Telephone of contact:
- E-mail of contact:

How long has the current fund administrator worked with the fund?
Since inception

Please provide the names and contact detail for administrators previously employed by the fund. Include an explanation for the change(s).

Are there provisions in the fund documentation relating to indemnification of the administrator?
Yes

Has ongoing due diligence of the administrator been conducted? If so, provide details (who, frequency, date of last onsite visit)?
Yes. Bill Hobson (COO) and Jennifer Cassell (CFO) visit the administrator 1–2 times each calendar year.

Does the administrator hold a credit rating and are they insured? Please provide details:

Valuation

Who calculates the NAV and what is the frequency of calculation?
The administrator calculates the NAV monthly.

Who is responsible for obtaining valuations and how are any difficult-to-price assets or instruments priced?
All portfolio holdings are level I assets. The administrator is responsible for obtaining all pricing.

Does the investment manager ever provide any instrument prices/NAV calculations?
No

What is the percentage of funds not held in exchange-traded instruments?
0 percent

Does the fund hold investments in which the underlying market has limited liquidity?
No

Are at least three independent prices available for non-exchange-traded investments?
Yes

Please list the sources and methodology of valuation for instruments that have limited liquidity or are non-exchange-traded:

Are any investments (such as trade finance, private placements, private equity, highly structured credit instruments, insurance, mezzanine loans, warrants, or options) priced using a yield-to-maturity, quantitative model, or other non-market-traded pricing practice?

If yes, please explain the pricing methodology:

Please describe how the fund directors ensure that the fund administrator obtains and verifies independent third-party valuations for these investments:

> *The fund directors review the NAV reports provided to them directly by the administrator.*

What is the procedure to price any investments where the purchase or sale of the investment would create a notable or material market impact?

Prime Broker

Details:

- Name:
- Address:
- Contact name:
- Telephone:
- Fax:
- E-mail:

Duration of your professional relationship. Provide details on any previous prime brokers firms used.

Are the assets held in the name of the fund? If not, please explain:
> *Yes*

Are all or any of the assets segregated from the prime broker's assets?
> *No*

Do you use multiple prime brokers? If so, please provide details:
> *No. We are currently evaluating several prime brokers so that we can add one in the next six months.*

How is cash held at the prime broker?

Does the prime broker have insurance? If so, please detail scope:

Can the assets of the fund be pledged or in any other manner used to support or benefit another entity's liabilities?

Does the company or any affiliate ever take "custody" of client assets?

What other services offered by the prime broker do you or have you utilized?

Are there provisions in the fund documentation relating to indemnification of the prime broker?

Has ongoing due diligence of the prime broker been conducted? If so, provide details (who, frequency, date of last onsite visit):

Does the prime broker hold a credit rating and are they insured? Please provide details:

Custodian

Details:

- Name:
- Address:
- Contact name:
- Telephone:
- Fax:
- E-mail:

Duration of the company's professional relationship with the custodian. Provide details on any previous custodians used.

How are subcustodians treated? Are you provided with notice when the custodian transfers assets to a subcustodian?

How is the risk of loss treated?

Are there provisions in the fund documentation relating to indemnification of the custodian or subcustodian?

Has ongoing due diligence of the custodian been conducted? If so, provide details (who, frequency, date of last onsite visit):

Does the custodian hold a credit rating and are they insured? Please provide details:

Auditor

Details:

- Name:
- Address:
- Contact name:
- Telephone:
- Fax:
- E-mail:

Duration of the company's professional relationship with the auditor: Provide details on any previous audit firms used:

Since inception

Have you confirmed that the auditor is in good standing in its domicile/jurisdiction?

Have the auditors ever issued qualified financial statements for the fund?

Has ongoing due diligence of the auditor been conducted? If so, provide details (who, frequency, date of last onsite visit):

Does the audit firm hold a credit rating and are they insured? Please provide details:

Legal

Details:

- Name:
- Address:
- Contact name:
- Telephone:
- Fax:
- E-mail:

Duration of the company's professional relationship with the legal advisers:

Third-Party Marketers

What external promoters or distributors, if any, have been appointed by the company for the fund?

What is the regulatory status of the external promoter and/or third-party distributor?

Duration of the company's professional relationship with any promoter:

Is there any business or personal relationship between the firm and its principals and the third-party marketing firm?

10. Data Overview
Fund Assets

Please list the size of the fund's net assets:
$275 million

What percentage of assets is represented by the largest three investors (please break out)?

Investor 1 (FOF): 12 percent

Investor 2 (FOF): 8 percent

Investor 3 (Endowment): 4 percent

Please list the size of assets by investment vehicle:
FOF: 60 percent
Pension: 5 percent
Foundation/Endowment: 22 percent
High Net Worth: 9 percent
Internal Investment: 4 percent

Provide a monthly history of the fund, strategy, and firm assets since inception (preferably in spreadsheet format):

Provide a monthly history of the fund's gross long and gross short exposures (preferably in spreadsheet format):

Fund Capacity

What is the maximum capacity of your fund?
$500 million

How did you determine the capacity figure?
The investment team had managed $750 million at GCH Advisors prior to starting FCM so we feel that $500 million is well within capacity constraints.

Has the capacity changed in the last five years?
No.

What is the projected time frame to reach capacity?

Will new money be accepted after capacity is reached?
We will soft close the fund for one year upon reaching $500 million to reassess the capacity figure.

How will front/back-office operations be affected in the event of significant increase in assets under management, and what measures will be taken?
We have hired additional staff over the last two years to stay ahead of asset growth. We feel we are adequately staffed at this time; however, we may add an additional investment analyst and admin. assistant if the opportunity to hire the right person arises.

Historical Redemptions

What were the five largest withdrawals in your fund since inception? Provide the following information for each:

- Date: December 2008
- Dollar amount: $11 million
- Percent of NAV: 12 percent
- Reason: The FOF client needed liquidity.

Internal Investment

What is the total amount currently invested by the principals/ management in the fund and other investment vehicles managed pari passu with the fund?

How is the co-investment structured and what are the key terms?

Has the management reduced its personal investment?

- Date:
- Amount:
- Reason:

Do internal investors have better liquidity terms than other investors?

Investors

Please provide a breakout of investors as follows:

- Pensions:
- Fund of Funds:
- Foundations:
- Endowments:
- Platforms:
- High Net Worth:
- Date:
- Internal Investors:

Fund Performance

Please provide historical performance since inception (monthly returns unless the NAV is calculated more frequently):

Is the fund's performance audited? If yes, by whom?

Is any portion of the Fund's historical track record the result of:

- Back-tested results:
- Performance from previous places of employment :
- Carve-outs from other funds:
- Indexes or other proxy returns:

List the five maximum drawdowns, in percent of equity for the fund, the recovery period, and explain what happened:

Miscellaneous

Are there any side letter agreements that can negatively impact the fund? If so, please give details:

Are there any special terms given to any investors?

Please list the following special terms:

- Best redemption terms
- Lowest fee granted
- Size of additional capacity
- Best portfolio transparency

11. Investment Strategy
Strategy and Competitive Advantage

Describe your strategy. Characterize your investment style in terms of:

- Strategy:
    Equity long/short; primarily U.S. oriented.
- Hedging:
    The firm generally looks to hold a short portfolio as a means of generating returns as well as portfolio hedging. However, at times of extreme stress, the fund managers can initiate a portfolio overlay hedge.
- Market exposure:
    The fund's net exposure generally runs in the 30 percent to 60 percent range but can run as low as −30 percent and as high as 75 percent.
- Portfolio concentration in terms of amount of instruments and exposure bias (min/max/avg. number of instruments, min/max/avg. long or short bias):
    Max long position is 10 percent; maximum short position is 6 percent.
- Geographical market focus:
    Primarily United States, but can invest up to 25 percent of assets outside the United States (including ADRs).
- Liquidity:
    Generally look to keep the portfolio liquid. Typically 75 percent of the portfolio can be liquidated within 5 trading days; 90 percent within 15 trading days; 100 percent within 30 trading days.
- Correlation:
    Our performance has been uncorrelated to the market and our peer group because we invest in nonconsensus names that are generally not held by other hedge funds.

What is your investment/trading philosophy?
Invest in companies with strong management, strong and/or improving future growth prospects, and positive cash flow. As we are not an event-driven fund, we do not necessarily look for

catalysts for future growth, but we do not avoid them either. We generally favor companies with light sell-side coverage and a low percentage of hedge fund ownership. For shorts, we generally look for companies that are overlevered, in businesses with limited growth opportunities, or companies that are selling at levels far in excess of what we deem to be their true value.

List the instrument types you use by percentage: *Equity: 95 percent; options, 5 percent.*

What makes your strategy unique?

> *We are bottom-up fundamental investors. We have a strong process but we feel our unique edge is our ability to find companies that are under the radar screen, size them within the portfolio appropriately, and know when to adjust position sizing. We generally invest in non-hedge fund names.*

What makes your strategy different from your peers?

> *We are bottom-up fundamental investors. We have a strong process but we feel our unique edge is our ability to find companies that are under the radar screen, size them within the portfolio appropriately, and know when to adjust position sizing. We generally invest in non–hedge fund names.*

What are the strengths/weaknesses of your investment strategy?

> *We are not contrarian investors, but since many of the names in which we invest are not generally "loved" by the hedge fund community, our return stream has been quite different from our peers. As such, we have experienced negative monthly returns when other funds have performed well (of course, the opposite has also been true).*

Why do you feel you will generate absolute returns?

> *We believe that smaller companies have the ability to perform in varying economic environments. We have the ability to invest across sectors and have demonstrated that we can generate absolute returns at FCM as well as GCH (where Ted and Jaime were co-PMs). The PMs have a long history of investing in this strategy/style and have delivered returns across multiple market and economic environments.*

In which markets do you believe your strategy performs best/worst? (Give examples of time periods):

- Volatility:
- Trends:
- Range trading:

What is your average holding period for:

- All investments?
- Profitable investments?
- Losing investments?
        Does the strategy have a long or short bias? *Long*
- What is the maximum net long or short exposure the fund has had?
        Highest net was 70 percent (Oct. 2010); lowest net was −2% (July 2008).
- What is the normalized net exposure?
        Average net exposure has been 46 percent since inception.

Do you believe that there are persistent structural inefficiencies in the area you invest in? Please explain. How do you think these market inefficiencies will change over time?

What investment criteria must new positions meet?
        (1) Strong management team, (2) positive cash flow), (3) future growth prospects, (4) minimum expected return of 30 percent, (5) competitive advantage.

What would be the maximum period of time when normal terms would be suspended?
        The fund is managed to be liquid and we have not since the firm's inception been in a position where the portfolio could not be fully liquidated within a quarter (which represents the fund's redemption liquidity).

Have the strategy or trading processes changed over time?
        No

Have you encountered position limit problems? If yes, please explain:

What is the percentage of assets in non-exchange-traded instruments? How long do you expect it would take to liquidate these assets under normal circumstances?

Describe your cash management policy:

Portfolio Construction

Who is responsible for managing the portfolio and how are decisions made (unanimous, majority, individual)?
        Ted Acoff is the portfolio manager and has sole responsibility for all buy, sell, and weighting decisions. However, he works closely with Jaime (research director) and the rest of the investment team when making any portfolio decisions.

To what extent is the portfolio construction dependent on computer models?

> *Portfolio decisions are not dependent upon computer models. The portfolio manager will run reports that depict the portfolio's VaR, liquidity, and factor exposures as a means of support.*

How do you invest new capital into the market?

> *We generally edge into new and out of existing positions over a few days but will sell or cover a position quicker in the case of a negative event or news (to stay ahead of potential future losses).*

How do you close out positions to meet capital redemptions?

> *See above.*

12. Investment and Portfolio Risk
Leverage

Discuss your leverage exposure policy and its management over different market cycles:

- What has been the maximum/minimum leveraged used?
  > *181 percent maximum gross exposure; 108 percent minimum gross exposure.*
- What has been the normalized leverage used?
  > *Average gross exposure since inception: 158 percent.*

What are your portfolio financing constraints/limits?

Liquidity

Discuss the nature of illiquid holdings in the fund and explain how they are valued:

What is the current liquidity of the underlying assets and what is the appropriate time period to liquidate?

Diversification

Discuss the depth of diversification (position, industry, sector, region, market cap, etc.):

Do you measure correlation between investments in the portfolio?

What are the main sources of marginal risk in your strategy?

Outsourced Risk Controls

Are any third parties involved in verifying adherence to risk limits, for example, the fund's administrator?

OTHER MATERIALS

In addition to the DDQ documented previously, we also asked for a copy of FCM's presentation and monthly letters for the past year. It is important to read all these materials in advance of the first call or meeting with the hedge fund. Most of the basic information regarding fees, liquidity, personnel, performance history, strategy, style, risk management, and operational efficiency can be answered in advance. This will make the initial call or meeting go more smoothly and elevate the discussion to value-added topics, such as determining if the hedge fund manager has a real edge or competitive advantage.

A hedge fund's presentation tends to offer a more visual and streamlined view of how the firm operates and how they manage the hedge fund as opposed to the DDQ, which is designed to be more expansive and detailed. However, the presentation can offer additional information that might not be covered in the DDQ, such as trade examples or more graphical illustrations of how the process works and how the team interacts. Additionally, it gives us a chance to compare how the process is described in both documents. As a hedge fund analyst, I am always looking to verify information, and one of the ways we can accomplish this objective is to compare different documents to make sure the message is consistent.

The DDQ and presentation tend to provide solid information about the firm, team, and process, but the monthly/quarterly letters are useful as a means of verifying that the firm actually does what they say they do, and the letters provide written documentation as to how the firm handled different market environments. However, not all monthly reports are created equal. Some hedge funds provide basic statistics such as performance and exposures (gross, net, long, short, etc.) while others provide varying degrees of written commentary about the period under review along with descriptions of current positions and attribution for the period. When this kind of information is available ahead of your initial call or meeting, it gives you the ability to research the information on your own (in advance) so that when you interview the hedge fund manager you have had an opportunity to formulate better, more informed (and tougher) questions.

For example, if the fund provides their top five or 10 long positions (they tend to avoid listing short positions in generic letters), you can do a number of things with just that information:

- Research the companies to develop a better understanding about how the manager thinks about research and portfolio construction.
- Track the real-time performance and news events of these holdings so that you can question the manager more effectively when you speak to him or her.

- Calculate the performance attribution by holding and as a group to better understand how much their top holdings have contributed to performance.
- Track the performance of this group of stocks to the appropriate benchmark to get a sense of how their highest-conviction names perform on a relative basis.

GET YOUR HANDS DIRTY (SO TO SPEAK)

I recognize that all or most of this information can be asked of and answered by the hedge fund manager, but I find that the process of digging into the manager's information (such as top holdings) and researching items on my own engages me in a way that helps me to absorb the information better and allows me to integrate the data more efficiently. As a result, I am more confident when I speak to the hedge fund manager and often can ask more intuitive questions that the manager may not be accustomed to answering (at least not this early in the process). In addition, I find that I am in a better position to challenge the hedge fund manager when I know the back story in advance.

Monthly letters and reports also provide a window into the manager's thinking at different points in time. For example, to better understand how hedge fund managers act (or react) in times of stress, I find it useful to review each of their monthly letters for 2008 and 2009. This two-year period includes a plethora of market moves (down in 2008 and up in 2009) but also has mixed signals regarding U.S. housing, global economic growth, and the feasibility of the European Union going forward, to name just a few. The monthly letters to me are worth their weight in gold because they give me an indication of how the portfolio managers dealt with these issues (without the benefit of hindsight and marketing fluff). For example, hedge fund managers can tell you in a meeting how calm they were and how they methodically adjusted risk down in 2008 and back up in 2009, but the monthly letters may paint a different picture; one that is not so calm, cool, and collected. It might highlight, for example, that the manager in question flipped exposures frequently and may have been more lucky than skillful during that time period...or the letters may confirm exactly what the manager tells you and match up precisely with how he or she has historically managed the fund.

FURTHER ANALYSIS

After reading the DDQ, presentation, and monthly letters, it is clear that our choice of the S&P as a benchmark was not appropriate. According to the materials reviewed, FCM targets small and mid-cap stocks and has managed the fund's net exposure within a fairly wide range. We can take this information and create additional tables and graphs to analyze (see Tables 4.1 and 4.2 and Figures 4.2 through 4.6).

The performance table in Table 4.1 highlights that FCM's performance has had many months in which its performance deviated significantly from the S&P 500, the Russell 2000, and the HFRI Hedged Equity Indexes (outlier periods have been highlighted in the table). Given the variance in returns, it is not surprising that FCM's correlation to each index ranged from 0.35 to 0.42.

The up/down charts in Figures 4.2 and 4.3 illustrate clearly that FCM underperformed significantly in up markets but did a good job of protecting on the downside.

FCM vs. Russell 2000

- Up capture ratio 15.2%
- Down capture ratio 13.8%

FCM vs. HFRI Equity Hedge

- Up capture ratio 62.2%
- Down capture ratio 24.6%

The up and down capture ratios measure the percentage gain/loss for FCM as a percentage of the gain/loss for the corresponding index. The ratio measures how much of the market move (either up or down) is "captured" by the fund.

Because the Russell 2000 has experienced much more volatility in returns than the HFRI Equity Hedge Index and FCM, the up and down capture ratios are smaller (FCM's returns were far less volatile). When compared to both the Russell 2000 and the HFRI Equity Hedge indexes, FCM's down-market capture is lower than its up-market capture—demonstrating the power of negative compounding on returns.

The exposure analysis highlighted in Figure 4.4 provides us with a great deal of insight into how the fund managers have adjusted risk (defined as net exposure) in the portfolio as the market environment shifted to bearish in late 2007–2008 and bullish in 2009–2011. In addition, it gives us a good

TABLE 4.1 Historical Performance Comparisons—Monthly

Month	Monthly Performance				Performance Differential		
	FCM	S&P 500	Russell 2000	HFRI Eq Hedge	vs. S&P 500	vs. Russell 2000	vs. HFRI Eq Hedge
Dec-06	0.42%	1.40%	0.33%	1.35%	−0.99%	0.08%	−0.93%
Jan-07	1.14%	1.51%	1.67%	1.16%	−0.37%	−0.54%	−0.02%
Feb-07	1.65%	−1.96%	−0.79%	0.63%	3.61%	2.45%	1.03%
Mar-07	1.30%	1.12%	1.07%	1.01%	0.18%	0.23%	0.29%
Apr-07	1.74%	4.43%	1.80%	1.86%	−2.69%	−0.06%	−0.12%
May-07	0.88%	3.49%	4.10%	2.24%	−2.61%	−3.21%	−1.35%
Jun-07	2.19%	−1.66%	−1.46%	0.89%	3.86%	3.66%	1.31%
Jul-07	0.17%	−3.10%	−6.84%	0.17%	3.27%	7.01%	0.00%
Aug-07	2.25%	1.50%	2.27%	−1.67%	0.75%	−0.02%	3.91%
Sep-07	3.62%	3.74%	1.72%	3.18%	−0.12%	1.91%	0.45%
Oct-07	0.45%	1.59%	2.87%	3.09%	−1.14%	−2.41%	−2.64%
Nov-07	−0.24%	−4.18%	−7.18%	−2.89%	3.94%	6.94%	2.65%
Dec-07	−0.22%	−0.69%	−0.06%	0.53%	0.48%	−0.15%	−0.74%
Jan-08	3.77%	−6.00%	−6.82%	−4.47%	9.77%	10.59%	8.25%
Feb-08	2.12%	−3.25%	−3.71%	1.31%	5.37%	5.82%	0.81%
Mar-08	0.42%	−0.43%	0.42%	−2.84%	0.85%	0.00%	3.26%
Apr-08	−0.21%	4.87%	4.19%	2.45%	−5.08%	−4.39%	−2.65%
May-08	4.93%	1.30%	4.59%	2.38%	3.63%	0.34%	2.55%
Jun-08	0.89%	−8.43%	−7.70%	−2.44%	9.32%	8.59%	3.33%
Jul-08	0.79%	−0.84%	3.70%	−2.84%	1.63%	−2.91%	3.64%
Aug-08	2.46%	1.45%	3.61%	−2.17%	1.02%	−1.15%	4.64%

(Continued)

TABLE 4.1 (*Continued*)

Month	Monthly Performance				Performance Differential		
	FCM	S&P 500	Russell 2000	HFRI Eq Hedge	vs. S&P 500	vs. Russell 2000	vs. HFRI Eq Hedge
Sep-08	-3.47%	-8.91%	-7.97%	-8.14%	5.44%	4.50%	4.67%
Oct-08	-2.41%	-16.79%	-20.80%	-9.46%	14.39%	18.40%	7.05%
Nov-08	-2.92%	-7.18%	-11.83%	-3.77%	4.25%	8.91%	0.85%
Dec-08	1.87%	1.06%	5.80%	0.22%	0.81%	-3.93%	1.65%
Jan-09	0.92%	-8.43%	-11.12%	-0.88%	9.35%	12.04%	1.80%
Feb-09	-2.61%	-10.65%	-12.15%	-2.20%	8.04%	9.54%	-0.41%
Mar-09	-1.97%	8.76%	8.93%	2.90%	-10.73%	-10.90%	-4.87%
Apr-09	-1.45%	9.57%	15.46%	5.44%	-11.02%	-16.91%	-6.90%
May-09	1.26%	5.59%	3.01%	6.37%	-4.33%	-1.75%	-5.11%
Jun-09	5.82%	0.20%	1.47%	0.18%	5.62%	4.35%	5.64%
Jul-09	-0.62%	7.56%	9.63%	3.20%	-8.18%	-10.25%	-3.82%
Aug-09	-1.56%	3.61%	2.87%	1.37%	-5.17%	-4.43%	-2.92%
Sep-09	2.28%	3.73%	5.77%	3.22%	-1.45%	-3.49%	-0.94%
Oct-09	-0.72%	-1.86%	-6.79%	-0.72%	1.14%	6.07%	0.00%
Nov-09	3.30%	6.00%	3.14%	1.57%	-2.70%	0.16%	1.73%
Dec-09	3.44%	1.93%	8.05%	2.07%	1.50%	-4.61%	1.37%
Jan-10	-1.98%	-3.60%	-3.68%	-1.27%	1.61%	1.70%	-0.71%
Feb-10	0.04%	3.10%	4.50%	0.92%	-3.06%	-4.47%	-0.88%
Mar-10	5.18%	6.03%	8.14%	3.15%	-0.86%	-2.96%	2.02%
Apr-10	2.38%	1.58%	5.66%	1.19%	0.80%	-3.28%	1.19%

May-10	−1.32%	−7.99%	−7.59%	−4.05%	6.67%	6.27%	2.73%
Jun-10	−0.34%	−5.23%	−7.75%	−1.85%	4.89%	7.41%	1.50%
Jul-10	−2.41%	7.01%	6.87%	2.36%	−9.42%	−9.28%	−4.77%
Aug-10	−0.72%	−4.51%	−7.40%	−1.37%	3.79%	6.68%	0.65%
Sep-10	4.24%	8.92%	12.46%	4.74%	−4.68%	−8.22%	−0.50%
Oct-10	2.73%	3.80%	4.09%	2.37%	−1.07%	−1.36%	0.37%
Nov-10	−1.82%	0.01%	3.47%	0.64%	−1.83%	−5.28%	−2.45%
Dec-10	3.75%	6.68%	7.94%	3.52%	−2.93%	−4.19%	0.23%
Jan-11	1.28%	2.37%	−0.26%	0.42%	−1.09%	1.53%	0.85%
Feb-11	2.50%	3.43%	5.48%	1.30%	−0.92%	−2.98%	1.20%
Mar-11	3.50%	0.04%	2.59%	0.50%	3.46%	0.91%	3.01%
Apr-11	0.97%	2.96%	2.64%	1.34%	−1.99%	−1.67%	−0.37%
May-11	−1.13%	−1.13%	−1.87%	−1.28%	0.01%	0.75%	0.15%
Jun-11	−0.67%	−1.67%	−2.31%	−1.26%	0.99%	1.63%	0.59%
Jul-11	0.58%	−2.03%	−3.61%	−0.33%	2.61%	4.19%	0.91%
Aug-11	−2.21%	−5.43%	−8.70%	−4.90%	3.22%	6.49%	2.69%
Sep-11	−1.52%	−7.03%	−11.21%	−5.97%	5.51%	9.69%	4.45%
Oct-11	−1.03%	10.93%	15.14%	4.89%	−11.96%	−16.17%	−5.92%
Nov-11	−2.61%	−0.22%	−0.36%	−1.60%	−2.39%	−2.25%	−1.01%

TABLE 4.2 FCM Historical Performance Comparison–Calendar Year

	Calendar Year Performance				Performance Differential		
Month	FCM	S&P 500	Russell 2000	HFRI Eq Hedge	vs. S&P 500	vs. Russell 2000	vs. HFRI Eq Hedge
2007	15.93%	5.49%	−1.57%	10.48%	10.44%	17.50%	5.45%
2008	8.18%	−37.00%	−33.79%	−26.65%	45.18%	41.97%	34.83%
2009	8.00%	26.46%	27.17%	24.57%	−18.46%	−19.17%	−16.56%
2010	9.75%	15.06%	26.85%	10.45%	−5.32%	−17.11%	−0.71%
2011	−0.54%	1.08%	−4.80%	−7.10%	−1.62%	4.27%	6.56%
FCM Correlation		0.35	0.39	0.42			

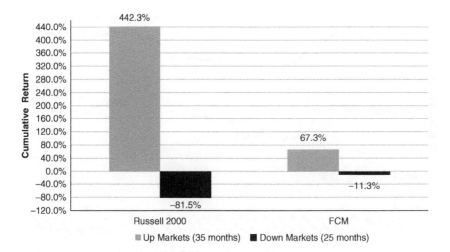

FIGURE 4.2 FCM Up/Down Chart versus Russell 2000 Index

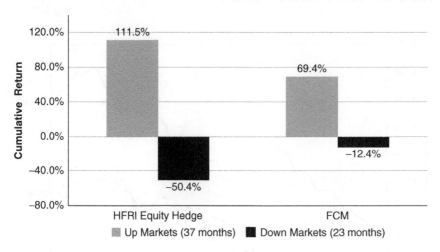

FIGURE 4.3 FCM Up/Down Chart versus HFRI Equity Hedge Index

understanding of what the normal gross and net exposures have been for the fund (we can compare this to the information they report in their DDQ and presentation). FCM did a very good job of adjusting exposures in 2008, bringing both gross and net exposure down significantly from their highs in October of 2007 to their lows in August/September 2008. It also shows that they were fairly early in putting risk back on in the fourth quarter of

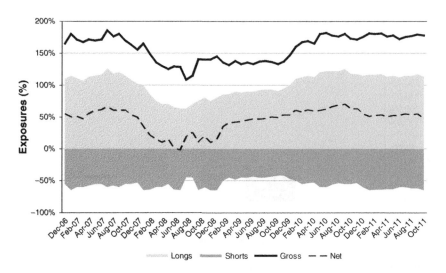

FIGURE 4.4   FCM's Historical Exposures

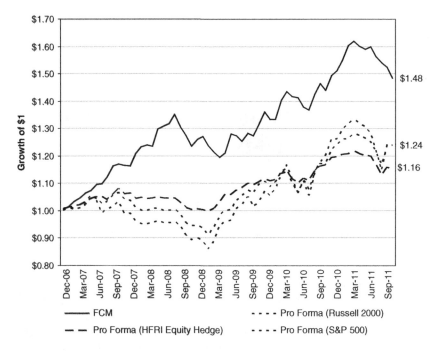

FIGURE 4.5   FCM Pro Forma Analysis

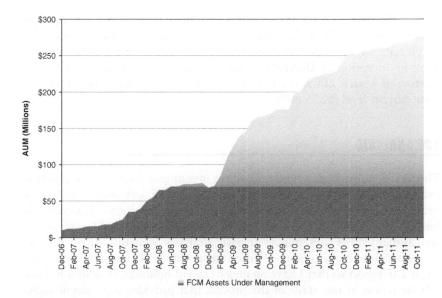

FIGURE 4.6 FCM's Historical Assets under Management

2008. However, if we view this chart along with Table 4.1 we can see that despite increasing the fund's net exposure, performance was somewhat light in 2009–2010 (when the equity market's performance was strong).

The data in Figure 4.5 compare the actual return for FCM compared to a pro forma return using the three indexes. The pro forma calculation is pretty simple—we multiply the fund's net exposure (average of net exposures over the current and previous month ends) by the return for the corresponding index for the month in question. We do this for the life of the fund and plot the return streams to see the impact of manager skill (alpha). FCM's actual returns look quite favorable to all three pro forma return streams. This implies that FCM's stock selection added value.

Monthly Pro Forma Calculation Example

$$FCM\ July\ R2k\ ProForma = FCM'Avg\ Net \times R2k\ July\ Return$$

Where:

$$R2k = Russell\ 2000\ Index$$
$$FCM's\ Avg\ Net = (June\ month\ end\ net + July\ month\ end\ net) / 2$$

The average net exposure is used to capture any month-to-month changes in net exposure. While it is not a perfect method, I believe it is more accurate than just applying the previous month end net exposure.

Finally, we can look at the fund's historical assets under management (Figure 4.6) to see how the fund and firm have developed over time. This graph indicates that the fund remained pretty small (under $100 million) from its inception in December 2006 through February 2009. However, starting in March 2009, the fund's assets have ramped up consistently to their current level ($275 million).

13F ANALYSIS

The SEC requires hedge funds that have investment discretion on assets in excess of $100 million in what are defined as 13F securities (a full list is available on the SEC's website) to report their long positions on a quarterly basis. These reports are free and publicly available on the SEC website (as well as many other sites that create basic analytics using the 13F portfolios).

When looking at equity-oriented hedge funds, I typically review the latest 13F report so that I have an idea of recent holdings. In addition, I run a basic report at this stage of the process that provides some detail about the positions, including:

- Sector/industry detail
- Selected valuation/growth ratios
- Recent performance metrics
- Market capitalization
- Average volume
- Recent stock performance

An example of this type of report can be seen in Table 4.3, which lists the 13F report for FCM as of September 2011.

The 13F portfolio analysis table provides many insights into the manager's thinking (especially when the reports are viewed sequentially over time) and provide an opportunity to research a few names in advance of a call with the fund manager so that I can ask better questions and be in a position to discuss the holdings with real knowledge of the underlying companies. Otherwise I can only be reactive as the manager describes the situation to me—by researching the name in advance, I can ask questions based on my research and try to elevate the depth of our conversation. As an added benefit, hedge fund managers are often impressed when they realize that the person they are speaking with actually knows something about their holdings. I personally find that hedge fund managers act differently when they know you know (or think you know) about their underlying portfolio holdings.

TABLE 4.3 FCM September 2011 13F Portfolio Holdings Report

Ticker	Company	Sector	Industry	Market Cap (mlns)	P/E	PEG	P/FCF	EPS Growth This Year	Short Ratio	ROE	ROR (Month)	ROR (Quarter)	Beta	Average Volume (1000s)
ALGT	Allegiant Travel Company	Services	Regional Airlines	1031	20.5	2.6	16.7	-12%	23.2	16%	8.9%	17.9%	0.49	126
BRKR	Bruker Corporation	Technology	Scientific & Technical Insts.	1980	24.4	1.6	50.5	17%	3.4	15%	-5.5%	-14.6%	1.41	722
DIOD	Diodes Incorporated	Technology	Semiconductor - Integrated Circs.	878	12.5	0.9	1186.1	874%	12.5	13%	-6.1%	6.0%	2.16	398
EXLS	Exlservice Holdings, Inc.	Services	Business Services	709	21.1	1.1	19.8	63%	5.1	13%	-11.6%	-0.1%	1.13	143
FDP	Fresh Del Monte Produce Inc.	Consumer Goods	Farm Products	1417	15.7	2.3	12.7	-55%	6.8	6%	-4.4%	5.5%	0.57	221
GLF	Gulfmark Offshore, Inc.	Basic Materials	Oil & Gas Equipment & Srvs.	1044	24.7	0.5	16.0	-168%	3.7	4%	-3.3%	-2.4%	1.38	243
GSIG	GSI Group Inc.	Technology	Scientific & Technical Insts.	313	13.4	1.1	10.3	99%	7.1	12%	-11.8%	2.1%	1.37	148
HGG	hhgregg, Inc.	Services	Electronics Stores	502	11.6	1.1	50.3	16%	15.4	17%	-12.4%	16.3%	1.25	520
HITK	Hi Tech Pharmacal Co. Inc.	Healthcare	Drugs - Generic	505	9.8		25.2	32%	6.7	29%	5.6%	14.9%	1.22	215
ISIL	Intersil Corporation	Technology	Semiconductor - Broad Line	1269	18.3	1.3	11.6	-33%	3.4	7%	-8.1%	-8.9%	1.27	1242
KKD	Krispy Kreme Doughnuts, Inc.	Services	Restaurants	422	20.7	0.6	23.3	4764%	4.5	24%	-12.2%	-22.7%	1.54	696
MCF	Contango Oil & Gas Co.	Basic Materials	Independent Oil & Gas	882	15.4		14.8	30%	9.9	14%	-4.8%	0.7%	0.87	113
MCRL	Micrel Inc.	Technology	Semiconductor - Integrated Circs.	613	14.7	2.9	14.5	217%	5.6	19%	-0.6%	2.8%	0.90	476
PRIM	Primoris Services Corporation	Industrial Goods	Heavy Construction	745	12.8	1.1	10.8	-17%	8.1	26%	5.1%	39.1%	0.98	196
SAPE	Sapient Corp.	Technology	Business Software & Services	1631	26.5	1.2	41.2	-52%	7.4	14%	-2.8%	11.9%	1.38	1099
SNX	SYNNEX Corp.	Services	Business Services	1048	7.6	0.8	18.6	31%	8.3	13%	-2.3%	11.8%	1.13	259
STEC	STEC, Inc.	Technology	Data Storage Devices	400	9.9	0.4	10.1	-60%	5.7	15%	-16.6%	-8.7%	1.57	1320
THO	Thor Industries Inc.	Consumer Goods	Recreational Vehicles	1325	12.9	1.1	15.9	-7%	8.4	13%	-5.3%	17.7%	1.97	577
TTEC	TeleTech Holdings Inc.	Services	Business Services	866	14.3	1.2	38.2	-28%	6.7	14%	-10.5%	-3.4%	1.26	173
TXRH	Texas Roadhouse Inc.	Services	Restaurants	962	16.6	1.1	17.3	20%	6.9	11%	4.0%	1.7%	0.95	1100
VICR	Vicor Corp.	Technology	Diversified Electronics	320	17.0	1.0	18.9	1088%	6.1	11%	-9.5%	-19.0%	1.59	114
ZUMZ	Zumiez, Inc.	Services	Apparel Stores	846	25.2	1.2	24.1	159%	10.0	15%	20.4%	48.3%	1.87	502
Average				896	16.6	1.2	74.9	317%	7.9	15%	-3.8%	5.3%	1.28	482

Fictional Capital Management — Due Diligence Journal

GCH Advisors?

Why did partners leave GCH? Get some references.

Only three partners. Team dynamic? Why do they keep nonpartners?

Why did analyst leave in '08? Role? Get contact detail if possible.

AUM small for long time but grown since '08.

Why institute stop-loss in '07? Based on specific event/issue?

Get detail about research done on stocks. What's edge?

How does PM manage the portfolio? DDQ doesn't really state.

How contrarian is the manager? How much loss will they take on longs?

How did they arrive at $500 million in capacity?

What power does COO have as risk manager?

Was fund managed differently when it was smaller (06-08)?

Ask for info on long vs short alpha.

FIGURE 4.7 Hedge Fund Journal Entries

HEDGE FUND JOURNAL

Because due diligence is a compressive and ongoing process I always keep a journal for each fund that I review. This "journal" in reality is a simple notepad in which I jot down all my thoughts, comments, and questions relating to my review of the underlying hedge fund. Since the introduction of the iPad, I have stopped using paper notepads and notebooks. Instead, I now use a note-taking app that allows me to keep all my notes on the iPad itself, gives me the ability to e-mail the notes, and allows me to tag them with identifiers so I can easily filter them at a later date.

In the journal shown in Figure 4.7, I typically jot down thoughts as I read through the manager's materials as well as questions that I would like to have answered (either through an additional information request or a call/meeting).

CHAPTER 5

Initial Interview

"Judge a man by his questions rather than his answers."

Voltaire

"I have no particular talent. I am merely inquisitive."

Albert Einstein

INITIAL CALL OR MEETING

Initial
Call or
Meeting

Step Three

After reviewing the materials that FCM sent over to us (DDQ, presentation, monthly letters) and concluding that they passed the initial data review, we can now schedule a brief call with the hedge fund manager to address any open questions and to gain a better understanding of the fund so that we can begin to determine what its competitive advantages may be (if any). I generally start the process with a call but will meet with managers face to face if they are from out of town and will be in my area or if I am at a conference and have a chance to meet them personally.

I purposefully keep these calls brief; generally 30 to 40 minutes because I do my homework in advance and, as a result, typically do not need to ask basic questions. To keep these calls on point, I send an e-mail in advance to explain what I would like to cover and to set the time frame for the call so that we are all on the same page.

General Discussion Topics

- Key investment professionals—emphasis on their experience and how they work together.
- Process—how it works and why it will continue to work.
- Risk controls—rules and who is in charge.
- Performance outliers—targeted questions regarding periods of extreme out/underperformance.

The goal of the initial interview is to get sufficient information to determine if the fund under review will make it to the next level (which in our workflow would mean more detailed quantitative analysis).

PHONE INTERVIEWS

There is no denying that face-to-face interviews are better when it comes to collecting data because you can observe body language, facial expressions, and general tone when sitting across from someone that you just cannot see on the phone. However, the phone interview is a vital component of the process, as it allows us to be very efficient with our time (face-to-face meetings generally last longer).

When I conduct initial phone interviews, I try to keep the number of participants to a minimum. In addition, I try to avoid multiline conference calls where different people call into a number from different locations. These calls have a tendency to get out of control. Lastly, I generally like to arrange calls when each participant is in the office and on a landline. Cell phones work well but when people are on the move, coverage can go in and out, and I have found that people can get easily distracted when they are on the move.

When I conduct these calls, I generally like to control the flow of the conversations but prefer that the investment manager do most of the talking.

BASIC INTERVIEW TIPS

1. Before conducting any interview, do your homework and know whom you are speaking with and the basic premise behind their investment strategy, process, and history. This way, you will be in a position to identify different lines of questioning should the opportunity arise. Knowledge is power.

2. Don't answer your own questions . . . let them answer. Resist the urge to jump in when they are answering—I often get the best information when I let people ramble on a bit.
3. Know when to be quiet (which should be most of the time if you are the interviewer). Ask your question, and then stop talking. This is a skill that very few people seem to be able to master. In addition, I have found that people generally are uncomfortable with silence and tend to keep talking (which can lead to new and interesting tidbits of information).
4. Ask questions in a nonsequential order. This keeps the interviewees on their toes and takes them away from their oft-recited script. Remember, hedge fund professionals have likely conducted hundreds of meeting and calls over their careers and have developed routines—try to get them out of their comfort zone (without being too obvious about it).
5. Don't let them change the question. If you want an answer to a specific question, don't be shy about asking it twice or pointing out that they have not yet answered the question.
6. Be flexible. Don't wed *yourself* to a script. Interviews can often take on a life of their own. I have seen analysts miss an opportunity to ask a *great* question because they were so caught up with asking a *good* question from their preprinted list.
7. Ask some generic questions and see where the answers lead. I like to ask questions that can be interpreted and answered in multiple ways because how the managers interpret them and choose to answer them gives me some information about how their minds work, which can help me to understand their strategy and process better.
8. Always ask "why." Question everything . . . even if you think you know the answer (you may sometimes be surprised by their response).
9. Ask for examples. Examples help to clarify. When asking for examples, do not review the ones they have listed in their presentation or other handouts . . . ask for a fresh one (take them off script).
10. Ask them what they don't do well. Most people like to talk about their successes and achievements. Ask them to list some mistakes. Also ask them to list the things they should improve upon (and don't forget to ask for examples).

In an attempt to make this book as realistic as possible, I have included the transcript from a mock interview that I conducted with FCM. I have cut out the introductions and other nonessential parts of the interview to make the length more manageable. My goal is to provide a realistic window into the interview process. In addition, I have added commentary in italics to give the reader an idea of what I am thinking as the interview proceeds.

Interview Transcript

Date: December 20, 2011
Participants: Frank Travers, Jaime Wernick

FT: Before we get into Fictional Capital Management, tell me about GCH.

We know from reading the DDQ that Jaime and Ted Acoff both worked at GCH previously. They began as analysts and eventually became co-managers of the firm's equity hedge fund. I did a database search for GCH and found that the fund stopped reporting in late 2008. I didn't run the performance for the years that Ted and Jaime were there because I wanted to get some history before doing so.

JW: Are you familiar with the firm?
FT: Not really. I've heard of them but never did any work on them; it looks like they shut down in 2009. Can you take me through their strategy and what you and Ted were responsible for?
JW: No problem. The firm started out as a long-only shop in the late 1980s and transitioned into hedge funds in the mid-1990s. The founder, Jonah Kellworth, was a pretty well-known value investor in the long-only world. When hedge funds started to expand in the 1990s, he brought on some people to build that side of the business and the alternatives side eventually gobbled up the long-only side. Ted started there in 1998 and I started in 2001. We were both hired as analysts and worked on the hedge fund.
FT: Who managed the hedge fund?

I want to know who managed the hedge fund because both Ted and Jamie reported to them and ultimately took over from them. If FCM moves through the due diligence process, I can contact them as potential references.

JW: Arty Gellberg and Mike Shell. Arty was the first portfolio manager but he left in late 1999 and Mike took over. When Mike left in 2003, Ted and I were promoted to co–portfolio managers.
FT: And you guys left three years later. Was there a problem at GCH?

The portfolio manager (PM) role seems to have had a revolving door. Three changes in less than 10 years.

JW: Yes and no. Jonah was a great guy, but he could be a bear to work with and he never really understood the long/short business. He was a great buy and hold value investor. He didn't appreciate the nuances of trading and never really liked shorting.

FT: So how did you and Ted interact with Jonah both before you were made portfolio managers and after?

JW: We got along great when we were analysts. Jonah was a fantastic analyst himself, but as the long-only business started to decline we had less interaction with him. I think it was tougher for Arty and Mike to deal with him.

FT: How was your relationship after you took over as PMs?

JW: That's when it all changed. He thought that he would have an easier time with us. Things had gotten heated with Arty and then Mike and they ultimately left. I assume because we were younger and because we were new PMs. Performance was pretty good and Jonah was a great marketer. He had loads of contacts and was able to raise assets despite the personnel turnover.

FT: Outside of marketing, what did Jonah do?

JW: His title was research director. He was a great analyst . . . on the long side.

FT: Why didn't *he* manage the fund and use you guys as support?

I don't quite understand the dynamic at GCH and want to gain a better understanding of what Jonah did versus what Ted and Jaime were responsible for. If I am going to look at the track record at GCH and use it to evaluate Ted and Jaime's past performance, I would like to know how much of that track record can be attributed to Ted/Jaime versus Jonah. In addition, if/when I reach out to Jonah for a reference I can compare his assessment to Jaime's.

JW: Like I said, he was a long-only guy. He recognized that his role was best suited to research and, to a lesser extent, marketing.

FT: How should I look at the GCH track record? How much of it was yours versus Jonah's or the rest of the team's?

Jaime stated that Jonah was the research director and was a strong analyst for the long side. When looking at the GCH track record, we will need to gain a better idea of how much weight we should place on it as a means of assessing Jaime and Ted's contributions. If we speak to Jonah, we should try to ascertain how much of the long attribution is his (and conversely how much of the short attribution was his). Additionally, we will need to speak with Arty and Mike to get additional viewpoints.

JW: Jonah definitely contributed but Ted and I ran that fund. We were responsible for all decisions from 2003 onward. Jonah was a great resource and someone to bounce ideas off, but his role was pretty limited. It ultimately led to our departure.

FT: Why did you guys leave?

I sense that there might be more to this story but I will leave that for another day.

JW: Ted and I had managed the fund for several years and had done a good job. Jonah's role diminished over time and we wanted equity in the firm. Jonah was unwilling to give us any. He gave us a share of the revenue, but it was never official and it was never in writing. We were essentially being paid a base salary and a discretionary bonus. It felt like the right time to go out on our own. Ted and I had a good working relationship and we weren't getting any younger. It seemed like a good time to launch our own business.

FT: I see that you launched the fund with $10 million. Was that your capital?

They launched with a pretty small amount of assets relative to other hedge fund launches at that time. If they had managed upwards of $750 million as stated in the DDQ, I wonder why none of that money followed them from GCH to FCM.

JW: Half was ours and the other half was from family and friends.

FT: How much were you managing when you left GCH?

JW: We left over the summer in 2006 so that would have been about $600 million or so in assets.

FT: None of it moved to FCM?

JW: I see what you are asking. First, Ted and I signed a no-compete clause in our contracts when we became portfolio managers at GCH that precluded us from soliciting assets from any clients for a year. Second, those clients were all brought on by Jonah and had been with him for years . . . in some cases for several decades. They were loyal to him.

FT: What are the names of the other analysts that worked at GCH?

I will do some digging later in the process, but it never hurts to get a head start. I will use the names of the people he provides as additional references.

JW: I can send that to you as a follow-up if you like.

FT: Great. So what was the strategy at GCH and how does it differ from what you do at FCM?

JW: The strategy is pretty similar. GCH was a value-oriented shop. We ran with a lower gross and a higher net. At FCM, we run with gross in the 150s and net in the 40 percent to 50 percent range. At GCH we ran with a gross that ran between 100 percent and 120 percent. We also had more of a long bias; typically more than 60 percent net.

FT: I assume turnover was different?

I want to probe how much of an influence Jonah was on them at GCH. Jamie had mentioned that Jonah was more of a buy and hold investor.

JW: Good point. We had much lower turnover at GCH. At FCM, turnover runs at two times to three times. We turn the short book over more frequently than the long book.

FT: 40 percent to 50 percent is your typical net range?

The DDQ states that turnover is a little lower so this is something to probe a bit further as follow-up or in a face-to-face meeting. We had run analysis on FCH's gross and net exposures (Figure 4.5) and know that the average net is 46 percent, but the fund has had a much wider range in practical terms. In 2008, the fund's net ranged from 2 percent to 35 percent. Excluding 2008, the typical net exposure was more like 50 percent to 60 percent. This is a good opportunity to explore their exposure management and to discuss what led them to go net short in 2008.

JW: Over the last few years it has been. The exception to that was back in 2008. We had taken both the gross and net exposure down over most of that year.

FT: Was that a macro call?

JW: Yes and no. We tell investors that we are bottom up but it was hard to ignore the macro environment back then. We actively spoke with clients and told them that we were nervous about the markets and that we would be taking down exposures. This was the only time in our history (at GCH and Fictional Capital) that we made such an overt top-down call. That said, our bottom-up fundamental work led us to the same conclusion. It was getting harder to find long positions in which we had any real conviction. Our short book has remained fairly consistent over the years, so the change in net exposure in 2008 was more a reflection of our inability to find conviction longs while maintaining consistent exposure in our short book.

FT: So did you reduce longs because of the macro environment or because you didn't have conviction in them any longer?

I want to understand how a bottom-up shop made such a strong (and correct) macro call and figure out if this is something that is part of their strategy and, if not, if it has changed their investment process at all. I have found that many hedge fund managers change aspects of their process following periods of weak performance.

JW: It was really a combination of both. Look, we are not active traders and we don't think we do great macro research, but the handwriting seemed to be on the wall from the top down and when we spoke to company managements, we started to hear some scary stuff. We tend to have bigger position sizes than your typical hedge fund, so unless we have conviction we don't put on positions. That's basic risk management, but it works for us.

FT: What changed in 2008 versus 2007?

I see that they had actually begun to take down their long book in 2007 so I thought it might be a good idea to probe further. In keeping with the interview tips, I am asking a question that I already know the answer to but want to see where his answer takes us.

JW: Well, that's another good point. Our concerns really started to come to the forefront in the fall of 2007. We had closed out of some longs and were looking through our pipeline and started to see that the level of conviction was not as strong. When we get to the process, we can talk about our ranking system and how we rank our stocks by a variety of factors—including conviction. The pipeline was full (as it always is) but we did not have any screaming buys, so the gross long exposure started to fall and took the net exposure down with it.

FT: So tell me how a new long position gets in the book.

As he is answering the previous question, I am referencing the exposures graph and underlying data from Figure 4.5, which illustrates how exposures changed over time. This data verifies what he is saying—gross long exposure declined from 100 percent in January 2008 and troughed at 63 percent in August of that year. It is interesting that long exposure actually ticked up during the fourth quarter. The question regarding new long positions should lead the discussion toward their investment philosophy and approach.

JW: Like I mentioned before, we have a portfolio management tool that we employ that guides us. We rank all pipeline ideas by potential upside, potential downside, correlation with other names in the portfolio, and our conviction. We also maintain this ranking for all stocks in the portfolio. Before adding any new name, we compare it to the names in the portfolio to see if it would be appropriate.

FT: Can you break down each component for me?

Seems like an interesting system. It was briefly mentioned in the DDQ and was represented in the presentation with a simple graphic.

JW: Sure. We build models for each stock that we research. Once the model for a company is built, we can make and tweak assumptions that will adjust the figures in the pro forma balance sheet, income statement, and statement of cash flows. We use the projected figures to calculate the potential upside and downside for the stock. We also run a scenario analysis to see how the stock has responded in various times of market stress and can manually adjust the upside and downside figures to reflect different scenarios.

FT: Do you sell when targets are hit?

Their DDQ states that they have a stop-loss for shorts but not for longs. I would like to better understand why and probe a bit deeper into the mechanics of their stops. Stop-loss programs often look great on paper, but fall short (no pun) in practice. I recognize that we have not finished discussing the ranking model and will move the discussion back to the ranking model in short order.

JW: Not always. We have a strict stop-loss in effect for short positions. We will automatically cover any short in which we have lost 20 percent.

FT: Absolute or peak-to-trough?

JW: I believe 20 percent from initial purchase price.

He should know the answer to this. He should not have to hedge his answer with "I believe." Let's probe a bit further.

FT: What about a position that is built over time? Or one in which you add to?

JW: Good question. This one is more situational. Ted and I will typically review any short that is down 120 percent based on its average cost, but we can also cover before then as well. The stop-loss rule is there as a backstop, meaning we want to make sure that we don't lose too much on any one position.

FT: But you don't have a stop loss for your longs. Correct?

JW: That's right. We try to stay true to our value roots and give longs more time to work out. That does not mean that we don't sell out of longs that are losing money because we certainly do. It means that we are willing to take some volatility in the short run when we have strong conviction in a name. This brings me back to the portfolio management tool. I think we got a bit sidetracked.

FT: Let's stay with the stop loss and general sell discipline a bit longer. Who makes the decision to sell or cover a position?

JW: Okay. Ted and I make those calls.

FT: The DDQ says that Ted makes all buy and sell decisions.

I do not doubt his answer, but he has stated something that does not jibe with their written materials.

JW: Technically he does, but we discuss everything first. We are a small shop and sit right next to each other, so we (the whole group) talk openly all the time.

FT: Can you overrule a decision?

I am not trying to be difficult with this line of questioning. My goal is to end the call with a clear understanding of who is responsible for doing what within the firm and to make an initial assessment of manager skill so that I can determine if there is any reason to continue the due diligence.

JW: No. Ted is the final decision maker. I was simply pointing out that many factors go into the decision. I have input as does the team.

FT: Thanks. Let's talk about ownership. You have three partners. Do you plan on expanding ownership to others at the firm?

I will let it drop at this point, but would like to explore the decision-making process more should we continue the process in the future. I would like to ask Ted how much of an impact Jaime has on his portfolio calls.

In addition, I can ask the analysts how Ted and Jaime interact and who makes the investment decisions. We can move the questioning to employee retention. They have only had one person leave the firm since launching, but I would like to know what they are doing to keep their existing employees.

JW: Not at this time. We do offer shadow equity to Joyce, Charlie, and Jacob.

FT: Meaning what exactly?

Shadow (or phantom) equity typically refers to a share in revenue without any actual ownership in the firm. This is common in the hedge fund industry but I would like to know how generously they pay their team.

JW: Joyce and Charlie are our analysts and Jacob is our trader. We think that we have a pretty strong group that works well together so we pay each what we think is a fair base salary as well as a percentage of the firm's net profits as an incentive. On top of that, we pay a discretionary bonus to all employees based on their performance for the year.

FT: What percentage of the profits do you pay to them?

JW: We don't really disclose that information, but I will say that the figure is in the 5 percent to 7 percent range.

FT: 5 percent to 7 percent for each analyst or for the three of them together?

JW: You are persistent. I'll give you that.

Brief silence.

JW: Last year we paid 7 percent of the net profits to the group of the three of them.

FT: So 7 percent in 2010. Did they get discretionary bonuses as well?

We can make a quick assessment of this figure by applying the average assets under management in 2010 ($222 million) and multiplying this by the portfolio gain for the year (10 percent) to arrive at a rough estimate for the gains for the year ($22 million). We can then apply the 20 percent performance fee and come up with an estimate for the performance fee received by FCM for the year ($4.4 million). According to Jaime, they paid 7 percent of this figure to the rest of the investment group ($311,000). So assuming that the three other team members each received an equal share, they each received a little over $100k in shadow equity for 2010. If we conduct an onsite visit, we can ask the analysts and trader if they are happy with their current compensation directly.

JW: Yes, but can we discuss that in person when you come in for an onsite visit? I am uncomfortable going into this on the phone this early in the process.

FT: Okay. What percentage did you pay out in 2009 and 2008?

JW: Again, we can go into this in more detail when we meet, but the shadow equity program did not come into effect until last year.

FT: Sorry, you made it sound like this had been in effect for a longer period.

By giving me a range, he implied they had done this more than once.

JW: I didn't mean it that way. I meant to say that we plan on paying between 5 percent and 7 percent. Last year things went quite well and we paid at the higher end of that range.

FT: Are they happy with this arrangement? Any concern that you are doing to them what Jonah did to you at GCH?

If they are happy with their team, they need to make sure that they keep them happy as well. There is a fair degree of turnover in this business and, while even good pay does not guarantee loyalty, it can't hurt. Jaime had expressed earlier that one of the reasons that he and Ted left GCH was because they did not have any equity in the firm.

JW: Good point. That's why we initiated it. Ted and I came up with the shadow equity program. I think the analysts are pretty happy. I think the situation with Ted and me was different. At GCH, we managed the fund while the team here supports us.

FT: How about the people in the operations group (Jennifer and Aaron)? Are they going to receive shadow equity at some point?

JW: Jennifer has been with us longer than Aaron so we will likely include her in this program.

FT: We are a few weeks from year end right now so have you decided to put Jennifer in the program for 2011?

JW: Not yet. Ted and I will make that decision shortly.

FT: You guys have seen pretty nice asset growth over the last two years. Has it changed your investment style at all?

JW: Not at all. We managed more than twice this amount at GCH.

FT: But your holding period was longer at GCH plus the market environment today is different from when you were managing money previously.

He knows this as well as I do. Past performance is not indicative of future results . . . and the same can be said of processes. When we analyze a hedge fund, we need to look forward, not backward. What works today might not have worked previously and vice versa.

JW: Both good points, but we are comfortable at current levels and feel we can manage up to $500 million at this time.

FT: Is today's portfolio as liquid as your portfolio was prior to the market crash . . . let's say summer of 2007 as an example?

If FCM progresses through the due diligence process, we will test this ourselves, but it is always good to ask up front so we have answers to compare later on. I also ask because I want to assess how well he knows his portfolio.

JW: Well, I don't have those statistics in front of me, but I would say it would be pretty similar.

FT: Do you have a liquidity requirement when establishing positions?

The DDQ stated they measure liquidity based on trailing 30-day volume but did not specify if they had any position restrictions.

JW: We don't buy anything that we can't sell out of in a few weeks.

FT: Can you be more specific?

JW: Sure. We try to maintain a liquid portfolio. We monitor position-level liquidity daily, and our goal is to ensure that 80 percent of the book can be liquidated within 10 days; the next 10 percent can be liquidated within 2 weeks; the next 5 percent can be liquidated within 3 weeks; and the remaining 5 percent can be liquidated within a month. That is our policy, but we have typically run much more liquid than that. For example, 95 percent of today's book can likely be liquidated in a few days and the rest within a week.

FT: Have you ever run the liquidity more like the guidelines?

JW: Yes. In 2008 we had seen liquidity dry up generally in the marketplace but we had net inflows that year and, as you pointed out before, assets increased considerably since. In addition, we had taken down our gross exposure throughout the year, so we were in pretty good shape from a liquidity perspective. In fact, we started to put some money back into the marketplace in the fourth quarter in 2008 when most people were panic selling, effectively providing some liquidity to the market.

FT: Give me a rough idea of your fund's historical long and short alpha.

His answer aligns perfectly with the data in Figure 4.5, which show clearly that they increased gross long exposure from 63 percent in August 2008 to 90 percent in March 2009. Time to switch it up a bit. We have focused on some pretty specific firm and fund topics, and I would like to move the conversation to some other areas.

JW: I can send you the exact figures but off the top of my head I can tell you that we have been profitable on both sides of the book over the life of the fund. However, most of the fund's historical attribution came from the long side.

FT: I assume the positive short attribution over the life of the fund was primarily due to 2008?

When we receive the historical attribution figures we can run a variety of analyses, but for now I would like to understand if 2008 drove the short performance, as the markets declined precipitously that year.

JW: Yes. A big piece of it came from 2008 but we did well in our short book in 2007 as well. 2009 and 2010 were tough on short positions as the market was strong—2009 in particular was rough.

FT: Please do send me the historical long and short attribution on a monthly basis if possible. How much of the short book are index hedges or overlay positions?

JW: We only put on stock shorts. We may use options at times to enhance a position when the pricing is appropriate—both long and short—but we don't think our clients pay us hedge fund fees to short an index. Anyone can do that themselves much cheaper.

FT: So you have never used an index short—an ETF, put option, or futures contract?

JW: We did use put options on the S&P 500 in the fourth quarter of 2008 and in January 2009. At that time, we had covered several short positions and felt it would be prudent to maintain our short exposure while the markets were tanking. This was a clear exception to the rule.

FT: You didn't have any new short candidates in the pipeline at that time?

JW: We had many, but we felt we were not being properly compensated for individual shorts. Correlations within the market surged and we believed it would be better to buy protection via the options market.

FT: But option premiums got pretty expensive at that time.

JW: True, but we felt it was more efficient to buy puts on the SPY and that left us with some cash to put to work later in the quarter.

FT: Any concern about a market cap mismatch?

FCM invests in small- and mid-cap stocks while the S&P 500 is a large-cap benchmark.

JW: Not with correlations as high as they were at that time. As you just said, correlations went to 1 and SPY options were cheaper than options on the Russell 2000. This was an efficient way to maintain our short exposure and it was ultimately a good decision.

FT: Tell me one thing that Ted can do better as a portfolio manager.

Time to switch things up again.

JW: I think Ted is a great PM. We have worked together for a decade and I think the proof is ultimately in the pudding... returns have been good since we opened up shop in late 2006.

FT: You've worked with him for a decade, so that puts you in a great position to assess weaknesses. Don't worry; I'm going to ask him the same question about you.

This is one of my favorite questions and I have had many people try to squirm out of answering it. People are generally okay assessing themselves or people that work under them but less comfortable when talking about peers or others above them in the organizational chart. I also think that this question helps to set the tone for future due diligence because it lets them know early in the process that I plan on asking tough questions and challenging their answers. When they know that tough questions will follow and that I will not let them squirm out of answers, things tend to go more smoothly.

JW: Let me think for a moment.

This is where silence can work well. I just sit back and wait for his response.

JW: All right. I have nothing bad to say about Ted... that's just the way it is. If I could change one thing about him, I would say that he tends to be a bit too conservative.

FT: Conservative about what? Give me an example.

That's a vague answer. I would like some detail.

JW: Pretty much everything. For example, we always talk about ways of improving performance, and I think that we can open things up a bit on the portfolio side and take on some additional volatility. We have a five-year track record and have a fairly low historical level of volatility. Clients love us when we protect capital (like we did in 2008) but they can get a bit impatient when we lag in strong up markets (like in 2009 and in 2010).

FT: What does he say in response?

Jaime's answer is a bit disconcerting. They have successfully managed a fund together for a long time and with strong performance results. Why would he want Ted to be more aggressive?

JW: That we have a process that works and there is no need to try to fix something that isn't broken.

FT: Sounds wise to me. You disagree with that?

JW: No, but I think we have room to take on additional risk.

His response about taking on more risk is a great answer. It gives me some insight into how Jaime thinks. In addition, it gives me an interesting line of questioning when I speak with Ted and the rest of the team.

FT: Is this a point of contention between the two of you? You're equal partners. Don't you have any say in the matter?

Now I'm just trying to get a reaction from him. He started answering the question with a vague answer but brought up something specific and provided too much detail for this never to have been discussed before.

JW: Of course I have a say. Ted, Bill, and I make all firm decisions together. We started FCM in a manner very similar to how we ran money at GCH and felt it would be best to do what we knew had worked in the past. Both Ted and I came up with that strategy. I have no issues with it. I'm just responding to your question.

I sense from his tone that we should move on. I can follow up if I conduct an onsite meeting at a later time.

FT: So I see that Bill (COO) was named the risk manager in 2009. Why?

JW: We felt at the time that it would be better to provide independent risk management. Prior to that Ted was the risk manager. I mean, we all watched the portfolio but Ted was ultimately responsible.

FT: Did something happen to prompt the change?

JW: Not really. Basically Bill presented the idea and both Ted and I agreed it was a more efficient way to run the fund. We have gotten good feedback from clients about the change. The industry is moving toward independent risk functions.

FT: What prompted Bill to come up with the idea in the first place? You had already been in business for a long time at that point.

JW: We wanted to grow our assets and had gotten advice from some consultants and large potential clients that it would be a good idea. Bill ran with it and pitched it to Ted and me.

FT: So what exactly does Bill do as the risk manager?

JW: Everyone at the firm has access to all risk reporting—from the prime broker as well as our internal system. Bill is charged with monitoring those reports and making sure that we stay within all stated guidelines.

FT: Has he ever had to take action?

JW: No.

FT: Let me rephrase the question. Does he have the power to take off a position if he finds it in violation of a risk limit?

JW: Well, we would take the position off if it were in violation.

FT: Who would?

JW: Either Ted or I would instruct Jacob to take off some risk if need be. We talked earlier about portfolio decisions, and this is an example of something that either Ted or I can do.

FT: Under what scenario would you do this and not Ted?

JW: If Ted were unavailable—on vacation, meeting with a client, or something.

FT: You mention in your presentation and DDQ that you try to avoid crowded hedge fund trades. Are you contrarian?

If we do an onsite meeting, decision making is something that I would like to explore more. We can move our call forward by bringing up a new topic.

JW: To some degree we are, but not on purpose. We definitely want to understand who is invested alongside us when we enter a position, and we have found that popular hedge fund names can rise or fall in price for reasons that make no sense to us. We don't cross off any name that has hedge fund ownership but find that because there are so many smaller companies that receive little buy and sell side attention that we have the opportunity to discover some hidden gems and sit back and wait for the rest of the marketplace to discover them. This is one of the reasons that we don't have a high level of correlation to the market or to our peers in the hedge fund world.

FT: So what is your edge?

JW: Well, I think that's for you to determine.

FT: I agree, but you have to have an opinion as well. No one knows FCM better than you guys, so I am interested in your opinion.

This is one of the most important investment-related questions that we will need to answer before making a decision to hire (or fire) any hedge fund manager. I always ask the hedge fund manager (and others on their team) what they view as their edge. Sometimes the manager comes up with something that I had not come up with and sometimes it just helps me to understand how they view their own process. I always find it especially interesting when different members of the hedge fund manager's team answer the questions with completely different answers.

JW: I think we are good at finding unknown and unloved stocks, researching them, and building a portfolio that is designed to make money on both the long and short side.

FT: That's a bit general. Anything specific?

JW: Like I said, I think you would be in a better position to rank us versus our peer group. If I had to pick just one thing, I would say that our stock ranking system is unique. It allows us to do our work and to rank the opportunities as objectively as possible. I always refer to 2008 as the best example. We did not have conviction in any longs, so the long book got smaller while we maintained our short book. Conviction level is a key determinant in our ranking system. Value managers always run the risk of catching a falling knife as prices fall, but our ranking system forces us to stop.

FT: What portfolio transparency do you provide?

JW: We provide a monthly investment letter that includes gross and net exposures, sector exposures long and short, top five positions as well as attribution. At year end, we write a year-end review that discusses winning and losing investments as well as additional information on our top holdings.

FT: I would like to review a portfolio if possible. Are you willing to provide full position-level transparency?

JW: We don't provide the full portfolio to anyone. We are happy to show you the portfolio and discuss any holdings when you are in our offices.

FT: How about an old portfolio from a year ago? Would you be willing to share?

JW: May I ask what your objective is?

FT: Sure. I would like to get a better understanding of how you construct your portfolio—both long and short—as well as get a sense for how the two books compare to one another. In addition, I would like to run an independent analysis of portfolio liquidity. I am happy to sign an NDA if that helps. Since you turn over your portfolio a couple of times each year, I don't think sharing this information would be giving away any inappropriate information.

Some managers have no problem sharing position-level transparency. For those that do, I have found that asking for an older portfolio (one that has likely been turned over several times) is more palatable. NDA is an acronym for a legal document called the nondisclosure agreement. As the name states, parties that sign an NDA are restricted from disclosing information as detailed in the legal agreement. Some managers require that an NDA be in place before sending over what they deem to be sensitive information while others do not require it. If this is what it takes to get the information, I generally have no problem with it.

JW: I would have to discuss that with my partners. Let me get back to you on that.

FT: Sounds good. Thanks for your time. I will likely have some follow-up questions and may request some additional information in the next few days.

MEETING NOTES

I have found that it is best to write notes every time that I have contact with an investment manager. This includes contact with noninvestment personnel (such as marketers, investor relations, etc.). I keep a handwritten account of all my manager notes in my iPad, but typing out a formal note is an effective way of keeping other people you work with fully informed. In addition, I have found that the process of writing the formal "manager note" is a good way of reviewing the conversation, collecting my thoughts, and summarizing my views. Meeting notes should always end with a list of outstanding questions and an action plan to move the due diligence process forward.

Key Points/Questions from the Manager Interview

- We will need additional background information on GCH. Jamie explained their history at the firm, but I can't help but feel that something is missing. Specific questions include:

- Why did the long-only business shut down?
- What was Jonah's role at the firm?
- How much of the fund's performance can be attributed to Ted and Jaime? I would also like to verify that they were actually portfolio managers.
- What were Ted and Jaime's roles at the firm and how did they evolve?
- The easiest way to get the backstory about GCH would be to contact former employees. This can include:
  - Jonah Kellworth (founder of GCH and director of research).
  - Arty Gellberg (former portfolio manager at GCH).
  - Mike Shell (former portfolio manager at GCH).
  - Other employees (Jaime will send list of analysts he worked with at GCH).
  - Contacts in the industry, including my contacts at the prime broker(s) that worked with GCH.
- Do an Internet search for GCH and all senior members to find information. Basic search including:
  - Database search (both internal and third party).
  - Hedge fund financial websites (from list in Table 3.1).
  - LinkedIn and other social media.
- Explore sell discipline and their stop-loss rules in particular. We can do this by speaking with other team members and by reviewing trade details for specific trades they have done.
- I was somewhat confused by Jamie's description of the decision-making process, particularly who is responsible for doing what. If we conduct an additional call or onsite meeting, this should be an important topic.
- I would like to better understand how their stock-ranking system works. Some real-life examples would be great.

Action Plan

- Request detailed monthly attribution since fund's inception.

  We requested this during the call and he agreed to send it. When we send our follow-up e-mail, we should ask for this in spreadsheet format and specify that we want to see monthly contribution to returns from the long book as well as the short book.
- Follow up with Jaime regarding full portfolio transparency.

  In the follow-up e-mail, reiterate that we will sign a NDA if needed and state that the purpose of this information is to better understand how they manage their portfolio. If they should decide not to provide lagged transparency from a year ago, ask if they would be willing to go back further. This information is not critical, but it would be very helpful in assessing how they construct their portfolios. Even if they send this information, I will look to verify portfolio positioning and liquidity through their service providers (prime brokers, administrators, and auditors) and/or through the due diligence mosaic built by analyzing the information, interviewing key personnel, and conducting references.

- While waiting for the decision regarding transparency, generate a historical 13F analysis.

We can perform the analysis shown in Table 4.3 for all quarters in which the firm has reported their holdings to the SEC via 13F filings. This analysis is not perfect because it is limited to long positions and only reflects the manager's long positions in stocks on U.S. exchanges at the end of the specified quarters. Managers have been known to adjust their portfolios at quarter end for the express purpose of rendering the 13F reports useless. In addition, for firms with higher levels of turnover, these reports can be less useful. Fortunately, FCM does not have a high level of turnover (they stated it was two times for the long book), so this analysis can be more effective. Lastly, we can use the quarterly 13F analysis as a check for the information that they provide to us in their monthly investor letters (at quarter end to match the 13F reports). By looking at the historical 13F analysis, we can determine if their typical long holdings exhibit the liquidity profile that Jamie told us in our call as well as give us a sense for the type of company that they hold in their long books. We can also calculate the theoretical performance for the long book for a given quarter using the positions at the end of the previous quarter and holding them constant for the following three months. We can then compare this figure with the actual long attribution that they agreed to provide as a means of determining the impact on the long book due to portfolio decisions during the quarter.

- Request independent risk report from prime broker.

Prime brokers generally provide risk reporting to their hedge fund clients. Some choose to use the risk system and resulting reports (and we know from their DDQ that FCM uses these tools) while others employ other third-party software or their own internal systems. I like to ask hedge fund managers if they would allow me to receive a sample risk report from their prime broker as a means of verifying what they are telling me. For an equity long/short fund, these prime brokerage risk reports often provide summary information such as:

- *Dollar exposures*
- *Notional exposures*
- *Beta-adjusted exposures*
- *Delta-adjusted exposures*

- *Liquidity analysis*
- *VaR*
- *Scenario analysis*
- *Portfolio stress testing*
- Request trade information (dates and amounts of all buys and sells) of their five biggest winners and five biggest losers of the last two years.

     This is one of my favorites. Again, the manager may require an NDA in place or refuse outright, but this information helps me to better understand how the hedge fund manager actually manages the portfolio. If the manager is sensitive about providing this kind of information about current open positions, then request the information for stocks in which they are no longer long or short—there should be much less sensitivity about former positions that have been closed out. When provided with this information, I like to create a graph of the underlying stock's price movements over the period in question and look to see if/when the hedge fund manager traded around major events (like earnings reports and other important news) that impacted the stock's price. I can compare this actual trading activity with what the manager tells me that they do. In any case, this information is usually a good launching point for questions when I am conducting an onsite meeting later on in the due diligence process.
- Request historical monthly sector and market cap breakdown.

     When we have this kind of historical detail, we can run pro forma analysis similar to what we did in Figure 4.5 (where we used net exposure to create a pro forma return using benchmark returns). We can also see if they have a tendency to favor certain sectors over others and whether or not their sector allocations or market cap allocations have led to positive or negative attribution over time. FCM positions itself as a generalist manager, meaning they do not have any specific sector specialization; rather, they look across all the sectors for the best stocks they can find. This kind of analysis can easily indicate which sectors have been their highest and lowest weights, which can help us to put their performance in a more accurate historical perspective.
- Request sample of older position(s)—model inputs and output; assumptions used; how scored/ranked in their ranking model.

     Most hedge fund managers prefer to show this kind of analysis to you when you visit their offices. They are less apt to send it to you via e-mail; however, there is no harm in asking. In either case, an analysis of their model inputs, outputs, and assumptions helps us to gain a much greater understanding of the type of work that they do and the level of detail that they go into when analyzing positions. Even when managers provide this information to me via e-mail, I still like to sit with the appropriate analysts when I conduct an onsite visit and go through live examples while sitting in their offices or at their desks. Portfolio managers and analysts are typically very proud of the work that they do, and since they never really get a chance to show this work off, I find that they are most accommodating and happy to provide lots of detail when you are at their offices. As a result, I find this type of analysis a great means of gaining information about the manager's research process and often about the process and team dynamic (if I ask the right questions). This type of analysis can also highlight deficiencies in a hedge fund manager's research process. Valuation models with broken links and/or information that has not been updated in a long while also provides valuable information.

- Request reference list for the principals.

   We will discuss reference calls in great detail in Chapter 11 but they are certainly worthy of a mention here. Reference calls are a great (and cost-free) way of obtaining new and verifying existing information. They are of critical importance when there are open or unresolved questions about any part of a fund or fund manager's history. In this case, I have several questions about Jaime and Ted's former employment at GCH. I will address this directly with them but will also speak with former co-workers. These reference calls can help to open up new lines of questioning and/or verify (or not) what Jaime and Ted tell me during our interviews.

- Reach out to one or more of the former GCH co-workers for a reference and more insight about the firm and Ted/Jaime's role there.

   We should always reach out to anyone who is listed by the hedge fund as a reference, but we should not stop there. It is often as important to assess who is not on the reference list provided by the hedge fund as who is listed on it. I am curious to see if Jonah is listed in the list of references that we requested from FCM. If he is not, then I will be cynical and ask myself why they would not list their former employer (who gave them their start as portfolio managers).

- Request beta-adjusted long and short exposures since inception.

   The pro forma analysis that we performed and highlighted in Figure 4.5 indicate that FCM has demonstrated a significant amount of alpha over the benchmark returns based on historical net exposures. I would like to perform the same analysis for the beta-adjusted exposures to more accurately assess performance.

CHAPTER 6

Quantitative Analysis

*"You can use all the quantitative data you can get, but you still
have to distrust it and use your own intelligence and judgment."*

Alvin Toffler

Quant.
Analysis

Step Four

Now that we have collected basic information from the hedge fund manager, conducted an initial review of the materials, and had a brief introductory interview with a senior investment professional, we have enough information at our disposal to decide if we want to move this manager further along in the due diligence process.

At this stage, we are at a tipping point. Should we decide that the hedge fund under review passes our initial tests, the amount of work that we will do going forward will increase significantly. We will need to perform an extensive quantitative analysis as well as a full-blown portfolio review. In addition, we will schedule an onsite meeting, where we will meet with all the key members of the investment, risk, and operations groups. When this has been completed, we will then conduct extensive reference checks and hire an investigative firm to perform a background check on all the key team members.

Upon completing our initial phone interview with Jaime Wernick in Chapter 5, we created a list of follow-up questions and compiled a list of things to request from FCM. That list was included in a follow-up e-mail, and FCM has decided to provide most of what we had requested. The lone exception was full position-level transparency. In this chapter, we will focus on the performance- and exposures-related data that they have sent to us.

PERFORMANCE MEASURES

In previous chapters, we have highlighted several different ways to visualize and compare historical performance including the following:

- Calendar year and annualized performance.
- Cumulative performance charts.
- Up/down charts.
- Correlation tables and rolling correlation charts.
- Pro forma returns based on exposures.
- Risk/return graphs.

In this chapter, we will expand this analysis and include the most frequently used and most relevant performance statistics. We will define each statistic and discuss how to interpret the statistics by using the data provided to us by FCM.

ABSOLUTE RETURN MEASURES

The performance measures that follow illustrate a number of different methods of highlighting the hedge fund's performance in isolation or in comparison to other hedge funds and/or benchmarks.

Histogram

A histogram is a simple and effective way of graphically representing a return distribution. Histograms are used to plot the density of a given hedge fund manager's returns. Figure 6.1 illustrates the return distribution for FCM compared to the S&P 500 Index.

This histogram plots the historical monthly returns in 1 percent increments between −5 percent and +5 percent. We can clearly see that FCM's returns are distributed more toward the middle of the range (with 70 percent of the returns falling +/−2 percent) and no monthly returns lower than −4 percent. The S&P 500, on the other hand, has numerous monthly returns on opposite ends of the chart (21 out of 60 returns exceeded +/−5 percent).

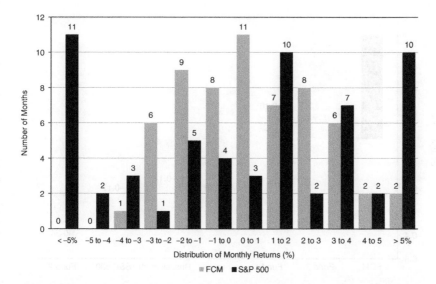

FIGURE 6.1 Histogram of Monthly Returns for FCM vs. S&P 500 from Dec-06 to Nov-11

Sharpe Ratio

This ratio measures the excess return per unit of risk and can also be referred to as the reward-to-variability ratio. When reviewing this ratio, the higher the result the better (which translates to higher risk-adjusted returns).

$$Sharpe\ Ratio = \frac{\{r - rf\}}{v}$$

Where:

    r = portfolio return (annual arithmetic mean return)
    rf = risk-free rate
    v = portfolio volatility (annualized standard deviation)

We know from our initial data review that FCM and Fund Three had the best performance for the period overall. The comparative statistics in Figure 6.2 clearly highlight that they also have the best return per unit of risk (standard deviation). Both the S&P 500 and the Russell 2000 indexes had negative Sharpe ratios.

The M^2 measure (named for Dr. Franco Modigliani and Leah Modigliani) uses the same information used in the calculation of the Sharpe

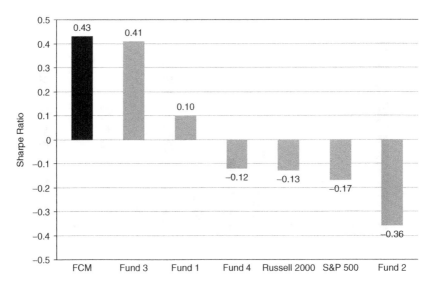

FIGURE 6.2 Comparison of Sharpe Ratios for Period from Dec-06 to Nov-11

ratio. It is basically the Sharpe ratio scaled by the standard deviation of the benchmark return.

$$M^2 Ratio = Sharpe\ Ratio \times v + rf$$

Where:

v = benchmark volatility (annualized standard deviation)

rf = risk-free rate

Information Ratio

The information ratio is similar to the Sharpe ratio. The main difference here is that the information ratio takes the excess return of the portfolio relative to a specific benchmark (not the risk-free rate) and calculates that figure as a percentage of the portfolio's tracking error relative to that benchmark.

$$Information\ Ratio = \frac{Premium}{Tracking\ Error}$$

Where:

Premium = annualized portfolio return – annualized benchmark return

Tracking error = standard deviation of the difference between the returns of the portfolio and the returns of the benchmark

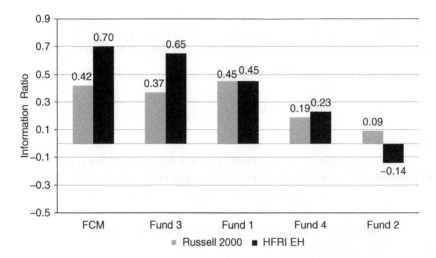

FIGURE 6.3 Comparison of Information Ratios for Period from Dec-06 to Nov-11

The information ratio is often viewed as a measure of a hedge fund manager's skill. The calculated statistic represents a way of measuring a hedge fund's alpha per unit of active risk. In Figure 6.3, we can view the hedge fund's information ratios compared to both the Russell 2000 and HFRI Equity Hedge indexes.

Once again, FCM and Fund Three come out looking better than the other fund alternatives when using both the Russell 2000 and the HFRI Equity Hedge Index as the benchmark; however, Fund One has the highest score when using the Russell 2000 as the benchmark.

MAR and Calmar Ratios

These ratios are used to measure return versus drawdown risk. They give the investor the ability to project potential opportunity gains versus the opportunity loss of investing with a specific hedge fund (by applying the annualized return as the potential gain and maximum drawdown as potential loss). This metric can be calculated for the life of a fund since its inception (minimum acceptable return [MAR] ratio) or over the previous three years (Calmar ratio). Table 6.1 illustrates the components of the MAR ratio calculation for each of the hedge funds in our universe as well as some indexes.

$$Calmar\ Ratio = \frac{Portfolio\ Return}{Maximum\ Drawdown}$$

Where:

Portfolio return = annualized portfolio return (last three years)
Maximum drawdown = absolute return of the largest drawdown (last three years)

$$MAR\ Ratio = \frac{Portfolio\ Return}{Maximum\ Drawdown}$$

Where:

Portfolio return = annualized portfolio return (since inception)
Maximum drawdown = absolute return of the largest drawdown (since inception)

TABLE 6.1 Data Table for MAR Ratio Calculation (ranked highest to lowest)

	Annualized Return	Maximum Drawdown	MAR Ratio
Fund 3	7.4	−8.2	0.90
FCM	8.2	−11.5	0.71
Fund 1	5.2	−38.9	0.13
Fund 4	3.0	−26.9	0.11
HFRI EH	1.0	−30.6	0.03
Fund 2	0.4	−24.8	0.02
Russell 2000	−1.3	−54.1	−0.02

Since we have used the full five-year track record elsewhere in this book, we will use the MAR ratio, which is calculated since the fund's inception. Figure 6.4 highlights that Fund Three had the highest MAR ratio because it experienced the smallest drawdown (−8.2 percent) of the group followed by FCM. The other three hedge funds as well as the benchmarks scored significantly lower due to their lower returns and larger drawdowns (which ranged from −25 percent to −54 percent).

Sterling Ratio

This ratio is virtually the same as the Calmar ratio with the only difference being that we subtract an arbitrary 10 percent from the maximum drawdown. This is done under the assumption that no matter how bad things have gotten in the past, they can always get worse in the future. In our calculation of the Sterling ratio, we will review the period since inception

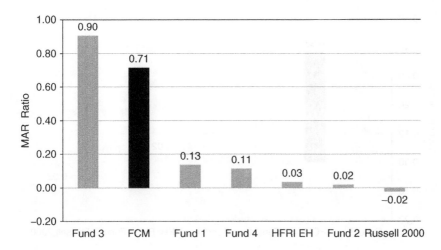

FIGURE 6.4 Comparison of MAR Ratios for Period from Dec-06 to Nov-11

to maintain consistency with previous measures. Table 6.2 illustrates the components of the sterling ratio calculation for each of the hedge funds in our universe as well as some indexes.

$$Sterling\ Ratio = \frac{Portfolio\ Return}{Maximum\ Drawdown + 10\%\ penalty}$$

Where:

Portfolio return = annualized portfolio return
Maximum drawdown = absolute return of the largest drawdown + 10%

TABLE 6.2 Data Table for Sterling Ratio Calculation (ranked highest to lowest)

	Annualized Return	Maximum Drawdown + 10% Penalty	Sterling Ratio
Fund 3	7.4	−18.2	0.41
FCM	8.2	−21.5	0.38
Fund 1	5.2	−48.9	0.11
Fund 4	3.0	−36.9	0.08
HFRI EH	1.0	−40.6	0.02
Fund 2	0.4	−34.8	0.01
Russell 2000	−1.3	−64.1	−0.02

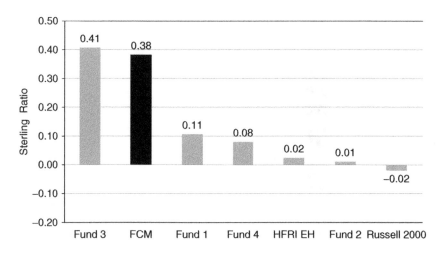

FIGURE 6.5 Comparison of Sterling Ratios for Period from Dec-06 to Nov-11

As we can see in Figure 6.5, the order remained the same as calculated by the MAR ratio (because the return and drawdown figures are identical—the only difference is the 10 percent drawdown penalty).

Sortino Ratio

The Sortino ratio (created by Frank Sortino) is similar to the Sharpe ratio; however, it substitutes downside deviation in the place of standard deviation in its denominator and changes the risk-free rate for a minimum acceptable return. As a result, it essentially modifies the Sharpe ratio by:

- Penalizing only those returns that fall below a user-specified target return.
- Measuring only downside volatility, whereas the Sharpe ratio measures both upside and downside volatility (standard deviation is a measure of total variability).

$$Sortino\ Ratio = \frac{\{r - m\}}{dd}$$

Where:

r = portfolio return (compound period return)
m = minimum acceptable return (user defined)
dd = downside deviation (similar to standard deviation but it considers only returns that fall below a defined minimum acceptable return instead of the arithmetic mean)

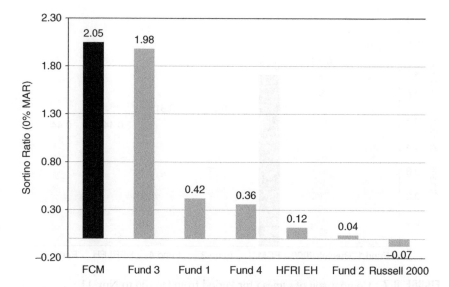

FIGURE 6.6   Comparison of Sortino Ratios for Period from Dec-06 to Nov-11

The user has the ability to input any minimum acceptable return (MAR) but for our purposes we will assume a MAR of 0 percent (which can be translated to setting the MAR to avoid losing money). As evidenced in Figure 6.6, FCM and Fund Three once again come out on top by a wide margin. You can rerun the analysis to set the MAR at specific levels, which may change the rank order.

Omega

This ratio does not assume a normal distribution of returns and takes into account skew. The Omega ratio calculates the likelihood of achieving a stated target return (similar to a minimum acceptable return). This is done by using the actual return distribution rather than a theoretical normal distribution.

The higher the calculated value, the higher the likelihood that the target return will be met or exceeded. This calculation involves partitioning returns into separate buckets (above and below the target return) and measuring the probability-adjusted ratio of gains to losses relative to the target return. Omega can be calculated for a discrete time period or we can create a rolling analysis to better assess manager skill over time. Figure 6.7 graphically illustrates the resulting Omega statistics for the funds under review.

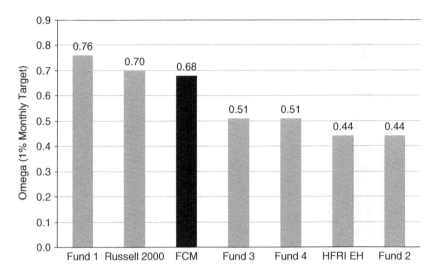

FIGURE 6.7   Comparison of Omega for Period from Dec-06 to Nov-11

$$Omega\ (L) = \frac{int\ [1 - F(r)], L, b}{int\ [F(r)], a, L}$$

Where:

Omega (L) = Omega given a defined threshold level

r = portfolio return

L = threshold level

$F(r)$ = cumulative distribution function of returns

a = lower bound of the return distribution

b = upper bound of the return distribution

ABSOLUTE RISK MEASURES

The risk measures that follow illustrate a number of different methods of highlighting the hedge fund's variance in returns in isolation or in comparison to other hedge funds and/or benchmarks.

Standard Deviation

This is one of the most common statistics used to measure the variability in returns for a hedge fund and their underlying benchmarks. Specifically, it measures how much dispersion exists from the average (mean) value. The statistic relies upon data that is normally distributed. A normal distribution of data means that most of the examples in a set of data are close to the "average," while relatively few examples tend to be at one extreme or the other.

The standard deviation is a statistic that tells you how tightly all the various data are clustered around the mean in a set of data. Standard deviation can be thought of as a "mean of the mean." When standard deviation is low, the bell-shaped curve of the distribution will be steep, and when standard deviation is high, the curve will be flatter.

$$Standard\ Deviation = \sqrt{\frac{Sum(r - avr)^2}{n}}$$

Where:

    n = number of returns
    r = period portfolio returns
    avr = average portfolio return

We can also measure "gain" standard deviation and "loss" standard deviation. The former measures the deviation of positive returns while the latter measures the deviation of negative returns.

The chart in Figure 6.8 illustrates that Fund 3 and FCM have the lowest levels of standard deviation while Fund One and the Russell 2000 Index exhibited the highest levels.

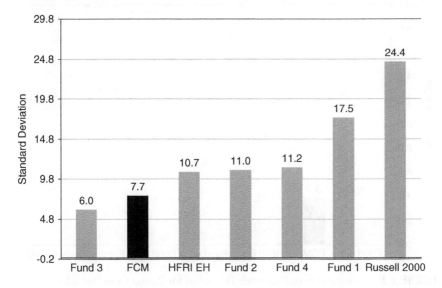

FIGURE 6.8 Comparison of Standard Deviation for Period from Dec-06 to Nov-11

Downside Deviation

This statistic is similar to standard deviation, but only includes returns that fall below a minimum acceptable return (MAR) versus the arithmetic mean used in standard deviation. For example, if the MAR is set at 10 percent, then downside deviation would only measure the variation in returns for each period in which returns fall below that figure. This calculation differs from "loss standard deviation," which measures the variation between each losing return and the average losing return.

$$Downside\ Deviation = \sqrt{\frac{Sum(r-m)\ where\ r < m}{n}}$$

Where:

   n = number of portfolio returns below a minimum acceptable return
   r = portfolio returns
   m = minimum acceptable return

Figure 6.9 looks similar to Figure 6.8, with Fund 3 and FCM exhibiting the lowest level of downside deviation.

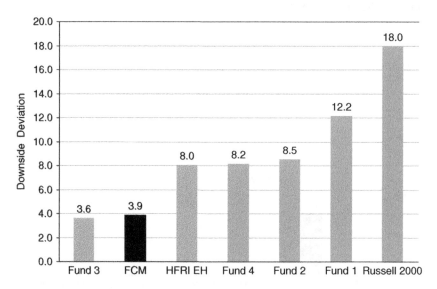

FIGURE 6.9 Comparison of Downside Deviation for Period from Dec-06 to Nov-11 (0% MAR)

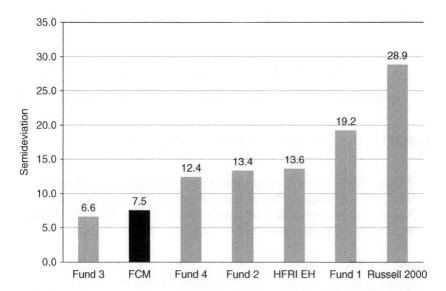

FIGURE 6.10 Comparison of Semideviation for Period from Dec-06 to Nov-11

Semideviation

This statistic measures the standard deviation of returns that fall below the mean return. It is calculated just like downside deviation except we modify the formula to include only those returns that fall below the mean return for the period instead of a minimum acceptable return. Figure 6.10 illustrates the calculated semideviation statistic for fund 3 compared to the other funds and benchmarks.

$$Semideviation = \sqrt{\frac{Sum\ (r - avr)\ where\ r < avr}{n}}$$

Where:

n = number of portfolio returns below a minimum acceptable return
r = portfolio returns
avr = average portfolio return

Skewness

Skewness is a measure of symmetry, or more accurately, the lack of symmetry. A data set is symmetric if it looks the same to the left and right of the mean. As such, skewness for a normal distribution is zero. The images in Figure 6.11 illustrate return distributions based on different types of skew.

FIGURE 6.11 Histograms Illustrating Positive and Negative Skew

- Positive skew—data skewed more to the left; the right tail is longer; smaller (more frequent) losses and higher (less frequent) gains.
- Negative skew—data skewed more to the right; the left tail is longer; higher (less frequent) losses and smaller (more frequent) gains.

$$Skewness = \sum \left(\frac{r - avr}{Std\ Dev\ r} \right)^3 \times \frac{1}{n}$$

Where:

n = number of portfolio returns
r = portfolio returns
avr = average portfolio return
Std Dev r = standard deviation of the portfolio returns

Interpreting Skewness Calculations   Because skewness is not measured in units of return like standard deviation, it should be interpreted as a measure of the shape of the return distribution.

- Skewness > 0: Right-skewed distribution (positive skew)—most values are concentrated on the left of the mean, with extreme values to the right.
- Skewness < 0: Left-skewed distribution (negative skew)—most values are concentrated on the right of the mean, with extreme values to the left.
- Skewness = 0: mean = median; the distribution is symmetrical around the mean.

Positive skewness indicates that positive returns were greater than anticipated and losses were smaller than anticipated. When analyzing skewness it is important to understand that an extreme outlier can significantly influence the resulting calculation. Skewness can be calculated using different return periods (such as monthly or quarterly returns), which can also impact calculated values.

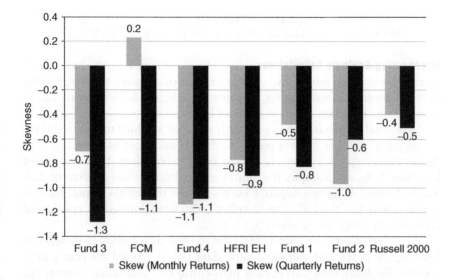

FIGURE 6.12 Comparison of Skewness for Period Dec-06 to Nov-11

Figure 6.12 uses historical monthly and quarterly performance for the hedge funds under review as well as the HFRI Equity Hedge and Russell 2000 Indexes. As you can see, the selection of period returns (monthly vs. quarterly) has a pretty big impact on the calculated statistic (particularly for FCM).

Kurtosis

Kurtosis is a measure of whether the data are peaked or flat relative to a normal distribution. Data sets with high kurtosis tend to have a distinct peak near the mean, decline rather rapidly, and have heavy tails. Data sets with low kurtosis tend to have a flat top near the mean rather than a sharp peak.

$$Kurtosis = \sum \left(\frac{r - avr}{Std\ Dev\ r} \right)^4 \times \frac{1}{n}$$

$$Excess\ Skewness = \left[\sum \left(\frac{r - avr}{Std\ Dev\ r} \right)^4 \times \frac{1}{n} \right] - 3$$

Where:

n = number of portfolio returns
r = portfolio returns

avr = average portfolio return

Std Dev r = standard deviation of the portfolio returns

Interpreting Kurtosis Calculations   Just like skewness, kurtosis has no real meaning relating to return; rather, it is a means of assessing the shape of the distribution for a given data set. The images in Figure 6.13 illustrate return distributions based on different levels of kurtosis.

A normal distribution has a kurtosis value of 3, which means that there are an equal number of data points to the left and right of the mean. The distribution's excess kurtosis is said to be negative when it has a value of less than 3. As an example, if a fund's excess kurtosis has a value of 2, it will be labeled as having negative kurtosis (even though the actual value is positive, it is less than 3). The distribution's excess kurtosis is considered positive when its value is above 3.

In a leptokurtic or "fat-tailed" curve, the distribution will tend to have higher peaks and will have more data points around the center than a normally distributed curve. In a platykurtic or "thin-tailed" curve, the distribution will tend to be flatter and have fewer data points around the center than a normally distributed curve.

- Kurtosis > 3—Positive kurtosis or "fat-tailed" distribution— distribution with greater peak with more data points clustering around the mean; more frequent large positive or negative returns.
- Kurtosis < 3—Negative kurtosis or "thin-tailed" distribution—flatter distribution of data points.
- Kurtosis = 0—normal distribution with equal number of data points to the left and right of the mean.

A hedge fund with a positive kurtosis value may be viewed as one that has experienced more extreme periodic returns at points in its history.

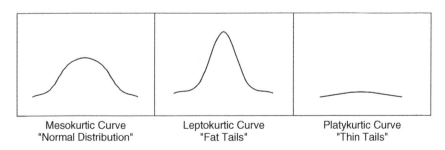

| Mesokurtic Curve | Leptokurtic Curve | Platykurtic Curve |
| "Normal Distribution" | "Fat Tails" | "Thin Tails" |

FIGURE 6.13   Histograms Illustrating Types of Kurtosis

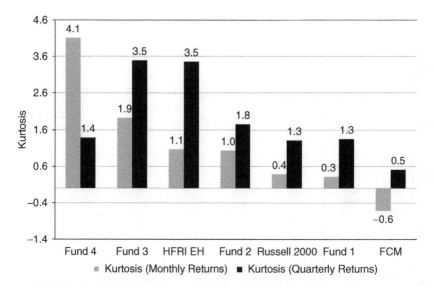

FIGURE 6.14   Comparison of Kurtosis for Period Dec-06 to Nov-11

As with all statistical performance-based measures, we should not assume that any past relationships will hold going forward, but this measure does provide a good method to understand a fund's performance history and helps to compare and contrast multiple hedge funds' overall level of risk (along with all the other measures outlined in this chapter).

As with skewness, we can calculate kurtosis based on monthly and quarterly return data. Figure 6.14 illustrates that only Fund Four had a positive kurtosis (value greater than 3) when using monthly data. However, when using quarterly data points both Fund Three and the HFRI Equity Hedge Index had positive kurtosis. FCM appears on the far right of the graph, indicating that its kurtosis values are the lowest within the group presented.

Drawdown Analysis

Drawdown simply refers to the current loss from the peak return and is illustrated in Figure 6.15 as the return from the fund's recent peak (point C) to its latest value (point D).

Maximum drawdown measures the largest peak to trough loss experienced by the fund and is represented in Figure 6.15 as the loss between points A and B.

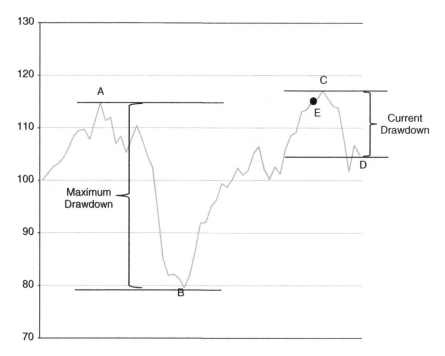

FIGURE 6.15 Example of Drawdown and Maximum Drawdown (HFRI EH Index for period Dec-06-Nov-11)

We can use maximum drawdown as a means of assessing a fund's historical losses and to compare both the magnitude of the loss as well as the time frame for the loss to other funds and indexes as shown in Table 6.3. The data from the table can be interpreted as follows:

- Maximum drawdown—largest loss over the five-year review period (Dec-06 to Nov-11). It can be illustrated in Figure 6.15 as the negative return achieved between points A and B.
- Length of drawdown—the number of months from peak to trough (between points A and B)
- Recovery from bottom—the number of months from trough to full recovery (referred to as the high water mark). This can be illustrated by counting the number of months between points B and E in Figure 6.15.
- Peak—the high point in a drawdown calculation (points A and C).
- Trough—the low point in the maximum drawdown calculation (point B).

TABLE 6.3 Maximum Drawdown Analysis

	Maximum Drawdown	Length of Drawdown	Recovery from Bottom	Peak	Trough
FCM	−11.5%	8	8	Aug-08	Apr-09
Fund 1	−38.9%	21	10	May-07	Feb-09
Fund 2	−24.8%	16	14	Oct-07	Feb-09
Fund 3	−8.2%	3	—	May-11	Aug-11
Fund 4	−26.9%	10	—	May-08	Mar-09
HFRI EH	−30.6%	16	24	Oct-07	Feb-09
Russell 2000	−54.1%	21	26	May-07	Feb-09

FCM's largest drawdown was −11.5 percent, and it occurred for the eight months between September 2008 and April 2009. It took an additional eight months for FCM to fully recover from that drawdown (reaching the high water mark in Dec-09). Fund Three and Fund Four have not yet fully recovered from their maximum drawdowns as of November 2011. But there is a big difference between the two. Fund Four declined −26.9 percent between May 2008 and March 2009 and has yet to recover more than 2.5 years later. Fund Three is currently undergoing its largest drawdown (−8.2 percent) and has only been in it for three months, and they have already made up most of the loss between Sep-11 and Nov-11.

Gain/Loss Ratio

This measures a hedge fund's average gain for all positive returns over a period as a percentage of the absolute value of the fund's average loss for all negative returns over the same period.

$$Gain \ to \ Loss \ Ratio = \frac{avg \ gain}{ABS \ (avg \ loss)}$$

Where:

$avg \ gain$ = average gain for all positive returns over the period

$ABS \ (avg \ loss)$ = absolute value of the fund's average loss for all negative returns over the period

This is a very simplistic analysis, but I think it provides useful information as we evaluate a fund's historical performance. In looking at the analysis in Table 6.4, we can see that only FCM's average gains exceeds the absolute value of their average losses when looking at the 60 months under review. The average monthly loss for FCM is similar to that of Fund Three,

TABLE 6.4   Gain/Loss Analysis (Monthly Returns)

	Average Gain	Average Loss	G/L Ratio
FCM	2.15%	−1.51%	1.4
Fund 3	1.38%	−1.50%	0.9
Fund 1	3.68%	−4.48%	0.8
Fund 2	2.24%	−2.74%	0.8
Fund 4	2.08%	−2.57%	0.8
Russell 2000	5.01%	−6.40%	0.8
HFRI Equity Hedge	2.06%	−2.97%	0.7

but it demonstrates a clear advantage over Fund Three when we look at average monthly gain (at 2.15 percent versus 1.38 percent for Fund Three). As a result, FCM's gain/loss ratio is significantly higher than that of its peers and the benchmarks.

REGRESSION-BASED STATISTICS

The regression-based statistics that follow illustrate a number of different methods of analyzing and reporting measures of association.

Beta

To understand the degree of association between two or more variables we can perform a regression analysis. To identify the degree to which the hedge fund's returns vary in relation to the variability in a specific index we calculate a statistic referred to as beta.

Statistically, beta is the slope of the regression line and is generally used as a means of assessing the index or market-related risk inherent in a fund (with risk being defined as variability of returns). Beta essentially measures a fund's sensitivity to market movements (when we specify an index as representative of the market) or the sensitivity to other return streams (such as other hedge funds). The regression analysis assumes a linear relationship between the variables resulting in a line of best fit.

When we run a regression, we can use the calculated values of alpha and beta to predict fund returns using the formula:

$$Predicted\ Fund\ Return = Alpha + (Beta \times Benchmark\ Return)$$

$$Beta = Correlation \times \left[\frac{std\ r}{std\ b} \right]$$

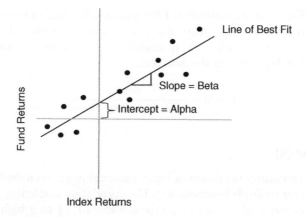

FIGURE 6.16 Regression Line of Best Fit Illustration

Where:

        Correlation = correlation between the fund and benchmark returns
        std r = standard deviation of the fund's returns
        std b = standard deviation of the benchmark's returns

As illustrated in Figure 6.16, beta is represented by the slope of the line. Interpreting beta:

- Beta = 1: variation similar to the benchmark.
- Beta > 1: fund returns vary more than the benchmark.
- Beta < 1: fund returns vary less than the benchmark.
- Beta = 0: fund returns not related to the benchmark.

Alpha

In the regression equation, alpha represents the value of the fund's return when the benchmark's return equals zero. It is used to measure a hedge fund manager's value added compared to a specific benchmark. As illustrated in Figure 6.16, alpha is represented by the Y-intercept.

$$Alpha = avg\ r - (Beta \times avg\ b)$$

Where:
  avg r = average fund return for the period
  avg b = average benchmark return for the period

T-Stat

This statistic measures the hypothesis that the slope of the regression (beta) is significantly different from zero. Using a 95 percent confidence level, a calculated T-stat value greater than 1.96 indicates that the beta is meaningful. The T-stat is an inferential statistical test. We can use the sample data (returns for the fund and the benchmark) to calculate a statistic to infer the strength in the relationship between the data sets.

$$T\text{-}Stat = \frac{Beta}{Beta\ Standard\ Error}$$

Correlation (R)

Correlation measures the extent of linear association between the fund and a benchmark (or multiple benchmarks). The correlation coefficient calculated in the regression analysis can range from a low of -1 to a high of $+1$. A correlation value at or near $+1$ indicates a high degree of association; a value at or near 0 indicates no association; a value at or near -1 indicates a negative degree of association (meaning they tend to move opposite to each other). (See Figure 6.17.)

$$Correlation\ (R) = \frac{Covariance}{std\ r \times std\ b}$$

Where:
     std r = standard deviation for the fund returns for the period
     std b = standard deviation for the benchmark returns for the period

According to the calculations presented in Table 6.5, FCM has produced alpha (value added) over the HFRI Equity Hedge and Russell 2000 indexes (Fund Three was a close second). FCM and Fund Three also had the lowest level of correlation to each index. The T-stats indicate that the results are significantly significant.

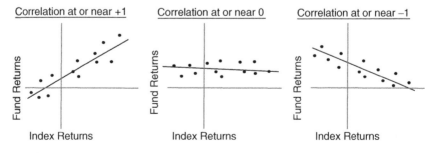

FIGURE 6.17 Graphical Illustration of Correlation

TABLE 6.5 Regression Results for Period Dec-06 to Nov-11

	Alpha	Beta	T-Stat	R	R^2
Relative to the HFRI Equity Hedge Index					
FCM	0.65%	0.30	10.41	0.42	0.18
Fund 1	0.37%	1.46	9.49	0.89	0.79
Fund 2	−0.04%	0.94	4.25	0.92	0.85
Fund 3	0.58%	0.24	9.96	0.42	0.18
Fund 4	0.21%	0.72	8.76	0.68	0.47
Relative to the Russell 2000 Index					
FCM	0.67%	0.12	22.63	0.39	0.16
Fund 1	0.47%	0.58	14.55	0.81	0.66
Fund 2	0.03%	0.34	17.57	0.76	0.58
Fund 3	0.60%	0.07	23.59	0.27	0.07
Fund 4	0.27%	0.21	21.83	0.45	0.20

Treynor Ratio

This statistic measures the return over the risk-free rate divided by beta. The formula is similar to the one we use to calculate the Sharpe ratio—the only difference is that we substitute beta in the denominator in place of standard deviation. So the Treynor ratio measures excess return per unit of benchmark or market risk (Sharpe measures excess return per unit of total risk). Figure 6.18 depicts the Treynor ratios for the hedge funds under review using the HFRI and Russell 2000 indexes as benchmarks (for the beta calculation).

$$Treynor\ Ration = \frac{r - rf}{Beta}$$

Where:

r = portfolio return (annual arithmetic mean return)
rf = risk-free rate

Fund Three comes out on top due to its low beta to both indexes. Both Fund Three and FCM have significantly higher values, meaning they have given investors a higher excess return per unit of market risk.

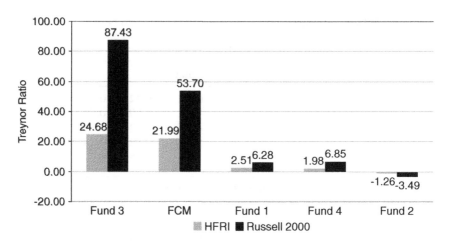

FIGURE 6.18   Comparison of Treynor Ratio for Period Dec-06 to Nov-11

PEER GROUP ANALYSIS

Peer group charts allow us to process a great deal of information in a quick and easy-to-read format. The goal is to create a universe of other hedge funds that have a similar mandate and to compare the performance of the fund under review to that universe.

We can slice the universe in a number of different ways. The most common are the following:

- Percentile ranking—for a given period we rank each of the hedge funds in the peer group universe from best performing to worst performing. The best fund would have a percentile ranking of 1 percent and the worst would have a percentile ranking of 100 percent.
- Quartile distributions—using the percentile ranking, we can create distribution ranges. A quartile distribution breaks the percentile ranking into four groups.
- Decile distributions—same as quartile distribution but there are 10 groups instead of four.

To account for outlier performance within the peer groups, it is common to set the top percentile at 5 percent (instead of 1 percent) and the bottom percentile at 95 percent (instead of 100 percent). This is done because just one outlier at either the top or bottom of the ranking can significantly skew

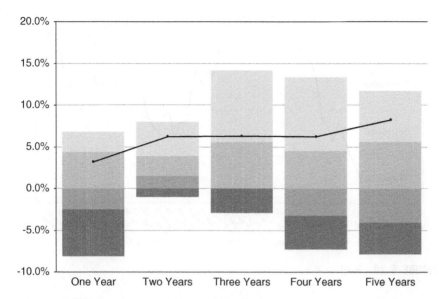

FIGURE 6.19 Peer Universe Quartile Distribution

the results. We can view the data in numerical format, but it is much easier and more efficient to display the results graphically.

Figure 6.19 highlights how FCM has performed relative to the peer group we created over multiple time periods. The fund has ranked in the first quartile in each period except the last year, where it is ranked in the upper part of the second quartile. Figure 6.20 shows the fund's results over one-year, two-year, and three-year rolling periods. Not surprisingly, the one-year rolling ranking has the greatest variability. This chart gives us an easy way to assess the percentile ranking from a historical perspective. Finally, we can take the data from Figure 6.20 and show the two-year rolling quartile distributions in Figure 6.21. Same data, but the chart provides a different perspective.

It is important to review the objectives and investment guidelines of the funds that comprise the peer group because if the peer group is not appropriate, then the comparison will yield results that may overstate or understate historical comparisons and weaken the analytical results. Peer groups should be built over time and adjusted as more information about the various funds within them is made available or discovered. Additionally, hedge funds can change over time, so a fund that may have been a good fit in the peer universe a year ago might not be a good fit today.

FIGURE 6.20   Rolling Percentile Ranking

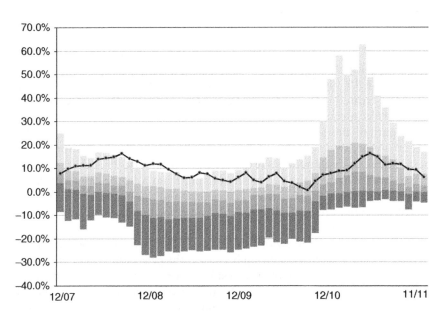

FIGURE 6.21   Rolling Two-Year Percentile Ranking within Quartile Distribution

Key Points/Questions from the Quantitative Review

- FCM has clearly experienced strong performance in absolute, relative, and risk-adjusted terms.
  - Highest Sharpe ratio.
  - Highest information ratio.
  - Second highest MAR ratio (behind Fund 3).
  - Highest Sortino ratio.
  - Highest Treynor ratio using monthly data.
- Fund Three had the lowest level of volatility, followed by FCM.
  - Standard deviation.
  - Downside deviation.
  - Semideviation.
- FCM's distribution of returns was attractive.
  - Positive skew using monthly data.
  - Lowest level of kurtosis (the return histogram shows returns were more normally distributed than the other alternatives).
  - FCM was the only fund with an average gain/loss ratio above 1.
- Regression-based statistics are appealing.
  - FCM and Fund Three exhibited low correlation to the indexes as well as the other fund choices.
  - FCM had the highest alpha values when compared to the HFRI Equity Hedge and Russell 2000 indexes.
- Strong peer group analysis.
  - FCM consistently appears in the first and second quartiles in the peer universe rankings over defined periods of time (one year, two years, etc.) as well as over rolling periods.

Action Plan

- Conduct initial reference calls.
- Conduct portfolio analysis.
  - 13F analysis.
  - Exposures analysis.
  - Create pro forma returns using exposures.
  - Analyze top holdings over time.
  - Create sample trade analysis.
- Verify portfolio exposures with the prime broker.

CHAPTER 7

Portfolio Analysis

"It's a proprietary strategy. I can't go into it in great detail."

Bernard Madoff

"It's not whether you're right or wrong that's important, but how much money you make when you're right and how much you lose when you're wrong."

George Soros

> Portfolio
> Analysis

Step Five

Having completed our quantitative performance analysis on FCM, we need to take our due diligence to the next level by analyzing the fund's holdings. The quantitative analysis does a good job of presenting the fund manager's results while the portfolio analysis should help to better understand the drivers of that performance.

When we conclude our portfolio analysis we should be in a position to understand:

- Historical return drivers (attribution).
- Strategy and style objectives and constraints.
- Sector and market cap exposures.
- Underlying portfolio liquidity.
- Make inferences about the decision-making process.
- Assess trading decisions.
- Identify potential outliers.

I find this part of the due diligence process one of the most enlightening. It provides me with evidence of the hedge fund manager's skill (or lack of skill) in analyzing and trading securities. When we hire an investment manager, we do so based on what we expect they will do for us in the future, not what they have accomplished in the past. Performance analysis allows us to look backward; portfolio analysis gives us the ability to properly assess whether or not the hedge fund in question is still positioned to perform well in the future. We will review positions made in the past as well as current positions held by the fund manager, but our understanding of the analytical techniques and processes employed will help to evaluate the manager's ability to perform in the future.

Of course we cannot predict what will happen, but by getting to know how the hedge fund manager, team, and organization work we can better handicap our odds of success. For example, if a hedge fund under review has experienced very strong performance historically and is still managed by the same person or team, we might be inclined to extrapolate that the manager "can" still do well in the future (all else being equal). However, if we discover while performing portfolio analysis that the manager's past performance was due largely to the fund's performance in health care stocks in years past and we further discover that the firm's health care analyst left a year ago to start his own hedge fund, we might have to reassess our opinion.

In the latter scenario, we might want to understand what the health care analyst's contribution to the portfolio was when he was employed by the fund and see if the firm had subsequently replaced that analyst with another (in which case we will need to evaluate the new analyst). We would have to make a judgment that the hedge fund can still perform well despite the fact that the person who researched the firm's biggest contributors to performance in the past is no longer with the firm. The point is that performance analysis alone would not have highlighted this issue.

ATTRIBUTION ANALYSIS

One of the things that we requested following the initial phone interview was portfolio attribution. FCM provided us with historical monthly long and short attribution. I have combined this information with the exposures data included in the due diligence questionnaire (DDQ) to create Table 7.1.

The exposures represent a snapshot of the fund's notional exposure in the long and short books at month end since inception. Notional exposure is presented because they have used options in the past (as we discovered in our phone interview) and we requested to see the "levered" or notional value of the option positions as opposed to the premium value.

TABLE 7.1 Exposure and Attribution Report for Period Dec-06 to Nov-11

Month	FCM	Russell 2000	Month End Exposures				Attribution			Estimated Returns	
			Longs	Shorts	Gross	Net	Longs	Shorts	Total Return	Longs	Shorts
Dec-06	0.42%	0.33%	110%	−55%	165%	55%	0.48%	−0.07%	0.42%	0.44%	0.13%
Jan-07	1.14%	1.67%	115%	−65%	180%	50%	2.13%	−1.00%	1.14%	1.90%	1.66%
Feb-07	1.65%	−0.79%	111%	−60%	171%	51%	0.35%	1.30%	1.65%	0.31%	−2.08%
Mar-07	1.30%	1.07%	107%	−60%	167%	47%	1.78%	−0.48%	1.30%	1.63%	0.81%
Apr-07	1.74%	1.80%	113%	−58%	171%	55%	2.33%	−0.59%	1.74%	2.12%	1.00%
May-07	0.88%	4.10%	115%	−55%	170%	60%	3.77%	−2.88%	0.88%	3.30%	5.10%
Jun-07	2.19%	−1.46%	116%	−55%	171%	61%	−0.46%	2.66%	2.19%	−0.40%	−4.83%
Jul-07	0.17%	−6.84%	126%	−60%	186%	66%	−7.21%	7.38%	0.17%	−5.96%	−12.83%
Aug-07	2.25%	2.27%	118%	−58%	176%	60%	3.21%	−0.96%	2.25%	2.63%	1.63%
Sep-07	3.62%	1.72%	120%	−60%	180%	60%	3.36%	0.27%	3.62%	2.82%	−0.45%
Oct-07	0.45%	2.87%	115%	−55%	170%	60%	2.79%	−2.34%	0.45%	2.38%	4.07%
Nov-07	−0.24%	−7.18%	108%	−55%	163%	53%	−5.62%	5.38%	−0.24%	−5.04%	−9.77%
Dec-07	−0.22%	−0.06%	102%	−53%	155%	49%	−0.17%	−0.04%	−0.22%	−0.17%	0.08%
Jan-08	3.77%	−6.82%	100%	−65%	165%	35%	−1.89%	5.66%	3.77%	−1.87%	−9.60%
Feb-08	2.12%	−3.71%	85%	−64%	149%	21%	−1.12%	3.24%	2.12%	−1.22%	−5.02%
Mar-08	0.42%	0.42%	75%	−60%	135%	15%	0.57%	−0.14%	0.42%	0.71%	0.23%
Apr-08	−0.21%	4.19%	70%	−60%	130%	10%	2.74%	−2.95%	−0.21%	3.78%	4.92%
May-08	4.93%	4.59%	70%	−55%	125%	15%	4.49%	0.44%	4.93%	6.41%	−0.77%
Jun-08	0.89%	−7.70%	65%	−64%	129%	1%	−4.52%	5.41%	0.89%	−6.70%	−9.09%
Jul-08	0.79%	3.70%	63%	−65%	128%	−2%	2.68%	−1.89%	0.79%	4.18%	2.92%
Aug-08	2.46%	3.61%	63%	−45%	108%	18%	3.18%	−0.72%	2.46%	5.05%	1.31%

(*Continued*)

TABLE 7.1 (*Continued*)

Month	FCM	Russell 2000	Month End Exposures				Attribution			Estimated Returns	
			Longs	Shorts	Gross	Net	Longs	Shorts	Total Return	Longs	Shorts
Sep-08	-3.47%	-7.97%	70%	-45%	115%	25%	-6.46%	3.00%	-3.47%	-9.72%	-6.66%
Oct-08	-2.41%	-20.80%	75%	-65%	140%	10%	-15.80%	13.39%	-2.41%	-21.79%	-24.35%
Nov-08	-2.92%	-11.83%	80%	-60%	140%	20%	-9.80%	6.88%	-2.92%	-12.64%	-11.00%
Dec-08	1.87%	5.80%	75%	-65%	140%	10%	5.13%	-3.26%	1.87%	6.62%	5.21%
Jan-09	0.92%	-11.12%	80%	-65%	145%	15%	-7.08%	8.01%	0.92%	-9.14%	-12.32%
Feb-09	-2.61%	-12.15%	85%	-50%	135%	35%	-9.01%	6.41%	-2.61%	-10.93%	-11.14%
Mar-09	-1.97%	8.93%	86%	-45%	131%	41%	3.17%	-5.14%	-1.97%	3.71%	10.83%
Apr-09	-1.45%	15.46%	90%	-48%	138%	42%	9.94%	-11.39%	-1.45%	11.30%	24.50%
May-09	1.26%	3.01%	88%	-45%	133%	43%	2.63%	-1.36%	1.26%	2.95%	2.93%
Jun-09	5.82%	1.47%	90%	-45%	135%	45%	4.42%	1.40%	5.82%	4.96%	-3.12%
Jul-09	-0.62%	9.63%	90%	-43%	133%	47%	6.61%	-7.23%	-0.62%	7.35%	16.42%
Aug-09	-1.56%	2.87%	92%	-45%	137%	47%	1.48%	-3.03%	-1.56%	1.62%	6.89%
Sep-09	2.28%	5.77%	93%	-45%	138%	48%	5.02%	-2.74%	2.28%	5.43%	6.09%
Oct-09	-0.72%	-6.79%	93%	-43%	136%	50%	-5.24%	4.53%	-0.72%	-5.64%	-10.29%
Nov-09	3.30%	3.14%	91%	-42%	133%	49%	3.56%	-0.26%	3.30%	3.87%	0.62%
Dec-09	3.44%	8.05%	95%	-42%	137%	53%	7.23%	-3.80%	3.44%	7.78%	9.04%
Jan-10	-1.98%	-3.68%	100%	-47%	147%	53%	-3.70%	1.72%	-1.98%	-3.80%	-3.86%
Feb-10	0.04%	4.50%	110%	-50%	160%	60%	3.36%	-3.32%	0.04%	3.20%	6.84%
Mar-10	5.18%	8.14%	112%	-55%	167%	57%	9.28%	-4.10%	5.18%	8.36%	7.81%
Apr-10	2.38%	5.66%	115%	-54%	169%	61%	5.65%	-3.27%	2.38%	4.98%	6.00%
May-10	-1.32%	-7.59%	112%	-53%	165%	59%	-7.23%	5.91%	-1.32%	-6.37%	-11.05%

Jun-10	-0.34%	-7.75%	120%	-60%	180%	60%	-7.58%	7.23%	-0.34%	-6.53%	-12.80%
Jul-10	-2.41%	6.87%	122%	-60%	182%	62%	3.05%	-5.46%	-2.41%	2.52%	9.10%
Aug-10	-0.72%	-7.40%	122%	-56%	178%	66%	-6.12%	5.40%	-0.72%	-5.01%	-9.30%
Sep-10	4.24%	12.46%	122%	-54%	176%	68%	13.09%	-8.84%	4.24%	10.73%	16.08%
Oct-10	2.73%	4.09%	125%	-55%	180%	70%	5.06%	-2.33%	2.73%	4.10%	4.27%
Nov-10	-1.82%	3.47%	118%	-55%	173%	63%	1.29%	-3.11%	-1.82%	1.06%	5.65%
Dec-10	3.75%	7.94%	117%	-54%	171%	63%	8.54%	-4.79%	3.75%	7.27%	8.79%
Jan-11	1.28%	-0.26%	115%	-60%	175%	55%	0.41%	0.86%	1.28%	0.36%	-1.51%
Feb-11	2.50%	5.48%	116%	-65%	181%	51%	6.21%	-3.71%	2.50%	5.38%	5.94%
Mar-11	3.50%	2.59%	116%	-64%	180%	52%	4.73%	-1.23%	3.50%	4.08%	1.90%
Apr-11	0.97%	2.64%	117%	-64%	181%	53%	2.83%	-1.86%	0.97%	2.43%	2.91%
May-11	-1.13%	-1.87%	113%	-63%	176%	50%	-2.19%	1.07%	-1.13%	-1.91%	-1.68%
Jun-11	-0.67%	-2.31%	115%	-63%	178%	52%	-2.23%	1.56%	-0.67%	-1.96%	-2.47%
Jul-11	0.58%	-3.61%	112%	-60%	172%	52%	-3.07%	3.64%	0.58%	-2.70%	-5.92%
Aug-11	-2.21%	-8.70%	115%	-60%	175%	55%	-9.23%	7.02%	-2.21%	-8.13%	-11.71%
Sep-11	-1.52%	-11.21%	115%	-62%	177%	53%	-11.57%	10.04%	-1.52%	-10.06%	-16.46%
Oct-11	-1.03%	15.14%	117%	-62%	179%	55%	14.90%	-15.93%	-1.03%	12.85%	25.70%
Nov-11	-2.61%	-0.36%	113%	-65%	178%	48%	-1.39%	-1.22%	-2.61%	-1.21%	1.93%
Avg			102%	-56%	158%	46%	32.75%	8.34%	41.09%	21.67%	-0.80%

There are many ways that people calculate gross and net exposures but we will keep things simple due to the nature of FCM's underlying strategy. For our purposes, we will use the following formulas to calculate gross and net exposures:

$$Gross\ Exposure = \frac{gnL + gnS}{NAV}$$

$$Net\ Exposure = \frac{gnL - gnS}{NAV}$$

Where,

    gnL = gross notional long value
    gnS = gross notional short value
    NAV = net asset value (amount of money invested in the fund)

The month-end exposures appear in graphical format in Figure 4.5 and the monthly long and short attribution is highlighted in Figures 7.1 through 7.3.

We were not provided with monthly returns for the long and short books, but we can use the information available to approximate the returns using the following formula:

$$Long\ Return = \frac{Long\ attribution}{avg\ long\ exposure}$$

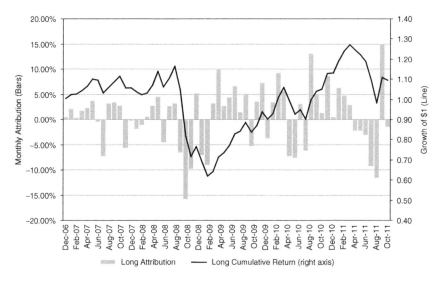

FIGURE 7.1 Monthly Long Attribution for Period Dec-06 to Nov-11

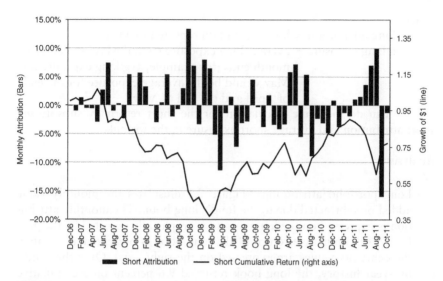

FIGURE 7.2 Monthly Short Attribution for Period Dec-06 to Nov-11

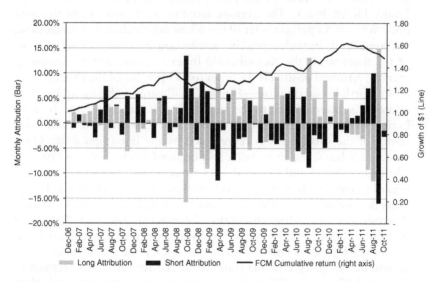

FIGURE 7.3 Monthly Long and Short Attribution for Period Dec-06 to Nov-11

Where,

> long attribution = long attribution reported by FCM
>
> avg long exposure = average long exposure from the last and current month ends (for example, avg long exposure for May would be the average exposure for the end of April and the end of May)

We can do the same calculation for the short return by substituting short attribution and average short exposure in the formula.

Analysis

■ Long portfolio attribution—Figure 7.1 illustrates the monthly value added or subtracted due to the fund's long book. The monthly attribution is expressed on the left axis and is graphically depicted by the grey bars. The cumulative return of the long book is presented as a line in the chart (its values are expressed on the right axis). Over the fund's five-year history, the long book returned 9.6 percent on a cumulative basis. Over the same period, the Russell 2000 was up 0.4 percent, the S&P 500 declined −0.9 percent, and the HFRI Index was up 5 percent. FCM performed significantly better than the long-only equity benchmarks and nearly doubled the performance of the corresponding HFRI Equity Hedge Index. The average monthly attribution from the long book was +0.55 percent. Out of the 60 months included in this review, the long book provided positive attribution 37 times (or 62 percent of the time) while the Russell 2000 Index (a proxy for the small-cap market) returned positively 35 times (or 58 of the time).

■ Short portfolio attribution—Figure 7.2 illustrates the monthly value added or subtracted due to the fund's short book. The monthly attribution is represented by the black bars (left axis) and the cumulative return of the short book is represented by the line (right axis). On a cumulative basis, the short book had declined as much as −63 percent (through Feb-09) and declined −23 percent over the entire five-year period (remember that the portfolio makes money when its short positions decline in value). This is a remarkable figure, as we have already determined that the Russell 2000 (+0.4 percent) and S&P 500 (−0.9 percent) experienced returns that were relatively flat. The short book experienced positive attribution in 26 out of the 60 months under review (or 43 percent of the time) while the Russell 2000 declined in 25 out of 60 months. While these percentages are consistent, it is clear that the fund's short positions significantly outperformed the (inverse of) the market.

TABLE 7.2 Long and Short Attribution for 2007

	Month End Exposures				Attribution			Estimated Returns		Index Returns	
	Longs	Shorts	Gross	Net	Longs	Shorts	Total Return	Longs	Shorts	Russell 2000	HFRI Eq Hedge
Jan-07	115%	−65%	180%	50%	2.13%	−1.00%	1.14%	1.90%	1.66%	1.67%	1.16%
Feb-07	111%	−60%	171%	51%	0.35%	1.30%	1.65%	0.31%	−2.08%	−0.79%	0.63%
Mar-07	107%	−60%	167%	47%	1.78%	−0.48%	1.30%	1.63%	0.81%	1.07%	1.01%
Apr-07	113%	−58%	171%	55%	2.33%	−0.59%	1.74%	2.12%	1.00%	1.80%	1.86%
May-07	115%	−55%	170%	60%	3.77%	−2.88%	0.88%	3.30%	5.10%	4.10%	2.24%
Jun-07	116%	−55%	171%	61%	−0.46%	2.66%	2.19%	−0.40%	−4.83%	−1.46%	0.89%
Jul-07	126%	−60%	186%	66%	−7.21%	7.38%	0.17%	−5.96%	−12.83%	−6.84%	0.17%
Aug-07	118%	−58%	176%	60%	3.21%	−0.96%	2.25%	2.63%	1.63%	2.27%	−1.67%
Sep-07	120%	−60%	180%	60%	3.36%	0.27%	3.62%	2.82%	−0.45%	1.72%	3.18%
Oct-07	115%	−55%	170%	60%	2.79%	−2.34%	0.45%	2.38%	4.07%	2.87%	3.09%
Nov-07	108%	−55%	163%	53%	−5.62%	5.38%	−0.24%	−5.04%	−9.77%	−7.18%	−2.89%
Dec-07	102%	−53%	155%	49%	−0.17%	−0.04%	−0.22%	−0.17%	0.08%	−0.06%	0.53%
Average	114%	−58%	172%	56%	0.52%	0.72%	1.25%	0.46%	−1.30%	−0.07%	0.85%
Cumulative					5.70%	8.50%	15.93%	5.13%	−15.99%	−1.57%	10.48%

TABLE 7.3 Long and Short Attribution for 2008

| | Month End Exposures | | | | Attribution | | | Estimated Returns | | Index Returns | |
	Longs	Shorts	Gross	Net	Longs	Shorts	Total Return	Longs	Shorts	Russell 2000	HFRI Eq Hedge
Jan-08	100%	−65%	165%	35%	−1.89%	5.66%	3.77%	−1.87%	−9.60%	−6.82%	−4.47%
Feb-08	85%	−64%	149%	21%	−1.12%	3.24%	2.12%	−1.22%	−5.02%	−3.71%	1.31%
Mar-08	75%	−60%	135%	15%	0.57%	−0.14%	0.42%	0.71%	0.23%	0.42%	−2.84%
Apr-08	70%	−60%	130%	10%	2.74%	−2.95%	−0.21%	3.78%	4.92%	4.19%	2.45%
May-08	70%	−55%	125%	15%	4.49%	0.44%	4.93%	6.41%	−0.77%	4.59%	2.38%
Jun-08	65%	−64%	129%	1%	−4.52%	5.41%	0.89%	−6.70%	−9.09%	−7.70%	−2.44%
Jul-08	63%	−65%	128%	−2%	2.68%	−1.89%	0.79%	4.18%	2.92%	3.70%	−2.84%
Aug-08	63%	−45%	108%	18%	3.18%	−0.72%	2.46%	5.05%	1.31%	3.61%	−2.17%
Sep-08	70%	−45%	115%	25%	−6.46%	3.00%	−3.47%	−9.72%	−6.66%	−7.97%	−8.14%
Oct-08	75%	−65%	140%	10%	−15.80%	13.39%	−2.41%	−21.79%	−24.35%	−20.80%	−9.46%
Nov-08	80%	−60%	140%	20%	−9.80%	6.88%	−2.92%	−12.64%	−11.00%	−11.83%	−3.77%
Dec-08	75%	−65%	140%	10%	5.13%	−3.26%	1.87%	6.62%	5.21%	5.80%	0.22%
Average	74%	−59%	134%	15%	−1.73%	2.42%	0.69%	−2.26%	−4.33%	−3.04%	−2.48%
Cumulative					−20.87%	31.66%	8.18%	−27.59%	−43.85%	−33.79%	−26.65%

TABLE 7.4 Long and Short Attribution for 2009

	Month End Exposures				Attribution			Estimated Returns		Index Returns	
	Longs	Shorts	Gross	Net	Longs	Shorts	Total Return	Longs	Shorts	Russell 2000	HFRI Eq Hedge
Jan-09	80%	−65%	145%	15%	−7.08%	8.01%	0.92%	−9.14%	−12.32%	−11.12%	−0.88%
Feb-09	85%	−50%	135%	35%	−9.01%	6.41%	−2.61%	−10.93%	−11.14%	−12.15%	−2.20%
Mar-09	86%	−45%	131%	41%	3.17%	−5.14%	−1.97%	3.71%	10.83%	8.93%	2.90%
Apr-09	90%	−48%	138%	42%	9.94%	−11.39%	−1.45%	11.30%	24.50%	15.46%	5.44%
May-09	88%	−45%	133%	43%	2.63%	−1.36%	1.26%	2.95%	2.93%	3.01%	6.37%
Jun-09	90%	−45%	135%	45%	4.42%	1.40%	5.82%	4.96%	−3.12%	1.47%	0.18%
Jul-09	90%	−43%	133%	47%	6.61%	−7.23%	−0.62%	7.35%	16.42%	9.63%	3.20%
Aug-09	92%	−45%	137%	47%	1.48%	−3.03%	−1.56%	1.62%	6.89%	2.87%	1.37%
Sep-09	93%	−45%	138%	48%	5.02%	−2.74%	2.28%	5.43%	6.09%	5.77%	3.22%
Oct-09	93%	−43%	136%	50%	−5.24%	4.53%	−0.72%	−5.64%	−10.29%	−6.79%	−0.72%
Nov-09	91%	−42%	133%	49%	3.56%	−0.26%	3.30%	3.87%	0.62%	3.14%	1.57%
Dec-09	95%	−42%	137%	53%	7.23%	−3.80%	3.44%	7.78%	9.04%	8.05%	2.07%
Average	89%	−47%	136%	43%	1.89%	−1.22%	0.67%	1.94%	3.37%	2.35%	1.88%
Cumulative					22.85%	−15.22%	8.00%	22.63%	39.33%	27.17%	24.57%

TABLE 7.5 Long and Short Attribution for 2010

	Month End Exposures				Attribution			Estimated Returns		Index Returns	
	Longs	Shorts	Gross	Net	Longs	Shorts	Total Return	Longs	Shorts	Russell 2000	HFRI Eq Hedge
Jan-10	100%	−47%	147%	53%	−3.70%	1.72%	−1.98%	−3.80%	−3.86%	−3.68%	−1.27%
Feb-10	110%	−50%	160%	60%	3.36%	−3.32%	0.04%	3.20%	6.84%	4.50%	0.92%
Mar-10	112%	−55%	167%	57%	9.28%	−4.10%	5.18%	8.36%	7.81%	8.14%	3.15%
Apr-10	115%	−54%	169%	61%	5.65%	−3.27%	2.38%	4.98%	6.00%	5.66%	1.19%
May-10	112%	−53%	165%	59%	−7.23%	5.91%	−1.32%	−6.37%	−11.05%	−7.59%	−4.05%
Jun-10	120%	−60%	180%	60%	−7.58%	7.23%	−0.34%	−6.53%	−12.80%	−7.75%	−1.85%
Jul-10	122%	−60%	182%	62%	3.05%	−5.46%	−2.41%	2.52%	9.10%	6.87%	2.36%
Aug-10	122%	−56%	178%	66%	−6.12%	5.40%	−0.72%	−5.01%	−9.30%	−7.40%	−1.37%
Sep-10	122%	−54%	176%	68%	13.09%	−8.84%	4.24%	10.73%	16.08%	12.46%	4.74%
Oct-10	125%	−55%	180%	70%	5.06%	−2.33%	2.73%	4.10%	4.27%	4.09%	2.37%
Nov-10	118%	−55%	173%	63%	1.29%	−3.11%	−1.82%	1.06%	5.65%	3.47%	0.64%
Dec-10	117%	−54%	171%	63%	8.54%	−4.79%	3.75%	7.27%	8.79%	7.94%	3.52%
Average	116%	−54%	171%	62%	2.06%	−1.25%	0.81%	1.71%	2.29%	2.23%	0.86%
Cumulative					24.50%	−15.20%	9.75%	20.26%	25.32%	26.85%	10.45%

TABLE 7.6 Long and Short Attribution for 2011 (Jan-Nov)

	Month End Exposures				Attribution			Estimated Returns		Index Returns	
	Longs	Shorts	Gross	Net	Longs	Shorts	Total Return	Longs	Shorts	Russell 2000	HFRI Eq Hedge
Jan-11	115%	-60%	175%	55%	0.41%	0.86%	1.28%	0.36%	-1.51%	-0.26%	0.42%
Feb-11	116%	-65%	181%	51%	6.21%	-3.71%	2.50%	5.38%	5.94%	5.48%	1.30%
Mar-11	116%	-64%	180%	52%	4.73%	-1.23%	3.50%	4.08%	1.90%	2.59%	0.50%
Apr-11	117%	-64%	181%	53%	2.83%	-1.86%	0.97%	2.43%	2.91%	2.64%	1.34%
May-11	113%	-63%	176%	50%	-2.19%	1.07%	-1.13%	-1.91%	-1.68%	-1.87%	-1.28%
Jun-11	115%	-63%	178%	52%	-2.23%	1.56%	-0.67%	-1.96%	-2.47%	-2.31%	-1.26%
Jul-11	112%	-60%	172%	52%	-3.07%	3.64%	0.58%	-2.70%	-5.92%	-3.61%	-0.33%
Aug-11	115%	-60%	175%	55%	-9.23%	7.02%	-2.21%	-8.13%	-11.71%	-8.70%	-4.90%
Sep-11	115%	-62%	177%	53%	-11.57%	10.04%	-1.52%	-10.06%	-16.46%	-11.21%	-5.97%
Oct-11	117%	-62%	179%	55%	14.90%	-15.93%	-1.03%	12.85%	25.70%	15.14%	4.89%
Nov-11	113%	-65%	178%	48%	-1.39%	-1.22%	-2.61%	-1.21%	1.93%	-0.36%	-1.60%
Average	115%	-63%	177%	52%	-0.05%	0.02%	-0.03%	-0.08%	-0.13%	-0.23%	-0.63%
Cumulative					-3.17%	-2.06%	-0.54%	-2.82%	-6.73%	-4.80%	-7.10%

The analysis shows us in clear terms that FCM has managed to make money in both their long and short books since inception. Now that we have determined that FCM has been profitable over its five-year history, we can disaggregate the attribution by calendar year to determine if any single year was responsible for the strong performance and determine where it came from (see Tables 7.2 to 7.6).

2007 Analysis
- Exposures
  - Gross range from 155 percent to 180 percent.
  - Net range from 47 percent to 66 percent.
- Attribution/Returns
  - Profitable in both the long and short books.
  - The Russell 2000 was down slightly for the year (-1.57%) and the HFRI Equity Hedge Index was up 10.5 percent.
  - Shorts declined -16 percent and were responsible for more than half of the positive performance attribution for the year (8.5 percent).
  - Short book performed exceptionally well in July (-12.8 percent versus -6.8 percent for the Russell 2000), June (-4.83 percent versus -1.5 percent for the Russell 2000), and November (-9.8 percent versus -7.2 percent for the Russell 2000).

2008 Analysis
- Exposures
  - Gross exposure ranged from 108 percent (August) to 165 percent (January).
  - Gross exposure subsequently increased to 140 percent in October (and stayed there through year end).
  - Net exposure changed significantly, starting at 35 percent in January, falling to -2 percent in July, and rising to 20 percent in November.
  - Timing was exceptional this year—FCM took down gross and net ahead of the market decline and started to add to both during the fourth quarter (a little early, but ultimately it was the right call).
- Attribution/Returns
  - The fund was profitable for the year as a whole.
  - Short attribution added 31.7 percent to returns and long attribution detracted -20.9 percent for the year as a whole.
  - The short book declined -43.9 percent for the year versus -33.8 percent for the Russell 2000, and the long book declined -27.6 percent for the year. Both books outperformed the small-cap marketplace.

- Significant outperformance in January (longs down only −1.9 percent and shorts down −9.6 percent while the Russell 2000 declined −6.8 percent). As a result, the fund gained 3.8 percent in a strong down month for equities.
- Due to low net exposure in April and performance within the long and short books that was roughly in line with the Russell 2000, the fund underperformed. The equity market performance was strong at a time when the attribution from the long and short books essentially cancelled each other out.
- The low exposure continued into June, and that proved to be beneficial, as the Russell 2000 declined −7.7 percent. The fund was only net long 1 percent, and the short book in June outperformed the market (declining −9.1 percent).
- In October and November the fund's performance was exceptional due to the low net exposure (10 percent in October and 20 percent in November). The short book's performance in October was additive (as it declined −24.4 percent versus −20.8 percent for the Russell 2000).
- Low net exposure in December led to underperformance that month, as the equity market turned in a strong performance (Russell 2000 was up 5.8 percent).

2009 Analysis

- Exposures
  - Gross exposure stayed in a narrow range (from 131 percent to 145 percent).
  - Net exposure increased from a low of 15 percent in January to a high of 53 percent in December.
  - Changes in exposure were more a function of a reduction in the short book. Gross short exposure fell from a high of −65 percent in January to a low of −42 percent in December (which was the lowest point in the firm's five-year history).
  - Average gross exposure for the year was 136 percent and average net exposure was 43 percent.
- Attribution/Returns
  - The long book added more attribution than the short book detracted. This was due to FCM's long bias throughout the year—as opposed to alpha driven by performance.
  - The long book gained 22.6 percent and the short book advanced 39.3 percent for the year versus a 27.2 percent gain for the Russell 2000 and a 24.6 percent return for the HFRI Equity Hedge indexes. The

long and short books underperformed the broad equity market for the year.

- It is clear that FCM's short book performed very poorly in 2009, and we should explore this with them when we conduct our onsite interviews.
- The fund's low net in January proved beneficial, as the Russell 2000 declined −11.1 percent. Outperformance in both books led to a marginally positive gain for the fund.
- In March and April, the fund's low net exposure and significant underperformance in the short book led to negative returns in each month at a time when the Russell 2000 increased 8.9 percent in March and 15.5 percent in April.
- FCM performed very well in June, driven by very strong performance in both books. The long book returned 5.0 percent and the short book fell −3.1 percent at a time when the Russell 2000 was up 1.5 percent. As a result, both long and short attribution was positive.
- In July and August, the fund's short book once again underperformed and led to poor relative performance. In July, the short book gained 16.4 percent versus a gain of 9.6 percent for the Russell 2000. In August, the fund's short book was up more than twice as much as the Russell 2000.
- In October, the short book turned around and performed very well, declining −10.3 percent when the Russell 2000 declined −6.8 percent.

2010 Analysis

- Exposures
  - Gross and net exposures looked similar to 2007 exposures.
  - Average gross was 171 percent.
  - Average net was 62 percent (the highest yearly average over the life of the fund).
- Attribution/Returns
  - The fund's performance was modestly behind the HFRI Equity Hedge Index but lagged the Russell 2000 by a wide margin (9.8 percent versus 26.9 percent).
  - A significant portion of the fund's underperformance relative to the Russell 2000 was driven by net exposure (February, March, April, July, September, December).
  - Poor long and short book performance hurt overall fund performance in February (longs were up 3.2 percent and shorts up 6.8 percent versus 4.5 percent for the Russell 2000).

- Strong long and short book performance in May, June, August, and November led to significant outperformance in each month.

2011 Analysis (through November)

- Exposures
  - Gross exposures remained in a tight range (172 percent to 181 percent).
  - Net exposure was lower in 2011 than 2010 and ranged from 48 percent to 55 percent.
  - Average gross was 177 percent and average net was 52 percent.
- Attribution/Returns
  - For the 11 months through November 2011, the fund's performance was −0.5 percent versus −4.8 percent for the Russell 2000 and −7.1 percent for the HFRI Equity Hedge Index.
  - Months in which the fund outperformed the equity market: January (shorts), March (both long and short), and July (both long and short).
  - The fund significantly underperformed in October, as the long book returned 12.9 percent and the short book returned 25.7 percent versus a gain of 15.1 percent for the Russell 2000.

FUNDAMENTAL ANALYSIS

As pointed out in the previous chapter, FCM declined to send us full portfolio transparency via e-mail. They offered to make available portfolio reports to us any time when we are onsite to conduct face-to-face interviews and meetings. This is not an uncommon occurrence. If I cannot get the fund manager to send the full portfolio transparency to me, I will simply write down all the information that I need when I visit them for further analysis at a later time. This is not an optimal solution, but one that will get me the information that I require nonetheless. As hedge fund due diligence analysts, we need to keep ourselves open to different ways of getting the job done. It is important to note that we should never skimp on our due diligence. If we decide that a certain level of information is needed to make an informed decision, we need to receive that minimum level. If we cannot receive it, then we can eliminate the hedge fund under review from consideration and move on to the next hedge fund in our pipeline (remember that there are nearly 10,000 hedge funds, so we should never get caught up on any single fund).

On a positive note, I have found that hedge fund managers tend to open up more once they get to know you better, and as we move through the due diligence process, we will request the information again.

If and when we receive full position-level transparency, we can do many things with it. For example, we can pull down fundamental stock data from a database (such as Bloomberg) and see how the manager's long and short books compare. When evaluating a value manager, we can look to verify that they invest in stocks with value characteristics. In addition, if we are provided with historical portfolio transparency, we can look to see how those characteristics have changed over time.

So in lieu of full portfolio transparency, we can start by looking up FCM's reported 13F filings. We had previously downloaded their latest 13F (for the end of the third quarter 2011) and uploaded some basic fundamental ratios as well as recent performance information.

Noteworthy Websites

There are a number of services that provide 13F information and analysis for a fee. For example, Bloomberg (which is generally subscribed by most institutional investors) provides very good portfolio analytics based on reported 13F holdings. However, there are a number of free or inexpensive resources that can be found on the Internet.

http://www.sec.gov/answers/form13f.htm
> This link takes you to the U.S. Securities and Exchange Commission's (SEC) website and specifically to the page that explains what a 13F is and provides further links.

http://www.sec.gov/divisions/investment/13flists.htm
> This is another link within the SEC's website. This page provides full lists of all 13F securities going back to the late 1990s.

http://www.secinfo.com/
> This is a great source for all public filings with the SEC. Users can search by fund, person, and geography or by specific SEC form. This website tracks all current and historical filings.

http://whalewisdom.com/
> An excellent website that gives the user the ability to search for any hedge fund or mutual fund and view their current and/or historical 13F holdings; the site also provides various tools to evaluate the underlying portfolios. The website tracks the most popular stocks held by hedge funds and reports a "heat map" designed to track stock holdings based on ownership as well as buying and selling trends. Lastly, this website provides reports based on historical portfolios that calculate changes in holdings between user-selected periods. When looking at a hedge fund portfolio, the

user can click on any holding to see which other hedge funds own the stock.

Prior to our initial phone interview, we simply used the information as it was presented in the 13F report. The goal at that time was to have a handy list of recent holdings that we could discuss during the call. However, now that we have decided to move FCM further in the due diligence process, we can make some adjustments to the data that will allow us to dig deeper.

In Table 7.7, we have displayed the results of the 13F analysis that we downloaded along with a sampling of valuation, earnings, liquidity, and price return data. The 13F filings also include the number of shares held in each security as well as the market value of each holding at that point in time. We can use either the market values or share-level data to calculate the hedge fund's weighting in each security. Because this report only lists long positions, we can only review a portion of the overall portfolio; however, given that FCM typically runs with a long bias (excluding the summer of 2008), this analysis can be valuable.

$$13F\ Weight = \frac{mktval\ s}{mktval\ p}$$

Where,

mktval s = reported market value for a given stock or other position

mktval p = sum reported market values for all positions

Since the 13F analysis does not factor in any leverage that the hedge fund manager might employ, we can adjust the 13F weight to scale the calculation up or down based on the fund's actual gross long exposure at that time (which the manager had previously provided to us).

Scaled Weight = 13F *Weight* × *long exposure*

The 13F weights and the scaled weights are listed in Table 7.7 in the fifth and sixth columns in the report. We can use the long and short exposure data received earlier to perform the scaling calculation (FCM's reported long exposure at the end of Sep-11 was 115 percent). As a result, when we add the scaled weights for the portfolio we will come up with a total value of 115 percent.

Now that we have calculated an approximation of the hedge fund's weights at the end of the third quarter for each position, we can calculate a weighted average for each of the valuation measures in the report. We also made four adjustments to data items within the report and have highlighted

TABLE 7.7 FCM's Adjusted 13F Long Portfolio for September 2011

Ticker	Company	Sector	Industry	13F Weight	Scaled Weight	Market Cap (mlns)	P/E	PEG	P/FCF	EPS Growth This Year	Short Ratio	ROE	ROR (Month)	ROR (Quarter)	Beta	Average Volume (1000s)
FDP	Fresh Del Monte Produce Inc.	Consumer Goods	Farm Products	6.0%	6.9%	1417	15.7	2.3	12.7	-55%	6.8	6%	-4.4%	5.5%	0.57	221
HGG	hhgregg, Inc.	Services	Electronics Stores	6.0%	6.9%	502	11.6	1.1	50.3	16%	15.4	17%	-12.4%	16.3%	1.25	520
HITK	Hi Tech Pharmacal Co. Inc.	Healthcare	Drugs - Generic	6.0%	6.9%	505	9.8		25.2	32%	6.7	29%	5.6%	14.9%	1.22	215
SNX	SYNNEX Corp.	Services	Business Services	6.0%	6.9%	1048	7.6	0.8	18.6	31%	8.3	13%	-2.3%	11.8%	1.13	259
THO	Thor Industries Inc.	Consumer Goods	Recreational Vehicles	6.0%	6.9%	1325	12.9	1.1	15.9	-7%	8.4	13%	-5.3%	17.7%	1.97	577
TTEC	TeleTech Holdings Inc.	Services	Business Services	6.0%	6.9%	866	14.3	1.2	38.2	-28%	6.7	14%	-10.5%	-3.4%	1.26	173
ZUMZ	Zumiez, Inc.	Services	Apparel Stores	6.0%	6.9%	846	25.2	1.2	24.1	159%	10.0	15%	20.4%	48.3%	1.87	502
EXLS	Exlservice Holdings, Inc.	Services	Business Services	5.0%	5.8%	709	21.1	1.1	19.8	63%	5.1	13%	-11.6%	-0.1%	1.13	143
MCRL	Micrel Inc.	Technology	Semiconductor - Integrated Circuits	5.0%	5.8%	613	14.7	2.9	14.5	217%	5.6	19%	-0.6%	2.8%	0.90	476
ALGT	Allegiant Travel Company	Services	Regional Airlines	4.0%	4.6%	1031	20.5	2.6	16.7	-12%	23.2	16%	8.9%	17.9%	0.49	126
BRKR	Bruker Corporation	Technology	Scientific & Technical Instruments	4.0%	4.6%	1980	24.4	1.6	50.5	17%	3.4	15%	-5.5%	-14.6%	1.41	722
GLF	Gulfmark Offshore, Inc.	Basic Materials	Oil & Gas Equipment & Services	4.0%	4.6%	1044	24.7	0.5	16.0	-168%	3.7	4%	-3.3%	-2.4%	1.38	243
GSIG	GSI Group Inc.	Technology	Scientific & Technical Instruments	4.0%	4.6%	313	13.4	1.1	10.3	99%	7.1	12%	-11.8%	2.1%	1.37	148
ISIL	Intersil Corporation	Technology	Semiconductor - Broad Line	4.0%	4.6%	1269	18.3	1.3	11.6	-33%	3.4	7%	-8.1%	-8.9%	1.27	1242
MCF	Contango Oil & Gas Co.	Basic Materials	Independent Oil & Gas	4.0%	4.6%	882	15.4		14.8	30%	9.9	14%	-4.8%	0.7%	0.87	113
SAPE	Sapient Corp.	Technology	Business Software & Services	4.0%	4.6%	1631	26.5	1.2	41.2	-52%	7.4	14%	-2.8%	11.9%	1.38	1099
STEC	STEC, Inc.	Technology	Data Storage Devices	4.0%	4.6%	400	9.9	0.4	10.1	-60%	5.7	15%	-16.6%	-8.7%	1.57	1320
TXRH	Texas Roadhouse Inc.	Services	Restaurants	4.0%	4.6%	962	16.6	1.1	17.3	20%	6.9	13%	4.0%	1.7%	0.95	1100
VICR	Vicor Corp.	Technology	Diversified Electronics	4.0%	4.6%	320	17.0	1.0	18.9	13%	6.1	11%	-9.5%	-19.0%	1.59	114
DIOD	Diodes Incorporated	Technology	Semiconductor - Integrated Circuits	3.0%	3.5%	878	12.5	0.9	21.9	13%	12.5	13%	-6.1%	6.0%	2.16	398
KKD	Krispy Kreme Doughnuts, Inc.	Services	Restaurants	3.0%	3.5%	422	20.7	0.6	23.3	13%	4.5	24%	-12.2%	-22.7%	1.54	696
PRIM	Primoris Services Corporation	Industrial Goods	Heavy Construction	2.0%	2.3%	745	12.8	1.1	10.8	-17%	8.1	26%	5.1%	39.1%	0.98	196
	Average (using 13F reported weights)			100%	115%	896	16.6	1.2	21.9	13%	7.9	15%	-3.8%	5.3%	1.28	482
	Weighted Average (using scaled weights)					1040	18.8	1.3	26.1	20%	9.2	17%	-4.1%	7.3%	1.47	535

them in gray. We did this because the reported values were extreme outliers and skewed the average and weighted results. To normalize this, the outlier values were replaced with the simple average for the group.

Adjustment Details:

- P/FCF for Diodes Inc.

    We changed this value from 1,186.1 to 21.9 (the average for the portfolio excluding this stock). This adjustment changed the weighted average P/FCF from 66.2 to 26.1.
- EPS growth for Vicor, Diodes, and Krispy Kreme.

    We changed Vicor (874 percent), Krispy Kreme (4,764 percent) and Vicor (1,088 percent) to 13 percent (the average for the group excluding these names). This adjustment changed the weighted average EPS growth from 263 percent to 26.1 percent.

Extreme outlier figures generally occur when the denominator in the valuation calculations is very small (or negative). For example, if we were to calculate the P/E ratio for a company that has a $25 price and just one cent in earnings, the calculated P/E would be 2,500. While this is an accurate calculation, it would likely significantly skew the overall portfolio results. This practice of "normalizing" outlier values is considered controversial by some and outright incorrect by some others, but I have found that it helps to make the numbers more meaningful when looking at them in a portfolio context.

EVALUATING PORTFOLIO DATA

Now that we have the third-quarter portfolio analysis, we can use the individual position-level data and the overall weighted portfolio-level data to learn more about FCM and to verify information received in various documents as well as in the interviews. I have also found these reports can lead to many new avenues of discussion when I meet with the hedge fund manager and team.

Sector Breakout

The first thing that we see when we look at the data in Figure 7.4 is that the fund at the end of Sep-11 was highly concentrated in just two sectors: services and technology. Neither the DDQ nor the fund presentation mentioned specific sector limits, so we should definitely inquire about this. In addition, when we review the historical 13F reports we should determine

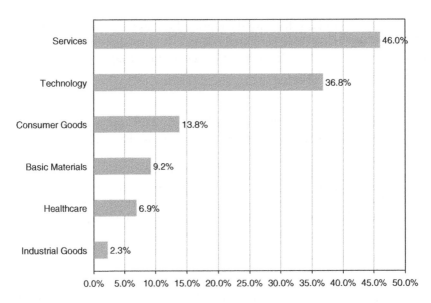

FIGURE 7.4   FCM 13F Portfolio (Sep-11)—Sector Weights

if this sector concentration has been consistent over time or if it is unique to this particular quarter.

To gain a better understanding of how the hedge fund manager has allocated within each sector, we can look at the industry breakout. The data in Table 7.8 show that FCM spread out its allocation within the services sector to five different industries with the biggest concentration in business services (three out of the eight companies in this sector represent nearly 20 percent of the overall long book's exposure and just over 40 percent of the exposure within the sector). Additionally, the business services stocks in the portfolio were among the larger weights within the portfolio.

The data in Table 7.9 indicate that of the eight portfolio companies in the technology sector, three of them specialize in semiconductors (representing 13.8 percent of the overall portfolio and just under 40 percent within the technology sector). The individual position size of the semiconductor companies is at the small-to-mid range of allocations (from 3 percent to 5 percent).

Sector Analysis—Follow-up Questions

■ Does FCM have any sector and/or industry constraints? If so, what are they? If not, how do they manage the risk to the portfolio?

TABLE 7.8 FCM 13F Portfolio (Sep-11)—Industry Weights within the Service Sector

Industry	# Co's	Portfolio Weight	Sector Weight
Apparel Stores	1	6.9%	15.0%
Business Services	3	19.5%	42.4%
Electronics Stores	1	6.9%	15.0%
Regional Airlines	1	4.6%	10.0%
Restaurants	2	8.1%	17.6%
Total	8	46.0%	100.0%

TABLE 7.9 FCM 13F Portfolio (Sep-11)—Industry Weights within the Technology Sector

Industry	# Co's	Portfolio Weight	Sector Weight
Business Software & Services	1	4.6%	12.5%
Data Storage Devices	1	4.6%	12.5%
Diversified Electronics	1	4.6%	12.5%
Scientific & Technical Instruments	2	9.2%	25.0%
Semiconductor	3	13.8%	37.5%
Total	8	36.8%	100.0%

- FCM runs a fairly concentrated long book (20 to 30 names). Do they typically manage the fund in a concentrated manner with respect to sectors as well? If so, do they favor any specific sectors?
- Do they hedge out any of this long exposure with specific stock shorts? Their DDQ states that they build the portfolio from the bottom up, but they have factored in the top down in the past (Jaime stated that they took macro factors into consideration in 2008 when they brought the fund's gross and net down). Do they pair up any of the longs with any of the shorts?
- We should request a sector attribution report and/or calculate our own sector attribution report. We should look to identify which sectors have helped and hurt the most. The analysis should span the entire five-year history, and we should break it out by calendar year to see if we can answer some of the open performance-related questions from the previous chapter.

- Are they investing in any specific themes within the sectors?
    - Business services represent 19.5 percent of total fund long exposure. In addition, one of the companies in the technology sector (Sapient Corp.) is listed as being in business software and services. We might want to look at this company as being part of business services overall, which would serve to further increase the exposure to that industry.
    - Semiconductors represent 13.8 percent of fund's total long exposure.
- Do any of FCM's team members have any specific training or expertise in technology? What is their edge in this space?
- With respect to the semiconductor allocation, how do they model current global growth (which is negligent outside of Asia) and the economic and political situations in the United States and Europe (which are tenuous) into demand for semiconductors?

Action Plan

- Request monthly sector exposure for the long and short books. They had previously sent us the net exposure by sector, but we will need the additional data to better evaluate the portfolio.
- Either call or e-mail to ask if they have any specific themes in the fund at this time. Extend the question to include the past 12 months as well.
- Conduct our own research on the stocks in the business services and semiconductor industries to determine for ourselves if there are any themes prevalent within the portfolio (we can determine if they are intended or unintended when we speak with them next).

Market Cap Breakout

The DDQ and presentation state that FCM focuses on small- to mid-cap securities. The market cap breakout in Figure 7.5 illustrates that the market capitalizations of the securities in the long book fell within $250 million and $2 billion. The weighted average market cap for the long book was just over $1 billion.

Market Capitalization Analysis — Follow-up Questions

- Is this distribution typical for them? Did the volatile market environment in 2008 (and to some degree ever since) have an impact on market cap distribution?

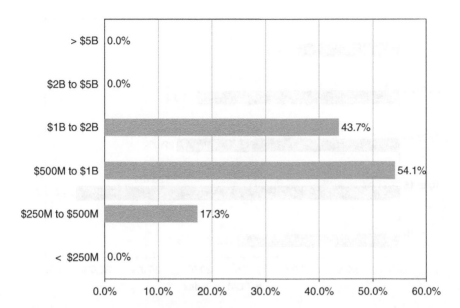

FIGURE 7.5 FCM 13F Portfolio (Sep-11)—Market Capitalization Distribution

- Have they ever invested in microcaps (we will define them as having a market cap below $250 million)? If so, was it a microcap at the time of purchase or did it decline in price and fall into the microcap range? In any case, did any microcap holdings violate their liquidity requirements?
- Have they ever invested in large-cap stocks? If so, find out which companies as well as the thesis behind each investment.

Price/Earnings (P/E) Breakout

We can see in Figure 7.6 that FCM's long book is skewed more toward stocks with P/E ratios less than 20. When compared to the appropriate index, the biggest deviation can be seen in the 10 times to 15 times range. I like to look at multiple portfolio valuation measures as a means of better understanding the hedge fund's investment philosophy. In our case study, FCM sells itself as a bottom-up, value-oriented fund. We can see from this chart that FCM does seem to favor stocks with lower P/Es, which is consistent with their value methodology. However, while I do find the portfolio level analysis useful, I often find great tidbits of information

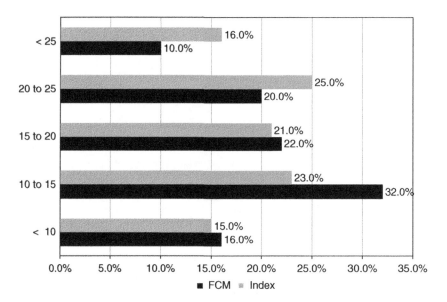

FIGURE 7.6   FCM 13F Portfolio (Sep-11)—P/E Distribution

pertaining to individual stocks that can lead to good questions when I speak with or meet the hedge fund manager.

Price/Free Cash Flow (P/FCF) Breakout

FCM's DDQ stated that the fund manager emphasizes free cash flow, so this ratio can be used as a means of identifying outlier companies for discussion when we speak the next time (likely during the onsite visit). This distribution in Figure 7.7 is not dissimilar to the small-cap market, but there are three companies with high P/FCF ratios: hhgregg (50.3), Bruker Corp (50.5), and Sapient (41.2). We should ask about these stocks the next time we speak to the manager.

Earnings Growth Last 12 Months (12-Month EG) Breakout

Nine of the companies in the long book had experienced negative earnings growth in the year ending Sep-11. On the positive side, there were three stocks that had demonstrated a high level of earnings growth in the past year (Zumiez, Micrel, and GSI Group). We can inquire about all or a subset of these stocks when we visit the fund manager. We can view the summary of the portfolio's earnings growth in specific ranges in Figure 7.8.

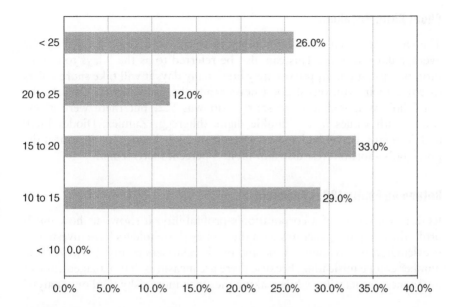

FIGURE 7.7 FCM 13F Portfolio (Sep-11)—P/FCF Distribution

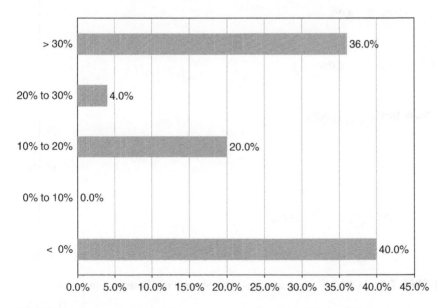

FIGURE 7.8 FCM 13F Portfolio (Sep-11)—12-Month EG Distribution

Short Ratio Breakout

The short ratio refers to the number of shares sold short divided by the average daily volume. This can also be referred to as the "days to cover" ratio because it tells approximately how many days it will take short-sellers to cover their positions if good news sends the price higher. Overall, the portfolio's weighted average short ratio was 9.2, but there were a few stocks with values in the double digits (hhgregg, Zumiez, Diodes Inc.), and Allegiant Travel had a short interest of 23.2. Figure 7.9 illustrates the portfolio's short interest distribution in 5 percent increments.

Return on Equity (ROE) Breakout

ROE is a measure of a corporation's profitability. It shows us how much profit the company generates with the money shareholders have invested. It is calculated by dividing net income by shareholders equity. However, the number can be misleading because there are measures that management can use to increase its value while making the stock more risky (DuPont analysis

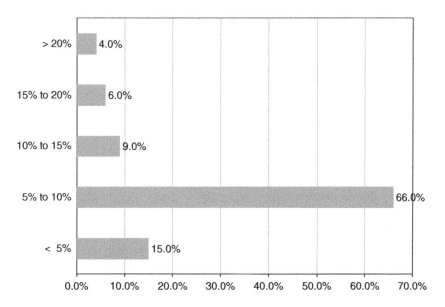

FIGURE 7.9   FCM 13F Portfolio (Sep-11)—Short Ratio Distribution

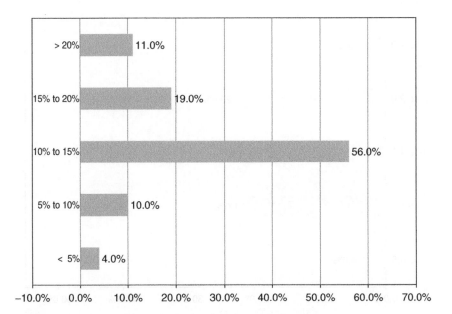

FIGURE 7.10 FCM 13F Portfolio (Sep-11)—ROE Distribution

can help by disaggregating the components of ROE). For our purposes, we can use this metric as a means of assessing how well the underlying company managements are creating value.

The breakout in Figure 7.10 illustrates that the ROE values are well distributed and that none of the companies in the long portfolio at Sep-11 had negative values (hence net income was positive).

Beta Breakout

The weighted average beta of the stocks in FCM's long portfolio at Sep-11 was 1.47 and appear normally distributed around the mean value. Only one stock had a beta below 0.5 (Allegiant Travel) and one had a beta above 2.0 (Diodes Inc.).

Liquidity Analysis

Portfolio liquidity is an essential component of understanding underlying risk inherent within a portfolio. FCM manages a small-to-midcap fund and

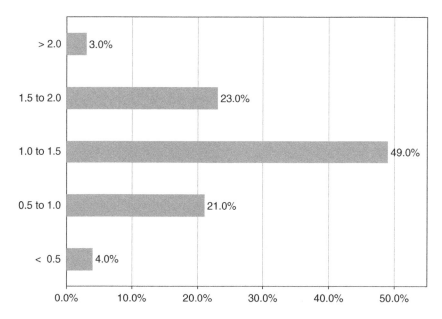

FIGURE 7.11 FCM 13F Portfolio (Sep-11)—Beta Distribution

we have determined that the latest 13F long portfolio is focused exclusively on small caps (market caps under $2B). In their DDQ, FCM states that they track and actively manage underlying portfolio liquidity. In our initial interview with Jaime Wernick, he stated that they look to keep 90 percent of the portfolio liquid within 10 days and that the entire portfolio can be liquidated within a month.

The analysis in Table 7.10 indicates that there are two positions (Vicor Corp and GSI Group) in which it would take more than 30 days to liquidate at the fund's current asset levels.

In this analysis, we use the 90-day average volume for each stock in the portfolio and multiply that by the latest stock prices to determine the average dollar value traded. This is listed in the table as Avg $ Volume (90 Day Avg). We then take the scaled weights for each stock in the FCM portfolio and multiply by the current assets in the fund ($275 million) as well as their stated maximum capacity ($500 million). We assume that the fund manager would not want to trade more than 25 percent of the average volume in any given day (to avoid impacting the price), so we apply a 75 percent discount to the average daily traded volume and divide that figure

TABLE 7.10 FCM 13F Portfolio (Sep-11) Projected Days to Liquidate Positions

Company	Stock Data Avg $ Volume (90 day Avg)	Scaled Weight	Mkt Value at $275M AUM	Mkt Value at $500M AUM	FCM 13F Long Portfolio Days to Trade at $275M AUM	Days to Trade at $500M AUM
Vicor Corp.	$ 844,238	4.6%	$ 12,650,000	$ 23,000,000	59.9	109.0
GSI Group Inc.	$ 1,372,355	4.6%	$ 12,650,000	$ 23,000,000	36.9	67.0
TeleTech Holdings Inc.	$ 2,772,792	6.9%	$ 18,975,000	$ 34,500,000	27.4	49.8
Exlservice Holdings, Inc.	$ 2,824,436	5.8%	$ 15,812,500	$ 28,750,000	22.4	40.7
Fresh Del Monte Produce Inc.	$ 5,002,250	6.9%	$ 18,975,000	$ 34,500,000	15.2	27.6
Micrel Inc.	$ 4,507,038	5.8%	$ 15,812,500	$ 28,750,000	14.0	25.5
SYNNEX Corp.	$ 6,727,396	6.9%	$ 18,975,000	$ 34,500,000	11.3	20.5
hhgregg, Inc.	$ 7,402,013	6.9%	$ 18,975,000	$ 34,500,000	10.3	18.6
Krispy Kreme Doughnuts, Inc.	$ 4,014,514	3.5%	$ 9,487,500	$ 17,250,000	9.5	17.2
Hi Tech Pharmacal Co. Inc.	$ 8,224,068	6.9%	$ 18,975,000	$ 34,500,000	9.2	16.8
Contango Oil & Gas Co.	$ 6,041,993	4.6%	$ 12,650,000	$ 23,000,000	8.4	15.2
Allegiant Travel Company	$ 6,176,772	4.6%	$ 12,650,000	$ 23,000,000	8.2	14.9
Primoris Services Corporation	$ 3,112,159	2.3%	$ 6,325,000	$ 11,500,000	8.1	14.8
Bruker Corporation	$ 8,540,240	4.6%	$ 12,650,000	$ 23,000,000	5.9	10.8
Gulfmark Offshore, Inc.	$ 9,053,575	4.6%	$ 12,650,000	$ 23,000,000	5.6	10.2
Zumiez, Inc.	$ 13,695,674	6.9%	$ 18,975,000	$ 34,500,000	5.5	10.1
Thor Industries Inc.	$ 14,511,293	6.9%	$ 18,975,000	$ 34,500,000	5.2	9.5
STEC, Inc.	$ 10,033,120	4.6%	$ 12,650,000	$ 23,000,000	5.0	9.2
Diodes Incorporated	$ 7,622,418	3.5%	$ 9,487,500	$ 17,250,000	5.0	9.1
Sapient Corp.	$ 12,452,958	4.6%	$ 12,650,000	$ 23,000,000	4.1	7.4
Intersil Corporation	$ 12,481,438	4.6%	$ 12,650,000	$ 23,000,000	4.1	7.4
Texas Roadhouse Inc.	$ 15,191,742	4.6%	$ 12,650,000	$ 23,000,000	3.3	6.1
				Average =	12.9	23.5

into the amount owned at both the $275 million and $500 million asset levels. For example:

Vicor Corp

90 Day Avg $ Volume	$844,238
90 Day Avg $ Volume after discount	$211,059

$$\text{Days to Liquidate Position (\$275M AUM)} = \frac{\$12,650,000}{\$211,059}$$

$$= 59.9 \ days$$

We can also observe that the average number of days to fully liquidate the long portfolio is 12.9 days at their current AUM level. In Table 7.11, we list the projected liquidity and compare it to the liquidity profile that Jaime gave us during our call. It is clear that the portfolio liquidity using our maximum 25 percent of daily liquidity assumption does not quite match up with what we were told previously.

Obviously, the projected liquidity profile gets even worse when we view the portfolio in the context of their maximum capacity of $500M in assets. We asked Jaime how they determined that $500M was the correct figure, and he stated that they have managed more than that previously (a peak of $750M). At the $500M asset level, four stocks would not be able to be liquidated within the one-month window and just under 10 percent of the 22 stocks in the long portfolio could be liquidated within ten days (a far cry from the 80 percent he gave us).

TABLE 7.11 FCM 13F Portfolio (Sep-11) Stated vs. Projected Liquidity at $275M AUM

Stated Liquidity Profile		Projected Liquidity
% of Portfolio Liquidated	# of Days	at Max 25% Avg Daily Volume
80	10	58
90	14	75
95	21	81
100	30	92

Liquidity Analysis—Follow-up Questions and Action Plan

- Use historical 13F reports to determine how liquid FCM's portfolio has been over time, particularly in 2008 when liquidity declined during the financial crisis.
- Request permission to receive an independent liquidity report from the prime broker. This report will take into account both the long and short books and provide an accurate assessment of underlying portfolio liquidity.
- Ask the manager if they can list any securities in the past that they have had a hard time trading (this can cover the short book as well).
- Ask them to explain how the portfolio would remain liquid at maximum capacity. Try to determine if they would have to alter their investment style by investing in larger and more liquid names. If this is the case, it may have a significant impact on future performance and may render much of their previous track record moot as a due diligence tool. This is a critical question. When equity long/short hedge funds are small, they can essentially invest in anything they want (because their small size allows them to invest in stocks that they would not be able to invest in when they get bigger). For example, if FCM was only managing $25 million, then they would be able to liquidate the Vicor Corp. position 5 days versus 60 days at the current asset level and 109 days at the $500 million asset level. In order to facilitate bigger assets, hedge funds can either invest in more liquid stocks (which could impact the strategy) or hold smaller positions in the less liquid stocks (which would lead to more positions and again potentially impact the portfolio).

Peer Group Comparison

The peer comparison in Table 7.12 gives us a good idea of how the funds in our initial peer group stack up against one another. We can (and will) conduct a historical portfolio analysis for FCM as well as the others in the peer group. Once this is done, we can review how FCM's fundamentals have changed over time and then compare its history with that of the others in the peer group (and any other funds that may be relevant).

A quick glance at the fundamental comparison does highlight that FCM's average market cap is significantly below all of the others and the average volume for its long book is multiples lower than the other four. FCM's portfolio also seemed to have lower earnings growth, a higher average level of short interest, and a higher P/E ratio than the others. We

TABLE 7.12 FCM 13F Portfolio (Sep-11) Compared to Peer Group's 13F Portfolios (Sep11)

	Market Cap (mlns)	P/E	PEG	P/FCF	EPS Growth This Year	Short Ratio	ROE	ROR (Month)	ROR (Quarter)	Beta	Average Volume (1000s)
FCM	1,040	18.8	1.3	26.1	20%	9.2	16.6%	−4.1%	7.3%	1.47	535
Fund 1	68,904	13.4	2.1	23.7	76%	2.1	18.1%	−0.7%	13.6%	1.05	16,107
Fund 2	7,167	13.0	1.2	18.4	61%	3.5	18.1%	−1.8%	10.8%	1.19	3,510
Fund 3	12,985	12.4	1.1	22.3	23%	4.0	35.2%	−3.3%	9.2%	1.02	4,092
Fund 4	189,800	10.1	1.1	29.4	138%	2.1	22.1%	0.2%	17.0%	0.93	12,100

know from the printed materials that FCM specializes in small- to mid-cap stocks, and we can see from this comparison that the other funds tend to focus on mid- to large-cap stocks. This helps to explain some of the historical differences in performance and regression-based statistics.

Historical Portfolio Analysis

We downloaded FCM's historical 13F reports from the websites mentioned earlier and we now have 13F reports beginning Mar-10 through Sep-11 (seven individual reports). While FCM has been around since late 2006, they did not have to start reporting their holdings to the SEC until March 2010.

In order to present the summary of the historical 13F analysis, we had to generate a full long portfolio report similar to what we have done in Table 7.10. As such, we can analyze each of the factors and highlight any specific companies that provide any outlier data points. We will also create and analyze historical charts that compare FCM to other relevant hedge funds over time. For the sake of brevity, we will not list each of the reports in this chapter.

The historical 13F analysis highlighted in Table 7.13 indicates that the long portfolio's market cap has stayed within a fairly tight range and that the fund has clearly been focused on small-cap stocks. When we receive information from the manager or prime broker regarding the composition of the current and past short portfolios, we will perform similar analyses.

When we have completed the analysis on both the long and short books, we can look to see how they line up against one another. For example, some small-cap managers have a hard time shorting smaller-cap stocks so they employ ETFs, index futures, or index options. When we review the short book, we will also need to get a better understanding of whether or not the manager is actually shorting stock or entering into swap agreements

TABLE 7.13 FCM 13F Historical Portfolio Analysis (Mar-10 to Sep-11)

	Market Cap (mlns)	P/E	PEG	P/FCF	EPS Growth This Year	Short Ratio	ROE	ROR (Month)	ROR (Quarter)	Beta	Average Volume (1000s)
Sep-11	1,040	18.8	1.3	26.1	20%	9.2	16.6%	−4.1%	7.3%	1.47	535
Jun-11	900	16.2	1.2	22.1	17%	8.4	21.1%	−3.5%	8.0%	1.32	515
Mar-11	956	19.0	0.9	23.4	22%	9.0	22.7%	−3.0%	6.8%	1.25	590
Dec-10	1,020	21.1	0.8	20.0	23%	7.4	17.4%	−4.9%	9.3%	1.32	625
Sep-10	1,500	22.0	0.8	21.2	25%	8.0	18.1%	−4.3%	6.1%	1.11	715
Jun-10	1,345	20.6	1.0	19.7	13%	7.2	13.4%	−2.8%	5.8%	1.19	672
Mar-10	1,208	18.2	1.1	18.3	18%	7.0	21.0%	−4.0%	10.2%	1.21	631

(as different financial instruments may have different risk profiles). Some small-cap hedge funds create a mismatch between their long and short books by shorting larger-cap names (which are generally more available as shorts than smaller-cap names). This is not a good or a bad thing. It is up to us as hedge fund due diligence analysts to determine if a specific fund is appropriate for their organization's overall portfolio of investments. Some investors have an issue with mismatched long and short books, while others view it as part of the manager's strategy and, as such, just simply part of the evaluation of the hedge fund.

FCM's current P/E ratio is in the middle of its historical range while the PEG ratio (P/E to growth) has been trending upward and is currently at its high point. The P/FCF ratio is interesting, as it has increased considerably over the review period and is at its peak as well. FCM's materials state that they consider free cash flow to be an important part of their company analysis, so when we meet with them we can ask why this ratio has been increasing, and we can point out specific stocks from our individual quarterly reviews that are outliers. As an example, hhgregg and Bruker Corp. each have P/FCF ratios in excess of 50 times in the Sep-11 13F analytical report (we can also identify others from previous reports). When looking at EPS growth, we see that the 13 percent figure from the Jun-10 report is an outlier, as it is at the low end of the range of values.

The short ratio is also at a peak, and the values in 2011 have all been higher than the values from 2010. FCM states that they tend to avoid typical hedge fund stocks. ROE is also near the low end of the range.

The overall portfolio statistics are less meaningful to me, as I tend to find more value in analyzing individual holdings and paying particular attention to outlier positions and other positions that don't seem to fit with a firm's stated investment philosophy, style, and/or methodology.

MERITS OF ADVANCED PREPARATION

It is important to know that by reviewing each of the historical reports, we incrementally add to our understanding of the hedge fund manager under review. The next time we speak with the manager or meet face to face, we will be armed with a number of specific questions relating to the manager's activity over time and we will be in a better position to spot inconsistencies in the manager's portfolio, process, and/or story.

In addition to giving us the ability to ask more enlightened questions, we are setting the tone for the interviews by letting the manager know that we have done our homework and are prepared to challenge him or her. I have found that hedge fund managers, who tend to be type-A personalities, typically enjoy being challenged (in a respectful way). If a manager tells you something about a portfolio holding and you know enough about it to play devil's advocate, the manager will take notice. I have found that the meetings tend to go better than if I just let the manager go through the presentation (remember that you can still play devil's advocate even when you do not know much about a particular holding by asking "Why?").

When we analyze performance and historical portfolios we are doing it to gain insight into:

- What type of investor the hedge fund manager is.
- How the manager acts in stressful situations.
- If the investment process is consistent.
- How the team interacts with one another.
- What each team member contributes to the final product.

We do this so that we can gain insight into how the hedge fund "may" act in the future. We can't buy past performance, but we can try to develop conviction in the underlying hedge fund and also determine how the hedge fund under review will interact with our other portfolio holdings (portfolio construction).

The graph in Figure 7.12 does a great job of highlighting that FCM has historically emphasized the technology and services sector. When we first reviewed the Sep-11 13F report, we asked if this had been consistent over time. We now have part of the answer (we will still need to dig into

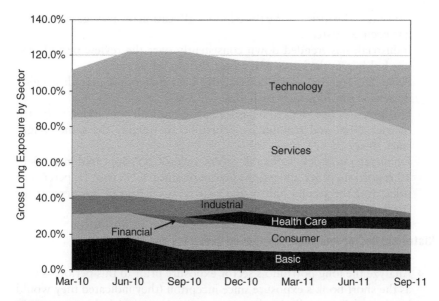

FIGURE 7.12 FCM 13F Historical Portfolio Analysis (Mar-10 to Sep-11)—Sector Exposure

the portfolios that predate the Mar-10 13F report (as that was the first 13F available to us).

Average Long Portfolio Sector Weights

Basic	12%
Consumer	14%
Financial	1%
Health Care	4%
Industrial	8%
Services	47%
Technology	31%

Analysis of Historical Long Portfolio Sector Analysis

- Technology: has stayed within a range and has trended toward the upper end of that range over the last year.
- Services: consistently the largest allocation within the portfolio; modest fluctuation in allocation.

- Consumer: historically the third largest allocation on average; allocation has been consistent.
- Industrial: has trended down consistently over the review period; just one holding in the latest 13F report (Primorsis Services).
- Basic: has trended down consistently over the review period; roughly decreased the allocation by half.
- Health Care: one stock (Hi Tech Pharmaceutical) was added in fourth quarter 2010 and remained in portfolio at roughly the same weight since then.
- Financial: one stock (Cohen & Steers: ticker CNS) appeared in the Sep-10 report; no other allocations before or since. CNS rose 18 percent in price over the second half of the year versus a gain of 3.6 percent for the Russell 2000 index.

Historical Sector Analysis — Follow-up Questions and Action Plan

- Analyze the long portfolio's sector exposure prior to this period as well as the short book's exposure since inception (they indicated they would let us see full portfolio-level transparency when we visit them onsite). In advance of the office visit, we should request historical sector exposures on a monthly basis for the long and short books.
- As a means of verifying the information presented to us by the hedge fund manager, we should ask for permission to receive summary exposure reports from the prime broker or the fund's administrator. Some service providers shy away from providing this type of information (because they do not want to assume any liability), but if the hedge fund manager directs them to provide it, they typically comply. The key here is to get the hedge fund manager to make this happen.
- Look for any capitalization mismatches between the long and short books.
- FCM had only allocated to one health care stock and one financial stock over the nearly two years reviewed. Is this consistent with the fund's history prior to March 2010? If they typically maintain a zero or low weight in these sectors, what was it about these two stocks that were attractive to them?
- Why has the allocation to industrials and basic materials traded lower over the review period? Is this the result of bottom-up stock selection or are there any macro considerations that have come into play (remember that they had applied macro views back in 2008 that also supported their bottom-up research)?
- We should look across the historical 13F reports to determine if there are any themes within the underlying industries (as we did when we

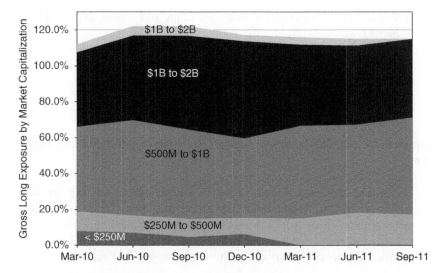

FIGURE 7.13 FCM 13F Historical Portfolio Analysis (Mar-10 to Sep-11)—Market Cap Exposure Distribution

reviewed the Sep-11 13F report). If any patterns develop, we should inquire about them and determine if they are incidental or not.

The same way that we analyzed historical sector exposure, we can view historical trends in market capitalization exposure (Figure 7.13).
Average Long Portfolio Market Capitalization Weights

< $250M	4%
$250M to $500M	13%
$500M to $1B	50%
$1B to $2B	47%
$2B to $5B	4%
> $5B	0%

Analysis of Historical Long Portfolio Market Capitalization

- < $250M (micro cap): the long portfolio has not had any allocation in this range in 2011 but had between 6 percent and 8 percent in 2010.
- $250M to $500M: this allocation increased from 2010 to 2011.

- $50M to $1B: this has stayed in a tight range and was at its period high at Sep-11.
- $1B to $2B: wider range of allocations and currently in the middle of the range.
- $2B to $5B: small allocation generally under 5 percent.
- > $5B: zero weight.

Historical Market Capitalization Analysis—Follow-up Questions and Action Plan

- We should determine if the fund has had larger allocations to micro cap stocks in the past (when their asset level was much lower). The long portfolio had three stocks in this range in the Mar-10 and Jun-10 13F reports and two stocks in the Sep-10 and Dec-10 reports. There were no microcap stocks in any of the three quarter-end 13F reports in 2011.

The analysis in Figure 7.14 is an extension of the liquidity analysis that we calculated and highlighted in Tables 7.10 and 7.12. While those tables represented the portfolio liquidity for FCM's long book using the Sep-11 13F report, the chart in Figure 7.14 shows the results of the analysis for the 13F reports from Mar-10 through Sep-11.

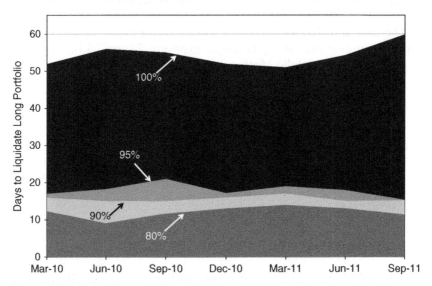

FIGURE 7.14 FCM 13F Historical Portfolio Analysis (Mar-10 to Sep-11)—Liquidity (Days to Liquidate)

This chart reinforces the Sep-11 analysis and clearly indicates that the projected portfolio liquidity (using our maximum 25 percent of average trading assumption) does not match what Jaime Wernick stated in our initial phone interview. In addition, it indicates that the number of days to fully liquidate the long portfolio has steadily increased from 52 days in Mar-10 to 60 days in Sep-11. This is definitely an issue and one that we will need to address when we conduct our onsite visit. As an action item, we should ask to review their internally generated liquidity reports and verify them against risk reports provided by the prime broker.

Trade Analysis

In Chapter 5, we asked the hedge fund manager to provide us with the trading history for one (or more) of their portfolio holdings. We asked to see this so that we could get a sense for how they act and react to company and market news and to get a flavor for how frequently they trade around positions. FCM provided several names, and we have highlighted the trading history for hhgregg, Inc. (which is a current holding) in Figure 7.15.

When I analyze a fund manager's trading history, I am also looking to understand what was going on within the company and in the marketplace in general when buys and sells were made. To do this, I simply track and highlight any days or date ranges in which there were any:

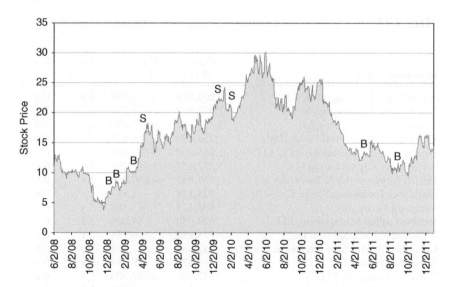

FIGURE 7.15   FCM Trade History for hhgregg, Inc. (HGG)

- Unusual volume for the stock.
- Extreme price moves (either up or down).
- Major market news.
- Company announcements.

I generally take this information and create a report that provides a quick snapshot for each event or news announcement. When discussing the stock and trading activity with the hedge fund manager, I will ask questions pertaining to the bullet points previously listed to see how well they know the position and to gain insight into how the fund manager (or team) analyzes various situations as well as how they react to both favorable and unfavorable news and events. As stated previously, I tend to get the most information from hedge fund managers when I do my homework in advance and go through real-life examples with them.

As a final point, because hedge fund due diligence analysts speak with hedge fund managers about their positions all the time, I can often refer to previous meeting notes that reference companies I plan on discussing with managers that I am currently reviewing. I always refer back to older meeting notes as a means of refreshing my knowledge about specific hedge funds as well as researching positions and themes that had previously been discussed.

TABLE 7.14 Top Institutional Holders of hhgregg, Inc. (HGG) at Sep-11

Institution Name	Shares Held	Shares Chg	% Out- standing	% in Portfolio
Adage Capital Management, L.P.	2,200,028	+585,000	5.9	0.1
Van Berkom & Associates Inc.	1,932,490	−13,254	5.2	2.5
T. Rowe Price Associates, Inc.	1,558,800	+237,400	4.2	0.0
Bank of America Merrill Lynch (US)	1,353,130	+1,314,421	3.7	0.0
Frontier Capital Management Co. LLC	1,286,000	+103,060	3.5	0.2
Lee Munder Capital Group LLC	1,252,857	+53,496	3.4	0.4
Fidelity Management & Research Co.	959,852	+100,000	2.6	0.0
BlackRock Institutional Trust Co. N.A.	928,138	−13,987	2.5	0.0
Vanguard Group, Inc.	896,123	+3,588	2.4	0.0
Sterling Capital Management, LLC	824,050	−64,000	2.2	0.2
Wells Capital Management Inc.	775,859	−66,881	2.1	0.0
Columbia Management Investment Co. LLC	702,665	+67,505	1.9	0.0
Wasatch Advisors, Inc.	663,670	−459,038	1.8	0.1
Royce & Associates, LLC	547,900	+547,900	1.5	0.0
Dimensional Fund Advisors, LP	468,530	+104,063	1.3	0.0

We can also use the position-level information we receive directly from the manager or from the 13F reports to see what other institutions own the stocks in FCM's long portfolio. The two leftmost columns in Table 7.14 are straightforward. The column "Shs Chg" represents the difference in the number of shares held at the end of Sep-11 versus Jun-11. The column "%Out" represents the amount of the company's outstanding shares that are held by the financial institution. The column "%Port" represents that stock's percentage of that financial institution's reported 13F portfolio.

These reports provide useful anecdotal information as they can give us an idea if FCM has invested in a manner similar to other funds (which can offer insight into their strategy and philosophy). We can also use this information to see if the underlying stocks could be negatively impacted if a major holder were to sell their stake in the company—this can be relevant when analyzing funds that specialize in small market caps.

CHAPTER 8

Onsite Interviews

"The most important thing in communication is hearing what isn't said."

Peter F. Drucker

"I never learn anything talking. I only learn things when I ask questions."

Lou Holtz

"Effective communication is 20 percent what you know and 80 percent how you feel about what you know."

Jim Rohn

At this stage, we have done a fair amount of work on FCM. The process started by setting search criteria and compiling a list of potential hedge funds to review. We then reviewed the list and after applying various quantitative and qualitative filters we narrowed the search universe to five hedge funds (Chapter 3). Upon receiving the basic materials to review directly from the manager (Chapter 4), we initiated a brief telephone interview to answer any outstanding questions we had at that time and to gain a richer understanding of the three Ps: people, process, and philosophy. We conducted an interview (Chapter 5) with the hedge fund's director of research, Jaime Wernick, and ultimately concluded that we would take FCM further in the due diligence process.

That's where things started to get a bit more intense. We requested additional performance, exposure, and portfolio information (most of which was sent immediately—the lone exception was position-level transparency). We then conducted a thorough quantitative analysis (Chapter 6), which served to answer some outstanding questions and to raise some new ones. Finally, we used the portfolio information that was available to us and

TABLE 8.1 Typical Due Diligence Time/Work Distribution

Due Diligence Component	% of Time/Work in the Due Diligence Process
Sourcing	Ongoing
Initial Data Request	1
Initial Data Review	3
First Interview	5
Quantitative Analysis	5
Portfolio Analysis	15
Onsite/Follow-up Interviews (covers investment, operations, risk)	30
Operational Analysis (includes legal and financial reviews)	15
Risk Analysis	15
Scoring Model	3
Reference/Background Checks	8

performed a variety of analyses to gain a better understanding of portfolio construction (Chapter 7).

While we are not yet done with our portfolio analysis, we have gathered enough information to determine that we are still interested in bringing FCM further along in the due diligence process. Now the hard work really begins. Despite the fact that we have done a good amount of work in the due diligence process thus far, the more time-consuming work is still ahead of us.

Based on the workflow in Table 8.1, we are only about 30 percent done at this stage. Let me make a few disclaimers here. The workflow in the table is an average based on my own experiences over the years. As I mentioned previously, due diligence is dynamic by nature and there is no set order to the workflow. The process goes faster for some hedge funds than for others (conflicting travel schedules and multiple geographical locations can certainly delay due diligence at times). Second, the onsite and follow-up interviews cover all aspects of the due diligence process (including investment, operational, and risk). Last, there is a great deal of overlap within the components of the due diligence process (i.e., we learn about investment methodology but we also learn about risk management when we perform the portfolio review—two for the price of one). As such, the percentages should be considered rough approximations.

From a broad perspective, we are looking to gain a better understanding of the following:

■ Investment process.
■ Strategy.

- Individual employee skill sets and experience.
- Team dynamic.
- Research capabilities.
- Assess if office space is adequate.
- Assess systems (investment, operational, risk, etc.).
- Assess overall infrastructure.
- Verify data previously presented (via e-mail, mail, verbally).
- Review investment and risk models.
- Review any documents that hedge fund is uncomfortable e-mailing (i.e., position-level transparency, compliance manuals, legal agreements with service providers, SAS 70 reports, etc.).
- Trading process and systems.
- Portfolio valuation.

ONSITE MEETING STRATEGIES

Onsite meetings can occur in one day or can span multiple days. When we conduct onsite meetings we should plan on doing interviews with all the key investment professionals, operational team members, risk team members, marketing, client service, and anyone else who may be essential in furthering our understanding of how the firm operates.

ONE-ON-ONE MEETINGS

When possible, I generally prefer to meet with team members individually at first for the following reasons:

- Test for consistency—I like to ask the same or similar questions of each team member so that I can determine if the answers are consistent. Some of the best information I have received in onsite meetings has come from this simple technique. The questions can be generic (What is your edge?) or specific (Name a mistake the firm has made in the last year and tell me what you have done to improve upon it.). However, it is important to note that a lack of consistency does not necessarily translate to a negative impression in the same way that a complete consistency does not automatically translate to a positive impression. For example, in the case of fund managers that have perfectly consistent stories, we need to determine if they are just good marketers who have honed the art of the presentation of if they are genuinely in sync with one another. This is where experience and the "art" part of due diligence comes into play. I particularly like to employ this "divide and conquer" method of interviewing when I don't feel I am getting the whole story from an individual or when I have doubts about an individual's or the firm's answers to questions.

- Keep meetings focused—Meetings with multiple people can certainly be beneficial and offer insight (which I will detail shortly), but they can also lose focus quickly. One-on-one meetings are easier to keep focused and on point. Different people have different presentational styles and possibly different agendas (on both sides of the table), and the result may lead to less informative meetings.
- Avoid groupthink—Groups sometimes take on a life of their own, which can be either good or bad. I have found that meetings with two people can go pretty well but when the meetings involve too many people, my questions and their answers can get somewhat murky.
- Avoid overshadowing—When meeting with multiple people (some of whom are senior and some of whom are junior), I have found that the junior team members often defer to their seniors. This dynamic provides information in and of itself (as I may then choose to explore the relationship between the senior and junior staff to determine how strongly the junior staff stand up to the senior staff when discussing stock research, portfolio management, risk management, etc.). However, I want to hear what everyone has to say, and if certain members defer all or most questions to other team members, then I have missed an opportunity to get their views. I enjoy speaking with junior team members because they can offer a different view of the firm. And because most junior team members are younger, they often don't know the "right" things to say (they have often not yet become good marketers and may not know the "company answer" to certain questions—which can lead to new informational avenues). In addition, some individuals are more introverted and others are not. I have done meetings with two co-portfolio managers in which one of them does all the talking. In this case, I generally request an additional meeting or call with the less talkative person.

When I conduct meetings, I typically use information from the first meeting to challenge the person whom I am meeting next and so on down the line. For example, if I am meeting with three team members in the following order (analyst, portfolio manager, risk manager), I may ask the analyst:

1. Name one thing you would change about the investment process.
2. Name one thing you would change about the risk process.

I can (and will) ask many other more specific questions that I can reference in later meetings while interviewing other team members. When subsequently meeting with the portfolio manager and risk manager, I can draw upon the analyst's answer to these questions to pose variants of the responses to the portfolio manager and risk manager that I (as an outsider) might never have thought to ask. Additionally, if either the portfolio or risk manager gives me any pushback during this line of questioning, I can state that this question came not from me but from within their own shop and see what develops from there. I am not looking to create controversy; rather, I am looking to challenge the professionals that I meet with to gain a fuller understanding of what they do and how they do it (and this type of questioning also gives me insight into the personalities of the people manning the hedge fund).

When I meet with professionals one-on-one, I like to ask the following general questions (which may be informative as stand-alone questions and answers but can also be recycled when I meet with the rest of the team):

- What is it you personally do best as *(fill in the blank)* at the firm?

  Simple question but one that many people have a hard time answering. I like to compare the answer to this question with how other team members answer the next question.

- What are your team members' strengths and weaknesses?

  Some people don't like to answer this question or, more specifically, the "weakness" part of the question. No one has any problem talking about strengths because it is part of the sales pitch. I expect that more junior team members might feel uncomfortable answering this about the senior team members, but I like to see how they respond anyway (and sometimes the answers are priceless). However, I expect senior members to have an opinion about what the firm and its people can improve upon—and I push them to answer when they are reluctant.

- What is the firm's edge?

  It is my job as a due diligence analyst to ultimately determine "if" a hedge fund has an actual edge, what it is, and whether it is repeatable in the future. That said, I like to hear what the various team members have to say about it for several reasons. First, any hedge fund manager should be able to briefly and succinctly explain what they do and what their competitive advantage is (the basic elevator pitch). Second, I like to compare answers. I often find that a basic question like this one can elicit different responses depending on whom I am talking to. This question, by the way, should not just be confined to people on the investment team. I ask everyone this question. For example, if a CFO's response to this question is "That's not really my area . . . why don't you speak with the portfolio manager because he would be in a better position to answer it?" I would follow up immediately by asking, "If you don't know what makes this firm special, why did you join and what is keeping you here?"

I like to ask questions that require people to think on the spot because I will not receive some preconceived answer (as mentioned earlier, hedge fund personnel are used to marketing meetings and generally have thought out the answers to most questions in advance...some even hire communications specialists to craft carefully worded responses to these questions). When I ask a question they have not yet heard or some variant of a question for which they do not have a well-rehearsed answer, I am more likely to get a much better (more telling) response.

■ Name three things the firm can do better. What are you doing to enable those changes?

Pick up any book on interviewing techniques and this question will be in it. It is an oldie but a goodie and can lead to some interesting answers (especially when you ask it of several different team members and use their own answers to play off one another).

■ What was the biggest mistake the firm has made? What, if anything, has the firm done to ensure it does not happen again?

This question is similar to the previous one. The difference is in this case we are looking for specific instances. For example, a long position that they held too long (or not long enough), an assumption in one of their stock models that was drastically incorrect, and so on.

MEETING WITH MORE THAN ONE PERSON

I prefer to meet with hedge fund professionals individually at first but find that group meetings can also be beneficial. For example, when we conduct our onsite interviews of FCM, I would like to meet with Ted Acoff one on one to better understand his role and skills, but given that he and Jaime have worked together at GCH and FCM for a decade together, I would also like to assess the dynamic between the two. At GCH, Ted and Jaime each started out as analysts and later became co-portfolio managers before leaving to start FCM. I am interested to know why they did not stick with the co-PM format, and since they are equal partners in the firm, I need to feel comfortable that they have a good working relationship.

I also tend to get good information from body language in meetings where I meet with two people (it becomes much harder to do when there are more than two). Let me start out by saying that reading body language can be tricky and it involves much more "art" than science. Some people read body language and they are not even aware that they are doing it. For example, I have heard from many experienced due diligence analysts that I have met in my career the following, "I don't know what it is, but I just don't trust that guy. His pedigree and performance are strong and everything else seems in order, but my gut just tells me to stay away." Over the course of my more than 20-year career analyzing investment managers, I have learned to trust my gut feelings (as well as those of others whom I respect). However, don't mistake a gut feeling for certainty, as we can never be certain that a hedge fund will perform as expected.

When I am doing a meeting with two hedge fund professionals, I often ask person 1 a question and look to see how person 2 responds while person 1 is answering (naturally this needs to be done discreetly). Just as a picture can be worth a thousand words, the reaction from person 2 can sometimes be more telling than anything either of them would ever say out loud. I have seen people shake their heads side to side (meaning "no") when the other person is answering a question in the affirmative. I have seen people's faces pucker up as if they have just bitten into a lemon in reaction to something that their teammate said. While "puckering" may be a bit extreme, eye rolling (as if to say "you've got to be kidding me") and head bowing (as if to say "I can't believe you are saying this") is much more common. When I detect some kind of reaction like the ones just mentioned, I don't assume any kind of malfeasance; instead, I make a note to probe the question/issue further (either on the spot, at a later date, or with other team members).

DIFFERENT PERSPECTIVES

If you are part of a due diligence team, you can do staggered meetings with the underlying hedge fund personnel. In other words, different members of your due diligence team can also meet with the appropriate hedge fund professionals to gain different perspectives. You can accomplish this by doing meetings with hedge fund personnel alongside another member of your due diligence team or you can do the meetings separately at different times. If your team is big enough, you can do both. The goal is to have several due diligence analysts meet with the hedge fund professionals and ask their own questions so that we can come together and compare notes and impressions. I strongly suggest having multiple people involved in the research and evaluation process because it helps to reduce individual biases and the different perspectives can add to our overall understanding of the hedge fund, which can lead to more informed (and hopefully) better investment decisions. I can point to numerous real-life examples where I have come out of a meeting with one impression and my teammate (who sat right alongside me) came out of the meeting with a completely different impression. In other less extreme instances, I finished a meeting not understanding an element of a hedge fund's process while my teammate seemed to understand it perfectly. In either case, doing the meeting together has led to additional questions and insights.

Alternatively, one person can interview hedge fund personnel at different times. It is important to mention that it is not uncommon to conduct several onsite meetings (and calls) while performing hedge fund due diligence. Experienced hedge fund managers realize that the due diligence process can involve multiple meetings and can take from a few months to several years to complete. You should never invest with any hedge fund unless you have strong conviction in the manager and are completely comfortable making the investment. If that happens after just a few meetings, great, but if it takes more meetings and a longer time, that is fine too. The only caveat is that we should look to maximize each onsite meeting that we do. Do your homework upfront, compile a question list, and take care of basic work in advance. For example, if you are meeting with a hedge fund manager after receiving their DDQ, presentation, monthly letters, and more, you should not have to ask what liquidity the fund offers or who the service providers are (because this information is likely spelled out in great detail in the aforementioned documents). If the documents are unclear, then you need to ask. I find it wasteful to demand someone's time and then ask basic questions that you should already know the answers to. Remember, any time during the trading day that you meet with investment personnel is time they have spent away from managing the fund.

MEETING NOTES

One of the most useful things that any hedge fund due diligence analyst can do is to take good meeting notes and organize them for future reference. A highly time-consuming aspect of our job as hedge fund analysts is to meet with portfolio managers, analysts, traders, risk managers, CIOs, CEOs, CFOs, CTOs, and so on. The information that we obtain in our phone calls and meetings with these professionals represents a critical component of our research and our ability to work efficiently in the future.

We previously highlighted general topics of discussion. In the following section, I have highlighted the specific questions that have come out of our initial interview, quantitative analysis, and portfolio analysis.

NOTE TAKING

Meeting notes are a key aspect of the due diligence process. They represent our record of conversations and meetings with the key members in the hedge funds that we review. When working in a team environment (as is the case in most institutional investment organizations), it is important to have discussions about various hedge fund manager meetings (at a minimum) and to provide written summaries of the meetings (which is the industry standard).

I have always been particular about my notes. I have used and kept my meeting notebooks for the last 15 years and have over 100 of them stored in my bookcase at home. Each book is numbered, as are the pages within each book. In the past, I had created a simple spreadsheet to track all my manager meetings and to provide reference information (manager name, notebook number, date of meeting, and pages within the notebook) so that I could easily find any notes of interest. I have also undertaken a seemingly never-ending project to scan all the notes and keep them on file for even easier reference.

However, in recent years I have found a much more efficient (and more expensive) method of taking and organizing my meeting notes. I now use my iPad and a stylus to handwrite my notes into one of the many note-taking "apps."

I currently use the "Note Taker HD" app because it provides me with the following functionality:

- Create tags for each meeting so that I can filter results by manager name, date, strategy, substrategy, country, state, city, and so on. I currently have about 500 meeting notes resident in the app and can filter them based on any one or a combination of tags previously mentioned. For example, if I would like to see all my meeting notes from last September I can filter by date. If I would like to see all equity long/short notes for funds resident in Singapore, I can simply filter by strategy and country. Needless to say, this functionality really comes in handy when I am sitting in a meeting with a manager (or client) and I am able to quickly access my notes from previous meetings.

- E-mail a PDF version of the note to anyone at any time right from the device.

- Back up my meeting notes in multiple locations.

- Upload PDF files to the app (I have used this for my older meeting notes, which have been scanned to PDFs). When I am done uploading my older notes to the app, I will have thousands of meeting notes spanning two decades immediately at my disposal.

However, there are dozens of other apps that you can employ should you use a tablet computer.

Question List for FCM

- We need to review position-level transparency onsite (record portfolio holdings at different points in time).
- We need permission to verify exposures and risk reporting with the fund's prime broker.
- We received a list of references for Ted and Jaime (upon our request). We need to ask for some references for Bill (who is a partner) as well as the other three members of the investment team.
- We need to address the issue of underlying portfolio liquidity. Jaime gave us a specific targeted liquidity profile when we spoke with him, but our 13F portfolio analysis indicates that the reported long positions do not meet Jaime's profile.
- The 13F analysis indicated that the fund had invested in smaller caps (microcap names in 2010) but eliminated them in 2011. We need to find out how prevalent microcaps were previously (2006–2009).
- The team managed the hedge fund with a small asset base until 2009, when assets started to ramp (and have done so consistently since that time). Did they manage the fund differently with fewer assets? Were they more concentrated? What was underlying portfolio liquidity when assets were small?
- Jaime indicated (as did the DDQ) that the fund's capacity is $500 million. When asked in the initial interview, Jaime's answer was not sufficient—he stated that they had managed more than that at GCH. Our liquidity analysis indicates that at $500 million in assets FCM's long portfolio reported as 13F holdings between March 2010 and September 2011 would have been much less liquid at the $500M AUM level. Ask them to mathematically justify the stated capacity.
- The fund is currently highly concentrated and, according to the 13F analysis, it has been throughout 2010 and 2011. Is this consistent with previous years? Are there any intended or unintended themes within the portfolio at this time? Have they had any themes in the past? What risk measures, if any, do they use to manage the concentration risk (both sector and position level)?
- FCM made Bill Hobson, CFO, the risk manager in mid-2009. Was there a specific event that led to this decision? How much power does Bill have as the risk manager? Bill does not appear to have any previous experience as a risk manager, so what does he bring to the table?
- They have a stop loss for shorts and none for longs. Why no stop loss for longs? Jaime did not adequately explain the stop-loss rules for shorts—ask Ted (PM) and the trader for clarification. Given they have no set stops in place for long positions, what was the biggest loss they

have ever taken (by percentage move in price and as impact to NAV for a single long position)?

■ FCM sells itself as bottom up but Jaime indicated that there was an element of top down in 2008, when they lowered both gross and net exposures (going net short for a two-month period). Was that a one time thing or have they employed top-down elements before then? Additionally, has their experience in 2008 changed the process or risk management at all? If yes, then explain.

■ FCM provided several trade examples (hhgregg was included in the previous chapter). Go through the examples in detail from the research perspective (with the director of research and the analysts), investment perspective (with the PM), and the trading perspective (with the trader).

■ Probe for more information regarding Ted and Jaime's time at GCH. I was unable to get a real handle on their time there when I spoke with Jaime. Reach out to their former co-workers from GCH and get more detail (it would be nice to have a few reference calls done in advance of the onsite meeting so that we have a better base of information from which we can operate).

■ How much money does each team member have invested in the fund? Has this number changed over time (to me this is more of an investment question than an operations question, as I gain confidence in the manager when I can see that they stand to lose right alongside me)?

■ Discuss ownership and if the three current partners plan on naming anyone else a partner.

■ Who markets and who handles client service for the fund?

■ The DDQ mentions that FCM has used consultants to assist in research efforts in the past. Outside of Smithson (mentioned in DDQ), have they used any other firms? What was the scope of their services? How were the consultants paid?

■ Have they invested in any non-U.S. companies? If so, how much and how did they perform the research?

■ In their materials, they emphasize that they require a strong management team for long positions. Do they personally meet with company management? What do they look for and how do they measure?

■ Have they ever invested in any illiquid instruments?

■ Explain further their strategy with regard to options. How do they account for the inherent leverage in options when they report exposures? Also, how do they define leverage?

■ How much of a role does Jaime play in the management of the portfolio? Their DDQ states that Ted makes all portfolio decisions, but Jaime was less than clear in our call.

- Do they monitor the portfolio on a risk-adjusted or beta-adjusted basis? If so, can they provide details?
- We had requested actual examples of how their ranking model worked, and Jaime indicated that it would be best to go through it in person. Make sure to follow up.
- What drove excess short performance in 2007?
- Go through 2008 and ask specifically about how the long book was able to perform as well as it did. What drove performance? Because there was earlier performance frequently throughout the year, spend time to go through positioning and portfolio drivers month by month.
- What prompted FCM to start putting exposure back on as early as September 2008 (when most others were frantically starting to reduce exposure)?
- What drove shorts in 2009/10/11 (significant outperformance again)? Given their history of strong attribution from shorts, what are they doing that differentiated them from peers?
- Discuss the outlier positions identified in the 13F analysis.
- Ask Ted (and possibly Jaime) what they think their former colleagues at GCH will say about them when we call. Also, ask if they have any recent contact information for Jonah (as we cannot seem to locate him via the normal channels).

ONSITE INTERVIEWS AT FICTIONAL CAPITAL MANAGEMENT (FCM)

Since FCM is a relatively small firm and they manage a single hedge fund, the onsite meeting will typically cover multiple areas of focus and, as a result, I may conduct interviews with people in the investment, operational, and risk-oriented areas. However, to keep with the flow of this book (which presents the various aspects of hedge fund analysis in separate stages/chapters), I will highlight only the investment-related interviews in this chapter and will include the operational interview in Chapter 9 and the risk interview in Chapter 10. Just keep in mind that we should always probe all areas when conducting interviews. In fact, make a point of asking your interviewees questions outside of their area of specialization. For example, when speaking to a portfolio manager or analyst make sure you ask how the firm conducts risk management (even though there is someone else charged with that specific task) and conversely, ask the risk manager how the firm conducts its research. Don't accept answers like "That's not my area, why don't you ask them directly?" Professionals that work at hedge funds are invariably well educated and bright—they have an opinion and we should do our best to extract it.

In the course of our due diligence, I will interview the PM (Ted), research director (Jaime), the analysts (Joyce, Charlie) and the trader (Jacob). However, I will not include transcripts for each of these meetings. Instead I will provide the following:

- Partial interview transcript of the meeting with Ted Acoff. I will leave out less relevant or repetitive sections and will summarize other sections.
- Meeting note that summarizes interviews with each member of the investment team.

Interview Transcript

Date: January 5, 2012

Participants: Frank Travers, Ted Acoff

Transcript begins after introductions and some small talk.

FT: Let's start with some history. Tell me about your role at GCH.

TA: I was hired by Arty Gellberg in 1998 as an analyst and eventually was named as co-portfolio manager after he left. Jaime and I managed the long/short fund.

FT: Where did Mike Shell fit in all this?

TA: Okay, so you know the firm?

FT: Not really. Jaime told me that Mike took over from Arty.

TA: Yeah. So he probably told you that Jonah was a hard guy to work for too. Arty and Jonah had a falling out and Arty left to start his own firm.

FT: Did anyone from your GCH days invest in your fund?

TA: Yes. Arty was a day-one investor. Nothing big, just a million to start, but he has added since then.

We will definitely reach out to Art Gellberg as a reference. He has experience working directly with both Ted and Jaime and had enough confidence to invest with them when they opened FCM.

FT: Did anyone else from GCH invest?

TA: No, just Arty. Getting back to GCH, Mike was brought in after Arty left and that lasted a few years. Jaime and I were then made co-PMs.

FT: Why didn't Jonah take over as portfolio manager?

TA: Jonah's skill set was in the long-only world. He was smart enough to realize that, and that's why he initially brought Arty on. In my opinion, he made a mistake hiring Mike. He was a good guy but Arty was a tough act to follow. Arty was a fantastic investor and I learned a great deal from him.

FT: Such as?

TA: Well, he ran a hedged book. He always used to say that hedge funds are supposed to hedge. Arty came from a technology background and, therefore, he tended to favor stocks in that sector. He brought me on to assist him based on my technology background. While many other hedge funds were long and strong technology in the late 1990s, we always hedged our long bets with technology shorts. We had positive performance but lagged during the bull market, but boy, did things turn around when the bubble burst. You will notice that Jaime and I always maintain a short book.

This explains FCM's allocation to the technology sector, which has been significant over our review period.

FT: What did Jaime do at GCH?

TA: Jaime was hired as the assets in the hedge fund started to ramp up. As I said just before, we had good performance in the late 1990s and our numbers in 2000 were quite good. That's another thing that Jaime and I learned from Arty. If you don't have conviction, get out of the way. Jaime was brought on as an analyst to assist Jonah in doing company research.

FT: What do you mean by "get out of the way"?

TA: To only invest when you have conviction, even if it causes a temporary lag in performance. We ran the book back in the late 1990s with a net long in the 20 percent to 40 percent range. We made money but really lagged the funds that stopped shorting. However, in the end we did the right thing. Markets collapsed in 2000 and the markets went through several tough years for equities. We came through the period looking pretty good.

FT: Did Jaime have any sector specialty?

TA: Not formally, but informally he was our go-to guy for consumer and retail. He focused mainly on those sectors at Jenners Blakely before joining GCH.

FT: After Mike left, you guys were named co-portfolio managers.

TA: Yes. I had been with the firm six years at that point and had a good relationship with Jonah. Jaime had been with the firm three or four years. Jaime and I were part of a five-person analyst team (not including

Jonah), and a significant portion of the fund's alpha in the previous years had come from our stock picks. While we hadn't been portfolio managers, we did play a key role in the composition of the fund and our selections had largely driven performance. When Bill left, Jaime and I met with Jonah and collectively decided on that course of action.

FT: You had no equity at this point. Did you get a share of the revenue?

TA: No equity but a generous revenue share.

FT: So you were happy with the arrangement?

TA: Not happy. We were thrilled. Jaime and I worked well together and always wanted to manage our own fund, so this was a great opportunity for us. We assumed that we would become partners at some point, though.

FT: Did you have complete say in overall portfolio decisions or did Jonah have any input?

This is an important question because it will dictate how much weight we place on their track record at GCH. It will also give me a point of reference when I speak with Jonah.

TA: We managed the portfolio but we had hard-coded portfolio parameters. Jonah always ran the firm's research effort and it was no different when Jaime and I took over.

FT: Did the strategy or the risk parameters change when you took over?

TA: Not really. They had changed when Mike took over because he ran the portfolio in a more diversified manner than Arty did. When we took over everything was essentially in place.

FT: Was the fund at GCH as sector concentrated as here at FCM?

TA: Yes, but not as much as here.

FT: How different then?

TA: Technology and consumer were the biggest allocations then as they are now but we had a sector limit of +/−20 percent net at GCH. No formal gross limits.

FT: And here?

TA: No formal limits. We go where the opportunities are, where we can find the best risk/reward.

FT: Any concern about sector concentration from a risk perspective?

TA: We are always concerned about portfolio risks, but we run a hedged book and have done a good job of sticking only to high conviction names. When we are not convicted, as in 2008, we take down exposure.

In 2008, we took down our long exposure and maintained our short exposure. We were a bit early in doing so and a bit early in putting the exposure back on, but it all worked out in the end.

FT: Is there an informal sector limit? Would you, for example, have 75 percent of the fund in technology?

TA: Conceptually, we would be 100 percent in technology if we could only find high-conviction names in that sector. However, we look across all sectors and there are always going to be attractive stocks in other sectors. The likelihood of that happening is pretty low.

FT: I reviewed your 13F filings and according to my research, most of your exposure since 2010 has been concentrated in technology and services. What was the exposure like before that?

We will verify this by reviewing their historical records later on and also by reviewing their audited financial statements and prime brokerage risk reports.

TA: On the long side we have generally found better ideas in those sectors along with consumer. I have been covering technology stocks my whole career and feel I have an edge there. Jaime has followed consumer and services companies for the last decade. We are comfortable in those sectors but, again, we will invest where we find the best opportunities.

FT: And on the short side?

TA: Prior to 2008, the short book was set up pretty similarly to the long book—short tech and consumer names. In 2008, we started to short financials, principally banks and mortgage companies. It worked well for us, as our long book fell less than the overall market and our short book turned in lights-out performance. The short book in general performed well, but the financials led the way.

Since we did not have any position-level information for 2008, we had questioned what drove the short performance, which was excellent. The fact that they were short mortgage companies explains a lot. However, it raises the question of expertise in that sector.

FT: Do you guys have any experience analyzing financials? There's a big difference between tech companies and banks.

TA: We were both long and short financials at GCH so we have a background in the sector. Remember, we may have had areas of specialization but we also covered stocks in other areas. Joyce was a big help with the banks in particular.

FT: Two questions: (1) when did you start to short the financials and (2) what was Joyce's role?

I thought his answer was weak and needed additional probing. They pride themselves on avoiding typical hedge fund names, but hedge funds went short financials in a big way after the bubble burst. I am curious as to the timing of the shorts in financials.

TA: I can look up the exact dates, but we actually started putting on some shorts in this area in late 2007 and did it throughout 2008. We never had a huge allocation but we did have decent turnover because the stocks hit their price targets generally faster than we would have expected. At the peak, I would say that we had maybe 15 percent to 20 percent gross short exposure in financials. Joyce's role was simple. She did a lot of the screening and was responsible for the company modeling.

FT: Was she directed to do that research or did she come up with the idea herself?

With this question, I am hoping to gain some insight into their research process. Additionally, I would like to know how much influence the analysts have on portfolio decisions.

TA: We decided as a group. We meet formally each Monday before the market opens to discuss the portfolio and pipeline. We have four analysts including Jaime and myself. Jacob, our trader, also does some analytical work. Jaime runs all research and he is charged with assigning research responsibilities to the analysts. Jaime and I also cover names. In this case, Joyce was responsible for looking at the financial sector and identifying potential shorts.

FT: So this was a top-down call?

TA: We are a bottom-up shop, but we find some of our ideas based on themes. Over the summer of 2008, it was pretty clear to us and to a number of others that the markets could crack. We were concerned that a crack in the markets led by a bursting of the property bubble could have huge ramifications in the financial sector. We narrowed that down to the banks and mortgage companies. We discussed it as a group and then Joyce was tasked with researching those groups and presenting a list of potential candidates.

FT: Long and short?

TA: No. At that time, we were pretty focused on the short side.

FT: So are you a bottom-up shop or not?

TA: We are definitely a bottom-up shop, but as I said, we still have to take into consideration the macro. There are no truly bottom-up shops. Whenever you model out a company's financial statements you have to make assumptions about interest rates, economic growth, FX rates, and so on. So we always need to pay attention to the macro environment.

FT: Did you lower long exposure in 2008 because of your macro views?

TA: That's a good question. We would like to think that everything we did came from pure stock selection. We had a hard time finding any longs in which we had strong conviction, so as we sold off various long positions as they hit their price targets or as we reassessed the company's prospects, we just didn't put on any additional longs. At the same time, we maintained our short exposure, so that essentially brought down gross exposure and flattened out our net exposure. Part of the reason we could not get comfortable with longs was due to the macro environment. So you tell me—was it top down or bottom up?

FT: Based on your description, seems like a combination of both.

TA: That's how I feel as well.

FT: Did your experience in 2008 change how you look at portfolio construction or stock selection?

TA: In what way?

FT: In any way.

TA: Well, I hadn't really thought about that much. Give me a second to think. Wow, that's a great question.

(After a few moments)

TA: I am going to have to think about that a bit more, but my initial response would be to say that our experience in 2008 taught us to trust our instincts and the process we have in place. I don't think we changed anything but I can say that we can now demonstrate that our method of investing works in both bad and good environments. It goes back to what I learned from Arty. If you don't have conviction, don't invest.

FT: So why was Joyce qualified to do the modeling on the financial companies? Does she have a financial background?

TA: She was an analyst at Creeson Capital for a few years before joining us and she was responsible for doing work on financials, among other sectors. We didn't hire her because of that experience, though. We hired her because we thought she had a strong analytical base and could grow with the firm.

I will make sure to inquire about Joyce's skills in this sector when I interview her later in the day. I will make a point of asking her for a reference so that I can verify the information.

FT: Sounds good. I believe that you had shorted ETFs in the latter part of 2008?

TA: You certainly do your homework. Yes, we did use some index ETFs as placeholders in the short book after covering some short positions.

FT: Doesn't sound bottom up to me.

TA: It's not, but remember what it was like in late 2008. It was crazy then. We started to gain more conviction in some names after the market cracked. We were able to get back in the market because we had taken down our long exposure and had dry powder available to invest at rock-bottom prices. We were a little early, but you can never pick either the top or the bottom. Things looked like screaming buys in the third quarter of 2008.

FT: How much of the short exposure in 2008 was stock shorts versus index shorts?

TA: We maxed out at about 15 percent or so.

FT: Fifteen percent gross or 15 percent of the short exposure?

TA: Gross.

FT: Your gross short exposure bottomed out at −45 percent in August and September moved back up to −65 percent in October. Was that from the short index exposure?

TA: You are spot on. After we covered some shorts that had fallen and met our price targets, we felt it was important to maintain the short exposure given the overall market, so we added some index shorts.

FT: Which indexes?

TA: Mostly S&P 500, but we also shorted XLF, the financials ETF a bit as well.

FT: XLF sounds like a macro call to me.

Jaime hadn't mentioned the XLF short when we spoke on the phone.

TA: Not really; we had covered a few financial shorts and liked that short exposure.

FT: Again, sounds like a macro call to me.

TA: I see where you are coming from, but it wasn't really like that. Three-quarters of the ETF exposure was in the S&P and the rest was in the XLF.

FT: So you're saying that one-quarter was a macro call, then? How long did you keep the index positions on?

I am challenging him on his assertion that establishing a short in the financial ETF was not a macro call. In fact, I can argue that the entire ETF position was a macro call, but I respect the fact that they were looking to control downside. I would like for him to at least admit to it.

TA: We didn't keep the ETF positions in the book all that long. XLF was a short position for about a month and the S&P short was through year end but shrank as the year wore on. Once we were able to find single-name shorts, we took off the index positions. As I said, this was a placeholder. We are believers in company fundamentals, but in the latter part of 2008 company fundamentals went out the window.

FT: So the ETF positions were your way of keeping the overall portfolio net exposure where you wanted it?

TA: If you want to put it that way, yes. You seem to view this as top down, but we look at it as a placeholder for our bottom-up selections.

FT: All right, let's move to the next topic. Tell me how you work as a team.

TA: As I mentioned, we meet weekly on Mondays, but since we are a small shop and we sit right next to one another, we are always in active dialogue. Have you seen our setup yet?

FT: I took a brief look. As we progress with the due diligence I would like to spend some time with you guys out by your desks to get a better sense of how you work individually and as a team, if possible.

I have found that sitting with the investment professionals can be a big help in understanding the team dynamic as well as a means of how they work individually. You cannot avoid spending time in hedge funds' conference rooms, but I have found the amount of intel I can get in this sterile environment can be limiting. Instead, I try to conduct interviews in people's offices and/or in their workspace (even when it is out on the trading floor). When you sit with someone in their own environment, you can glance at what they are currently working on, which is always a great source for questions. In addition, when they reference some work that they had done in the past, you can ask them to pull it up right on their screen (which is a great way of verifying what someone is telling you).

TA: Not a problem at all. As to our relationship, Jaime is a great research director. He takes care of managing the analysts and I work more with Jacob, our trader. Jaime maintains a steady pipeline of ideas and is skilled at getting the most from the analysts.

FT: Who comes up with pipeline names?

TA: Mostly Jaime and I. Joyce is getting good at identifying potential candidates as well.

FT: And Charlie?

TA: He's talented but still young. He is very bright and a wizard with financial models; he has excellent Excel skills. Jaime comes from an investment banking background so he is also well versed in creating detailed models as well. They work quite well together.

FT: Back to Joyce. How many of the names in the current portfolio did she source?

TA: We have about 50 positions right now and I would say that she was responsible for maybe a handful of them.

FT: Long or short?

TA: A couple of each.

FT: Why are you the portfolio manager and not Jaime?

Jaime and Ted had co-managed the fund at GCH previously, so I am still curious how they decided to break out the responsibilities.

TA: What do you mean?

FT: You co-managed assets at GCH. Why did you change things up here?

TA: One decision maker is cleaner.

FT: Why you and not him?

TA: We talked about it and agreed it was the best way to organize the firm. I may be the one making the final calls, but Jaime plays a large role in all decisions.

FT: Can you put on a position that he does not like?

TA: No. He is the director of research and he is responsible for the buy and sell lists.

FT: What does that mean?

TA: I cannot invest in any position long or short unless he has approved it from a research standpoint. It is our internal system of checks and balances. I might be the portfolio manager but I can only invest in names that Jaime has ultimately approved.

FT: Do you have any names that have been approved that you have not invested in?

TA: Absolutely. We have a number of stocks at any given time that we like but either don't currently have the conviction in or just have better alternatives.

FT: So you are looking for a better price point?

TA: In some cases, yes. But we don't put on a position unless we have conviction in the name and it has a better risk/reward profile than names currently in the book. We have a stock ranking system that takes these factors into account.

FT: Do you have to sell one position to buy another?

I am definitely interested in the ranking system but would like to stay on point here.

TA: Not necessarily. If we have strong conviction in a name, we can add it to the portfolio. That will have an impact on our gross exposure. That's what happened in late 2008 and throughout 2009. We had low gross exposure and as we found additional high-conviction stocks we mostly added them to the portfolio. We sold or covered names also, but not as a one-on, one-off technique.

FT: What's your maximum allowable gross exposure?

TA: Per the OM, we can max out at 250 percent but realistically, we don't plan on bringing the total gross over 200 percent.

FT: So why is it set at 250 percent?

This is a personal pet peeve of mine. If you tell me you will not do something, why say you "may" or "can" in the legal documents? If you are not used to reading hedge fund documents, you will learn quickly that they often give hedge fund managers a wider mandate than they typically need. As a due diligence analyst, we need to factor in not just what managers say they will do, but what they can "actually" do according to the contract. We will cover this more in the operational analysis chapter, but it is worth mentioning here.

TA: We wanted to make sure we had a cushion just in case.

FT: You can't have it both ways, though. Either you will or you won't exceed 200 percent. Which is it?

TA: Two hundred percent is an informal limit. We have been in operation for five years and have never gone over that limit. We've never had exposure in the 190s at all.

FT: But you could. Under what scenario would you increase exposure over 200 percent and take it to the formal maximum?

TA: I can't think of any reason why we would want to do it.

FT: What is your current gross exposure?

TA: Roughly 175 percent.

FT: Net?

TA: Fifty percent.

FT: Let me circle back to the previous question. Why are you the PM?

TA: You don't quit, do you? When we were at GCH, I was the one who tended to think more about portfolio construction and Jaime tended to think more about the research side of things.

FT: Who owns the track record?

TA: We both do.

FT: Legally?

TA: Yes. It's in our agreement.

FT: You guys have had strong performance in your short book. What do you suppose has driven that?

TA: I think we have had strong performance in both the long and short books. When we look at a short, we basically look for the opposite of what we think makes a strong long candidate. We look for companies that have weaknesses somewhere in the chain, less than top-notch management teams, have made bad investments, and have no history of generating consistent free cash flows. If you look at our short book, you will see that most of the names have a low level of short interest. We tend to be early when we invest in both the long and short books. We tend to avoid well-traveled hedge fund names.

FT: Let's go through some current short examples. Tell me how they are sized in your portfolio, what the investment thesis is, and why no one else seems to be seeing what you do.

We go through several examples of current shorts and then some current longs in the portfolio for about half an hour. Ted seems to have an encyclopedic knowledge of the names. This includes several of the long positions that I had researched ahead of this meeting. The transcript picks up after this discussion.

FT: Thanks. Let's talk a bit about portfolio transparency. I spoke with Jaime and he indicated that you guys are not comfortable e-mailing older portfolios to me. Why is that?

Nothing like being direct. They are a fundamental long/short shop and in my view should have no issue sharing older information. After all, they have likely turned over the portfolio many times since then so there should be no sensitivities. Besides, they have already stated that they will let me see the portfolio in its entirety while onsite.

TA: I wasn't aware of that. I don't think we have ever sent full portfolios with all long and short positions to anyone in the past.

FT: There's always a first time. In any case, you guys are now starting to market to more institutional investors and I expect that they will ask for the same information. I am not asking for today's portfolio. Besides, we just went through a number of current positions anyway. I am simply trying to get a handle on how you have managed the fund historically. I am happy to sign an NDA if that makes you more comfortable.

TA: I can't give you an answer right now. Let me discuss it with Jaime and Bill.

I can tell from his body language that there is a good chance that they will provide the lagged transparency.

FT: Great. Thanks. I noticed in reviewing your 13F long portfolio that you had some stocks that had market caps below $250 million back in 2010 but none since. Was that typical of the portfolio when it had fewer assets?

TA: It seems as if you know a good deal about our portfolio already. Yes, I would say that it was typical. I don't recall the exact breakout, but we had a few smaller companies in the portfolio in the earlier years.

FT: What's a few?

TA: A couple at times; maybe as many as five or six at peak.

FT: I understand that you don't have any formal liquidity guidelines.

Now that we have confirmed that they have held smaller, less liquid stocks in the fund when it was smaller, we really need to understand how liquid the fund was in the early days and determine if they are currently managing the book as they had back then. It is important when reviewing past performance to always understand how the manager achieved that past performance. If the fund invested in securities that it can no longer invest in (due to size or any other reason), then we may have to discount that performance to some degree. We can certainly give them credit for strong performance, but since they are essentially managing a different fund, we have to take that into account.

TA: Right. Nothing we state in the presentation, but we do try to maintain a liquid portfolio. We have quarterly liquidity with 90 days' notice. We can fully liquidate our book in a month if need be.

FT: What do you base that on?

TA: Our own analysis. We track our holdings in real time and at the end of each day we calculate the projected portfolio based on a share of daily volume.

FT: I did the same and found that it would take you more than a month to sell several different positions. I assumed a daily maximum of 25 percent of average daily volume. Where am I going wrong?

TA: I can ask Jacob to come in and go through the liquidity with you if you like, but I can assure you that we can liquidate within a month. We also have the prime broker report as a backup.

FT: That would be a good check for me. It would be great if the prime broker could send me a copy of that report.

This was a perfect segue into asking for the prime brokerage report. Instead of just asking for it, the discussion has led us naturally to that point.

TA: I'm not sure that they would do that.

FT: I have received liquidity and exposure reports from your prime broker while conducting due diligence on a number of other hedge funds in the past. If you direct them to send it, they will. They may be a pain about doing it, but they will.

TA: Okay. I'll ask Bill to take care of that.

FT: Great. Since we are on the subject, I would like to see a copy of their risk report as well.

TA: I'll talk to Bill and you guys can work out the details. Okay?

FT: Sounds good. Let me ask you about how you and Jaime work together. If you currently have a long technology position in the portfolio and Jaime no longer likes the name, do you sell?

I would still like to get a better sense of how Ted and Jaime work together. I had already asked this question but wanted to probe further.

TA: Jaime doesn't just wake up one day and no longer like any position. We talk about our positions all the time. You had mentioned that you want to observe us and I think that would answer many of your team-related questions. To address your question a little differently, if Jaime and I had discussed a specific holding and we decided that it no longer fit for some reason, then we would sell or cover the position.

FT: You had mentioned earlier that you could only invest in stocks that Jaime had approved. That this method represented your internal check and balance. That works for stocks when they make their way into the portfolio. How about when they leave the portfolio? How does that work?

TA: You want to know more about our sell discipline?

FT: Yes.

TA: Jaime and I (and the rest of the team, for that matter) discuss positions daily. When we make an initial investment we set a price target, write a brief thesis for the trade, and score the stock based on our ranking model. Should the price target be met or the thesis change for any reason, we discuss the position and more than likely sell or cover.

FT: What would be the exception?

TA: If things change for the worse or if our initial analysis was wrong, we would likely just get out of a position. If we were right and a stock reaches our price target, we may decide to just take some profit and reset the target higher for a long or lower for a short.

FT: Why not just get out completely?

TA: We have given up some performance in the past for doing that.

FT: Do you adjust the price target because something has changed or because your initial modeling was incorrect?

TA: Usually because something has changed, but we are not perfect. Sometimes we like a stock due to our growth projections only to determine that we underestimated the growth rate. Products can take on a life of their own and when they gain momentum, they can really take off and surprise to the upside—or downside when news is bad.

FT: But aren't you playing with fire to some degree? Unrealized gains have a nasty habit of turning lower or into realized losses.

TA: They can, but we generally reduce the position, take some chips off the table.

FT: Do you have a formal stop-loss policy?

TA: We do for shorts but not for longs. We review any short that moves −20 percent against us.

FT: So it's not a real stop?

TA: It's more of a rule that forces us to review the position.

FT: So again, no stops. Right?

I don't really care if they have a stop or not, but I want to understand what they do. When someone implies that they have a stop in place, I want to know if they actually follow through or if it is a mere suggestion. Jaime stated that the −20 percent stop for short positions was a hard rule; Ted is now telling me that it is not.

TA: No hard stops, but we are typically pretty sensitive to losses and often take off at least part of a position that has moved more than −20 percent against us.

FT: Just shorts?

TA: We give long positions a little longer leash because there is a limit to the downside there and unlimited potential losses with shorts.

FT: So what would make you reduce a position or eliminate it after it has moved −20 percent?

TA: Do you require your managers to have hard stop losses? You are really hammering this one.

FT: No. I'm asking because I don't quite understand your policy. Maybe I misunderstood Jaime, but I got off the call thinking that you had a more formal stop in place for shorts.

TA: Okay. Let me explain. We have found that we are often early to spot potential long positions and, as such, we can see some price weakness early on. We will absolutely sell a long position in which the thesis has changed or if there is something going on with the stock that we cannot figure out.

FT: Such as?

TA: Such as a continued slide in price with absolutely no reason at all. We can take pain to a certain level, but we have learned through the years that sometimes small-cap stocks decline in price for what appears to be no good reason. This usually is a good indicator of things to come. The unexplained loss has an impact on our overall conviction level, which leads to a reduction in exposure to that name or an outright sell. On the short side, we are much less tolerant of losses. When shorts move against us, their weight in the fund gets bigger, and that will impact how we view the risk in that stock. That's why we establish smaller positions in shorts—in the 2 percent to 3 percent range versus 4 percent to 6 percent for longs. I generally reduce short positions by half if they move −20 percent against us and probably more than half of the time just cover the position completely.

FT: I assume that if left to Jaime he would not be so quick to act?

TA: Did he say that?

FT: No. I am just reading between the lines.

I am guesstimating based on Jaime's assessment that Ted is too conservative.

TA: Well, then you are reading Jaime pretty well. I tend to be more conservative than Jaime. That is not to say that he's aggressive, but we have had numerous discussions about position weights and sell discipline.

This had also come up in my call with Jaime. I would like to understand this dynamic better.

FT: Can you expand on that?

TA: Okay. Jaime and I often discuss position sizing. He tends to want to size up positions more frequently than I do.

FT: Where does he want position sizing to go?

TA: Nothing radical, but if normal longs are 4 percent to 6 percent, he would like them to be in the 6 percent to 8 percent range. We are both in agreement about the sizing of shorts.

FT: So what is your objection to moving the long position sizes up? It seems at first glance that you have good stock selection skills. Why not leverage that?

TA: I agree. I think we have done a good job selecting stocks as well, but we also pick some that don't work out. Using our weighting scheme, we typically have about 20–25 or so longs and 20–25 shorts. This is similar to what we had done at GCH—although we were more diversified there. So that's a system that has worked well for over seven years. Why fix something if it's not broken?

FT: Is this disagreement something that might cause a rift between you two at some point?

I will ask Ted directly and see if I can get any additional information when I speak to Bill (CFO) and the analysts later on.

TA: No. Nothing even close. We have a great relationship. We have been working together for a decade and are good friends personally as well as professionally. There are absolutely no issues between us. I think that an active dialogue about how we manage the fund is healthy.

FT: Talk to me about your stock ranking system. How does it work and how long have you been using it?

TA: Sure. Turn to page 15 of the presentation and we can walk through it.

FT: Okay.

I have included the graphic from their presentation here for reference:

hhgregg, Inc.

Upside	75%
Downside	−20%
U/D Ratio	3.75
Correlation (1–5)	4
Conviction (1–5)	4
Score	**60**

TA: As you can see, we have four components: upside, downside, correlation, and conviction. The upside and downside are based on the financial models that we build for each of our companies. We simply take the estimated upside and divide by the absolute value of the downside. In this example, we believe that hhgregg, Inc. has an almost 4 to 1 upside versus downside. We then apply our assessment of correlation and our level of conviction. We multiply the bottom three numbers in the table to come up with our score.

FT: How do you rank correlation between 1 and 5?

TA: Simple gradations. If correlation is high, we give it a score of 1; if it is low or negative, it gets a score of 5. We want to reward stocks with low correlations and penalize stocks with high correlations. We start by looking at historical figures and adjust based on our understanding of the company's product mix and growth prospects going forward instead of just relying upon historical relationships. It's as much art as science.

FT: And conviction?

TA: Again, not rocket science. We assign a conviction value for each stock, with a score of 5 being the highest conviction and 1 the lowest.

FT: Who makes those assessments?

TA: The team has input, but Jaime and I essentially set the levels. As research director, Jaime is ultimately responsible for the ranking model.

FT: Do you change any of the scores over time?

TA: Yes. When we make changes to our model's assumptions or when events lead us to change either the correlation or conviction level. It is such a simple method of pulling multiple facets of our work together. It ranks stocks based on attractiveness (that's the up/down ratio and conviction values) and factors in the portfolio dynamic (correlation) and applies our assessments of those factors to a conviction level.

FT: Do you compare the ranking of potential holdings to existing portfolio holdings?

TA: Absolutely. We generally only add a new name to the portfolio if it has a score above the lowest ranked stock currently in the portfolio.

FT: To add a new name, do you take an existing name out?

TA: Sometimes. We have room to grow our gross, so if we find a name that has a high score and we believe it adds value to the portfolio, we may just add it.

FT: Do you do this for longs and shorts?

TA: Yes. We run it the exact same way. I'm surprised that more people don't do things like this. I can tell you that this simple ranking methodology has helped us on numerous occasions.

FT: Do valuations factor into your ranking? That seems to be missing.

TA: Valuations are factored in with the conviction value. We have thought about separating conviction into components but each time we have tried we found that it didn't work as well.

FT: More art than science?

TA: Well put.

FT: When you measure correlation for a long or short, do you do it against the whole portfolio or do you match longs with longs and shorts with shorts?

TA: That's a great question. We do both, but when we assign a value to the correlation score we tend to focus much more on a stock's correlation within its appropriate book—so for a long candidate we tend to put more weight on its correlation to the stocks in the long book.

FT: Why is that?

TA: As I mentioned before, we tend to run with a long bias. Long positions have a higher average weight in the fund and a longer holding period. We like to think of our fund as being two funds really—one long and one short. We certainly look how the two books interact with one another, but our longs are designed to provide alpha as are our shorts. The short book is not a real hedge to the long book, meaning we don't try to offset specific exposures. We short a stock when we believe the price will go down, irrespective of what we are doing on the long side. We are more concerned about creating a highly correlated long or short book. We try to avoid doing that by using the ranking model and conducting portfolio stress tests and scenario analysis.

FT: Good segue into portfolio themes. Do you have any at this time?

TA: No. We are bottom-up investors.

FT: If you don't mind my saying, it looks to me as if you have a few themes in the portfolio. You have 20 percent of the long book in three outsourcing companies (Synnex, TeleTech, and Exlservice) and 14 percent of the long portfolio in semis (Intersil, Micrell, and Diodes).

TA: True but each name was initiated based on bottom-up research.

FT: I didn't ask how they got in the portfolio; looking at the portfolio from the top down, these appear to be obvious clusters. Would you say that these two examples are not intended themes but maybe unintended?

TA: We understood when we added each name that we were adding exposure but, again, this is all bottoms up. We can go through each name if you like.

FT: I would like to, but for now let's stay more top down. I assume that the correlation value in your ranking model for each of these stocks was and is high because they are in the same industries?

TA: Maybe we should just go through each name?

FT: Not yet. Let me ask the question a different way. You have three companies in the outsourcing industry and three in the semiconductor industry. Outsourcing companies can be uncorrelated, I assume (and when I ran the correlation for the three of them they were only mildly correlated), but semiconductors tend to be much more correlated as a group. Let's focus on semis for now.

TA: Okay. We have three positions in semiconductor companies, but you can see that we have weighted them at the lower end of our range. We did this because of your comments regarding correlation. That said, each of these three companies specializes in a different area within the broad semiconductor universe. But even if the correlation was high, we are comfortable with each name and have weighted the three of them in a way that we think reflects your concerns. Moving to the three outsourcing companies, they are as different as can be. The correlation within the group should be low and each of them has a low level of correlation to the long book in general. We started by researching Synnex and found the other two as we progressed through the research. Most databases list them as peers, but they are really in completely different businesses.

FT: Can you walk me through your views on these companies with an emphasis on their ranking in your model?

TA: Sure.

Ted walks me through the six names in the outsourcing and semiconductor industries. Once again, he clearly demonstrates that he knows the names well. In addition, I am impressed with their ranking system. It is simplistic, but seems to make sense when we walked through the examples.

FT: What's your edge? Why should I hire you guys?

TA: I think our edge is that we focus on stocks that others don't. We tend to be nonconsensus thinkers and as a result our returns look very different from other long/short funds. I think we do great research, but lots of firms do great research. I would say that our ranking system is a differentiator as is our consistent long and short philosophy, meaning we look to make money on both sides of the book. We've been pretty successful thus far.

FT: You have done a good job with your longs, but what makes you good on the short side?

TA: I can't really answer that. We look for shorts the same way we look for longs, only in reverse. I think we have done comparatively well with our shorts because we apply our proven strategy and avoid the herd. We are not contrarian, but we really don't like to invest just because everyone else is investing. I think that keeps our universe of long and short opportunities fresh, much fresher than your typical hedge fund.

We have covered a number of things in our meeting and before moving on to the next interview, Ted takes me to his desk and walks me through the systems that he uses to build and monitor the portfolio.

The interview ends at this point.

Meeting Note

In a typical due diligence visit, I would meet with multiple investments, operational, and risk professionals. To keep this chapter moving, I have summarized the interviews that I conducted with the rest of the investment team members. The summaries are in meeting note format. A formal typewritten note accomplishes three goals:

1. Allows other members of my firm to learn about the details of my interviews.
2. Forces me to think about the information that I received in my interview(s). My handwritten notes can be a bit of a jumble. A formal note that is distributed to other team members forces me to think about the meeting and summarize the main points as well as my key findings.

3. Creates a nice historical record that can be referenced at a later date. When I have conducted multiple meetings with a hedge fund manager over a period of time and plan on visiting them again in the near future, I always review old meeting notes to make sure that I am completely up to speed and that I have not forgotten anything.

Example

To:	Research Team
From:	Frank Travers
Date:	January 6, 2012
Re:	Onsite Meeting with Fictional Capital Management

Location

FCM's office is bare bones. The space is small (about 1,500 square feet) and has no reception area (you basically walk into the trading room when you enter the office). There is a small computer room and pantry area, but the conference room is located outside their offices and is shared with several other firms on the floor. The COO/risk manager has the only office and he shares it with the CFO. The trading area is essentially one long room with six connecting desks laid out in pairs facing one another. The investment team sits right next to one another and the CFO's operational assistants sit next to them.

Ted Acoff

I spent about two hours meeting with Ted (about half in the conference room and the other half at his desk). The meeting started with a discussion about Ted and Jaime's time at GCH, where they had worked together previously. They both started as analysts and after several PM changes were made co-portfolio managers. They managed the portfolio together for three years before leaving to launch FCM. Having spoken to both Ted and Jaime about GCH, it appears that they were able to take the investment philosophy from that firm and bring it mostly intact to FCM. They do not seem to have made many changes. They did formalize a stock ranking model at FCM, whereas it was not something that was used in its current form at GCH. In addition, at FCM they tend to run the portfolio in a more concentrated manner.

The strategy is equity long/short, primarily in the small-cap space (they can invest in mid-caps but I have not seen any evidence that they have done so in the past). They typically invest in U.S. listed companies but have invested in foreign companies through American depository receipts (ADRs) in the past (very infrequently based on the portfolio review that I was able to do at the office). The strategy is listed as being generalist, but it is clear that they are most comfortable in the technology, services, and consumer sectors. The historical portfolio review indicated that these three sectors tend to make up at least 75 percent of their exposure—both long and short (refer to the attached 13F analysis for more detail on recent long portfolio exposures). I was given access to their historical portfolio information and took down a sampling of long and short portfolio positions at randomly chosen month-end periods. I will conduct a more detailed analysis (to be distributed upon completion). In addition, FCM is working with their prime broker to provide independent verification of exposures, liquidity, and risk statistics.

FCM has been in existence for five years and has made money in each of them (including 2008). They have exhibited strong performance on both the long and short side of the book and have done so in a consistent manner. For example, positive attribution from the short portfolio was significant in multiple years—not just in 2008 as one would expect (refer to the attached performance history and analytical reports for additional information). The firm is currently managing $275 million in assets, with most of the assets coming in after their strong 2008 performance (AUM graph included in attachments). Average market capitalization appears to be about $1B based on the 13F analysis as well as the onsite portfolio review, but they have invested in smaller, less liquid names in the past (prior to 2011) and, as such, we will need to assess how much of their performance came from these less liquid names and determine if they intend to dip that low in market cap in the future. I asked both Ted and Jaime and they stated that they would likely not invest in "micro" cap stocks due to the issue with portfolio liquidity. On that topic, I spoke with Ted (and previously with Jaime on the phone) about underlying position-level liquidity and came away with a strong sense that they would have no issues meeting quarterly redemptions at current asset levels. If we hire FCM we will need to keep a close eye on liquidity to ensure that they stay liquid as promised.

I discussed a number of current as well as previous holdings and have summarized each below:

[The summary of position detail would appear here]

FCM uses a simplistic but seemingly effective stock ranking system that employs the following formula:

$$\frac{projected\ upside}{abs\ val\ projected\ downside} \times correlation \times conviction$$

Correlation ranges from a score of 1 to 5 (with a score of 1 signifying high correlation to the portfolio and a score of 5 signifying low or negative correlation). Conviction represents an arbitrary number between 1 and 5 also (with a score of 5 signifying very strong conviction). They treat their long book and short book as two distinct portfolios; short positions are not used to hedge out exposure from the long book. Instead, they aim to profit from both longs and shorts. This formula is used to calculate a figure for each long and short in the portfolio with long positions ranked against other long positions and short position ranked against short positions (they provided a hard copy of the current rankings for each position in the long and short portfolios, which is included in the attachments).

We discussed performance drivers for each year and I have summarized the main points below:

2007 performance drivers

2008 performance drivers

2009 performance drivers

2010 performance drivers

2011 performance drivers

Ted had a very thorough understanding of current portfolio drivers and was able to provide detail going back to the fund's inception without any notes or use of the computer, which I found pretty impressive. When we went to his desk, he was able to open historical portfolio reports and provided evidence to back up what he had said in the conference room.

We also spoke about the fund's sector concentration. Ted informed me that they are sector agnostic but that he has more of a background in technology and Jaime has more of a background in services and consumer, which explains the fund's historical bent in that direction. I asked how they were comfortable investing in only a few sectors, and he stated that they would invest in a single sector if that was where they found the best opportunities. He went on to say that they have always managed the fund with both longs and shorts and that they would not take the net exposure above 65 percent net long (which they have only exceeded once—in October 2010). Their average net exposure over the life of the fund has been 46 percent and they are comfortable managing the net in the 40 percent to 60 percent range. However, they can take exposure down considerably (and did in 2008). In that year, they found it difficult to find high-conviction long positions and, as a result, their gross long exposure dropped (while they maintained their gross short exposure). This served to decrease both gross and net exposure in late 2007 through 2008 (the fund's net had troughed at −2 percent in July 2008).

Ted stated that while they are not strict contrarians, they do try to avoid crowded hedge fund names and do their best not to be impacted by either positive or negative sentiment coming from Wall Street. They have found that they perform well when they buy high-conviction longs and sell high-conviction shorts. For them it's that simple. When they find more high-conviction stocks, the gross increases, and when they can't find high-conviction stocks, the gross contracts. They have no problem reducing either their long or short books if that is what their stock research tells them. However, in speaking to them it seems pretty clear that they did take top-down factors into consideration in 2008. Specifically, they employed ETFs on the S&P 500 and XLF (financials ETF) after they had covered a number of short positions that had reached their price targets. The ETF positions were used as placeholders until they were comfortable using single-name shorts (until fundamentals mattered again). Additionally, they shorted several bank and mortgage company stocks in late 2007 and 2008. I inquired about their expertise in this area and was told that they had covered financials at GCH and that Joyce (analyst) had taken the lead on these names based on her prior experience with her former employer (I will cover this in detail when I summarize my interview with Joyce).

As a form of checks and balances, Jaime (research director) must approve all stocks before Ted (portfolio manager) can invest either long or short in any names. Ted and Jaime had previously been co-portfolio managers at GCH and I had gone into the meeting concerned that this split might be problematic, but after meeting both Ted and Jaime (as well as the rest of the team), those concerns have been resolved in my view. Jaime has control over the buy/sell list and Ted has control over the portfolio. The interaction that I was able to observe between Ted and Jaime (and from the interviews that I had with their employees) leads me to believe that the two have a strong and mutually respectful relationship. Ted had mentioned that he and Jaime are not just partners but close friends—their families have spent time together, and they think they operate better as a team than either one would operate on their own.

Jaime Wernick

I did not spend much time with Jaime, as I had already spoken to him and had a full day planned meeting with the other members of his firm. However, we did spend some time going through portfolio holdings and reviewing company models on his terminal. All financial models were built out in

Excel and the models themselves were built largely by the team (several were taken from the sell side and adjusted to reflect FCM's assumptions). The models were quite detailed and were generally projected out one to two years (see attachment for hard copy examples of the models and projections created by FCM for hhgregg, Inc. and Fresh Del Monte). Jaime and Ted sit across from each other and it is easy to see how they would be in constant communication. Jaime informed me that he and the team meet formally on Mondays and basically meet right in the trading area, with each person sitting right at his or her desk. The meeting lasts about two hours and occurs between 7:00 am and 9:00 am (leaving time to get up to speed before the markets open at 9:30 am). Topics covered in their formal meeting:

1. Review current portfolio exposures.
2. Discuss upcoming events and current news for all existing holdings.
3. Discuss current pipeline and debate stocks in the final stages of research.
4. Set the research agenda for the upcoming week.

Jaime stated that, given their close proximity, they discuss positions all day long. He gave me a flavor of how it works by asking Joyce about a name they are currently researching (Diamond Foods, Inc—ticker DMND). I observed the two of them go back and forth regarding the model and, specifically, the assumptions that Joyce was using to determine near-term growth. Apparently, they have had a debate about this in the past and Joyce took five minutes to walk Jaime through the model's output. Jaime asked a number of questions—some of which Joyce knew the answer to and others that she did not—and she agreed she needed to make some additional calls and tighten up the model before presenting in the upcoming Monday meeting. I assume that some of this was for show (as I was just a few feet away observing), but the tone and body language indicated to me that this was a fairly typical conversation between the two.

I asked Jaime to show me his research files on some older positions. I asked if he could open the research files for the bank and mortgage companies that they had shorted in 2007/2008. I watched him scan through the directory—they keep all their research on the "r" drive under a folder name titled "previous holdings" (there was also a folder entitled "current holdings"). He opened the previous holdings folder and there appeared to be several hundred subfolders sorted by stock ticker. He scanned the list and opened half a dozen reports. I was able to see that the models were similar to the ones we had reviewed for current holdings. They were all complete (no blank or messed-up cells). I did not have enough time to read through them in detail but they appeared to be in order.

Joyce Modlin

I wanted to meet with Joyce away from the team so asked if we could chat back in the conference room. My meeting with her went quite well. She is still young but she was very impressive. She took me through her experience at Creeson Capital and provided me with names of people I could speak with as a reference (she said she would follow up later with their contact details). The first part of the interview related to her experience and her stock research skills and the second part related to her interaction with the others at the firm.

Strong academic background (Columbia, Wharton) and seemed to have been well schooled at Creeson Capital. We spent time discussing the bank and mortgage stocks that FCM had shorted in 2008. She stated that the idea to look at those companies came from Ted and Jaime but that she feels that she played a role as well. I asked how much of the grunt work on those names she did and she responded that she did it all (under Jaime's guidance). Her knowledge of those names (which by this time had been out of the portfolio for about three years) was solid. She was not as good a presenter as Ted was but she clearly knew her stuff. I have summarized the key points from the stocks we discussed below:

[The summary of position details would appear here]

I asked what she liked and didn't like about working at FCM. She stated that she liked working closely with Ted and Jaime (at Creeson Capital she was just another analyst among a large group of analysts). She feels that she can have an impact on the portfolio by suggesting new research ideas and/or completing research on new names for possible inclusion in the portfolio. I asked when she thought she would be made a partner and I could see that this was an issue with her. She said she would hope at some time in the future they would make her a partner but she was not in any hurry. I asked if she was okay receiving a small percentage of the revenue, and her response was that she expected her compensation to grow as assets have grown (assuming performance is strong). She said that she joined a small firm so that she could (1) play an important role within the firm and (2) grow along with the firm (as an analyst and in terms of compensation).

I asked what she would suggest to Ted and Jaime that they could do to make FCM a better place. She replied that she would like a more formal growth plan so that she (and the others) could see where they were going within the firm. I asked her how important the stock ranking model was to her and she (surprisingly) said that it was just one of many tools. She believes the firm's competitive advantage is their stock research and level of concentration. I asked her to explain. She feels that FCM does strong, nonconsensus research and "put their money where their mouths are" by being more concentrated. She felt that Creeson Capital was too large and overdiversified (with nearly 200 positions across the long and short books)—when they did solid research and were right about a given stock, it never really had much of an impact on performance due to its small weighting. I asked if she felt FCM could be even more concentrated (following Jaime's comments on the phone) and she replied that she felt they managed the portfolio well—she wouldn't change a thing. I asked how many names currently in the portfolio were hers and she replied 12. As this was twice the number that Ted had given me, I asked if they were all hers or if she was directed to do research. Her response was that she was the lead analyst on 12 names right now and that she had another 15 or so she was working on.

I asked her to take me back to her desk and show me how she researches a stock. We went back to their offices and she opened a current research file (Acco Brands) and walked me through her work. Her files were in a folder labeled "pipeline" on their "r" drive. I was able to see that they had a large number of subfolders for stocks currently in the pipeline (somewhere between 30 and 40).

Charles Reiter

I sat with Charlie for a brief time at his desk to go through his experience and see some work samples. He spent a few years as an investment banker at Giles & Massey and was hired by FCM in 2011 as a junior analyst. He took me through two current holdings for which he has primary responsibility (Hi Tech Pharma and Krispy Kreme). His work appeared to be as detail oriented as that of the others. As I did with Joyce, I asked him to open up his work files for those names and found the files to be complete.

Jacob Holder

Jacob has been with FCM for four years and is largely an execution trader. He has the authority to buy and sell within discrete ranges set by Ted. He is not authorized to put on any risk and can only take off risk if the order comes from Ted. He has room to trade into and out of positions but that is about all. I asked if he had enough work to do trading and he replied that he spends about half of his time trading and the other half assisting Jaime in stock research. Jacob has a decade of experience at three different investment firms and likes his role at FCM, as it keeps him in the flow of trading as well as keeping him involved in company research. I asked him if he was responsible for any names, but Jaime popped his head up and said that Jacob's main function is trading and he assists others in their research as opposed to taking the lead on company research. I watched Jacob as Jaime said this and could see that he did not like Jaime's response. We then spent a few moments going through some recent trades and discussed how he legged into Revlon (a recent purchase) over the last few days and how he had covered Select Comfort (a former short) just yesterday. When Jacob started to discuss Select Comfort, Jaime popped up again and said that this was an example of a short that moved against them quickly and they got out (at a 10 percent to 12 percent loss). I asked why they covered (as it was well within the −20 percent drawdown) and he stated that they just got the growth assumptions wrong. They did not expect that people would continue to buy expensive beds while unemployment hovered at 9 percent but that assumption has been wrong thus far. Based on Jacob's workload as an execution trader in a firm that does not trade all that much, I would not be surprised to see him leave at some point (unless his role as an analyst is elevated at some point).

Follow-up List

- Conduct operational due diligence.
  - Interview COO and CFO.
  - Verify arrangements with service providers (administrator, prime broker, auditor, etc.).
  - Perform thorough document review.
  - Perform legal review of firm and fund.
  - Perform review of annual fund audits.

- Conduct a risk assessment of the fund.
  - Qualitative assessment of investment personnel and risk manager.
  - Quantitative assessment.
  - Risk philosophy, methodology, limits.

- Reference checks for key team members (emphasis on the principals).
  - Start with "on list" references.
  - Search for "off list" references and contact them.

- Use position-level information from the onsite meeting to:
  - Assess historical liquidity.
  - Verify historical attribution/exposure data previously provided by the fund manager.
  - Better understand investment strategy and style.
  - Assess shorting skills.

- Verify the stock-level information that they provided.
- Speak with COO to determine if FCM will provide access to portfolio and risk reports from the prime broker and/or administrator
- Determine quality of the fund's more recent clients (performance chasing?).
- Conduct background checks on the three principals.

CHAPTER 9

Operational Due Diligence

"Nothing is so firmly believed as that which we least know."
Michel de Montaigne

"The greatest obstacle to discovery is not ignorance—it is the illusion of knowledge."
Daniel J. Boorstin

Operational
Analysis

Step Six

When we think about the myriad number of things that can cause a hedge fund to fail, what immediately comes to mind are issues surrounding the investment professionals, process, and fund performance. When investors analyze a hedge fund, they tend to focus on the return they expect from the hedge fund in the context of the underlying fund risk. After all, very few hedge funds are hired because they employ multiple offsite data services or because their compliance manual is particularly well written. However, operational due diligence (ODD) is a critical aspect of hedge fund due diligence. The following case study is a perfect example of why ODD is important.

CASE STUDY: BAYOU FUND

While there are many good examples that illustrate the importance of operational due diligence, the plight of Samuel Israel III, Daniel Marino, and James Marquez is quite remarkable and reads more like fiction than fact. The story of Bayou Group is a cautionary tale of hedge fund fraud involving falsified pedigrees, fake auditing results, clear conflicts of interest, multiple staged suicides, fictitious investment returns, international intrigue, and a nationwide manhunt.

Sam Israel III was able to raise an estimated $450 million from investors into his family of hedge funds between 1996 and August 2005. Israel came from a "good" family (his grandfather built a commodity business that merged into Donaldson, Lufkin & Jenrette) and he had worked alongside a legend in the hedge fund industry, Leon Cooperman of Omega Advisors, heading that firm's execution trading in futures and equities. Investors seemed to be attracted to Bayou's steady and conservative return stream (as opposed to extreme returns that might be viewed as "too good to be true"). In addition, Bayou did not charge a base (management) fee, instead charging clients only 20 percent of profits, which is not a common practice among hedge funds. Lastly, Bayou employed a top-tier auditor to perform its annual fund audits, which were made available to all clients and prospects and assured their clients that Bayou's brokerage arm, Bayou Securities, was periodically audited by the NASD and SEC (implying further regulatory scrutiny of the Bayou funds).

Sounds like a potentially attractive investment on paper; unfortunately, Israel's fund was a complete scam, and many of the things that Bayou touted to investors as "best practices" and reasons to trust them were either nonexistent or falsified.

Red Flags

- No independent auditor—Bayou claimed that Grant Thornton was its auditor, but in reality the fund was audited by an accounting firm called Richmond Fairfield Associates, which listed Daniel Marino as its managing agent (a clear conflict of interest). Additional scrutiny of this firm indicated that it employed just three employees (including Marino) and did business out of a residential address. Bayou was Richmond Fairfield's only client and the financial statements it prepared for the Bayou funds were fake.
- No independent board of directors—Bayou's BOD consisted of just Israel and Marino. It did not include any independent oversight. In 2004, the BOD approved the transfer of $100 million from the hedge fund to Israel's personal account for trading in his own name.
- Previous regulatory issues and litigation—An ex-partner had previously accused the firm of securities fraud, alleging the misappropriation of $7 million from a fund trading account. Additionally, the NASD had previously fined both Israel and Marino.

- Falsified pedigree—in company marketing materials, Israel had indicated he had graduated from Tulane University when he had not and that he had worked as head of execution trading at Omega Advisors for the previous four years (he worked at Omega for just 18 months and it was later determined that his role was more administrative in nature).
- Affiliated broker dealer—Bayou's marketing materials claimed that the commissions generated by their affiliated broker dealer were credited back to the fund, but this was difficult to analyze and the cross ownership increased the potential for fraudulent activity. This commission rebating was a method Israel employed to prop up his fund's poor performance.
- Decreasing investor communication—toward the end, communication with clients went from good to bad to nothing.
- Significant dispersion between the fund's onshore and offshore funds—while a certain level of dispersion is acceptable, the difference between the two was significant, and it is reported that Bayou communicated to certain clients that they had diverted profitable trades from the onshore fund to the offshore fund to improve its performance and help attract new assets.

Daniel Marino wrote the following passage in a six-page suicide letter: "If there is a hell I will certainly be there for eternity." He did not follow through with the suicide and is now spending time in jail for his crimes. After Israel did appear for his prison sentence in June 2008, the press speculated that he might have committed suicide when his abandoned car was found on the Bear Mountain Bridge ("Suicide is painless" was written in dust on the car's hood). He didn't follow through either. In fact, he hid from authorities until he turned himself in to a small-town police station nearly a month later. Just to show that people who commit fraud can also be duped, in a last-ditch effort to make back all the money that he had lost while managing the fund, Israel attempted to invest the last $100 million in the Bayou fund in a scheme referred to as "prime bank investment fraud." Israel was deceived into thinking that he could achieve eye-popping returns by investing the money with an elite group of traders that would buy securities privately at a large discount, then turn around and sell the securities to the market at face value (he was told that the $100 million investment would return over $10 billion over a 10-year period).

DEFINITION

Operational due diligence is as important to the overall hedge fund evaluation process as investment due diligence. The graphic in Figure 9.1 is meant

FIGURE 9.1 Interconnectedness of Different Components of
Due Diligence Process

to illustrate that the three broad components of due diligence are meant to
work together, and if any one aspect of the due diligence process is weak, it
will weaken the whole process.

Each component of the process is connected to the others and should not
be performed in a vacuum. While most institutional firms have professionals
that specialize in each of the three areas, it is important to recognize that
a great deal of information about a hedge fund's operations can be gleaned
while conducting investment-related due diligence and vice versa. In addition,
because investment due diligence typically involves interviewing a different
group of people within a hedge fund than either risk or operational due
diligence, a due diligence team that works together and shares information
can compare and contrast information from multiple perspectives.

I consider operational due diligence to embody all aspects of analysis that
do not implicitly include investment and risk analysis (though there may be
and likely will be crossover). When conducting operational due diligence it
is important to understand that there are three types of negative results:

- Failure to meet minimum standards—hedge fund investors should set a
  series of minimum standards and apply them to all hedge funds currently

in their portfolios and any funds that come under review. Minimum standards can include things like independent administration, defined and appropriate valuation policies, independent board of directors, and so on.

- Red flag(s)—assuming a hedge fund meets the minimum standards, there may exist one or more major red flags, any of which would dismiss the investment. Examples include past regulatory sanctions, insufficient operational staff, liquidity mismatch, and the like.
- Multiple yellow flags—in this scenario, a hedge fund meets all minimum standards and has not triggered any red flags (significant issues) but has multiple small issues that when taken together might produce a negative opinion. Examples include mistakes in documents, poorly constructed marketing materials, non-key personnel turnover, and so forth.

IMPORTANCE OF OPERATIONAL DUE DILIGENCE

The pie chart in Figure 9.2 breaks out an analysis of hedge fund failures compiled by Capco Research[1] in a working paper entitled "Understanding and Mitigating Operational Risk in Hedge Fund Investments." The paper was published in 2002 but its message is as meaningful today as it was

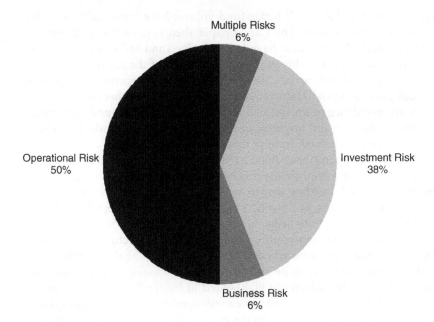

FIGURE 9.2 Analysis of Past Hedge Fund Failures

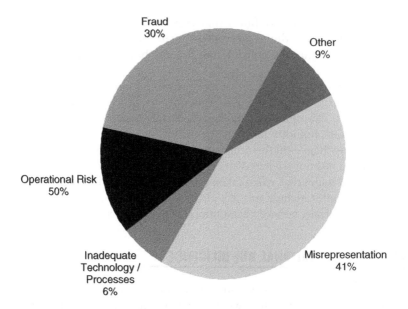

FIGURE 9.3   Analysis of Hedge Fund Operational Issues

then—more than half of all hedge fund failures have historically been due to noninvestment causes. The Capco paper then goes on to break out the main operational issues that have led to hedge fund failures (Figure 9.3). The interesting aspect of this analysis is that many of the reasons often cited as operational failures can be caught in a detailed and thorough operational due diligence analysis. Unfortunately, there is no set checklist that will guarantee avoidance of operational issues or fraud. Hedge funds are staffed by some of the best and brightest people in the investment industry, and as due diligence has evolved, so have misleading and fraudulent activities.

A dedicated operational due diligence effort that is geared toward evaluating a hedge fund prior to investment and then maintaining a high level of vigilance is the only and best way to avoid or to greatly diminish the prospect of operational failures. In Ernst & Young's "Coming of Age: Global Hedge Fund Survey 2011,"[2] both hedge funds and hedge fund investors were asked what the three most important criteria were when selecting hedge funds. Hedge fund managers were asked to put themselves in the shoes of the hedge fund allocator in this exercise and investors were asked to rank their own criteria. The results, which are highlighted in Figure 9.4, are enlightening. Hedge fund managers believe that the most significant factor in getting hired is long-term performance (72 percent of them thought it ranked in the top

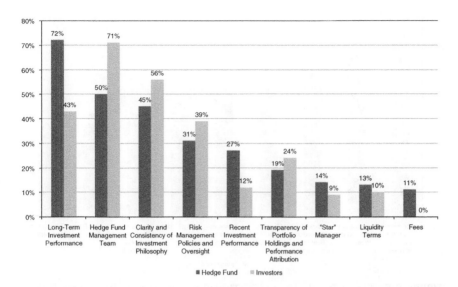

FIGURE 9.4 Survey Results: Key Criteria When Selecting Hedge Funds

three), while only 43 percent of the investors ranked long-term performance in their top three. Hedge fund investors ranked the investment team as the most important criterion (71 percent), followed by clarity and consistency of investment performance (56 percent). What I found particularly interesting is that criterion labeled "risk management policies and oversight" was voted as in the top three criteria by just 31 percent of the hedge funds surveyed and 39 percent of the hedge fund investors surveyed. Just a few years after the 2008 financial crisis and risk policies/management have already been knocked out of the top three considerations by two-thirds of the investors when they evaluate a hedge fund.

In the same Ernst & Young "Coming of Age" report, investors were also surveyed to determine what red flags caused them to drop a hedge fund from consideration after it had passed their initial screening. Figure 9.5 ranks the responses from most to least important. The top five red flags were all noninvestment related. The number one red flag was concern over risk management and policies. So the respondents do not consider risk management to be in the top three reasons to hire a hedge fund, but they consider it the top reason not to hire a fund. I believe that the results of this survey are critically important in understanding just how important operational due diligence is in overall hedge fund evaluation. A talented hedge fund manager with a storied pedigree who manages a hedge fund with a true edge that is projected to generate significant alpha may be passed on as an investment based on

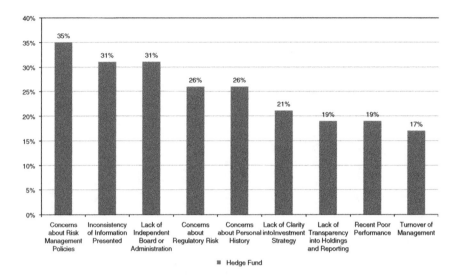

FIGURE 9.5   Survey Results: Red Flags That Cause Investors to Pass on Investing with a Hedge Fund

operational weaknesses. Operational due diligence is akin to wheels on a car; no matter how nice the car looks and how finely tuned the engine, it will not get anywhere without the wheels.

Potential Operational Issues

- Code of ethics violation.
- Reputation.
- Culture.
- ADV disclosures.
- Policy revisions.
- Personnel turnover.
- Investor concentration.
- Reduction in internal investment.
- Negative media.
- Less than full-service administration.
- No offsite BCP/DR (or no formal plans/policy at all).
- Affiliated broker-dealer.
- No formal valuation policy.
- Outside interests.
- Financial stability of the company.
- Scalability of the business.

- Insufficient technical and/or personnel resources.
- Conflicts of interest.
- Key man risk.
- Financial statement concerns.
- Timing of financial statements.
- Compliance procedures.
- Fund expenses.
- Restatement of NAV.
- Business risk.
- Firm's profitability.
- Tax treatment.
- Shadow reconciliation.

CATEGORIZATION OF OPERATIONAL DUE DILIGENCE

Operational due diligence covers a wide array of major and minor topics. Table 9.1 breaks out the major review categories in five different areas (the five P's).

Documents to Request

Here is a fairly comprehensive list of documents to request when conducting an evaluation of a hedge fund's operations. Based on the domicile of the fund under review, some of these documents might not apply. Several of these documents would likely be requested during the investment portion of the due diligence process (presentation, DDQ, monthly letters) so it is important to keep interdepartmental communication open.

- Offering of private placement memorandum.
- Subscription documents.
- Articles of association.
- LP agreement.
- Certificate of incorporation.
- Certificate of good standing.
- ISDA agreements.
- Audited financial statements.
- Due diligence questionnaire.
- Pitchbook.
- Historical investor letters.
- Historical risk reports.

TABLE 9.1 Operational Categories—The 5 P's

People	Providers	Process	Policy	Product
CFO	Administrator	Trade Life Cycle	Compliance Manual	Base Fee
COO	Prime Broker(s)	Cash Flows	Code of Ethics	Incentive Fee
CCO	Auditor(s)	Shadow Reconciliation	Valuation	Subscription Fee
CTO	Information Technology	Business Continuity	Board of Directors	Redemption Fee
Business Planning	Legal	Disaster Recovery	Personal Trading	Subscription Frequency
Turnover	Internal Systems	Cash Controls	Transparency	Redemption Frequency
Powers	External Systems	Cash Management	Reporting	Redemption Notice Period
Reputation	Insurance	Outsourcing	Anti–Money Laundering	Lockup
Pedigree	Custodian		Know Your Client	Penalties
Board of Directors	Brokers		Other Business Interests	Gates
	Banks			Side pockets
	Stock Loan & Repo			

- Historical exposure reports.
- Performance information (with appropriate disclosures).
- Compliance manual.
- Personal trading procedures manual.
- Anti–money laundering and know your client policy.
- Communication policy.
- Organizational chart.
- Fund structure chart.
- Business continuity plan.
- Disaster recovery plan.
- Valuation policy.
- Insurance coverage and providers (copies of insurance certificates).
- ADV I, II, Schedule F (if currently or previously registered with the SEC).
- Employee turnover list (all hires and fires—dates and responsibilities).
- Service provider list (with contact details).
- Client breakout (by type and size).
- Details of side letters and managed accounts.
- List of any regulatory violations.
- Disclosure of any conflicts of interest.
- Disclose of any outside businesses.
- AUM history (all funds).

People

When conducting operational due diligence on a hedge fund one of the critical areas to evaluate is the size and quality of the fund's operational team. There is no set formula that will determine the number of people that will be able to efficiently and effectively run a fund's operations because that is dependent upon a number of factors, such as instruments used by the fund manager, number of offices, location of offices, number of counterparties, number of funds managed, and so on. When I evaluate a hedge fund's operations I generally look for the following:

1. Dedicated operations personnel.
    Hedge funds should emphasize a clear separation of duties among the front, middle, and back offices. Portfolio managers and analysts should spend their time focusing on managing the fund, not worrying about International Swaps and Derivatives Association (ISDA) agreements.

2. Fund is able to meet minimum standards.

   Minimum standards can include independent administration, valuation policy, independent auditor, specific levels of transparency, and so on. It is important for any hedge fund under review to have the right plans and policies in place to meet (and preferably exceed) these minimum standards.
3. Operations personnel have appropriate backgrounds.
4. Operations personnel can properly discharge their duties.
5. Clear and well-thought-out growth plan (both systems and people).

A small equity long/short fund that does not trade often would not need a large back office, whereas a global macro shop with multiple portfolio managers trading dozens of global financial instruments with offices in the United States, London, and Hong Kong would require a full team of operations specialists. In the case of the former, I would prefer to see at least one dedicated individual who would likely have a COO/CFO title but would prefer two to three people (CFO, COO, admin support). In the case of the macro hedge fund, I would expect full separation of duties within the back office, which would result in a much larger team.

When evaluating operational professionals, we apply the same standards that we use when we evaluate investment professionals. A CFO should have had actual experience as a CFO at a hedge fund. In fact, it is important to understand what kind of hedge fund the CFO previously worked for. For example, we would want a CFO with experience negotiating ISDA agreements working at a macro fund but should be somewhat leery if the CFO only had prior experience at an equity long/short fund, where ISDA agreements are not as relevant. It is not uncommon for smaller hedge funds not to have dedicated chief compliance officers and chief technology officers. Smaller hedge funds typically assign these functions to existing operational personnel or outsource them to firms that specialize in compliance or information technology.

When evaluating a hedge fund's operations it is important to understand the firm's culture and working environment as well. Is the firm a good place to work? Does the firm retain employees or is turnover high? In the "documents to request" section, I listed a line item that asks the hedge fund to list all hires and departures for a period of time. I like to review this list going back three to five years if the firm/fund has been around that long. Small firms should have no problem providing this information, but larger shops (and there are hedge funds with more than 1,000 employees) may give you some pushback. In that case, ask for hires and departures of key personnel (but be clear as to what "key" means to you). Companies are typically happy to provide lists of people that they have hired, so scour that list and when you see that someone important was hired on a certain date, ask if that was to replace anyone (this is a backdoor way of asking about departures).

When reviewing operational documents, write all comments and questions in your hedge fund journal (Figure 4.11). I list each professional separately and write down their respective responsibilities as well as my interpretation of their actual powers. It is one thing to have a fancy title; it is something quite different to have actual authority. As an example, FCM's COO is also the risk manager; however, we found out when we spoke to Jaime that he does not have the power to take off any risk. Instead, he can only bring issues to the portfolio manager's attention. While this may not be a reason to drop them as a candidate in our search, it is certainly not optimal.

Providers

In the sections that follow, we will define and discuss each of the service providers that were detailed in Table 9.1.

Administrator   One of the minimum standards mentioned previously is for a hedge fund to have an independent administrator. Administrators provide a number of services, but one of the most important is to independently calculate a hedge fund's net asset valuation (NAV) on a monthly basis (or more frequently depending on the individual hedge fund's liquidity terms). The vast majority of hedge funds today employ independent administrators for this function, but there are still a few holdouts. However, it is important to understand what level of service an administrator has been hired to provide to the fund. Full-service administration means the administrator values the positions and calculates the fund's NAV on its own, independently from the hedge fund. Other variations include "NAV Light," where the administrator does not keep its own independent records; instead, they simply do a sanity check on the NAV that the hedge fund calculated themselves or use security prices provided to them by the hedge fund. When evaluating the NAV calculation services that an administrator provides to a hedge fund, it is important to understand whether or not the administrator checks reported positions back to the prime broker statements to confirm that the assets actually exist. Does the administrator obtain prices on its own or check the prices provided by the hedge fund? If they do check prices, do they check all prices or do a sampling?

There are a number of independent administrators in existence today and there are also a number of others that are part of larger organizations (such as banks). When evaluating administrators it is just as important to know and evaluate the person or team that is in charge of working with the hedge fund under review as it is to assess the firm itself.

Primary Administrator Services
- Calculation of the net asset value.
- Fee calculations.
- Preparation of semiannual and annual accounts.
- Keep the fund's financial books and records.
- Pay fund expenses.
- Reconcile broker statements.
- Settlement of daily trades.
- Pricing of securities.
- Calculation and payment of dividends and distributions.
- Oversee orderly liquidation and dissolution of fund.
- Partnership accounting.
- Performance calculation.
- Distribution of statements to clients.
- Distribution of offering materials to prospective clients.
- Oversee subscriptions and redemptions.
- Apply anti–money laundering and know your client rules.

In addition to understanding the type of administrative services employed, it is imperative to work with hedge funds that use top-tier (top-quality) service providers. Table 9.2 highlights the 10 largest administrators based on assets under administration for the end of the second quarter of

TABLE 9.2 Largest Administrators by Assets as of 2Q 2011

Rank	Administrator	2Q 2011 Assets ($B)	# of HFs
1	Citco Fund Services	507	2,017
2	State Street Alternative Investment Solutions	417	830
3	BNY Mellon Alternative Investment Services	283	1,350
4	Goldman Sachs Administration Services	213	538
5	Citi Hedge Fund Services	187	979
6	GlobeOp Financial Services	174	n/a
7	Northern Trust	150	244
8	Morgan Stanley Fund Services	128	n/a
9	SS&C Fund Services	125	n/a
10	HSBC Securities Services	124	646

2011. The list was compiled by Hedgefund.net in their "2Q 2011 HFN Hedge Fund Administrator Survey."

The size of the administrator does not dictate how good they are, but it does imply top-notch systems and less business risk. When evaluating a hedge fund's administrator, it is important to make sure that they have the expertise and infrastructure to properly perform their functions. In addition, it is important to conduct site visits with service providers to establish and maintain relationships with the individuals that work on the hedge funds in your portfolio and under review as well as to continuously monitor their services and systems (which will evolve over time).

In recent years, there has been some consolidation in this industry and I expect that trend to continue. In addition, fund administrators also provide aggregation and certification services to hedge fund investors. For example, as hedge fund investors we are always looking to verify information that is sent to us. If a hedge fund provides you a monthly report that lists its assets under management, liquidity of underlying investments, counterparty balances, and so on, then it would be valuable to receive independent verification from the administrator.

These reports are valuable but they are produced by the hedge fund manager and, as such, there is no independent verification that the information is accurate. To fill this void, some administrators have begun to provide transparency reports that independently verify these important figures (for a fee, naturally). After all, the administrator is in a great position because they see all positions and independently price them. These reports provide hedge fund investors with the following:

- Levels of independent pricing.
- Asset and liability balances.
- Aggregated pricing data (Level I, II, II assets).
- Fund liquidity.
- Percentage of valuations independently obtained.

When conducting operational due diligence on a hedge fund's service providers, contact them yourself to verify the inception date of the relationship, services provided, changes to services provided, and any issues that have arisen. Remember that the administrator works for the fund, not the investor, so ask the hedge fund manager to call the administrator in advance so that they will speak more openly with you. In addition, when you continuously speak with operational service providers you will create your own network of people whom you can call upon when you have questions or issues.

Questions to Ask

- What is the administrator contracted to do for the firm/fund? Provide a detailed list of all current and past services provided.
- What are the terms of your agreement with the administrator?
- How often do you reconcile trades/prices?
- Do they provide full NAV calculation? If not, describe what they do.
- What is the estimated delivery schedule you have in place with the administrator? (When do they deliver initial NAV estimates, final NAV figures, etc.?)
- How long have you employed the administrator?
- Provide the name and contact details for the person or people that work on your account.
- Are you happy with the level of service that you receive? Are you happy with the people specifically assigned to your account?
- Have there been any personnel changes at the administrator relating to people that worked on your account? Ask for details. This is important because we need to understand who is doing the work on the fund we are reviewing. Turnover at the administrator may be meaningful if the turnover is related specifically to the fund under review (i.e., people have had a hard time working on the account and, as a result, we see a history of turnover). In addition, I find it encouraging when a hedge fund knows exactly who is (and was) working on their account and can put the service in a historical perspective—it gives me a better sense that they are on top of things.
- How much does the administrator charge and what is the expense (in basis points) charged to the fund annually? Has this changed? Provide a historical accounting of the charges expensed to the fund.
- Have you changed administrators? If so:
  - Name the previous administrator(s).
  - Specific reason(s) for change (be on the lookout for changes due to disagreements over valuation, NAV calculation, etc.).
  - Date(s) of change.
- Have you had any disagreements with any of the administrator's work? If so, what was the issue and how was it resolved?
- Can the administrator provide copies of all historical annual fund audits? This is done as an independent check (recall that Bayou basically created their own fictitious audited financial reports and passed them off as real). Audit firms are generally hesitant to send out the financial statements to investors (remember that the auditors work for the fund, not the investor); however, they do send the financial statements to a fund's administrator—so if we receive the audited financial statements

from a fund's administrator (not from the hedge fund directly), we can view that as an independent check—but ask them to verify this.

- When speaking to the administrator directly, ask:
  - How many hedge funds does the firm service?
  - With regard to the people assigned to the hedge fund under review, how many hedge funds do they service?
  - What is their procedure for calculating pricing and NAV calculation? Who actually crunches the numbers? Who signs off on their work?
  - What records do they maintain?
  - Have they ever had any disagreements with the hedge fund regarding NAV calculation (or anything else)?
  - Has the hedge fund ever overridden the administrator's process or NAV calculations?
  - Have they experienced personnel turnover relating to professionals that work on the hedge fund's account?

Auditors   One of the best sources available to verify information reported to us by hedge funds can be found in the fund's annual audited financial statements. It is important to read all audited financial statements. For example, if you invest in a hedge fund's onshore feeder, then you need to review the annual audits of that feeder, but you should also review the audit of the offshore fund and any other fund audits that may be available. You can compile this information in the due diligence journal to verify statements made by the hedge fund manager or to open a new line of questioning. When reviewing audited financial statements make sure you check to see if the auditor's opinion is qualified or unqualified (or adverse). In addition, make sure to read all the footnotes. Some of the best information can often be found in the footnotes.

Audit firms prepare these annual (and sometimes more frequent) audits, but they also assist hedge funds in maintaining their books and records, and assist with a fund's internal accounting, tax planning, and regulatory compliance.

When assessing a hedge fund's audit firm, it is critical to evaluate the overall quality of the firm doing the audit. The big four accounting firms are at the top of the pyramid, followed by national audit firms and then regional firms. In addition to assessing the quality of the firm, it is important to understand the quality of the actual individuals at the firm that are conducting the audit on behalf of the hedge fund. As with all service providers, you should contact the audit firm to verify the services they are providing, the length of service, and to verify the number of annual audits that they completed for the hedge fund. For newly established hedge funds, you can check to see if an engagement letter has been signed.

Questions to Ask

- What is the auditor contracted to do for the firm/fund? Provide a detailed list of all current and past services provided.
- What are the terms of your agreement with the auditor?
- How long have you employed the auditor?
- Provide the name and contact details for the person or people that work on your account.
- Are you happy with the level of service that you receive? Are you happy with the people specifically assigned to your account?
- Have there been any personnel changes at the auditor relating to people that worked on your account? Ask for details. It is important to know who had done the work previously and why they are no longer working on the account (especially if they are still working at the firm).
- How much does the auditor charge and what is the expense (in basis points) charged to the fund annually? Has this changed? Provide a historical accounting of the charges expensed to the fund.
- Have you changed auditors? If so:
  - Name the previous auditor(s).
  - Specific reason(s) for change.
  - Date(s) of change.
- Have you had any disagreements with any of the auditor's work? If so, what was the issue and how was it resolved?
- Ask the hedge fund if they could direct the auditor to e-mail you the historical audited financial statements directly (not likely to happen, but worth a try).

Prime Broker   Banks and securities firms offer bundled packages of services to hedge funds that are referred to as "prime brokerage." Prime brokers provide hedge funds with custodial services (clearing, custody, and asset servicing), financing (leverage of client assets), trading, securities lending, capital introduction, systems, research, office space, risk management, and other assorted consulting services.

Questions to Ask

- Provide a list of all current prime brokers under contract with the fund.
- Provide a historical accounting of any prime brokers employed by the fund.
- If they have added or fired any prime brokers in their history, ask why.
- Ask for a detailed list of services provided by each prime broker employed by the fund (many hedge funds employ multiple prime brokers).

- What are the terms of your agreement with the prime brokers?
- Does the hedge fund use any of the systems and/or software provided by the prime broker? Ask for details (which systems, when they started to use them, why they use them).
- Does the hedge fund trade through their prime brokers? If so, provide details (activity, costs).
- Provide the name and contact details for the person or people that work on your account.
- Are you happy with the level of service that you receive? Are you happy with the people specifically assigned to your account?
- Ask the hedge fund manager if they would direct their prime broker(s) to provide summary level risk reports (so that we can verify assets under management, liquidity, exposures, risk levels).
- Is the prime broker the custodian of the hedge fund's assets? If so, does the prime broker employ subcustodians (provide details)?
- Are assets held at the prime broker in the fund's name? Are cash balances at the prime broker held in the fund's name?
- Does the prime broker provide trade-level and position-level information directly to the administrator?
- How much leverage will the prime broker provide and what is the basis on which it is provided?
- What other resources does the prime broker provide to you?
- Provide details for the following:
  - Stock borrow.
  - IPO allocations.
  - Fees for trade execution, clearance charges.
  - Stock lending costs.
  - Financing rates.
  - Capital introductions.
  - Research.
  - Systems.
- Has the prime broker ever closed or altered credit lines? When? Why?
- Have you negotiated for better fees and/or services with your prime broker(s)?
- Do you work through any intermediary parties (i.e., introducing prime brokers)?
- If the hedge fund employs a multiprime model, how do they aggregate data? (Make sure that the administrator receives information from each of the hedge fund's prime brokers.)

Information Technology Hedge funds can employ many systems in the day-to-day management of their hedge fund as well as the day-to-day management of the firm's operations. Examples of systems that may be used include trade flow, research, accounting, and client relationship management (CRM). These systems can be off-the-shelf third-party systems or they can be unique, internally programmed systems. It is important to understand who provides and supports the systems.

Information technology is a critical aspect of a hedge fund's day-to-day business and, as such, it is important to evaluate a hedge fund's information technology (IT) service providers. Often smaller hedge funds will outsource their IT function to an external firm. In this case, we should determine the quality of the service provider as well as the level of services that they provide. Contact the service provider directly and verify everything that the hedge fund has indicated that they do. Verify the term of the relationship and, if it is a new relationship, ask the hedge fund whom they used in the past (and call them, too). Get detailed information about the IT service provider directly from the provider (as opposed to the hedge fund) so that you can evaluate whether or not they are of appropriate quality and can fulfill the hedge fund's needs. Ask the provider what the systems were like when they were first hired and try to glean any additional information about the hedge fund from their unique perspective. Last, ask service providers if they work with any other hedge funds. Ask if they have been impressed or underwhelmed by any of them. While I can't say that I have gotten much information about hedge funds from IT service providers, on one occasion I was able to get information that led me to drop a particular fund from consideration (you never know where actionable information can come from, so ask everyone for their views).

A useful method of evaluating the hedge fund manager's internal processes is to inquire about the search process that they employed when looking to add or change service providers. Ask how they determined the universe of candidates, how they narrowed it down to the finalists, and ultimately, how they selected the winner. Ask how they negotiated the terms and how they rate and track their service providers. This can offer some insight into how the operations group works, which is one additional data point to consider when evaluating their overall quality.

Questions to Ask
- Who is responsible for information technology internally? (Interview them separately.)
  - What are their qualifications?
  - Are they dedicated or do they wear multiple hats?
- If the hedge fund has multiple offices, do they have a person responsible for IT in each office or is it managed in one specific office? If multiple people are tasked with this responsibility, ask for details.

- Provide a detailed list of all systems and software used within the firm. (Make note of which versions of third-party software they use and compare to the latest versions.)

- Designate what is proprietary and what is third party.
- Who designed and programmed the proprietary software and systems? Are they still with the firm? If not, who manages the software and updates code?
- When was the last time the systems and hardware were updated?
- How often are proprietary and third-party systems updated or upgraded?
- Do you test your systems periodically? If so, provide details.

- Do you have a review and/or testing policy? If so, provide details.
- Do you plan on doing any updates and/or upgrades in the future? If so, ask for details (what, when, why, cost).
- Ask for a detailed list of the hardware the firm employs.
- How does the firm decide whether or not to update or upgrade hardware and software? Who decides? What are the criteria used?
- Does the hedge fund see any current weaknesses in their information technology (systems, relationships, personnel)? If so, what are they and how do they plan to resolve the issue(s)?
- Has the hedge fund engaged the IT service provider to come into their offices on a regular basis for systems maintenance or do they call the provider only when they have a problem? Ask for details (and verify with the service provider directly).
- Has the IT provider assigned a specific individual to the hedge fund manager's account or do they randomly assign technicians based on availability?

Legal Law firms help in the creation of hedge fund company structures as well as the creation of the underlying hedge fund vehicles. Hedge funds with both onshore and offshore funds will employ multiple law firms to handle their affairs based on jurisdiction (a Cayman lawyer for funds registered in the Cayman Islands, etc.). Most law firms that specialize in hedge fund creation tend to work from templates and make changes based on each hedge fund's individual constraints (if you read enough offering memorandums, you will likely be able to identify which law firm assisted in its creation).

Questions to Ask

- Who are the firm and fund's legal advisors? (Make sure to get names for onshore as well as offshore entities.)
- What services do the law firms provide?
- Have you changed law firms in the past? If so, who and why?
- Does the law firm provide any compliance services? If so, ask for details.
- Has the hedge fund ever been visited or audited by any regulatory body? If so:
  - Which regulatory body?
  - What date(s)?
  - What were the findings?
- Has the firm or any employee of the firm ever been sanctioned by a regulatory body?
- Are internal communications monitored? If so, provide details.

Insurance   Check the business efficacy and ratings for any insurance providers. As with other service providers, review any insurance certificates and verify directly with the insurer that the documents are real and that the policy terms provided to you by the hedge fund are accurate. Types of insurance typically include errors and omissions (E&O), directors and officer liability (D&O), and/or general partner liability. Hedge funds may also take out insurance coverage on specific key individuals within the firm.

Questions to Ask

- What kind of insurance coverage does the firm/fund have?
- What are the terms?
- Who are the providers?
- Who/what is covered?
- Who is paying for the insurance (fund or firm)?
- Who (or what entities) are the named beneficiaries?
- Does the insurance policy exclude specific events?
- Ask to receive a copy of the insurance certificates.

Custodian   Custodians hold a hedge fund's cash and securities. Prime brokers often provide custodial services to hedge funds. It is important to determine whether or not the cash and securities held by the custodian are in the name of the underlying hedge fund or in the custodian's name. If the assets are held in the custodian's name, then, in case of a liquidation (such as Lehman), it may become harder for the hedge fund to reclaim those assets.

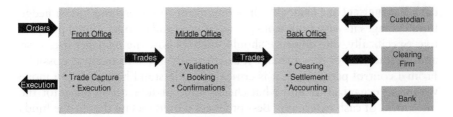

FIGURE 9.6 Simple Example of Life Cycle of a Trade

Process

The next category we will review focuses on a hedge fund's internal processes.

Trade Life Cycle The trade life cycle refers to the workflow associated with a particular investment decision. The life cycle starts with trade origination and follows through to settlement. Within a hedge fund, it will typically involve the trading group (trade origination and execution) and the operations group (trade validation, confirmation, clearing, and settlement). Figure 9.6 is a very simplified representation of how a trade can be accomplished within a hedge fund.

Questions to Ask

- Who makes the trade decisions?
- How are the decisions communicated?
- Who has the authority to trade?
- How are orders placed?
- How are orders tracked/documented/confirmed?
- Who reviews/confirms the trades?
- If there is more than one fund, how are trades allocated among them? How is this checked?
- How often does a trade break? Provide examples.
- How do you remedy trade breaks?
- Who reconciles trades?
- Describe the reconciliation process.
- What trading system (trade capture system) do you employ? Has this changed over time?
- Do you employ straight through processing (electronically process trades without any manual intervention)?
- What is the settlement timing (time needed to process the trade after the trade date)?
- Has the settlement timing changed? If so, why?

Cash Management and Controls   It is important to understand how a hedge fund manages its cash both from an investment and an operational perspective. Specifically, due diligence should uncover how the manager uses cash and whether or not they manage it as efficiently and effectively as possible. From a control perspective, it is critical to understand how cash can move within an organization and what checks and balances are in place for the movement of cash externally. Best practices would dictate that hedge funds require multiple signatories to approve the movement of cash. In addition, it would be optimal for at least one of those signatories to be someone other than the portfolio manager—it would be even better for one of the signatories to be someone completely independent from the hedge fund itself (such as a senior member of the fund's administrator). You may recall from the Bayou Capital example at the beginning of this chapter that the hedge fund manager was able to move $100 million out of the fund to a personal account because the firm did not have any independent checks and balances (or any independent board members).

Questions to Ask
  ▪ What is the typical level of cash? (Ask for historical levels of cash.)
  ▪ Does the level of cash fluctuate over time? If so, why?
  ▪ Where is the cash held? (Ask for a list ranked by dollars held.)
  ▪ Who manages margin requirements? Ask to see real-life examples of how this is tracked.
  ▪ Who is in charge of the cash reconciliation process? Describe the process.
  ▪ Does the hedge fund use any third-party cash management services? If so, provide details of the relationship and how it is monitored internally (who is in charge and what is the process).
  ▪ What is the process employed to move cash internally (who and how)? A cash flow diagram is an easy way to represent this process. This should include details regarding:
    ▪ Who can move cash?
    ▪ Have the signatories changed over time? If so, provide details (who and why).
    ▪ Does the process change based on the dollar amount of the cash movement (i.e., additional signatures for dollar amounts over a specified amount)?
    ▪ How many signatures are required?
    ▪ Are there any "backup" signatories? If so, who?
    ▪ What records are kept and what is the review process?
    ▪ Does the board of directors review cash movements before or after they are made? If not, why?

- What checks and balances are in place? How long have they been in place?
- Have the checks and balances changed over time? If so, how and why?
- Can we review the cash movement documentation for the last three months (or last five cash movements)? This should be verified when conducting your onsite visit (ask to see their files and/or verify on their systems).
  - Create a time line and check against their stated policy and process.
  - Check to see how signatures are collected—physically or via e-mail). If by e-mail, how do they verify that the signatory actually sent the e-mail?

"Shadow" Reconciliation   Outsourcing creates great economies of scale for hedge funds. A hedge fund can take advantage of specialized expertise and advanced technology without committing monetary and human resources by employing third-party service providers. However, many hedge funds either conduct their own shadow accounting or hire another third party to check what their primary service providers are doing. Hedge funds typically shadow the following:

- Trade booking.
- Pricing.
- Valuation.
- Securities reconciliation.
- Cash reconciliation.
- MIS reporting.
- Preparation of books of accounts.
- Creation and distribution of client statements.

Questions to Ask
- Do you shadow any of the work done by your service providers?
- Do you shadow these activities internally?
  - Who does the shadow accounting?
  - What is the process?
  - Have you had any "material" differences with the work done by the third-party firm? (Has pricing been accurate? Have NAV calculations been in line?) Ask them to define what they view as material.
  - If there have been any material differences, how were they resolved? (Request details for each difference and pay attention to how they were resolved—did the administrator "cave in" and use the hedge fund's figures?)

- If there have been material differences, speak to the third party directly and ask how they were resolved (to verify what the hedge fund told us previously).
- Do you employ any additional third-party firms to provide shadow accounting?
  - What firm(s) do you employ?
  - What do they do?
  - Do they have any actual authority or do they just provide a check?
  - Have you used any other firms in this capacity? (As indicated previously, always check to see if there have been changes in service providers—this can be an indication of past issues.)
- If they do not employ shadow procedures, ask how they verify the external work.

Business Continuity   Business continuity refers to a hedge fund's plans and procedures to keep the hedge fund running in real time in the case of a disruption. A disruption can be a loss of power in the middle of the work day, Internet connectivity issues, or any other event that can temporarily disrupt normal operations.

Questions to Ask
- What are your business continuity plans and procedures?
- Can you provide me with a copy of your policy?
- Have you ever had a business disruption? If so, ask the following for each occurrence:
  - What was the issue?
  - Was there any impact to the business or fund (i.e., was there trade slippage, did they miss any trade opportunities, did they lose any data permanently)?
  - How long did it take for your firm to be fully functional during the disruption? Ask to see specific evidence (for example, ask to see trade stubs for trades that occurred while the disruption was still in effect).
  - Which service providers were involved either in the disruption or the solution? (Ask so that you can verify the information with the service providers later on.)
  - What did you learn from these disruptions?
  - Did you change your process as a result of any of these occurrences? If so, how?
  - Have you changed service providers as a result of these occurrences? If so, ask for details.

- Do you conduct periodical tests of your business continuity procedures? If yes, ask:
  - How often?
  - When were they conducted? (Get specific dates.)
  - What was the test procedure?
  - What were the test results?
  - Do you test the procedures internally or use an outside consultant? If so, whom did you use and can I see their results?
- If they have not and do not plan to test business continuity procedures, ask how they can be comfortable in the event that something should disrupt their business.
- If the firm has multiple offices:
  - How do they coordinate between them?
  - Who is in charge at each office?
  - What is the policy and procedure for each office?

Disaster Recovery   Disaster recovery is different from business continuity. Business continuity deals with short-term, temporary disruptions, while disaster recovery refers to significant "disaster" events (such as an earthquake or building fire). Needless to say, all hedge funds should have both business continuity and disaster recovery plans and procedures in place and they should be regularly tested.

Questions to Ask

- What are your disaster recovery plans and procedures?
- Can you provide me with a copy of your policy?
- Where are data files stored? How frequently are they saved?
- Do you have any redundant servers in place (in case one server malfunctions)?
- Are your servers located on or offsite (or both)? (Ask for details.)
- Do you save copies of all data offsite? If so:
  - Where are the data stored?
  - Which firm(s) do you employ? What are the terms?
  - How frequently do you save the data?
  - Specifically, what data are stored?
  - How many years' worth of data do you store offsite?
  - How can you access the data if needed?
  - How long will it take to extract the data to be fully functional?
- Who is in charge of disaster recovery should there be an event?

- Who created the disaster recovery plan and procedures?
  - If an external consultant was used, ask for their contact details so you can verify the information the hedge fund provides.
  - Is the consultant still under contract? What are the contract terms?
  - If the consultant is no longer under contract, how do you keep the technology up-to-date and in line with best practices?

If the policy and procedures are created and maintained internally, ask for the qualifications of the person in charge. Make a point of speaking directly to that person and assessing their ability and whether or not they are up to the task (experience, authority, actual responsibility).

- Do you have alternate office space ready in the case of an event? Smaller hedge funds may designate a partner's home as alternative office space, while some larger firms may have rented office space in place as an alternative. Ask for full details.
- In the case of a disaster:
  - How long will it take to become fully functional?
  - What systems will be restored? Fully or partially restored?
  - What data will become available? When will it become available?
  - What will not be available?
- Do you conduct periodical tests of your disaster recovery procedures? If yes, ask:
  - How often?
  - When were they conducted? (Get specific dates.)
  - What was the test procedure?
  - What were the test results?
  - Do you test the procedures internally or use an outside consultant? If an outside consultant is used, whom did you use and can I see their results?
- Have they ever had an actual disaster scenario? If so, ask for details.
- If they have not and do not plan to test disaster recovery procedures, ask how they can be comfortable in the event of a disaster.
- If the firm has multiple offices:
  - How do they coordinate between them?
  - Who is in charge at each office?
  - What is the policy and procedure for each office?

Policy

The next category we will review focuses on a hedge fund's internal policies.

Compliance Manual   A culture of compliance is a must at any hedge fund. Hedge fund fraud is more likely to occur at a firm that does not effectively review and monitor its employees' activities. It is important that a hedge fund have a thorough and well-thought-out policy, including remedies in the case of any violations. Compliance can be managed internally, but many hedge funds employ outside compliance consulting organizations as a means of providing checks and balances. Outside firms are also used for cost considerations (smaller hedge funds might find it more cost effective to use an outside firm instead of hiring an additional person or people).

Questions to Ask

- Who is the firm's compliance officer?
- Do they have a formal written compliance manual?
- Ask for a copy of the compliance manual. If they will not send it, then ask to review it in full when you conduct your onsite visit.
- If the compliance function is outsourced, ask for details about the third-party firm:
    - Name of firm?
    - Length of service?
    - Details of services provided:
        - Advisory only?
        - Regular compliance checks? Ask for details.
        - Mock regulatory audits?
- Do you have a formal compliance manual? If so, ask for a copy.
- Who wrote the compliance policy? Has it changed over time? If not, ask for details.
- What is the firm's policy regarding gifts received by employees? Who is in charge of this function? How is it tracked?
- What is the policy regarding use of soft dollars? How is it tracked?
- How frequently are compliance checks done? What is the process and how is the process monitored?

Code of Ethics   A code of ethics is designed to encourage integrity and give clients a window into how the hedge fund views its responsibilities as a fiduciary of its client's capital. Hedge funds should have formal (preferably written) policy guidelines. This code should apply to all employees of the firm and should be actively monitored and tracked by the head of compliance. As part of the process, the hedge fund should be able to state that all employees have read the code of ethics and signed a document stating that they have and will comply with all of its terms (this should be done at least annually). The code of ethics typically covers:

- Protection of client confidentiality.
- Employee trading policy.
- Gift policy.
- Entertainment policy.
- Outside business interests.

Questions to Ask

- Do you have a formal, written code of ethics? Ask for a copy. If they are not comfortable giving you a complete copy, ask for the table of contents (to check that all the major concepts are covered) and request to review the document in detail when you are onsite. When you do your onsite visit, make sure you receive the full document and read it to ensure that it is complete and consistent with what the hedge fund reported to you.
- Has anyone ever violated any of the provisions of the code of ethics? Ask for details (ask specifically how the situation was remedied).
- How do you monitor employees for violations?
- Are all employees required to read the code and certify that they have not committed any violations? If so, with what frequency?

Valuation Policy   One of the most important aspects of the operational due diligence process is to determine and verify a hedge fund's pricing and valuation policies. Pricing and valuation policy will dictate a hedge fund's monthly net asset value, which is the price at which new investors buy into a fund and existing investors redeem out of a fund. This is the primary reason why we require hedge funds to employ the services of independent administrators, who are contracted to use the formal pricing and valuation policy in their determination of a hedge fund's NAV.

However, pricing and valuation policy can get quite complicated depending on the types of securities that a hedge fund buys and sells. For example, liquid equity investments are fairly easy to price, but distressed debt is often more thinly traded. Some hedge funds invest in less liquid securities that require complicated statistical pricing models to be used as a best estimate of current pricing. It is important to understand how all securities are priced, how these prices are obtained, and how many pricing sources are used. For example, in the case of pricing a liquid equity it is important to know if the last trade is used for pricing or if the midpoint or an average price is used.

Many larger hedge funds that invest in complex or illiquid investments form an internal pricing and valuation committee. These committees are typically charged with setting policy and keeping the policy up-to-date (due to the ever-changing and growing hedge fund landscape). They can meet monthly, quarterly, or annually to review pricing as an additional check and balance. Some hedge funds employ the services of specialized firms that provide specific valuation services (this is often done to assure clients that the hedge fund is doing everything in its power to assure pricing independence and accuracy).

Every hedge fund should have a formal, written valuation policy. The administrator should also have a copy of the formal valuation policy, and we need to review the policy and verify that is actually being followed.

Questions to Ask

- What is your valuation policy? Ask for a written copy of the formal guidelines (make sure to verify the policy and adherence to it with the fund's administrator).
- How do you ensure that the valuation policy is actually being carried out by the administrator? The answer will likely be that they verify the procedure by doing their own internal daily reconciliation with the administrator (which would identify any issues immediately).
- Do they employ any additional valuation testing?
- Do they use any third-party valuation services? If so, who and what were they responsible for doing? Ask for their contact details so you can verify this information.
- Do any of the firm's investment professionals play a role in pricing or valuation? If so, explain.
- Have you had any discrepancies with the administrator (daily/weekly/monthly)?
- Do you have an internal (or external) pricing or valuation committee? If so:
  - Who are its members?
  - What is their authority?
  - Have they ever found any issues with the policy?
  - Have they ever suggested any changes to the policy? If so, were they enacted (provide details)?
  - How frequently do they meet?
  - Has the committee membership ever changed? If so, why and when?
- Does the hedge fund price any of the fund's securities? If so:
  - Provide a list of current securities internally priced.

- Provide the pricing methodology (show how they were priced and provide backup).
- Why does the firm price them internally (why not use an independent third party)?
- Does the firm now (or has it ever) employed the services of a third-party valuation service? If so, provide details.
  - Have you ever had to restate the fund's NAV? If so, provide details for each occurrence (what happened, pricing discrepancy, how it was resolved, did it impact any client allocations).

Board of Directors   In a recent court case involving the Weavering hedge fund, two independent board directors were found to be guilty of willful neglect and failing to carry out their duties. The directors were both related to the hedge fund manager (brother and stepfather) and were charged with "doing nothing for almost six years."[3] The case is currently being appealed, but this case may have awakened interest in the concept and practice of a hedge fund's board of directors.

These boards can be made up of full-time hedge fund employees (executive board members) and non–hedge fund employees (non–executive board members). There is no set rule as to the number of board members required, but most funds seem to have at least two members (with an unofficial industry average of three to five members).

The responsibilities of a board of directors typically include the following:

- Review performance.
- Monitor investment and risk guidelines.
- Check and monitor NAV calculations.
- Review pricing and valuation policies.
- Monitor marketing and client service functions and communications with clients/prospects.
- Review anti–money laundering policies and know your client policies and procedures.
- Periodically review performance of the fund's service providers.
- Review proposed side letters and monitor existing side letters for compliance.
- Review fund disclosures.
- Exercise discretionary powers (i.e., accepting subscriptions below the minimum stated on the offering memorandum).

- Review proposed changes to offering materials and other legal documents.
- Meet at least annually (and preferably three to four times each year) either in person or telephonically.

When reviewing the quality and effectiveness of a fund's board of directors, it is important to review what each board member brings to the table. A board with experienced professionals that cover various specialties within the hedge fund world would have a clear advantage, as they would be able to review most issues and render timely and accurate opinions. In addition, it is important that the director's roles and specific responsibilities be spelled out in writing (and signed by all relevant parties). When reviewing a board, it is important to understand who is independent from the day-to-day operations of the hedge fund. As we have seen in the Bayou case, a board with no independent oversight can result in fraudulent behavior. Last, a cottage industry involving "professional" directors has become quite lucrative in recent years. When evaluating a hedge fund's board members, try to determine how many boards each member is part of (it is not uncommon for these professional directors to have board seats with many hedge funds).

Questions to Ask

- Who are the firm's and fund's board of directors?
- What are their qualifications (ask for their biographies)?
- Ask for the contact details for all board members so that you can speak with them directly to verify what the hedge fund tells you.
- When was each one appointed?
- Have there been any changes to the board? If so, who, when, and why?
- How much is each director compensated for being on the board?
- Do any of the board members have any personal or professional affiliation with the hedge fund or any of its personnel?
- For each board member, list the total number of boards on which they are members.
- What are the duties of the board (ask for a detailed list)?
- How often does the board meet? Are in-person meetings required or can they be done via the phone?
- Is a board vote required to be unanimous?
- Ask to see letters of representation provided to the fund's audit firm.
- What are the director's indemnification provisions?
  - Is D&O insurance in place? Are there any policy exclusions? Review the details.

Personal Trading   This is typically covered in the firm's compliance manual or code of ethics. Hedge fund personnel should have the majority of their personal "liquid" wealth invested in their own hedge funds, but for a number of reasons they may also maintain personal trading accounts (to invest in securities outside of their fund's mandate, for example).

Questions to Ask

- Does the firm have a personal trading policy? If so, provide a copy.
- Does the policy require preclearance before trading?
- Who manages the process?
- Who approves trades?
- What is the procedure?
- How are trades approved?
- Do you receive quarterly brokerage statements from your employees? If so, how do you check the information for policy violations?
- Do you receive the statements from the brokers directly or from your employees?
- Are your employees required to certify that they have not violated the personal trading policy? If so, how frequently? Who is in charge of the reviewable process?
- Do you use any automated software to monitor compliance? If so, provide details.
- Do you employ any third party to monitor compliance? If so, provide details.
- Have there ever been any violations of your personal trading policy? If so, provide details. How was the issue resolved?

Transparency and Reporting   This is certainly a hot-button topic. There has always been a tug of war between a hedge fund's desire to minimize transparency and investors' desire to receive full position-level transparency. The media often portrays hedge funds as being dark pools of capital in which investors are largely kept in the dark about their activities. But I have found that most hedge funds are willing to work with their clients to provide a level of transparency that makes everyone comfortable.

From the investor's perspective, a certain level of transparency is required to effectively perform due diligence on any hedge fund. In this book, we have gone through a number of steps in the due diligence process, and a common thread among all the various aspects of the evaluation process has involved information flow. We need historical performance (and all disclosures) so that we can put the fund's track record in a proper historical perspective. Performance, however, is a backward measure. One of the most important things we do as due diligence analysts is determine the likelihood of a hedge fund's success going forward. To accomplish this goal, it is important to understand how the hedge fund operates and evaluate actual investment decisions (not just the resulting performance). Obviously, we cannot do this unless we receive information on trades and investments. The ultimate goal is to develop an opinion regarding the hedge fund manager's style and skill so that we can make an informed investment decision. After all, how can we evaluate a hedge fund manager's track record if we have no idea of how they have invested in the past? Once we make a decision to hire a hedge fund manager, then the real work begins. We then need to regularly monitor their performance and stay on top of portfolio exposures and risks. Once again, without some level of portfolio transparency this would be impossible.

From the hedge fund manager's perspective, they spend the vast majority of their time trying to find exceptional investments so that they can achieve their stated risk/return objectives. Fund management is a competitive business and they are typically not willing to share the fruits of their labor with competitors. Hedge fund manager monthly letters and quarterly reports can often be found on a number of financial websites (without the manager's permission or consent). The only way the letters can be posted is if someone on their distribution list (clients, prospects, consultants, etc.) posts them to these sites. Once a hedge fund manager's positions are released into the marketplace, competitors may steal their ideas—essentially riding on the back of their hard work. If this information were to be released to the marketplace while the fund manager is still building a position, it might cause a rise in the stock's price, which would negatively impact a hedge fund building a position in that name. Hedge funds are generally reluctant to share full details of their short books for several reasons. First, they are always concerned with being involved in a short squeeze. Second, if a company's management finds out that a particular hedge fund is short their stock, they may shut down communication with that fund going forward. Last, many quantitatively oriented hedge fund managers are reluctant to share full transparency because it may be possible to reverse engineer their methodology (their "secret sauce"). Quantitative hedge funds differentiate themselves based on their ability to find messages in vast arrays of data in ways that others have not yet figured out. If they were to provide full transparency, then their competitors might be able to find out what they are doing and piggyback on their success (which may actually reduce the efficacy of the trading strategy and, hence, their entire business). In addition, quantitative hedge funds with highly active trading methodologies may perform hundreds of thousands of trades in a given period of time. How many investors are in a realistic position to process this amount of data?

In recent years we have seen the emergence of several third-party risk firms. These firms collect actual position-level information from hedge funds and their service providers. They take the collected information and create detailed risk reports that aggregate the data and provide investors with an independent view (and check) on hedge fund risk and exposures (without disclosing specific position-level transparency to investors). These risk aggregators can also be hired to pull information from multiple hedge funds and provide investors with a risk report that aggregates all the underlying positions across multiple portfolios. These services are not free and they are not perfect, but they satisfy a need and desire for risk analysis and independent investment verification.

Outside of these third-party risk aggregators, each hedge fund investor has to decide what is the minimum acceptable level of transparency they need to make an informed investment decision about what is required to adequately monitor the investment going forward. It is important to make sure that transparency is discussed and agreed to by all parties before hiring the manager.

In addition, it is important to speak with the hedge fund professionals directly about their investments, exposures, liquidity, and risks. Phone calls and face-to-face meetings will help you to put the due diligence jigsaw puzzle together. Always take detailed meeting/call notes and check their verbal statements back to monthly/quarterly investor letters, risk reports, liquidity reports, and so forth.

Questions to Ask

- What level of transparency do you provide to investors? Ask for historical transparency reporting.
- Will you provide position-level transparency on a lag basis? Some hedge fund managers have an issue with providing a full view into the current portfolio but are willing to provide dated portfolios (on one-, three-, five-month lag).
- Ask for position-level transparency for previous years (so that we can verify that they have invested consistently over time).
- What risk reporting do you provide? Ask for historical risk reporting.
- Will you allow your prime broker to provide us with summary exposure and risk reports?

Product

The offering memorandum will provide most of the product-level information we will need when conducting our operational review. When we conduct our interviews with the hedge fund's operational staff, we can ask them to explain the hedge fund's fees, liquidity terms, minimum investment amounts, side pockets, gate lockups, and notice periods. However, we ultimately must use the offering memorandum as the final say in all matters.

Base (Management) Fees   Management fees are calculated as a percentage of the fund's net asset value. These fees are typically expressed on an annual percentage basis, but calculated and paid monthly or quarterly. For example, a 2 percent management fee is expressed as an annual percentage of the fund's NAV but can also be expressed as 0.17 percent on a monthly basis (2 percent divided by 12). Management fees are generally viewed as a means of covering the operating costs (or "management" costs) of operating the business. However, some funds earn management fees far in excess of their operating costs, which have caused some investors to question the validity of a defined (preset) management fee. In recent years, a small number of hedge funds have initiated a sliding management fee schedule (one that gets lower as assets reach certain milestones). Also, smaller or recently launched hedge funds have created what is known as a founders class for investors willing to subscribe to the fund when it is still in its early stages. These founders share classes often include incentives such as lower management or performance fees, increased transparency, and future capacity rights.

Incentive/Performance Fees   The initial design of the hedge fund fee schedule was meant to incentivize managers to perform well because the greater the hedge fund's return, the greater the fees paid to the manager. A hedge fund that charges a 20 percent performance fee would collect 20 percent of all fund profits for a given year. If a hedge fund manages $100 million and achieves a 10 percent return, then the fund has generated a profit of $10 million, which would translate to a performance fee of $2 million (20 percent of the $10 million profit) to be paid to the fund managers. It is industry standard for hedge funds to employ a high water mark (loss carry forward provision), which means that the performance fee only applies to net profits (profits after losses in previous years have been recovered). A hedge fund that experiences significant losses in a given year will not receive a performance fee until it has made back all the losses, which sometimes leads hedge fund managers to close the fund rather than suffer through many years without performance fees.

One critique of performance fees is that once they are paid to the manager, they are nonrefundable. For example, if hedge fund managers have great performance in year one, they will collect a performance fee. However, if performance in year two is poor, they do not collect any additional performance fee (but they do not have to return the previous year's performance fee even if the cumulative two-year performance record is negative). In this scenario, clients have lost money and have paid the manager an incentive fee (in year one). To remedy this, some hedge funds (not many) include a "clawback" provision in their terms. A clawback provision would force the hedge fund manager to effectively return previously earned fees (partially or in full) should the fund's cumulative performance turn negative. In addition, a small percentage of hedge funds have a hurdle rate in place, which means that a performance fee is only paid on the fund's performance in excess of a fixed percentage or predefined benchmark rate. Performance fees are typically calculated on either a fund-level basis or a per-share basis. When calculated on a fund-level basis, the performance fee is calculated based on the overall fund level and is based on the fund's NAV adjusted for subscriptions and redemptions. When calculated on a per-share basis, performance fees are calculated at the individual shareholder level.

When reviewing performance fees it is important to understand the method of calculation and the frequency of payment. Many people assume that performance fees are paid annually upon the conclusion of a calendar year. While this is true most of the time, it is not always the case. Some hedge funds collect performance fees quarterly (and some even receive them monthly). A more frequent payment schedule can lead to a mismatch based on the hedge fund's investment horizon or level of volatility. In addition, some hedge funds end their fiscal year in a month other than December.

Other Fees   When reviewing a hedge fund's offering documents, it is also important to determine what other fees and expenses investors will be charged with (if any). Some funds charge a fee for subscriptions and redemptions. Some funds charge a penalty for redemptions within a specific time period following initial investment. When conducting your operational due diligence, ask specifically for the hedge fund to list and discuss all expenses charged back to the fund. Naturally you will need to verify this information by reading the documents yourself. While the practice is not common, some hedge funds may expense some or all expenses related to the "management" of the fund (which can include employee salaries).

Subscriptions/Redemptions   Most hedge funds accept subscriptions on a monthly basis (on the first business day of the month). Some may offer more frequent subscriptions (weekly, twice per month, or daily). Hedge funds also have minimum requirements for initial and subsequent investments (but may be willing to waive the minimum if asked).

Liquidity is one of the most important things to evaluate when performing due diligence on a hedge fund. We perform liquidity analysis on the fund's actual portfolio holdings during the investment due diligence process, and we verify through the operational portion of the due diligence process that the position-level liquidity matches the stated fund liquidity. For example, a hedge fund that focuses on distressed debt (which can be less liquid and even illiquid at times) that offers clients monthly liquidity with 30 days' notice has a clear liquidity mismatch. It's one thing for a hedge fund to advertise a certain level of investor liquidity; it's another thing to actually deliver that liquidity to investors (2008 was a painful lesson in liquidity mismatch between hedge fund holdings and investor liquidity for many hedge funds and their investors).

In addition to assessing the frequency of hedge fund investor liquidity, it is important to know and understand the required notice period. For example, a hedge fund with quarterly investor liquidity and a 30-day notice means that to redeem from a hedge fund at the end of a given quarter, the investor must submit written notice at least 30 days in advance.

When reviewing the offering memorandum, look for language that creates an exception to the liquidity terms stated elsewhere in the document. It is common in most hedge fund offering memorandums to include provisions whereby the hedge fund can suspend redemptions should they see fit to do so. For example, this exception may be triggered if the hedge fund manager determines that the act of redeeming assets may impair the remaining investors in the fund (such as in the financial crisis of late 2008 or due to an unusually large redemption).

Lockups Hedge funds may impose a lockup on new investors. The hedge fund lockup provision means that during a certain initial period, an investor may not make a withdrawal from the fund. A "soft" lockup is one where the investor can redeem all or a portion of their assets while still within the lockup period, for a fee. When reviewing soft lockup provisions, make sure that any penalties paid due to early redemption are paid to the fund—not the fund manager. A "hard" lockup is one in which the investor has no liquidity options within the lockup period (the money cannot be redeemed).

Know and understand these terms —lockup period, type of lockup (hard or soft), and penalty for early redemption (if under a soft lockup). In addition, determine in advance if the lockup terms pertain just to your initial investment or all investment tranches (if you make multiple investments over time). Last, you must determine if the lockup period expires completely or is "rolling" (meaning the lockup starts over again). For example, a rolling two-year lockup means that investors can redeem once every two years. If you miss your redemption window at the end of two years, you must wait another two years to redeem again.

Gates A gate is a restriction placed on a hedge fund that limits the amount investors can withdraw from the fund during a specific redemption date or over a redemption period. The purpose of a gate provision is to prevent a run on the hedge fund, which could cripple its operations. Gates are initiated because a large number of withdrawals from a fund could force the manager to sell off a large number of positions (potentially at unfavorable prices). It is a measure designed to protect investors that do not redeem from the fund.

Gates can be triggered at the fund or investor level. An example of a fund-level gate would be if a hedge fund manager can withhold redemptions if more than 25 percent of the fund's assets are scheduled for redemption. An example of an investor-level gate would be if an investor is limited to redeeming 25 percent of their invested assets each quarter. In this case, it would take an investor four quarters to fully redeem. An individual investor-level gate may be overridden by a fund-level gate.

Check if the hedge fund under review has ever gated investors. If they have, ask for details and determine on your own if the suspension of redemptions was justified. In late 2008 and into 2009, a number of hedge funds gated their clients and suspended redemptions. Some of these hedge funds gated for the right reasons, while others (in my personal view) gated to save their business (meaning they could have liquidated positions and satisfied client redemptions but chose not to). I will never invest with those funds and will avoid any funds managed by former senior members of those firms for ethical reasons.

Side Pockets The term "side pocket" refers to a portion of the hedge fund that is segregated from the main fund for certain illiquid investments. Side pockets can be accounted for at the fund level (meaning all investors own a pro rata share of the side pocket) or at the individual investor level (only investors that "opted" for side pockets when they subscribed own a piece of the side pocket). When making a new hedge fund investment, you must determine if the fund has a side pocket already in place and if investors will be required to invest in the side pocket or if they can opt out. Many hedge funds will completely segregate the side pocket, which means it will not be available to new investors.

When reviewing a hedge fund with side pockets already in place, you need to determine if the side pocket was used by design or if the hedge fund inappropriately invested in illiquid securities and was forced to create a side pocket. In the latter case, you will need to determine what led to the side pocket and assess whether or not it could happen again. A hedge fund that is supposed to invest only in highly liquid investments and goes outside of their mandate to invest in illiquid securities and is then forced to put the illiquid securities in a side pocket might be viewed as undisciplined or may have committed style drift.

When evaluating the liquidity of a hedge fund, you should also be aware of hedge fund positions that are not in a side pocket, but should be there (and may move there at a later date). This is another reason why transparency is critical. It is always best to be prepared and to think through all possibilities and contingencies.

Assets under Management   It is important to understand how much capital a given hedge fund firm is managing in the product under review as well as at the firm overall (if they manage multiple products). Asset size is a quick and effective indicator to determine if a hedge fund manager is profitable or not. A hedge fund managing $800 million with a staff of 12 people and a strong performance history (performance history is important because it will help determine the incentive fee figures) is likely above breakeven. In addition, when hedge funds manage a fund with a small amount of assets, it may have an impact on portfolio positioning, liquidity, and performance. For example, if a hedge fund manages a small amount of money in its early days, then it can invest in smaller and less liquid investments (that it will likely not be able to invest in when it grows larger). When reviewing assets, it is just as important to understand where the assets have come from as much as how much they have.

Questions to Ask

- Provide a monthly history of assets for all funds managed by the firm (including any managed accounts).
- Do you currently manage any assets on a hedge fund platform? If so, which platform(s)? What are the terms? Hedge fund platforms often negotiate better liquidity terms for their clients, which will impact our review of the hedge fund.
- Did you manage any funds in the past that have been closed? If so, why? Please include the monthly asset history for any closed funds (along with a monthly performance history as well).
- How much of the assets under management represent internal capital? An associated question should be to ask for the percentage of each hedge fund professional's liquid net worth that is currently invested in the fund. Ask if internal capital has ever been reduced. If so, when and why?
- Ask them to provide a list of the fund's 10 largest clients (name of client and amount of investment). If they are not comfortable sharing client names, ask them to list the top 10 investors by investor type instead

of name (institution, fund of fund, foundation, endowment, platform, high net worth, etc.).

- Ask them to provide a percentage breakout of all fund and firm assets under management by client type.
- Ask them to provide a list of the largest redemptions in the fund's history. Who redeemed? How much did they redeem? Why did they redeem?

OPERATIONAL DUE DILIGENCE TIPS

Minimum standards—before performing extensive investment, risk, and operational due diligence, do a quick check of the firm/fund documents to ensure that they meet your minimum standards. This can save a great deal of time down the road. If a hedge fund may be deficient in one or more areas, make an inquiry and then decide to move the fund up or out.

Read ALL documents—hedge funds produce prodigious amounts of paper (offering memorandums, presentations, DDQs, monthly letters, quarterly letters, risk reports, subscription and redemption documents, compliance manuals, code of ethics, personal trading policies, etc.). Read every word of every document. Skimming is evil. It is okay to skim the documents in the early stages to get a quick read, but eventually you must read and understand everything.

Cross check information—operational due diligence covers the entire firm, not just the people who work in operations. Operational "best practices" should be inherent in the culture of the entire organization. Speak to portfolio managers, analysts, traders, risk managers, economists, and the like. This will provide you with different viewpoints and may possibly alert you to inconsistencies within the firm.

Cross check information internally—in an institutional setting, operational due diligence is often done by dedicated operations professionals, while investment and risk evaluations are typically conducted by other professionals dedicated to those areas (a "silo" approach whereby everyone has a specific function). All meeting/call notes, reports, and analyses should be available and reviewed by everyone involved in the due diligence process (across the distinct groups). Comments about trade flow made by a trader (and uncovered during investment due diligence) may contradict comments made by the firm's CFO (during the operational due diligence process). Internal communication is essential if these inconsistencies are to be uncovered.

Liquidity, liquidity, liquidity—make sure you fully understand the hedge fund's liquidity (this includes lockup, side pocket, and gate provisions). It is also critical to assess the liquidity of a hedge fund's underlying investments and match them to the liquidity they offer to clients—be aware of a potential liquidity mismatch.

Skin in the game—hedge fund managers should be invested in their hedge fund right along with their clients. Be wary of any hedge fund managers that do not have the majority of their "liquid" net worth invested in their fund(s). Track the hedge fund's amount of internal investment and be on the lookout for redemptions.

Review history—when evaluating a specific hedge fund, make sure to conduct a historical review of the firm as well as any other current and former funds managed by the firm. If the firm manages multiple products, review them as well. There are numerous historical instances of one fund within a firm complex taking down the whole business. Speak with existing and former employees, clients, and service providers to help you put things in a historical perspective.

INTERVIEW WITH FCM OPERATIONAL STAFF

So far in the operational due diligence process, we have collected and reviewed all relevant documents (as previously listed) and conducted an introductory phone call with Jennifer Cassell (CFO) to answer most of the outstanding questions emanating from the review of the documents. Now we are ready to personally interview the operations staff.

I will not include a transcript of the interviews as I did in the previous chapter, but will include all the relevant insights in the following meeting note.

Example

To: Research Team

From: Frank Travers

Date: January 6, 2012

Re: Onsite Meeting with Fictional Capital Management

Interviews with Operational Staff—Bill Hobson (COO) and Jennifer Cassell (CFO)

I met with Bill and Jennifer in their shared office. Bill is a founding partner and Jennifer joined the firm in January 2009. Bill was an accountant at a small regional accounting firm for five years after graduating from New York University (NYU). He started his career in the hedge fund space in 1997, when he joined Bellman Capital as their controller. He stayed there for five years until he accepted the COO position at GCH Advisors in late summer of 2002. He described the move as a clear upgrade in responsibilities. When Ted and Jaime decided to leave GCH, they asked him if he would join them as a partner in their new endeavor. Bill owns 20 percent of the firm's equity. I asked him how the break with GCH went and he candidly told me that it did not go well. Jonah took the departure personally. He felt that he had given all three of them their "big break" in the business and was upset when they decided to leave together. I told him that I would contact Jonah at some point for a reference and asked him what he thought Jonah would say. Bill replied that he was not sure. Some other clients had spoken to Jonah for a reference in the past and he has been inconsistent. According to Bill, Jonah has said good things about Ted and Jaime's ability to analyze stocks and manage a portfolio.

Bill described his job as handling all business affairs, including marketing and client service. Prior to Jennifer and Aaron joining the firm, he handled everything on the operations side from trade reconciliations to creating the monthly client reports. I asked how much time Ted and Jaime spend on non-investment-related things and he stated that they spend 100 percent of the trading day managing the portfolio. He meets with them weekly to discuss business affairs on Mondays after the market has closed (they typically meet in the conference room and systematically discuss all ongoing and upcoming initiatives). They have worked closely together as a group for eight years (since he first joined GCH back in 2002) and have settled into a comfortable and efficient routine.

I asked Bill why he left GCH to start FCM with Ted and Jaime. He responded that he thought Ted and Jamie were the best analysts and portfolio managers that he had ever worked with and he thought they would be able to translate the success they had had at GCH to the new endeavor. It has taken a few years to get assets to a more comfortable level, but they seem to have momentum now and the firm is performing well on both sides of the business—portfolio-wise and operationally. Jennifer and Aaron report directly to Bill.

Jennifer took over all of the accounting, financial, and trade-related jobs from Bill when she joined in 2009. Bill mentioned that FCM had strong performance in 2008 and started to get some serious attention from institutional investors, so they decided to stay ahead of the game and hire a CFO to assist him. Jennifer has a degree in accounting from Dartmouth University and is a CPA. She spent the first 10 years of her career at two of the big four accounting firms, with the last five dedicated to the hedge fund space. Bill was very comfortable hiring Jennifer because he had worked with her for several years while he was at GCH. Jennifer was the lead auditor who worked directly on GCH financial statements and advised on tax-related matters for the firm. When FCM decided to hire a dedicated CFO, the first person he called was Jennifer.

I asked Jennifer what attracted her to FCM and she said that she had a great relationship will Bill from the GCH days and that she and Bill had discussed the possibility of her joining the firm over the years. She had kept track of FCM and had met with Ted and Jaime many times and felt that she would fit in well with the team. In addition, she was eager to make a move away from fund audits and move over to the hedge fund side of things.

Jennifer described her job as doing everything operationally so that Bill can focus on managing the business and raising assets for the firm and that the investment team can focus on what they do best. In the course of the interview, it was apparent to me that Bill and Jennifer have a strong working relationship. Bill was knowledgeable about everything that Jennifer was doing and Jennifer was likewise knowledgeable about everything that Bill was working on.

I asked what Aaron did for the firm and Jennifer told me that he was hired right out of school earlier in the year (March 2011) and he has a steep learning curve ahead of him, but he is a hard-working kid and she gains more confidence in him daily. He is charged with doing the daily cash and trade reconciliations and calculating the daily shadow NAV. Jennifer reviews his work daily and compares his calculations to that of the administrator to identify any issues as early as possible.

I asked Bill to describe the current marketing strategy. He replied that the firm has achieved a solid five-year track record, including a positive return in 2008. He feels that their uncorrelated return stream should attract the attention of investors that are tired of hiring hedge funds that "all buy the same stuff." He told me that they had taken in an additional

$20 million on January 1, which brings total fund assets to about $300 million. He has been busy responding to requests for information (RFIs) in the past few months and they have had three other institutional investors conducting onsite due diligence in the fourth quarter. He can't guarantee any subscriptions, but he expects at least one of them to invest and estimates that they will write a $30–$40 million check. If all three come in, then they may see upwards of $60–$70 million come into the fund.

I asked why they are not managing more than $300 million (given the strong track record). He responded that the firm was pretty small prior to 2009 and they did not market the fund much. Bill stated that bringing Jennifer on board freed up his time to professionalize their marketing materials and to get the word out to potential clients. He added that performance in 2008 was excellent and people actually started to call them when they saw the returns in their database searches. He has also pressed their prime broker to do some capital introductions for them. In the last year, the prime broker invited them to speak at three conferences (two in NYC and one in Florida). They attended all three and feel they were able to gain access to consultants, funds of funds, and other investors very efficiently. They met two of the three potential investors he mentioned earlier via these conferences.

I asked him what the fund's capacity was and he stated that they should close around $500 million. I asked him if "should" meant they "would" (as stated in their DDQ and confirmed by both Ted and Jaime). He responded that they planned on closing the fund at $500 million. He went on to say that they are still a fair ways off from $500 million and his focus now is on getting the fund to its full capacity. He feels that if performance stays strong, they may get there in 12 to 18 months (given the current level of interest).

I asked Jennifer when she thought she would be made a partner and she stammered a bit before replying that I should ask Bill. Bill replied that they were not likely to make anyone a partner this year but they would revisit the concept next year. I asked Bill if the firm granted any shadow equity to anyone (I already know that they do grant shadow equity to the investment team from my earlier call with Jaime and meeting with Ted). Bill seemed a little uncomfortable answering the question (I assumed because Jennifer was sitting right there) so I said to Bill that we could discuss compensation at a later time.

I have summarized the key aspects of the remainder of the interview:

Fees

- Class A: 1.5 percent base fee and 20 percent performance fee.
- Class B: 1.0 percent base fee and 20 percent performance fee.

Liquidity
- Class A: quarterly redemptions with 90 days' notice (no lockup).
- Class B: quarterly redemptions with 90 days' notice (one-year hard lockup for each tranch).

Other Funds/Managed Accounts
- None

Side Pockets/Gates
- None

Payment of Proceeds after Redemption
- 90 percent paid within 30 days; remainder paid upon completion of the annual audit.

Trading
- They have a dedicated trader (see attached bio) and they estimate that they make between 10 and 15 trades each day.
- They primarily trade equities but can trade listed options and ETFs.
- Life of a trade:
  - Jacob Holder has authority to trade on behalf of the fund (Ted Acoff can also trade in his absence).
  - All trades are placed with third parties (they have no affiliations with any brokers/dealers).
  - They currently use the prime broker's order management system (which we have reviewed and feel is adequate). They are currently in the process of upgrading to a new system and expect to be up and running by the end of the quarter. Roughly 70 percent of their trades are executed by their prime broker.
  - FCM has relationships with approximately 30 or more executing brokers. The trader (Jacob) is responsible for broker selection (however, Ted Acoff, the PM, will make suggestions occasionally).
  - Each trade is allocated at the time of the order.
  - On a daily basis, Jacob and Aaron (admin. assistant) reconcile all trades with the executing brokers' trading desks (via telephone and/or e-mail). Upon approval from Jacob and

Jennifer, Aaron e-mails a trade summary including price per share, number of shares, commission, and executing broker to the prime broker.

- For manually executed trades, Jacob receives confirmation of trades from the executing brokers either by telephone or e-mail. These trades are reviewed by Aaron and Jennifer as part of their daily approval process. Executing brokers independently send confirmations to the prime broker for confirmation.
- FCM reviews all reports and communicates any adjustments to the prime broker and the administrator via e-mail. Records of all activity are maintained on the firm's main and backup servers.
- The administrator reconciles trades and cash movements with the prime broker and FCM on a T+1 basis.

Records
- The administrator keeps the official books and records for FCM. Cash and positions are reconciled daily by the administrator to counterparty statements.

Cash Procedures
- All unencumbered cash is held at the prime broker. FCM generally runs with low unencumbered cash.
- All cash movements are initiated and authorized by the fund's administrator.
  - Movements < $10,000: the administrator alone can approve.
  - Movements > $10,000: three signatures are required.
    1. The administrator.
    2. Either Ted Acoff or Jaime Wernick.
    3. Bill Hobson.
- In addition, the prime broker must approve all cash movements.

Pricing and Valuation
- Given the strategy (exchange-traded U.S. equity), FCM does not have a formal pricing and valuation committee.
- The fund's administrator is 100 percent responsible for obtaining prices and determining valuation. The administrator's primary source for pricing is Bloomberg, but they compare Bloomberg pricing to at least two additional sources to ensure accuracy.

- FCM has never restated a monthly NAV.
- 100 percent level I assets.

Administrator Services

- Fund accounting on a daily/monthly basis.
- Fund shareholder services and fund accounting (monthly).
- Independent NAV calculation.
- Independent portfolio verification.

Disaster Recovery/Business Continuity

- Formal, written policy in place. Action plan was created by external consultant (see attachment for copy of policy and consultant write-up).
- Bill Hobson charged with maintaining the plan internally.
- FCM employs a third-party IT firm (see attachment for details). This firm manages FCM's systems remotely and visits the office monthly for a hands-on maintenance review.
- All mission-critical systems (shared drives and e-mail server), data, and systems information is stored daily at a backup location geographically separate from the primary systems and records.
- All critical computer equipment (including PCs, servers, communication, and telephone equipment) is protected by local and central uninterrupted power supply. Critical systems have swappable disk drives in a RAID configuration in the event of a disk drive failure (see attachment for additional details).
- All workstations and servers are backed up each night.
- The month-end backup tapes are maintained by the third-party IT firm (who verifies the backup). Current day's transaction files and critical contact information is pushed to a secure, remote FTP site at the end of each business day.
- The third-party IT firm has conducted two tests of the system since they were hired in March 2009.

Compliance

- Personal trading is not allowed at FCM. Employees are encouraged to invest in the hedge fund or can invest in mutual funds or ETFs (see attached personal trading policy). There have been no violations of this policy to date.

- Bill Hobson was in charge of firm compliance until September 2011, when the firm outsourced the function to a third party (see attachment for details).

NOTES

1. Capco Research, Working Paper, "Understanding and Mitigating Operational Risk in Hedge Fund Investments," 2002.
2. Ernst & Young, "Coming of Age: Global Hedge Fund Survey 2011."
3. Judy Gross, "Hedge Fund Boards of Directors Play Vital Role," Forbes Online, September 30, 2011.

CHAPTER 10

Risk Due Diligence

"Risk comes from not knowing what you're doing."
Warren Buffett

"Even a correct decision is wrong when it was taken too late."
Lee Iacocca

"In these matters the only certainty is that nothing is certain."
Plinius the Elder

Risk
Analysis

Step Seven

Risk resides everywhere. There are dozens of risks inherent in every hedge fund...from a simple long/short equity strategy to a complex globally diversified derivatives strategy. Following the advice of Plinius the Elder would lead one to always question the presence and potential impact of risk within an investment company and its underlying hedge funds.

Before we can go into any discussion of risk, it might be a good idea to define it. Traditionally, risk has been defined as a simple statistical measure of volatility. After all, when we refer to a risk/return graph, the "risk" portion of the graph is typically depicted as annualized standard deviation. In Chapter 6, "Quantitative Analysis," we learned that hedge funds can be measured using dozens of risk-related statistics (drawdown, downside deviation, semivariance, etc.), and we have also covered numerous other operational and investment risks in other chapters in this book. The implication is that risk is multifaceted; therefore, we must evaluate it from a variety of different perspectives.

When I was outlining this chapter for the book, I wanted to come up with a new and innovative definition for the term "risk." I thought about risk for a while and tried to come up with a more professional way of stating that I consider risk to be the possibility of something bad happening or something going wrong. After a while, I realized that I had already come up with the best definition.

Risk = the possibility of something bad happening

What I like about this definition is that it is simple, to the point, and somewhat liberating. It does not paint us into the corner of focusing solely on quantitative measures. In addition, it should remind us that risk is evolving and our means of evaluating it must evolve as well. The following list is by no means complete, but it should provide a clearer picture of how risk is inherently part of every aspect of a hedge fund. Risk management should be viewed across the firm and should be ingrained in the firm's culture.

Types of Risks

- Asset liquidity
  The liquidity of a hedge fund's underlying assets.
- Basis
  The risk that offsetting investments will not experience price changes in entirely opposite directions from one another.
- Business
  Is the business profitable (can it stay in business)?
- Client concentration
  If one (or a few) large client(s) redeem, will there be a negative impact on the fund's remaining investors? Will the redemption from a large client negatively impact the firm's profitability?
- Commodity
  Will fluctuations in commodity prices impact portfolio positions?
- Correlation
  What happens if the correlations among portfolio companies or between the portfolio companies and the overall market were to increase dramatically?
- Counterparty
  How sound is the underlying quality of the hedge fund counterparty or counterparties? What happens if they experience difficulties (such as Lehman's demise)?

- Credit

  What impact would an increase or decrease in credit spreads have on the portfolio and the market?
- Currency

  What impact would currency fluctuations have on the portfolio as a whole and on the earnings power of underlying portfolio companies? What impact will currency rates have on explicit FX positions held by the fund?
- Derivatives

  Does the fund invest in complex derivatives? If yes, then what are the "true" risks?
- Downside

  What is the risk of an extreme portfolio drawdown?
- Geographic

  Does the hedge fund have any specific geographic exposures (United States, Asia, Europe, emerging markets, frontier markets)? What are the implications?
- Interest rate

  What are the implications to the portfolio of changes in the structure of interest rates?
- Key person

  Is the firm or fund overly dependent upon one (or a select few) individual(s)? What happens if they leave the firm?
- Leverage

  How much leverage does the fund employ? How does that impact the portfolio?
- Liquidity mismatch

  Does the fund's underlying portfolio holdings match investor liquidity?
- Market

  To what degree is the fund correlated to the market?
- Model

  Does the fund manager rely upon models to research, measure risk, and/or value the portfolio? If so, what happens in the case of a model failure?
- Operational

  Does the firm have sufficient personnel, systems, policies, and oversight in place to avoid any operational failures or overt fraud?
- Position concentration

  How concentrated is the underlying portfolio? Can any single position (or a relatively few number of positions) have a significantly negative impact on the fund's performance?

■ Pricing

Are prices readily available and are they independently sourced? If underlying securities are illiquid, how are they priced and could less frequent pricing impact the portfolio's net asset value (NAV)?

■ Regulatory

This is an external risk and one that is almost impossible to accurately assess. When running a fund through stress testing and scenario analysis, we should apply potential regulatory changes (such as a potential ban on short selling). At a minimum, we should be aware of all pending regulatory concerns and understand how they might impact our hedge fund portfolios.

■ Reputation

Reputation applies to the underlying hedge fund manager as well as the hedge fund investor. For example, several funds that invested in the fraudulent Madoff hedge fund ultimately went out of business because they had damaged their reputation as professional hedge fund investors. Hedge fund managers also face reputational risk, which can lead to redemptions and even the possibility of a run on assets.

■ Tail

Tail events seem to occur with much more frequency than mathematical models would have us believe. What risks would the fund face in a tail event? What protections (if any) are in place?

■ Transparency

What is the risk of not receiving adequate transparency from a hedge fund manager? After we hire a hedge fund, we are responsible for tracking its progress and monitoring it on a regular basis.

GRAPHICAL DEPICTION OF HEDGE FUND RISKS

Figure 10.1 is a simple graphic that ranks the level of risk (from low to high) for a number of key risk factors that may impact hedge funds. A score of 1 implies low risk and a score of 10 implies high risk. Note that most of these risks are nonquantitative and that a number of them represent pure qualitative assessments (also known as "educated" opinions). This chart is by no means scientific, but I believe that it clearly depicts a more accurate and complete view of the risks inherent in FCM's hedge fund than looking at performance-based statistics alone. As I have stated a number of times throughout this book, hedge fund due diligence is a marathon, not a sprint. There is no single metric that can tell you to hire any hedge fund. Firing a hedge fund is a different matter completely; there are a number of single variables that can lead to a manager's termination (style drift, personnel changes, etc.).

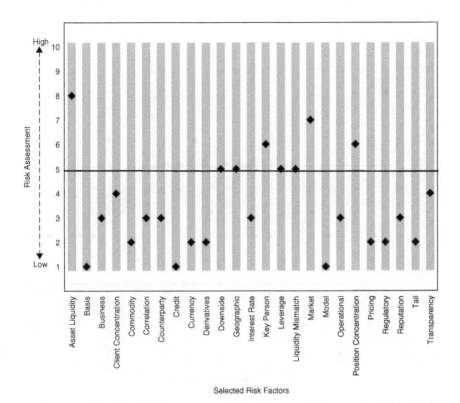

Selected Risk Factors

FIGURE 10.1 Analysis of Selected Risk Measures for FCM

The graphic in Figure 10.2 takes the same risk scores highlighted in Figure 10.1 (which highlights the scores in absolute terms) but compares them to the scores for the other hedge funds in our peer group. The grey bar represents the range of scores achieved by the other hedge funds (from low to high). The marker signifies where FCM scores for each risk measure relative to the entire group. This chart allows us to quickly and efficiently see how FCM (or any other manager) compares to its peers and gives the reader the ability to quickly see where the problem issues are.

In the Capital Market Risk Advisors (CMRA) 2011 risk survey, respondents were asked to rank their greatest focus when conducting and assessing risk management. The results of this survey are illustrated in Figure 10.3. Several things in the survey results are enlightening. First, many top risk concerns are non-investment-related risks. Second, it is interesting that only 32 percent of respondents view operational risk as a major focus. Given the importance of operational due diligence, this figure is somewhat

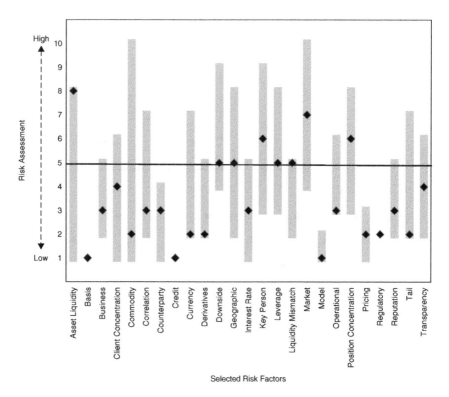

FIGURE 10.2 Analysis of Selected Risk Measures for FCM vs. Peer Universe

disappointing. In Figure 10.4, the CMRA survey measured the percentage of respondents that had a formal risk management plan in place over the last three years. The number of respondents with formal policies in place had increased significantly over the period (from 60 percent in 2009 to 87 percent in 2011). This clearly underscores the growing importance of risk management and formal risk management policies today.

RISK DUE DILIGENCE

Now that we have established that risk is prevalent across all areas within a hedge fund, we can define the risk due diligence process as it relates to our case study of FCM. We have already analyzed a number of performance-based (Chapters 4 and 5) and exposure-based risk measures (Chapter 7). In addition, we covered operational risks (Chapter 9). We will aggregate all of

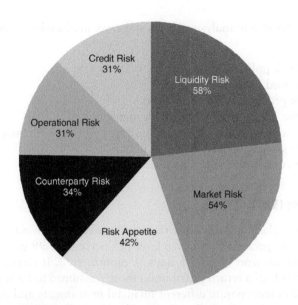

FIGURE 10.3 CMRA 2011 Risk Governance
Survey—Risk Focus

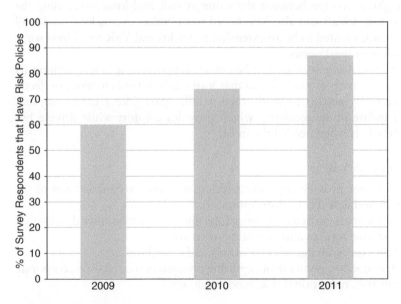

FIGURE 10.4 CMRA 2011 Risk Governance Survey—% of Respondents with
Formal Risk Policies

these risks later in our analysis. At this stage, we are looking to evaluate the following:

- Formal risk policy and procedures.
- Systems used to monitor risk.
- Test risk procedures for robustness.
- Assess the qualifications of the risk manager.
- Determine the independence and authority of the risk manager.
- Evaluate stated exposure and risk limits.
- Test for compliance with stated risk limits.

Value at Risk (VaR)

VaR describes the maximum loss one can expect from an adverse market move within a specified confidence level (95 percent or 99 percent) over a specified time horizon (1 day, 5 days, 1 month, etc.). It characterizes the extreme quantile of a return distribution mostly assumed to be normally distributed. It can incorporate different financial instruments and asset classes to generate a single estimate for expected loss.

Conditional VaR (CVaR) is a measure that assesses the likelihood that a specific loss will exceed the calculated VaR figure. It is derived by applying the weighted average between the value at risk and losses exceeding the value at risk. CVaR can also be referred to as "mean excess loss" and "tail VaR." It was created to be an extension to traditional VaR to address some of its inherent weaknesses.

While VaR has its uses and has many supporters, it is not without its problems. I have personally found that VaR analysis tends to work perfectly until we really need it to work, then it falls apart (like a car airbag that doesn't inflate in an accident,[1] which provides comfort while driving but ultimately fails when needed the most).

Problems with VaR

- It does not provide any information about the extreme left tail of the profit and loss (P&L) distribution.
- It relies upon particular assumptions about the probability distribution of extreme returns and normality of returns.
- It relies on estimates of correlations and volatilities.
- It does not do a good job of capturing nonsystematic risks (i.e., corporate event risk, operational risk, model risk, etc.).

Despite its shortcomings, VaR and CVaR can be used as another tool in our due diligence toolbox. Using the same 13F data that we used to evaluate the portfolio previously, we can calculate a portfolio value at risk (VaR) for each of the 13F reports available to us (quarterly beginning March 2010 through September 2011). In this chapter, we will review the latest 13F report (Sep-11) and perform analysis across a variety of measures.

The value at risk analysis in Table 10.1 displays the results for FCM's long portfolio (including leverage) over a one-day time horizon with a 95 percent confidence level. At the total portfolio level, VaR was calculated to be $9.75 million (meaning we can be 95 percent confident that the maximum loss we can expect the portfolio to experience over a single day would be

TABLE 10.1 FCM 13F Portfolio (Sep-11): One-Day VaR Analysis—All Positions

		Historical VaR 95% Confidence Interval One-Day Time Horizon			
Ticker	Stock Name	Market Value	VaR	VaR %	CVaR
STEC	STEC, Inc.	$ 12,610,000	$ 763,623	6.1	$ 1,023,659
KKD	Krispy Kreme Doughnuts, Inc.	$ 9,487,000	$ 550,054	5.8	$ 662,955
VICR	Vicor Corp.	$ 12,650,000	$ 708,076	5.6	$ 946,813
GSIG	GSI Group Inc.	$ 12,650,000	$ 665,869	5.3	$ 777,427
ZUMZ	Zumiez, Inc.	$ 18,975,000	$ 944,215	5.0	$ 1,252,568
DIOD	Diodes Incorporated	$ 9,487,000	$ 456,306	4.8	$ 617,472
HGG	hhgregg, Inc.	$ 18,975,000	$ 886,975	4.7	$ 1,161,618
PRIM	Primoris Services Corp.	$ 6,325,000	$ 293,371	4.6	$ 373,114
GLF	Gulfmark Offshore, Inc.	$ 12,650,000	$ 585,969	4.6	$ 847,335
THO	Thor Industries Inc.	$ 18,975,000	$ 864,557	4.6	$ 1,083,920
HITK	Hi Tech Pharmaceutical Co. Inc.	$ 18,975,000	$ 860,013	4.5	$ 1,033,079
BRKR	Bruker Corporation	$ 12,650,000	$ 520,635	4.1	$ 723,710
SAPE	Sapient Corp.	$ 12,650,000	$ 500,382	4.0	$ 676,671
ISIL	Intersil Corporation	$ 12,650,000	$ 484,283	3.8	$ 621,803
MCRL	Micrel Inc.	$ 15,812,000	$ 598,347	3.8	$ 759,644
ALGT	Allegiant Travel Company	$ 12,650,000	$ 467,230	3.7	$ 534,317
SNX	SYNNEX Corp.	$ 18,975,000	$ 692,872	3.7	$ 921,506
MCF	Contango Oil & Gas Co.	$ 12,650,000	$ 457,862	3.6	$ 663,036
TTEC	TeleTech Holdings Inc.	$ 18,975,000	$ 683,425	3.6	$ 966,669
TXRH	Texas Roadhouse Inc.	$ 12,650,000	$ 400,486	3.2	$ 557,515
FDP	Fresh Del Monte Produce Inc.	$ 18,975,000	$ 588,124	3.1	$ 747,338
EXLS	Exlservice Holdings, Inc.	$ 15,812,000	$ 468,026	3.0	$ 647,808
Total Portfolio		$ 316,208,000	$ 9,751,678	3.1%	$ 13,961,126

$9.75 million). The levered market value of the long portfolio was $316 million, so we can calculate the VaR percentage (VaR divided by portfolio market value) to be 3.1 percent (meaning we can be 95 percent confident that the maximum single-day loss we can expect from the portfolio would be −3.1 percent). The conditional value at risk (CVaR) for the portfolio was calculated to be $13.96 million, which translated to a potential percentage loss of −4.4 percent (CVaR divided by portfolio market value).

This analysis also lists the VaR and CVaR calculations for each of the positions in the portfolio as well. The individual VaR and CVaR figures will not sum to the portfolio total because the portfolio takes into account position weighting and the underlying correlation between the individual stocks. The individual stocks have been sorted according to VaR percentage.

Additional Observations

- The smallest positions in FCM's 13F long portfolio by market value (Krispy Kreme, Diodes, and Primoris) account for three of the top eight when ranked by VaR percentage.
- The largest contributors to CVaR were (in order): Zumiez ($1.25 million), hhgregg, Inc. ($1.16 million), Thor Industries ($1.08 million), Hi Tech Pharmaceutical ($1.03 million), and STEC ($1.02 million).

Table 10.2 aggregates the 13F long portfolio according to GICS (Global Industry Classification Standard) sector classifications. There are several key observations in this analysis. The first is that information technology (IT), which is the largest sector by market value by a wide margin, had the lowest VaR percentage (3.0 percent). The second is that the energy sector,

TABLE 10.2   FCM 13F Portfolio (Sep-11): 1-Day VaR Analysis—Sector

GICS Sector	Historical VaR 95% Confidence Interval One-Day Time Horizon			
	Market Value	VaR	VaR %	CVaR
Energy	$ 25,300,000	$ 1,049,742	4.2	$ 1,433,030
Health Care	$ 31,625,000	$ 1,202,630	3.8	$ 1,583,197
Consumer Discretionary	$ 79,062,000	$ 2,973,096	3.8	$ 3,897,500
Industrials	$ 31,625,000	$ 1,107,545	3.5	$ 1,603,762
Consumer Staples	$ 18,975,000	$ 588,124	3.1	$ 747,338
Information Technology	$ 129,622,000	$ 3,922,282	3.0	$ 5,647,659
Total Portfolio	**$ 316,209,000**	**$ 9,751,678**	**3.1%**	**$ 13,961,126**

which is the second smallest sector by market value, had the highest level of VaR percentage (4. percent). While the energy sector makes up only about one-fifth of the market value relative to information technology, its VaR represents one-fourth that of the VaR for the IT sector. Clearly, FCM's energy stocks exhibit more volatility than the stocks in any other sector.

Table 10.3 displays the results of the one-day VaR analysis for FCM's 13F portfolio aggregated by GICS industry. The largest industry by market value, retail, had the third lowest VaR percentage of the 15 industries in the analysis (3.5 percent). Semiconductors, an industry we had highlighted when we had analyzed portfolio exposures in previous chapters, is the second largest industry by market value, but had a relatively low VaR percentage (3.8 percent). None of the top five industries according to VaR percentage have more than one underlying stock in their respective groups, so we can conclude that VaR seems to be driven more by individual stock holdings than any specific industry themes.

Table 10.4 breaks out the VaR analysis according to defined beta ranges. As expected, the higher the beta, the higher the VaR figures.

Tables 10.5 through 10.8 display the results of the FCM 13F long portfolio VaR analysis for a one-month time horizon with a 95 percent

TABLE 10.3   FCM 13F Portfolio (Sep-11): One-Day VaR Analysis—Industry

	Historical VaR 95% Confidence Interval One-Day Time Horizon			
GICS Industry	Market Value	VaR	VaR %	CVaR
Computers	$ 12,610,000	$ 763,263	6.1	$ 1,023,659
Electrical Components/Equip	$ 12,650,000	$ 708,076	5.6	$ 946,813
Diversified Holding Companies	$ 6,325,000	$ 283,371	4.6	$ 373,114
Transportation	$ 12,650,000	$ 585,969	4.6	$ 847,335
Home Builders	$ 18,975,000	$ 864,557	4.6	$ 1,083,920
Pharmaceuticals	$ 18,975,000	$ 860,013	4.5	$ 1,033,079
Health Care Products	$ 12,650,000	$ 520,635	4.1	$ 723,710
Internet	$ 12,650,000	$ 500,382	4.0	$ 676,671
Semiconductors	$ 50,600,000	$ 1,898,260	3.8	$ 2,396,188
Airlines	$ 12,650,000	$ 467,230	3.7	$ 534,317
Software	$ 18,975,000	$ 692,872	3.7	$ 921,506
Oil & Gas	$ 12,650,000	$ 457,862	3.6	$ 663,036
Retail	$ 60,087,000	$ 2,126,939	3.5	$ 2,986,788
Commercial Services	$ 34,787,000	$ 1,113,299	3.2	$ 1,533,900
Food	$ 18,975,000	$ 588,124	3.1	$ 747,338
Total Portfolio	$ 316,209,000	$ 9,751,678	3.1%	$ 13,961,126

TABLE 10.4 FCM 13F Portfolio (Sep-11): One-Day VaR Analysis—Beta

One-Day Time Horizon				
Beta Ranges	Market Value	VaR	VaR %	CVaR
1.5 to 1.7	$ 41,112,000	$ 1,830,368	4.5	$ 2,473,026
1.3 to 1.5	$ 47,397,000	$ 1,876,808	4.0	$ 2,658,358
1.0 to 1.3	$ 161,287,000	$ 5,189,635	3.2	$ 6,988,490
0.7 to 1.0	$ 37,950,000	$ 1,131,184	3.0	$ 1,592,414
0.5 to 0.7	$ 28,462,000	$ 775,847	2.7	$ 1,038,527
Total Portfolio	$ 316,208,000	$ 9,751,678	3.1%	$ 13,961,126

TABLE 10.5 FCM 13F Portfolio (Sep-11): One-Month VaR Analysis—All Positions

		Historical VaR 95% Confidence Interval One-Month Time Horizon			
Ticker	Stock Name	Market Value	VaR	VaR %	CVaR
STEC	STEC, Inc.	$ 12,610,000	$ 3,580,021	28.4	$ 4,801,385
KKD	Krispy Kreme Doughnuts, Inc.	$ 9,487,000	$ 2,579,982	27.2	$ 3,109,537
VICR	Vicor Corp.	$ 12,650,000	$ 3,321,172	26.3	$ 4,440,945
GSIG	GSI Group Inc.	$ 12,650,000	$ 3,123,202	24.7	$ 3,646,454
ZUMZ	Zumiez, Inc.	$ 18,975,000	$ 4,428,759	23.3	$ 5,875,067
DIOD	Diodes Incorporated	$ 9,487,000	$ 2,140,264	22.6	$ 2,896,199
HGG	hhgregg, Inc.	$ 18,975,000	$ 4,160,280	21.9	$ 5,448,473
PRIM	Primoris Services Corporation	$ 6,325,000	$ 1,376,032	21.8	$ 1,750,059
GLF	Gulfmark Offshore, Inc.	$ 12,650,000	$ 2,748,438	21.7	$ 3,974,353
THO	Thor Industries Inc.	$ 18,975,000	$ 4,055,130	21.4	$ 5,084,038
HITK	Hi Tech Pharmaceutical Co. Inc.	$ 18,975,000	$ 4,033,817	21.3	$ 4,845,569
BRKR	Bruker Corporation	$ 12,650,000	$ 2,441,994	19.3	$ 3,394,502
SAPE	Sapient Corp.	$ 12,650,000	$ 2,346,998	18.6	$ 3,173,866
ISIL	Intersil Corporation	$ 12,650,000	$ 2,271,491	18.0	$ 2,916,515
MCRL	Micrel Inc.	$ 15,812,000	$ 2,806,497	17.8	$ 3,563,048
ALGT	Allegiant Travel Company	$ 12,650,000	$ 2,191,502	17.3	$ 2,506,169
SNX	SYNNEX Corp.	$ 18,975,000	$ 3,249,856	17.1	$ 4,322,248
MCF	Contango Oil & Gas Co.	$ 12,650,000	$ 2,147,562	17.0	$ 3,109,913
TTEC	TeleTech Holdings Inc.	$ 18,975,000	$ 3,205,548	16.9	$ 4,534,079
TXRH	Texas Roadhouse Inc.	$ 12,650,000	$ 1,878,446	14.9	$ 2,614,977
FDP	Fresh Del Monte Produce Inc.	$ 18,975,000	$ 2,758,546	14.5	$ 3,505,326
EXLS	Exlservice Holdings, Inc.	$ 15,812,000	$ 2,195,236	13.9	$ 3,038,487
Total Portfolio		$ 316,208,000	$ 45,739,423	14.5%	$ 65,483,496

TABLE 10.6 FCM 13F Portfolio (Sep-11): One-Month VaR Analysis—Sector

GICS Sector	95% Confidence Interval One-Month Time Horizon			
	Market Value	VaR	VaR %	CVaR
Energy	$ 25,300,000	$ 4,923,725	19.5	$ 6,721,506
Health Care	$ 31,625,000	$ 5,640,836	17.8	$ 7,425,852
Consumer Discretionary	$ 79,062,000	$ 13,945,057	17.6	$ 18,280,893
Information Technology	$ 129,622,000	$ 18,397,134	17.2	$ 26,489,870
Industrials	$ 31,625,000	$ 5,194,848	16.4	$ 7,522,309
Consumer Staples	$ 18,975,000	$ 2,758,546	14.5	$ 3,505,326
Total Portfolio	$ 316,209,000	$ 45,739,423	14.5%	$ 65,483,496

TABLE 10.7 FCM 13F Portfolio (Sep-11): One-Month VaR Analysis—Industry

GICS Industry	Historical VaR 95% Confidence Interval One-Month Time Horizon			
	Market Value	VaR	VaR %	CVaR
Computers	$ 12,610,000	$ 3,580,021	28.4	$ 4,801,385
Electrical Components/Equip	$ 12,650,000	$ 3,321,172	26.3	$ 4,440,945
Diversified Holding Companies	$ 6,325,000	$ 1,376,032	21.8	$ 1,750,059
Transportation	$ 12,650,000	$ 2,748,438	21.7	$ 3,974,353
Home Builders	$ 18,975,000	$ 4,055,130	21.4	$ 5,084,038
Pharmaceuticals	$ 18,975,000	$ 4,033,817	21.3	$ 4,845,569
Health Care Products	$ 12,650,000	$ 2,441,994	19.3	$ 3,394,502
Internet	$ 12,650,000	$ 2,346,998	18.6	$ 3,173,866
Semiconductors	$ 50,600,000	$ 8,903,630	17.6	$ 11,239,120
Airlines	$ 12,650,000	$ 2,191,502	17.3	$ 2,506,169
Software	$ 18,975,000	$ 3,249,856	17.1	$ 4,322,248
Oil & Gas	$ 12,650,000	$ 2,147,562	17.0	$ 3,109,913
Retail	$ 60,087,000	$ 9,976,229	16.6	$ 14,009,277
Commercial Services	$ 34,787,000	$ 5,221,837	15.0	$ 7,194,629
Food	$ 18,975,000	$ 2,758,546	14.5	$ 3,505,326
Total Portfolio	$ 316,209,000	$ 45,739,423	14.5%	$ 65,483,496

TABLE 10.8 FCM 13F Portfolio (Sep-11): One-Month VaR Analysis—Beta

	Historical VaR 95% Confidence Interval One-Month Time Horizon			
Beta Ranges	Market Value	VaR	VaR %	CVaR
1.5 to 1.7	$ 41,112,000	$ 8,585,187	20.9	$ 11,599,518
1.3 to 1.5	$ 47,397,000	$ 8,803,012	18.6	$ 12,468,806
1.0 to 1.3	$ 161,287,000	$ 24,341,547	15.1	$ 32,778,923
0.7 to 1.0	$ 37,950,000	$ 5,305,725	14.0	$ 7,469,086
0.5 to 0.7	$ 28,462,000	$ 3,639,044	12.8	$ 4,871,123
Total Portfolio	$ 316,208,000	$ 45,739,423	14.5%	$ 65,483,496

level of confidence. This analysis indicates that the maximum value at risk was $45.7 million, which translates to a VaR percentage of 14.5 percent based on the portfolio's total market value of $316 million. The CVaR was estimated to be $65.5 million, or 20.7 percent on a CvaR percentage basis.

Stress Tests and Scenario Analysis

A stress test uses extreme stress scenarios as a means of estimating how a current portfolio would perform under the same or similar conditions. Types of scenarios include historical scenarios (i.e., September 2011) and market scenarios (i.e., a 20 percent drop in equity markets). Other scenarios can include extreme moves in interest rates, credit spreads, commodity prices, FX rates, volatility, and so on.

In addition to calculating and reviewing VaR statistics, we can also use the same 13F data to conduct portfolio stress tests for each of FCM's quarterly 13F reports (from Mar-10 to Sep-11).

The analysis in Table 10.9 estimates the one-day impact on FCM's 13F long portfolio based on market stresses in September 2011 brought on by the terrorist attacks.

This stress test covers the two weeks from Monday, September 11, 2001, through Monday, September 24, 2011.

Global equity markets experienced large declines in value over this period:

- S&P 500 declined −8.2 percent.
- Russell 2000 declined −10.7 percent.
- Germany's DAX declined −13.5 percent.

- U.K.'s FTSE 100 declined −8.3 percent.
- Japan's Nikkei 225 declined −6.3 percent.

TABLE 10.9 FCM 13F Portfolio (Sep-11): One-Day Stress Test (Sept. 11)

| | | Stress Test
Event: September 11, 2001
One-Day Time Horizon | | |
Ticker	Stock Name	Market Value	$ P&L	% P&L
ZUMZ	Zumiez, Inc.	$ 18,975,000	(3,508,053)	−18.5
HGG	hhgregg, Inc.	$ 18,975,000	(3,322,380)	−17.5
TXRH	Texas Roadhouse Inc.	$ 12,650,000	(1,982,230)	−15.7
KKD	Krispy Kreme Doughnuts, Inc.	$ 9,487,000	(1,200,864)	−12.7
DIOD	Diodes Incorporated	$ 9,487,000	(1,177,374)	−12.4
VICR	Vicor Corp.	$ 12,650,000	(1,522,864)	−12.0
MCRL	Micrel Inc.	$ 15,812,000	(1,573,696)	−10.0
ISIL	Intersil Corporation	$ 12,650,000	(1,258,012)	−9.9
STEC	STEC, Inc.	$ 12,610,000	(1,244,511)	−9.9
ALGT	Allegiant Travel Company	$ 12,650,000	(1,238,380)	−9.8
SNX	SYNNEX Corp.	$ 18,975,000	(1,815,330)	−9.6
GLF	Gulfmark Offshore, Inc.	$ 12,650,000	(1,168,432)	−9.2
BRKR	Bruker Corporation	$ 12,650,000	(1,098,483)	−8.7
SAPE	Sapient Corp.	$ 12,650,000	(1,030,336)	−8.1
GSIG	GSI Group Inc.	$ 12,650,000	(983,294)	−7.8
THO	Thor Industries Inc.	$ 18,975,000	(1,361,128)	−7.2
TTEC	TeleTech Holdings Inc.	$ 18,975,000	(1,331,473)	−7.0
HITK	Hi Tech Pharmaceutical Co. Inc.	$ 18,975,000	(1,313,680)	−6.9
PRIM	Primoris Services Corporation	$ 6,325,000	(408,443)	−6.5
EXLS	Exlservice Holdings, Inc.	$ 15,812,000	(958,516)	−6.1
MCF	Contango Oil & Gas Co.	$ 12,650,000	(297,513)	−2.4
FDP	Fresh Del Monte Produce Inc.	$ 18,975,000	(106,694)	−0.6
Total Portfolio		**$ 316,208,000**	**$ (29,901,686)**	**−9.5%**

Stress Test Observations

- Total losses based on the recent 13F long portfolio were estimated to be −29.0 million, which translates to a −9.5 percent return for the day.
- Seven of the 22 stocks in the portfolio experienced double-digit losses.
- Seventy-three percent of the stocks outperformed the Russell 2000.
- None of the 22 stocks increased in price; however, Fresh Del Monte was nearly flat (−0.6 percent).

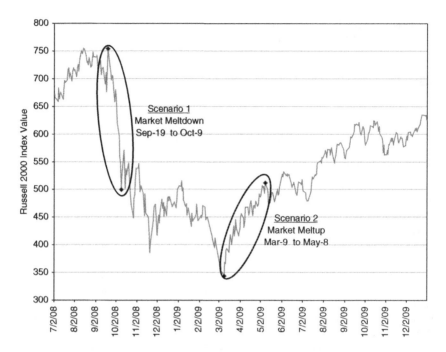

FIGURE 10.5 Scenario Analysis 2008 Meltdown and 2009 Meltup

In addition to reviewing standard stress periods, we can create an analysis to compare the performance of the portfolio over a variety of handpicked time horizons. The chart in Figure 10.5 depicts the performance history of the Russell 2000 Index from mid 2008 through the end of 2009. This is an interesting period of time, as we witnessed a severe drawdown in equity markets in 2008 and a complete reversal in 2009. Two distinct periods of time have been identified in the chart.

Scenario One

■ Market meltdown: from September 19 to October 9.

Scenario Two

■ Market meltup: from March 9 to May 8.

These two scenarios represent short-term rapid movement in the Russell 2000 and can be used as an indicator to see how the current (and previous) 13F long portfolios would have performed in these two very different scenarios.

In Table 10.10, we can review the performance of each of the portfolio positions during the market meltdown. The total (levered) portfolio would have declined −38.0 percent in value versus −33.8 percent for the Russell 2000. The unlevered portfolio would have fallen right in line with the Russell 2000 (−33.0 percent). The individual stocks in the portfolio would have fallen from −22.1 percent (Primoris) to −38.4 percent (Zumiez).

In Table 10.11, we analyze scenario two, which depicts a short-term extreme move upward by the Russell 2000 in the spring of 2009. Using FCM's 13F report for the period ending Sep-11, we analyze what their

TABLE 10.10 FCM 13F Portfolio (Sep-11): Meltdown Scenario

Scenario Analysis
2008 Market Meltdown
(9/19/08 to 10/9/08)

Ticker	Stock Name	% P&L	Contribution
ZUMZ	Zumiez, Inc.	−38.4	−2.6%
TTEC	TeleTech Holdings Inc.	−34.9	−2.4%
THO	Thor Industries Inc.	−34.7	−2.4%
HGG	hhgregg, Inc.	−33.4	−2.3%
FDP	Fresh Del Monte Produce Inc.	−31.7	−2.2%
EXLS	Exlservice Holdings, Inc.	−37.8	−2.2%
SNX	SYNNEX Corp.	−30.7	−2.1%
VICR	Vicor Corp.	−45.4	−2.1%
GLF	Gulfmark Offshore, Inc.	−44.6	−2.0%
BRKR	Bruker Corporation	−41.5	−1.9%
GSIG	GSI Group Inc.	−40.6	−1.9%
SAPE	Sapient Corp.	−35.9	−1.7%
DIOD	Diodes Incorporated	−47.2	−1.6%
MCRL	Micrel Inc.	−27.1	−1.6%
KKD	Krispy Kreme Doughnuts, Inc.	−43.2	−1.5%
HITK	Hi Tech Pharmaceutical Co. Inc.	−20.0	−1.4%
ISIL	Intersil Corporation	−28.7	−1.3%
MCF	Contango Oil & Gas Co.	−27.8	−1.3%
ALGT	Allegiant Travel Company	−24.9	−1.1%
STEC	STEC, Inc.	−21.3	−1.0%
TXRH	Texas Roadhouse Inc.	−19.6	−0.9%
PRIM	Primoris Services Corporation	−22.1	−0.5%
Total Long Portfolio (with leverage)		**−38.0%**	
Total Long Portfolio (w/o leverage)		**−33.0%**	
Russell 2000 Index		**−33.8%**	

TABLE 10.11 FCM 13F Portfolio (Sep-11): Meltup Scenario

Scenario Analysis
2008 Market Meltup
(3/9/09 to 5/8/09)

Ticker	Stock Name	% P&L	Contribution
KKD	Krispy Kreme Doughnuts, Inc.	250.9	8.7%
THO	Thor Industries Inc.	120.5	8.3%
GSIG	GSI Group Inc.	154.8	7.1%
ZUMZ	Zumiez, Inc.	83.0	5.7%
SNX	SYNNEX Corp.	77.7	5.4%
STEC	STEC, Inc.	97.7	4.5%
HGG	hhgregg, Inc.	59.3	4.1%
GLF	Gulfmark Offshore, Inc.	87.2	4.0%
BRKR	Bruker Corporation	76.5	3.5%
SAPE	Sapient Corp.	67.1	3.1%
HITK	Hi Tech Pharmaceutical Co. Inc.	42.3	2.9%
VICR	Vicor Corp.	61.5	2.8%
DIOD	Diodes Incorporated	80.6	2.8%
TTEC	TeleTech Holdings Inc.	38.1	2.6%
TXRH	Texas Roadhouse Inc.	40.5	1.9%
EXLS	Exlservice Holdings, Inc.	30.0	1.7%
FDP	Fresh Del Monte Produce Inc.	22.7	1.6%
MCF	Contango Oil & Gas Co.	32.1	1.5%
ALGT	Allegiant Travel Company	25.5	1.2%
MCRL	Micrel Inc.	16.9	1.0%
ISIL	Intersil Corporation	14.9	0.7%
PRIM	Primoris Services Corporation	10.4	0.2%
Total Long Portfolio (with leverage)		**75.2%**	
Total Long Portfolio (w/o leverage)		**65.4%**	
Russell 2000 Index		**49.1%**	

performance would have been in this market meltup. The levered portfolio would have achieved a 75.2 percent return versus a 49.1 percent return for the Russell 2000. The unlevered return would have been 65.4 percent. Both the levered and unlevered portfolio returns would have been far in excess of the index. Each of the 22 stocks in the portfolio would have experienced gains during the period under review, with three stocks (Krispy Kreme, Thor Industries, and GSI Group) each advancing in excess of 100 percent. These three stocks alone provided 24.1 percent of attribution to the levered portfolio return of 75.2 percent (which translates to about a third of the total return). A total of 13 stocks outperformed the Russell 2000 return.

In Chapter 7, "Portfolio Analysis," we reviewed liquidity based on quarter-end 13F portfolios and used the most recent average volume for each period to estimate how long it might take to liquidate the underlying portfolios. In Table 10.12, we apply the average volume for each stock during the market meltdown to determine how this stress period would have impacted the Sep-11 13F portfolio. We compare the results of this liquidity analysis to the analysis previously calculated. Focusing on the portfolio averages, we can clearly see that liquidity in scenario one represents a significant drop from the normal liquidity measured previously. In fact, we have estimated that the average number of days to liquidate the portfolio (assuming a $275 million portfolio value) in scenario one would increase the number of days to liquidate the portfolio from 12.9 days to 50 days (a 257 percent increase). Using a $500 million net asset value (FCM's stated maximum capacity), the number of days to liquidate increased from 23.5 to 91. On average, the number of days to liquidate increased by 387 percent.

Individual Stock Outliers (at $275 million NAV)

- Primoris: 470 days to liquidate.
- Hi Tech Pharmaceutical: 265 days to liquidate.
- GSI Group: 113 days to liquidate.

However, overall the fund's liquidity does not appear to be a mismatch with its investor terms. Investors in FCM's class B shares receive a lower base fee but also agree to a one-year hard lockup, so we should determine how much of current assets are locked up when we assess overall liquidity. Even if none of the assets under management were under lock, we estimate that the fund managers could liquidate most or all of the fund's holdings within a 90-day time frame (an average of 50 days assuming $275 AUM and 91 days assuming $500 AUM). Additionally, in our calculations we assumed that the fund manager would not trade more than 25 percent of a stock's average daily volume. In a liquidation environment, it is entirely possible that the manager may be able to sell or cover in excess of 25 percent on any given trading day, which would serve to reduce overall liquidation time.

Outside of full fund liquidation, this analysis indicates that FCM would be able to comfortably liquidate a significant portion of the fund's holdings within the quarterly investor liquidity time frame at current asset levels but might experience difficulty at $500 million.

Using the calculations from scenario one and scenario two, we can create an up/down analysis shown in Table 10.13 similar to the one we

TABLE 10.12 FCM 13F Portfolio (Sep-11): Meltdown Scenario (Liquidity Analysis)

Company	Assuming $275M in Fund Assets			Assuming $500M in Fund Assets		
	Recent 30 Day Average Volume	9/19/08 to 10/9/08 Average Volume	Difference (# of Days)	Recent 30 Day Average Volume	9/19/08 to 10/9/08 Average Volume	Difference (# of Days)
Vicor Corp.	59.9	40.8	(19.2)	109.0	74.1	(34.9)
GSI Group Inc.	36.9	112.5	75.6	67.0	204.5	137.5
TeleTech Holdings Inc.	27.4	11.1	(16.3)	49.8	20.2	(29.6)
Exlservice Holdings, Inc.	22.4	39.2	16.8	40.7	71.4	30.6
Fresh Del Monte Produce Inc.	15.2	6.0	(9.2)	27.6	10.9	(16.7)
Micrel Inc.	14.0	11.7	(2.3)	25.5	21.3	(4.2)
SYNNEX Corp.	11.3	12.7	1.4	20.5	23.1	2.6
hhgregg, Inc.	10.3	51.0	40.7	18.6	92.7	74.0
Krispy Kreme Doughnuts, Inc.	9.5	19.8	10.4	17.2	36.0	18.8
Hi Tech Pharmaceutical Co. Inc.	9.2	265.3	256.0	16.8	482.3	465.5
Contango Oil & Gas Co.	8.4	3.9	(4.5)	15.2	7.1	(8.1)
Allegiant Travel Company	8.2	6.0	(2.1)	14.9	11.0	(3.9)
Primoris Services Corporation	8.1	469.6	461.5	14.8	853.9	839.1
Bruker Corporation	5.9	5.6	(0.3)	10.8	10.2	(0.5)
Gulfmark Offshore, Inc.	5.6	3.9	(1.7)	10.2	7.1	(3.0)
Zumiez, Inc.	5.5	12.2	6.7	10.1	22.3	12.2
Thor Industries Inc.	5.2	4.8	(0.5)	9.5	8.7	(0.8)
STEC, Inc.	5.0	8.2	3.1	9.2	14.9	5.7
Diodes Incorporated	5.0	4.2	(0.8)	9.1	7.6	(1.5)
Sapient Corp.	4.1	4.6	0.5	7.4	8.4	1.0
Intersil Corporation	4.1	1.2	(2.8)	7.4	2.2	(5.2)
Texas Roadhouse Inc.	3.3	6.7	3.4	6.1	12.2	6.1
Portfolio Average	12.9	50.0	37.1	23.5	91.0	67.5

TABLE 10.13   FCM 13F Portfolio (Sep-11): Up/Down Scenario Analysis

		Up/Down Ratio 2009 Meltup/2008 Meltdown		
Ticker	Stock Name	Meltdown	Meltup	U/D Ratio
KKD	Krispy Kreme Doughnuts, Inc.	−43.2%	250.9%	5.81
STEC	STEC, Inc.	−21.3%	97.7%	4.59
GSIG	GSI Group Inc.	−40.6%	154.8%	3.81
THO	Thor Industries Inc.	−34.7%	120.5%	3.47
SNX	SYNNEX Corp.	−30.7%	77.7%	2.53
ZUMZ	Zumiez, Inc.	−38.4%	83.0%	2.16
HITK	Hi Tech Pharmaceutical Co. Inc.	−20.0%	42.3%	2.11
TXRH	Texas Roadhouse Inc.	−19.6%	40.5%	2.07
GLF	Gulfmark Offshore, Inc.	−44.6%	87.2%	1.96
SAPE	Sapient Corp.	−35.9%	67.1%	1.87
BRKR	Bruker Corporation	−41.5%	76.5%	1.84
HGG	hhgregg, Inc.	−33.4%	59.3%	1.78
DIOD	Diodes Incorporated	−47.2%	80.6%	1.71
VICR	Vicor Corp.	−45.4%	61.5%	1.36
MCF	Contango Oil & Gas Co.	−27.8%	32.1%	1.15
TTEC	TeleTech Holdings Inc.	−34.9%	38.1%	1.09
ALGT	Allegiant Travel Company	−24.9%	25.5%	1.03
EXLS	Exlservice Holdings, Inc.	−37.8%	30.0%	0.79
FDP	Fresh Del Monte Produce Inc.	−31.7%	22.7%	0.72
MCRL	Micrel Inc.	−27.1%	16.9%	0.62
ISIL	Intersil Corporation	−28.7%	14.9%	0.52
PRIM	Primoris Services Corporation	−22.1%	10.4%	0.47
	Total Long Portfolio	**−38.0%**	**75.2%**	**1.98**
	Russell 2000 Index	**−33.8%**	**49.1%**	**1.45**

had used in Chapter 6, "Quantitative Analysis." The up/down ratio is calculated by dividing the return for each stock derived in the "up" scenario by the absolute value of the return derived in the "down" scenario. We then aggregate the individual stocks to determine the portfolio's up/down ratio. Of the 22 stocks in the portfolio, only five of them did not rise in the up market more than they fell in the down market (Exlservice, Fresh Del Monte, Micrel, Intersil, Primoris). The average ratio for the portfolio was 1.98 times versus 1.45 times for the Russell 2000 index. Not surprisingly, Krispy Kreme was up nearly six times the amount it was down over the respective periods.

FACTOR DECOMPOSITION ANALYSIS

Another statistical method of analyzing portfolio exposures is to decompose portfolio returns and/or portfolio holdings based on predetermined factors. To do so at the portfolio level, we can create a series of risk factors based on geography, size, style, industry, currency, and commodity exposures. Industry factors can be based on GICS industries or subindustries. Style factors include value, growth, momentum, size, or leverage (among others).

By regressing individual portfolio holdings against a series of risk factors and aggregating the information at the total portfolio level, we may learn more about potentially "hidden" portfolio exposures and risks underlying the portfolio. We can perform this analysis on a single portfolio and create a single point in time analysis or project the portfolio backwards to evaluate how the underlying risk factors have changed over time. If we have multiple historical portfolios at our disposal, we can perform this analysis for each point in time to evaluate the consistency of the results and to help determine the consistency of the hedge fund manager's investment process and style.

The math behind this analysis is beyond the scope of this book, but I have included a graphical representation (Figure 10.6) to illustrate how a typical factor decomposition model can help us to better understand how a given hedge fund manager operates.

The analysis begins with an estimation of the portfolio's total risk (far left of the illustration). The regression then attempts to determine how much of the risk is due to the predetermined factors (factor risk) and how much of the risk cannot be explained by the factors (nonfactor risk). The results

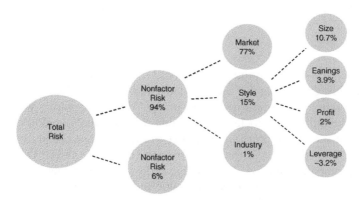

FIGURE 10.6 FCM 13F Portfolio (Sep-11): Position-Based Factor Decomposition

of this analysis indicate that most of the risk in the underlying portfolio of stocks based on the Sep-11 13F portfolio can be explained (it is estimated that 94 percent can be explained by the factors).

Decomposing the factors, we can see that the vast majority of the factor risk is related to the market (77 percent), followed by style factors (15 percent) and specific industry factors (1 percent). This should not be surprising, as the 13F portfolio only represents FCM's long positions and is fully invested (it is actually more than fully invested because the portfolio is levered to 115 percent gross long exposure).

Further decomposition of the style factor indicates that size (10.7 percent) is the primary component, followed by earnings (3.9 percent) and profitability (2 percent). This is a sampling of the factors that had the greatest impact on overall style factor risk. A dozen or so additional factors were measured and resulted in little or no impact on risk.

When conducting due diligence on underlying hedge fund risk, we need to assess the underlying risks inherent in the fund itself as well as to evaluate the people in charge of tracking risk. In our case study of FCM, we have already conducted multiple phone and face-to-face interviews to better understand investment and operational risks. In the remaining part of this chapter, we will include a meeting note based on our interview with Bill Hobson, who is FCM's COO as well as risk manager.

Questions to Ask When Interviewing Risk Professionals

- Do you have a written risk management policy? If so, please provide a copy.
- Has the policy ever changed? If so, when and why?
- Who is your risk manager?
  - Is the risk management function independent from the investment and trading functions?
  - What are the risk manager's objectives?
  - Whom does the risk manager report to?
  - Does the risk manager have the authority to take down risk?
  - Can anyone at the firm override the risk manager? If so, who? Has that ever happened? If so, provide details.
  - Does the risk manager fill any other roles at the firm? If so, how much time is spent on non-risk-related functions?
- Has the role of risk manager changed? If so, when and why?
- Has the risk manager changed? If so, who and why?
- What risk systems do you use internally (both proprietary and third party) to capture, calculate, and aggregate risk? Ask to see the risk

systems firsthand at their computer terminal. Also ask if they would send you sample copies of internal risk reporting (ask for a redacted version if they are uncomfortable giving you this type of information).

- Does the fund have any formal risk limits?

  - Position level
  - Sector level
  - Geographical level
  - Strategy level
  - Drawdown
  - Stop-loss
  - VaR

- Have the risk limits ever changed? If so, when and why?
- Are the risk systems tied into the trading or portfolio management systems? If so, how do they check to ensure that risk data have not been tampered with?
- Which employees at the firm have access to risk reports? Which employees have access to the system itself?
- Does the firm use any externally generated risk reports (i.e., prime broker risk reports or third-party risk aggregators)? If so, do you reconcile the results to internally generated reports? If so, who prepares the reports? Ask to see a sample of the external reporting. Make sure to verify with the external service provider the extent of the serviced provided.
- Does the firm employ an external risk consultant to review risk reports or to evaluate the efficacy of the risk management process?
- How are data fed into the risk management system (internal trading/portfolio management systems, prime broker, administrator)? If the source is internal, how do they verify accuracy?
- Has the risk manager ever identified any violations of stated risk policy? If so, what was the violation and how was it resolved?
- Do you calculate portfolio VaR? If so, please explain the methodology used. Please provide an example of the current portfolio VaR. How often is this analysis performed? How are the results used?
- Do you calculate portfolio stress tests or scenario analysis? If so, please explain the methodology. Please provide an example of the latest portfolio stress test and scenario analysis. How often is this analysis performed?

- Do you estimate tail event risk? If so, please describe the methodology. Please provide an example of this analysis. How often is this analysis performed?
- What involvement do any members of the investment or trading staff have in the risk management process? If any, please define.
- Do you measure factor sensitivities? If so, please describe the methodology. Please provide an example of this analysis. How often is this analysis performed and how is it used?
- If applicable, please describe the risk management process in the context of the latest market tail event (i.e., financial crisis in 2008). Go through the risk reports generated for each month and compare to actual portfolios.
- What is your plan for improving risk management in the next 12 to 24 months?
- What is your current risk budget? Do you expect it to increase or decrease in the next 12 to 24 months? Ask them to detail and explain the proposed change.
- Is the risk manager accessible to clients for update calls and periodic meetings?
- Are you willing to share aggregated portfolio risk reports?
- Are you willing to direct your external risk provider (or prime broker) to provide me with periodic copies (i.e., monthly) of the aggregated risk reports so that I can verify you are operating within your stated guidelines?

INTERVIEW WITH FCM RISK MANAGER

When conducting due diligence on underlying hedge fund risk, we need to assess the underlying risks inherent in the fund itself as well as to evaluate the people in charge of tracking risk and the systems they employ. In our case study of FCM, we have already conducted multiple phone and face-to-face interviews to better understand investment and operational risks. In the remaining part of this chapter, we will include a meeting note based on our interview with Bill Hobson, who is FCM's COO as well as risk manager. This note would normally be part of the meeting note that was included at the end of the previous (operations) chapter. However, because this book is structured in such a way that each aspect of the due diligence process is broken out in individual chapters, I have included it here to remain consistent with the book's flow.

To: Research Team
From: Frank Travers
Date: January 6, 2012
Re: Onsite Meeting with Fictional Capital Management
Interview with FCM's Risk Manager—Bill Hobson

After completing the operational interviews with Bill Hobson (COO) and Jennifer Cassell (CFO), I spoke with Bill (who is also the risk manager) about FCM's risk management policies. I started by asking him what his qualifications for the position were. He stated that he did not have any formal risk management training, but that he did not have to calculate any of the risk metrics, as the firm uses its portfolio management system to monitor positions and risk exposures in real time and also uses the daily risk reports generated by the prime broker.

Their internal portfolio management system is a top-of-the-line third-party system that many other equity long/short hedge funds use and one that I have reviewed on multiple occasions in the past (see my attached full review of the system for detailed information about how the system operates). While the portfolio management system is top notch for entering orders and managing portfolio exposures, it is not independent from the risk reporting. Trades are entered by the trader (Jacob), reconciled by Aaron, and approved by Jennifer daily, but there is no separation between the trading, portfolio management, and risk systems/reporting.

When I pointed this out to Bill, he replied by showing me copies of the risk reporting that he can pull down from the prime broker's risk system on a daily basis. The prime broker receives the trades independently from FCM and since the portfolio is a straightforward equity long/short strategy, they provide reporting that is more than adequate. In addition, Bill pointed out to me that Aaron reconciles all trades each evening and prepares a report of all daily trades for him to review as well. Bill compares the trade reports provided to him by Aaron to the risk reports generated by the prime broker's system to insure against errors or fraud.

I asked to see all the risk reporting for the previous trading day (including internal reports, Aaron's trade reconciliation report, and prime brokerage reports). We spent time going through each and I was satisfied that they have a robust system of checks and balances. Bill then signed into the prime broker's system and gave me real-time access to the reports. During the investment due diligence process, I had requested access to the prime broker's risk reporting to verify that the fund is positioned as they had reported to me via monthly letters and verbally during the interviews. I used this as an opportunity to verify position sizing, exposures, beta-adjusted exposures, liquidity, and VaR statistics. Bill printed out a copy of the current prime broker's risk report for me to take back to the office. I asked if he could instruct the prime broker to provide me with some historical reports and he said that he would speak to them. I then asked if he could also instruct either the prime broker or the administrator to provide me with some lagged portfolios (full position-level transparency). He said that he would speak with his partners and get back to me, but he indicated that he thought he would be able to do it.

After going through the reporting and systems, we discussed how he applied them to his job as risk manager. He stated that the firm employs basic risk measures: individual position limits (10 percent for longs and 5 percent for shorts), portfolio exposure limits (250 percent maximum gross), and a −20 percent stop-loss provision for short positions. They do not have any formal limits on total fund net exposure but they expect that it will be in the 40 percent to 60 percent range most of the time. I asked if they had any limits on sector or industry exposure and he responded that they invest where they find opportunity to profit—they do not have any limits. I asked if they would ever invest in just one sector and he replied that it was unlikely but that they did not have any rule against it. He suggested that I ask Ted or Jaime (which I had already done and was given the same answer).

I asked why he was named as the risk manager in 2009. He told me that he had suggested to Ted and Jamie that the firm become more institutional and part of that process should involve the segregation of the portfolio management function from the risk management function. He suggested that he take over the role and both Ted and Jaime agreed it was a good idea. I asked what the board thought and he said that it was well received. He went on to say that in late 2009, they had changed one of the independent board members to include a person (Ashton White) with a risk background to round out the board's skills. He mentioned that by doing so, they now have three independent board members (in addition to Ted, Jaime, and himself) that oversee the firm/fund's operations. I asked who they had replaced and he told me the previous member, Andy Dearns, was with a firm that provided professional board oversight. They determined that it would be better to have people on the board with specialized skills so that they could always strive toward best practices. I asked if he could provide me with the contact details for the three independent board members so that I could call them as part of the reference-checking procedure. I also asked for the contact details for the former board member so that I can call him to verify the circumstances of his departure. Bill said he would e-mail them to me.

I then asked him what kind of authority he had as the risk manager. He replied that if he were to find a violation of stated policy he would speak to Ted and Ted would instruct Jacob to remedy the situation. I asked why he (Bill) could not de-risk in the case of a violation, as that is clearly industry best practice. He replied that FCM is a small firm with one portfolio decision maker (Ted), and if there were an issue it would be discussed among the entire group in real time. He went on to say that Jacob sits right next to Ted and that any discussion about position or portfolio limits would involve Jacob and the rest of the team as well (considering that they all sit a few feet from one another). They are comfortable with the system as it currently stands and don't see any reason to change things at this time.

I asked if there was a specific reason why the change in the risk management function occurred in 2009 and he said that they did not respond to any issue or crisis. I asked him to walk me through the process for the last violation that he uncovered. Bill stated that he has never had to speak with Ted about violating any risk limits. He said that Ted keeps positions well within the guidelines and when any stock starts to get a little outsized, the team is "all over it." For example, he spoke about a recent long position that had performed well and had grown from being a 7 percent position to an 8 percent position (well within the 10 percent maximum), and it was a daily topic of conversation among the group. Ultimately, Ted reduced the position by half as it was nearing the team's target price. He said that he feels that Ted is great at taking profits; he is not a greedy investor.

I asked how much of his liquid net worth is invested in the fund and he informed me that all his money (outside of his home and some working capital to pay bills in the bank) is invested and has always been invested in the hedge fund.

I asked him if they had a formal written risk management policy and he replied that they did and that he would send me a copy (although he said that it states little more than what we had just discussed). I asked if their board member with the risk background conducts any independent checks on risk and he said that he has not thus far. The board does review the portfolio, fund performance, trading commissions, and the risk policy but they had not asked for a separate risk assessment. He told me that it might be a good idea to do so and wrote it down in his notebook.

I asked if the firm uses VaR, stress testing, or scenario analysis and he replied that they look at the statistics provided to them by the prime broker (and which are included in the risk report he printed out for me), but that they truthfully do not find these reports to be particularly helpful to them. He went on to say that they have a very simple strategy that puts them in what they believe to be attractive long positions and what they believe to be highly unattractive, overlevered, poorly managed short positions. He stated that they do not find any real value in VaR analysis because it is backward looking and because it tends to understate portfolio risk, which can lead to complacency. He gave me a quick primer on their stock conviction ranking system and said that he believes that this ranking system along with the firm's desire to actually "hedge" the fund with active short positions keeps them protected. They all know that the fund can be volatile at times but that is expected, and they "manage the portfolio based on a proven investment philosophy and methodology."

NOTES

1. David Einhorn, "Private Profits and Socialized Risk," *Global Association of Risk Professionals Review*, June/July 2008.

CHAPTER 11

Reference and Background Checks

"Trust but verify."

Ronald Reagan

"One must verify or expel his doubts, and convert them into the certainty of yes or no."

Thomas Carlyle

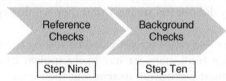

Reference Checks	Background Checks
Step Nine	Step Ten

Reference checking is one of the most misunderstood and underutilized aspects of the due diligence process. Reference checks are usually relegated to the very end of the process following dozens and even hundreds of hours of accumulated investment, operational, and risk-related due diligence. This does not make sense from either a psychological or efficiency standpoint. If we were to wait until the end of the due diligence process only to find out that a reference check with a hedge fund manager's former employer raised significant potential issues, we might end up throwing away quite a bit of time, effort, and money. In addition, my experience has taught me that it is human nature to minimize and potentially marginalize smaller issues raised during reference checks after so much effort has already been expended.

The solution is alarmingly simple: Start making reference checks earlier in the due diligence process. I would suggest making a few reference checks after you have conducted your first interview with the hedge fund manager(s) and have determined that you would like to move them through the due diligence process. This is an efficient use of time because making reference checks earlier in the process can also help us to better understand what the manager's skill set is as well as to point out additional lines of questioning. Make a few additional reference calls after you have completed the first round of onsite or face-to-face visits and have decided once again to pass the hedge fund along to the next stage in the due diligence.

ONLIST AND OFFLIST REFERENCES

Hedge fund managers often include the contact information for a few references right in the due diligence questionnaire. If not, then they will generally have a list of references all ready, complete with names and contact details (e-mail and/or phone numbers). This list consists of people that the manager had previously contacted and asked if they would provide references for them. As such, we can assume that the people from this list will provide fairly positive reviews. After all, why would they agree to be put on a manager's reference list if they weren't going to say positive things? More directly, why would the hedge fund manager list this particular group of references if they did not feel strongly that they would say positive things?

- Onlist reference—a reference provided to you by the hedge fund manager. The hedge fund manager has likely spoken to the references in advance to request permission to send out their contact information.
- Offlist reference—a reference that we source ourselves.

I make a point of calling all onlist references because they are easy to reach and I already know that they are willing to speak to me. In addition, I can often find out good information from these people—in many cases, surprisingly good information. Whenever I speak to a person as a reference for a hedge fund employee, I always try to put things in perspective by understanding who the person is and what their relationship is to the person being reviewed. Often some of the people you would most want to speak with have already been precleared and available as references, such as former bosses, co-workers, clients, associates, and so on.

When a hedge fund provides me with an extensive list of references that covers the entirety of their careers, I can take this as a good sign that there are not likely to be any skeletons in their closet. But as Ronald Reagan so famously said, "trust but verify." I have made reference calls to people on a hedge fund manager's "pre-approved" reference list who had no idea that they were on the list and who, in some cases, hadn't spoken to the individual in question for years. I have also had other onlist references provide negative reviews of the individual in question. The fact of the matter is that you just don't know what you are going to get until you make the calls.

Onlist references can also be good source of additional offlist references. Whenever I speak to anyone, onlist or offlist, as a reference for an individual I always ask if they can give me the names of anyone else that I should speak with. If I am speaking with a former co-worker, then that person should be in a great position to detail the names of everyone else that they had worked with (and can often save you the search time by providing their contact details).

Offlist references are, in my view, the most valuable. When a hedge fund manager who has been in the industry for 15 years and has worked at three different firms hands me a list of three people to call as references, I have to wonder why the list is so small. The reason might not be nefarious at all. Perhaps it includes the three people that know him best or are the people to whom he had reported at his previous places of employment. A good due diligence analyst will seek out the other people that were not included in the reference list. Sometimes the most important thing is not who *was* listed but who *was not* listed.

INTERNET AND SOCIAL MEDIA

One of the best ways to find out information that you can use to conduct reference checks involves simple searches on the Internet. I am an avid user of Google and search for information in it on a daily basis. When researching a hedge fund, type the name of each person at the firm into Google along with a relevant secondary word or phrase (to distill the resulting list to websites that are more applicable). For example, do not search for a portfolio manager named "John Smith" by his name alone because the search will result in millions of useless websites that have nothing to do with *your* John Smith. To remedy this issue, include a unique word or phrase to narrow the results. Including "John Smith" + "Excelsior Capital" in your search will more than likely reduce your search results. When using Google and other search engines to look for information about hedge fund employees, make sure you use every possible derivation of their name. For example, search for "Alexander Smith" and "Alex Smith."

When looking to find additional references for individuals at a hedge fund you are reviewing, create a detailed biography for each person under review. Include the following information:

- Name.
- Educational background (schools, grades, majors).
- Titles held (CFA, CPA, etc.).
- Affiliations past and present.
- Published papers, articles, books.
- Appearances on radio and television.
- Presentations at industry conferences.
- Current place of employment.
- Current title.
- Current role.
- Current responsibilities.
- Previous places of employment.
- Previous titles.
- Previous roles.
- Previous responsibilities.

Start to collect the data by reading the firm's presentation and due diligence questionnaire. Fill in additional blanks when you interview the person in question and the people that work with him or her. Make sure to include any and all factual information that you can find.

Now when you search the Internet and speak with references you have a detailed list of facts to verify. If a person represents that he has graduated from a certain university in the fund's presentation but lists a different university in the bio for a conference at which he spoke a decade earlier, you have a discrepancy to look into.

When searching with Google and other search engines, make a point to also check the news section of the search sites. In addition, if you are serious about a given hedge fund include the firm name and the names of key individuals in a Google alert. This function will e-mail you whenever the firm's or individuals' names appear either on the Web or in a news story. You can set these alerts to inform you instantly or at a specific preset time each day.

Outside of search engines, I have found social media to be an extremely useful means of locating additional references to check. My go-to service for finding professional connections is LinkedIn. LinkedIn is a social media website that caters to professionals across all industries on a global basis. Per the company's website, LinkedIn had 135 million members as of November 2011, and they estimate that nearly four billion professional searches were conducted on the platform in 2011 alone. LinkedIn provides a certain level of membership free of charge and then charges for some of its advanced features. I use the free service and have found it nearly indispensable.

Investment professionals have really embraced this website, and I find that many (if not a majority) of people that I come into contact with in the hedge fund industry have a LinkedIn profile. This makes reference checking so much more efficient. Using the John Smith example from before, I can search for John Smith and Excelsior Capital to find the profile for the person I am looking for. Once I click into the profile, I can verify that it is for the right person by comparing the biography in the profile to the biography of the person that we have created. If the individual in question has filled in the proper details, I can simply click on one of his previous places of employment and LinkedIn will provide me with a list of all current and former employees of the firm. I can cross check the dates to make sure that a potential reference worked at the same company at the same time that John Smith worked there. LinkedIn then gives me the ability to contact that person directly.

Using the biography for each hedge fund professional that I create, I then use that information to systematically scan LinkedIn to find every professional connection that I can. I reach out to each of these people and ask if they would speak with me as a reference. I generally hear back from nine out of 10 professionals that I reach out to on LinkedIn within a week and generally have no issue arranging reference calls from there.

Last, I would caution readers to understand that any information that they post to a website, share via Facebook or Twitter, or communicate through any other Internet websites might be found (legally) at a later date by a determined researcher (or forwarded by someone who is/was on their "friend" list). I have found some pretty funny things while conducting these kinds of detailed Internet searches (vacation pictures, book reviews, political commentary, etc.).

CONTACTING REFERENCES

There are two schools of thought when it comes to contacting references. The first method is to call them without any advance warning and request an interview on the spot. The thinking here is that if the person agrees to speak with you on the spot, you might catch them off guard and they may provide better information. The second method is to reach out in advance to set up a call at an agreed upon date and time. I am not a fan of the former, as I think it sometimes has a detrimental effect. In addition, some of the references that I conduct take some time and I try to make sure that

From: Frank Travers

To: John Smith

Sent: December 15, 2011

Subject: Reference for Ted Acoff (Fictional Capital Management)

John,

We are currently conducting reference checks on one of your former collegues at Zebra Capital: Ted Acoff, who is now with Fictional Capital Management.

I am an analyst at Hedge Fund Analysis, Inc., a hedge fund due diligence advisory firm, and we are currently considering making an investment in Ted's hedge fund.

My firm places a great deal of importance on reference checks and I would genuinely appreciate any time you could spare to speak with me.

Please feel free to e-mail me or call me with a date/time that works for you.

Regards,

Frank J. Travers, CFA

Hedge Fund Analysis, Inc.

frank.travers@hfanalysis.com

FIGURE 11.1 Sample Reference E-mail

the reference has set aside ample time to speak with me so that the call does not get rushed. I generally prefer to e-mail the reference in advance so that I can communicate the reason for the call and its importance. If they do not get back to me, I will eventually call them to arrange a call at a later date.

The sample e-mail in Figure 11.1 can be used for offlist references. You can use the same template for onlist references; just change the first sentence to "We are currently conducting reference checks for Ted Acoff of Fictional Capital Management and your name was provided to us by Ted as a reference."

Who Should Check References?

Too many firms hand this task off to junior analysts or administrative professionals. In my opinion, this is a mistake. Reference checks can be among the most difficult interviews you will perform as a due diligence analyst. They can also be among the most useful information sources available to you. The psychology of reference checking is subtle, as people are normally predisposed to say positive things about others or to say nothing at all. Reference interviews can really challenge the skills of the interviewer. Onlist references can be every bit as challenging as offlist references.

Type the term "reference check" in Google and many of the results will include many reference checklists or forms. Conceptually, these checklists sound like a good idea because they can help to keep you on track during an interview, and if things go off topic, you can refer back to the checklist to get things "back on track." The problem is that some of the best information that I have gotten from references came from conversations that strayed off topic. While there are certainly some specific questions that you will need to ask (to verify biographical information, for example), I prefer to ask relatively open questions and see where they take the conversation.

Asking open-ended questions and subtly steering the conversation from time to time in different directions is an art form. As a former colleague of mine used to say, "just get them talking." This comment was given somewhat tongue in cheek at the time but the advice is sound nonetheless. Try to build an honest rapport with the reference and see how things develop. As mentioned in previous chapters, learn the art of asking a question and then shutting up (so that you can actually hear the answers).

Reference interviews are as much about hearing what is *not* said as they are listening to what is actually said. When you ask a question, listen to the answer, and if you sense that it is lacking or fuzzy in some way, push that line of questioning further. Pay attention to the reference's tone of voice as an indicator of the person's true feelings.

Think about the profile of the typical person that you will be calling for a reference. Since many of the calls we make will be with former colleagues, it is safe to assume that many of them will have a work history similar to that of the person we are checking (i.e., if we are doing reference checks on a portfolio manager, we will likely call upon other portfolio managers, analysts, traders, etc.). Do you really think that a junior analyst is the appropriate person to represent your firm when speaking to these people? Do you further believe that the junior analyst has the requisite knowledge base and experience to question a 20-year veteran portfolio manager?

So, the answer to the question of who should conduct the reference checks is simple—you should (the person leading the due diligence effort). You can lean on other senior members of your team, but reference checks should be taken seriously and should be conducted by experienced interviewers. After all, who knows the details better than you do? It is remarkable how much more effective an interviewer you will be when you have studied the individual's background and have evaluated the hedge fund in question. This knowledge will lead you to instinctively ask better questions and will put you in a much better position to spot a false or disingenuous answer.

A last piece of advice is to avoid putting your words in other people's mouths. Instead of asking "Do you agree with me that John's stock modeling skills are his greatest asset?", you can ask the same question in different ways. For example, you can ask the question in a very open manner, "What is John's edge?" or more directly, "What do you think of John's stock-modeling skills?" If you ask the first question, you have essentially tipped your hand to the reference as to your views. The reference may use that information to frame subsequent answers (which will sound good to you because they will mirror your own views). A simple rephrasing of the same question will force the reference to come up with his or her own answer and may even lead you down a different path. For example, when asked what John's edge is, the reference may respond that John's risk management techniques are his real edge. You can then follow up by asking specifically about John's stock-modeling skills and see where that takes you.

PROBLEMATIC REFERENCES

Not all conversations with references will go smoothly and result in high-conviction answers to your questions. As stated earlier, reference checking can be difficult but they are definitely worth the effort. When dealing with difficult people, remember to be professional at all times—and be friendly (you will catch more bees with honey than you will with vinegar). Keep in mind that not all reference interviews will result in new information. In fact, I would argue that most reference interviews essentially rehash much of the same information—this is a good thing.

Types of Problem References

Following are some of the most common types of problem references you will encounter:

- The Stonewaller
    Not every reference will be open and forthcoming. Some people are afraid of potential litigation or they might be uncomfortable sharing information when they don't know how that information will be used (this is especially true in the case of a potentially negative reference). This is one of the main reasons why I do not like to call and put people on the spot, as I have found that this technique often turns

people off, and I get more measured or "politically correct" answers. If we contact the reference in advance and arrange a call or meeting, then we can infer that the reference is willing to speak to us (or the person would not have agreed to chat). However, some references are difficult to pry information from. My advice is to be patient and remain friendly. Remind the reference how important reference interviews are in your due diligence process and imply that nonanswers may even raise a yellow flag. Assure the reference that anything said to you will not be communicated outside of your firm.

- The Politician

When people try to avoid answering direct questions, they often sidestep the question by steering the conversation in another direction (just as politicians do). Be on the lookout for this type of behavior because it may be a great indicator of where the "skeletons are buried." If you ask a reference "What was John's relationship with his boss, Michael, like?" and the reference goes on to tell you about John's relationship with everyone *except* Michael, then you should push the issue further in this conversation and make a point to push it in other reference calls. To remedy this situation, gently steer the conversation back to your original question. If that does not work, then you might consider being direct and telling the person that he or she is not answering the question.

- The Evader

What do you do when you have contacted the reference and he or she has not gotten back to you? If the reference is onlist, then simply alert the person you are checking and ask him or her to reach out on your behalf to set up a call. This only works for onlist references because the reference likely has a relationship with the reference subject and had agreed in advance to provide a reference. When you are trying to secure an offlist reference, the key is to be persistent (without being annoying). Use an e-mail to explain what you are trying to accomplish with the reference and to assure complete confidentiality. If the person does not respond, call him or her directly. It is harder to dismiss someone when you are standing right in front of them or when they are speaking with you on the phone (whereas e-mails can easily be ignored).

- Negative References

Not all references checks will be positive. Most reference checks that I conduct are generally positive, and my goal in doing them is to get a complete and accurate picture of the person being checked out. I am always on the lookout for information that is new or inconsistent with previously gathered data or opinions that have been formed. However, every once in a while I receive a very negative reference. Whenever you receive a negative reference, you need to take the time to fully understand the issues involved. While conducting the reference call let the person know that the information they are providing may result in us declining to invest in the hedge fund under review (so that they know the potential consequences). Ask the person directly if they have any personal issues with the reference subject and ask if it would be okay to contact them again at a later time to clarify any open questions. In addition, ask them if they can think of anyone else that feels the way they do or can confirm what they are telling you.

After the negative reference call, communicate the results internally and decide what the best course of action should be. Not all negative references will lead to failing a hedge fund. Remember that some people have their own agendas and we will need to better understand what they are. For example, if a portfolio manager's former mentor and boss provides a negative reference, it might be because the reference truly doesn't think the portfolio manager in question is talented or because they were personally offended when that person left the organization to start their own hedge fund (thus becoming a competitor). In this example, you should find out from others who worked (and still work) at that organization what their relationship was like and if the former boss had taken the portfolio manager's departure personally. Ultimately you will have to make a judgment call in the matter, so you should exhaust all possible options before doing so.

Generic Questions to Ask

I don't want to contradict my previous statement that reference checklists are not optimal, but I have included a series of basic questions that you can ask. I do this to inform the less experienced analyst as well as to set the tone for the actual reference summaries to follow in the next section. In the questions that follow, I assume we are asking the reference questions about Ted Acoff, the portfolio manager at FCM.

- Can you tell me about yourself?
- How do you know Ted?
- What is your relationship with Ted and FCM?
- Are you related in any way to Ted or anyone else at FCM?
- Are you an investor in FCM? (If not, ask them why later in the interview.)
- What can you tell me about FCM?
- If the person had worked with Ted previously:
    - Can you tell me about the firm where you worked together?
    - What was your role there?

- What was Ted's role there?
- What was Ted's greatest strength?
- What was Ted's greatest weakness?
- Who did not get along with Ted? (This is a variant of "How well did Ted get along with everyone?")
- How had Ted evolved over the years?
- What surprises you the most about Ted?
- What are some of the things that you think Ted can work on to improve?
- Can you give me the names of anyone else you think I should speak with as a reference? (If they give you names, ask for some contact details if they have it.)
- What do you like about the FCM hedge fund?
- Can you suggest the names of other hedge funds that you think are of high quality?
- If the reference is a current client of FCM:
  - Why did you hire FCM?
  - What do you see as their edge?
  - What risks have you identified about the fund?
  - In what ways have you been disappointed with FCM?
  - How accessible is the team?
  - What information does FCM share with you?
  - Can you tell me something that they can or should be doing better?
  - Whom do you view as their closest peers?
- If the reference is a former client of FCM (or a previous firm):
  - Why did you redeem from FCM?
  - Did the fund meet with your expectations?
  - How did the investment team grow as investors while you were a client?
  - Can you tell me something that they can or should be doing better?
  - Whom do you view as their peers?
- What do you think of the entire team at FCM (investment and operations)?

WHOSE REFERENCES SHOULD YOU CHECK?

You must perform reference checks on all key hedge fund employees. In the FCM example, we will need to conduct checks on Ted Acoff (fund manager) and Jaime Wernick (director of research) for certain. Bill Hobson (COO and risk manager) is also important to the firm's operations. All three of these members are partners in the firm as well.

We should focus our reference checking on these three because they manage the fund and run the business. In addition, we should conduct some level of reference checking for the two analysts, the trader, and Jennifer Cassell (CFO). My rule of thumb when deciding whom to reference check is to include anyone who can have a significant impact on the management of the fund or firm. Since Ted, Jaime, and Bill had all worked together for several years at GCH, many of the reference calls that I make will likely apply to all three.

HOW MANY REFERENCE CALLS ARE ENOUGH?

This is more art than science. There is no scientific formula that we can apply to answer this question. The simple answer is that we should continue checking references until we are satisfied that we can verify their statements and provide sufficient support to our own internal assessment. For example, if we were to determine that a hedge fund manager is particularly good at identifying strong investment opportunities in the energy sector, we should look to find multiple independent verifications that this assertion is true (or at least that others who have experience with the portfolio also feel the same way based on their experience).

I created a simple tool to help me analyze references in the context of four main categories: relevance, character, experience, and skill. When I am done with a given reference call, I always write a formal note (just as I do when I do a call or meeting with a hedge fund manager) and distribute the note internally. Personally, I keep track of all reference checks by filling in a reference scorecard (like the one in Table 11.1).

The reference scorecard allows me to track all the checks that are made and to summarize what I took away from each check. I list the name of the person that I spoke with and how they know the reference subject. I then indicate who the reference subject is and whether or not it is an onlist or offlist reference. Each reference check is then scored based on the following four criteria:

1. Relevance
     Relationship to the manager (personal connection = lower score; independent = higher score); how well they know the person; perceived conviction.
2. Character
     Personality; morals; ethics; behavior; ability to work with others; attitude in tough times.

TABLE 11.1 Reference Scorecard

| | | Reference Scorecard | | | Make-Believe Capital Advisors | | | | |
| | | | | | Scores: Low = Zero; High = Five | | | | |
	Name	Relationship	Reference for	Type	Relevance	Character	Experience	Skill	Total
1	Alfred Pennyworth	Former co-worker at II Capital	John Smith	Off	5	5	5	5	75
2	Jason Todd	Former co-worker at II Capital	John Smith	Off	5	5	5	5	75
3	David Cain	Classmate at Yale	John Smith	Off	5	5	5	5	75
4	Sasha Bordeaux	PM at ABC Capital	John Smith	Off	5	5	5	5	75
5	Scott Balkan	Current client	John Smith	Off	5	5	5	5	75
6	Julie Madison	Former co-worker	John Smith	Off	5	5	5	5	75
7	Lew Moxon	Former co-worker at II Capital	Jane Doe	Off	5	5	5	5	75
8	Henri Ducard	Classmate at Yale	Jane Doe	On	5	5	5	5	75
9	Dan Turpin	Former co-worker at II Capital	Jane Doe	Off	5	5	5	5	75
10	Chu Chin Li	Former co-worker at II Capital	Jane Doe	Off	5	5	5	5	75
11	Perry White	Current client	Jane Doe	Off	5	5	5	5	75
12	Kenny Braverman	Former client	Jane Doe	On	5	5	5	5	75
	Total								900

3. Experience

Matches resume; rating at position(s); relevance to current endeavor.

4. Evaluation

Alpha generator? Hard worker? Leader? Work quality? Good business sense? Proven skill set?

Each of the latter three categories' (character, experience, and evaluation) scores is multiplied by the relevance figure to come up with the total score for each reference. The reasoning is that the scores should be scaled by how relevant we view each individual reference. For example, if we were to conduct a reference with a person's former co-worker (who also happens to be his brother-in-law), then we might assign a lower relevance score to that reference. On the other hand, if we do an offlist reference with someone who had worked right alongside the reference subject for 10 years and who knows a great deal about how the subject had invested previously and can comment on their strengths and weaknesses, we would assign a higher score to the relevance category.

I have found that when a given hedge fund's total score in the reference scorecard (including all references for all reference subjects) exceeds a total of 500 points, I am generally comfortable with the number of references completed (this translates to a minimum of seven references, assuming perfect scores of 5 in each category). For larger firms, the score would have to increase to reflect the additional key people for whom we would need to conduct reference checks.

BACKGROUND CHECKS

In the hedge fund industry, background checks are generally done by third-party investigative firms. These firms are experts at probing into people's backgrounds and extracting data from dozens of informational databases. Most investigative firms that conduct background checks have arrangements with other background firms located in most countries around the world and often employ them as subcontractors (at an additional cost to the buyer) when it is necessary to dig into the background of someone who was born overseas or has lived or worked in a different country. Background checks can include reviews of:

- Educational records
- Certifications
- Past employment history

- Identity/address verification
- Criminal history
- Litigation history
- Financial information
- Regulatory filings
- Print and online media

Background checks represent an independent accounting of the historical records for the key people within a hedge fund. However, these evaluations and resulting reports can be expensive, so when conducting hedge fund due diligence it is customary to only do background checks for senior decision makers within the firm. In the case of FCM, I would recommend paying for third-party background checks for each of the three partners (Acoff, Wernick, and Hobson). A positive result would be to receive a "clean" report from the investigative firm and to then compare the data in the report to the data we have collected during the due diligence process.

SUMMARY OF REFERENCE CALLS FOR FCM

The following summarizes the background reference calls to Jonah and Arty.

Jonah Kellworth

Jonah was difficult to reach. It was only after Ted Acoff called him and asked him to speak with me that the call took place. It was a short call and he did not give me a chance to ask many questions. He started the conversation by saying that he might not be the best person to speak with because he did not like the way that they (Ted, Jaime, and Bill) left GCH. He believed that they stayed long enough to get a track record and went off to do their own thing. I asked him how much notice they gave him and he replied that they were good about that—they offered to stay and help with the transition, but he didn't take them up on the offer. I asked what happened after they left and he replied by asking me, "What do you want to know about Ted and his guys?" Message taken. I then asked him to tell me how he views Ted and Jaime as investors. He replied that he thought they were very good analysts, Ted in particular. He was impressed with how they had managed the fund after Bill's departure and stated that performance was strong when they co-managed the fund.

I asked him what he viewed as their weaknesses and he said that Ted was a great technology analyst (that was his background), but was not as strong in other areas. He said he cannot speak to their ability today, as he has not kept in touch with either of them. He did not answer my question regarding Jaime so I asked him specifically what Jaime's strength and weaknesses were, and he said that Jaime was a good analyst but Ted was the brains behind the operation. I asked him how he got along with them when they were still working at GCH, and he said he thought things were fine. He hadn't heard about any issues from them. He stated he was surprised and disappointed that they left. I asked him if he had considered making them partners at GCH, and he stated that he had offered an equity stake to Ted and Jaime but not Bill when they told him that they wanted to leave, but they had already made up their minds to go.

I asked what he thought of Bill and he replied that he did what he was supposed to do. He finished his work on time and as far as Jonah could recall, they hadn't had any client complaints about NAV or reporting (which Bill spearheaded).

I asked him what he thought Ted and Jaime's edge was and he responded that he didn't know if they had one. He told me that answering that question was my job, not his.

As a final question, I asked if he could think of any reason why I should not invest with FCM, and he said that when they worked at GCH they did a good job and he had no issues with their investment skills. His issue was with their decision to leave after he took a chance at promoting them from analysts to portfolio managers.

Arty Gellberg

Arty was a day-one investor in the fund and had added some additional dollars over the years (he currently has $2.1 million invested in the fund). He told me that Ted was the best analyst he had ever recruited and that he had always expected great things from him. He said that Ted is a whiz with technology and telecommunications companies. His modeling skills are good, but his true skill is seeing through all the smoke screens that companies put out and finding the one or two key issues that will either make or break a company's future growth prospects. He also stated that Ted is a natural skeptic and that buoyed his ability to spot great short ideas. He mentioned several specific examples from their days together at GCH.

I asked Arty to name FCM's weaknesses. He did not hesitate in saying that the fund is concentrated in a few sectors and that investors need to understand that, while the fund has done well since launch, it can be volatile at times given its concentration. I asked why he stayed if he had concerns, and he said that he is not concerned personally because he knows what to expect and has a long investment time frame. He is concerned that some of the newer clients might be performance chasing and might end up being hot money (meaning they may leave at the first signs of a drawdown).

I asked him to comment on the relationship between Ted and Jaime and he replied that they are good friends. He has personally seen them work together and since he was an early investor, he has watched them grow as investors and as business owners. He thinks that their fund is a throwback to the old days of hedge fund investing when funds actually hedged out long exposure with shorts. He was thrilled with their performance in 2008 and feels that their process kept them out of trouble. I asked him if he had any concerns about the financial exposure in 2008, and he replied that they did a solid job analyzing the banks and mortgage companies themselves, but he was reassured because they hired a consultant to work with them on the sector as well. I asked him to tell me about the consultant but he did not have any information.

I asked him to talk about the other team members, and he said that Bill was a good COO and that he has been very impressed with Jennifer, the CFO. He thinks the analysts are pretty good and that the decision to give some stock research to their trader (Jacob) was a wise move, as they don't trade enough to really justify a full-time trader.

In the remaining reference calls, we were able to verify all factual data and support our conclusion that Ted Acoff and Jaime Wernick are strong analysts and that they work well as a team. We did uncover some new tidbits of information that will require additional information and follow-up.

Action Plan

- Complete the hedge fund scoring model.
- Follow up with FCM on any open questions.
- Order background checks for Ted, Jaime, and Bill.
- Find out more about the consultant that FCM used to assist in the valuation of their financial holdings in 2008. This information came from a call with Arty Gellberg and it was not brought up by either Ted or Jaime in my calls/meetings with them.
- Find out more information about when and why Jacob was given stock research responsibilities. This was mentioned when I met with the team during the onsite visit, but my sense from Arty is that there is a little more to the story.
- I asked John Grenel (former colleague at GCH) to name some winning and losing stock positions from back when Ted and Jaime worked there and he gave me several names. He mentioned that GCH really blew it with Cicso and Liberty Media and since they are both in Ted's area of expertise, I would like to ask Ted to speak about each of these positions. Neither of these names had been brought up when I asked Ted directly for the names of some losing trades from his days at GCH.

CHAPTER 12

Hedge Fund Scoring Model and Decision Making

"In any moment of decision the best thing you can do is the right thing, the next best thing is the wrong thing, and the worst thing you can do is nothing."

Theodore Roosevelt

"Informed decision-making comes from a long tradition of guessing and then blaming others for inadequate results."

Scott Adams

> Scoring
> Model

Step Eleven

At this point in the process, we have gone through all of the major steps involved in sourcing, screening, and evaluating a group of hedge fund managers. An institutional investment firm would at this time likely present all potential hedge fund candidates to its investment committee for discussion and, eventually, a decision to hire or not (or to place the hedge fund under review on a buy list or "bench").

In the previous chapter, we reviewed the procedure for performing reference and background checks. In this chapter, we will assume that references were largely positive and that the background check came back from the investigative firm with a "clean" report (meaning no issues).

I have found that one of the best ways to collect and to synthesize all of the information that we have received in the due diligence process is to

summarize all the key components of the process into what can be referred
to as a hedge fund scoring model.

HEDGE FUND SCORING MODEL

Scoring models have been around for many decades. I have found them to
be useful in my hedge fund evaluations for the following reasons:

- **Consistency**—force the reviewer to think about all the hedge funds
  under review in a similar context.
- **Attribution**—each variable in a scoring model can be aggregated to a
  broad level (investment, operations, risk), allowing for multidimensional
  analysis.
- **Tracking**—once a hedge fund has a score, it is relatively easy to update
  on a regular basis. This allows the reviewer to track the scores and
  monitor for changes over time.
- **Peer Analysis**—once a group of funds have been scored, the reviewer can
  look for trends within the various strategies or look for inconsistencies.
- **Apportioning**—scoring models give the reviewer the ability to emphasize those attributes deemed the most relevant when evaluating hedge
  funds and deemphasize those attributes deemed less important.

However, it is important to understand that scoring models are just one
of many tools that due diligence analysts have in our toolboxes.

In this chapter, I will highlight a simple hedge fund scoring model that
extracts various key elements of the process that have been highlighted
throughout the book. The model employs a total of 42 variables that cover
the key areas from the three main categories: investment, operations, risk.

List of Variables

- Edge
- Experience/Pedigree
- Investment Process
- Professional Turnover
- Investment Team
- Transparency
- Attribution
- Capacity
- Consistency
- Drawdown Potential Systems
- Administration
- Audit

- Business Continuity and Disaster Recovery
- Board of Directors
- Business Risk
- Internal Controls
- Operations Experience/Pedigree
- Internal Investment
- Liquidity Match
- Pricing/Valuation
- Audits
- Compliance
- Fees
- Liquidity
- Regulatory
- Leverage
- Risk Limits
- Risk Manager Authority
- Risk Process
- Systems
- Portfolio Concentration (position, sector, etc.)
- Internal Quantitative Risk
- Absolute Return
- Relative Return (indexes)
- Relative Return (peer group)
- Volatility
- Drawdown
- Correlation

The model is broken out into four components: investment, operational, risk, and performance-related. Each variable is weighted according to its level of importance. A variable that has a grade = 1 is viewed as the most important and will receive a higher multiple. A variable with a grade = 2 is viewed as important but not as important as variables in grade 1. All variables in the investment, operational, and risk categories receive a grade of either 1 or 2. All the variables in the performance-related category receive a grade of 3, which means they are viewed as the least important. As I have stated elsewhere, we should not hire hedge funds based on past performance (but neither can we ignore it).

Each variable is scored on a scale of 0 to 5, with 0 being the worst score and 5 being the best score. To apply the grade system, we:

Grade = 1: Multiply by three
Grade = 2: Multiply by two
Grade = 3: Multiply by one

This simple grading system allows us to emphasize those variables that we view as the most important. Each of the four categories is scored separately and then they are aggregated to compile a total score for each manager. Tables 12.1 through 12.5 display the summary results for each variable broken out by category. To understand how the individual variables were scored, I have included brief commentary for each.

Investment Variables

Variable:	Edge (Grade 1)
Definition:	Qualitative assessment of the hedge fund's edge—process, systems, people, or some combination? Level of conviction?
Score:	*3 out of 5*
Commentary:	*FCM performs solid research but does not seem to have any distinct advantage over other fundamentally oriented firms. They do employ a ranking model that is somewhat unique and they tend to take a nonconsensus view, which has led to lower correlation to their peer group.*
Variable:	Experience/Pedigree (Grade 1)
Definition:	Number of years in the industry; number of years in specific role. Quality of past experience.
Score:	*4 out of 5*
Commentary:	*Ted Acoff (PM) and Jaime Wernick (Research Director) have worked together since 2001 and, more importantly, since 2003 when they co-managed a similar product at GCH. Ted has 18 years of experience in the industry and eight as a portfolio manager (GCH and FCM). Jaime Wernick has 16 years of industry experience, including two as co-PM with Ted and five as research director at FCM.*
Variable:	Process (Grade 1)
Definition:	Efficient and effective use of people and systems.
Score:	*4 out of 5*
Commentary:	*FCM manages its human and systems resources well. Ted and Jaime have developed a system of internal checks and balances that has worked well for them for a number of years. The firm is small and they benefit from working closely with one another. They meet formally once each week, but are in contact in real time. Their ranking model is used effectively and has been in place since their days at GCH.*
Variable:	Professional turnover (Grade 1)
Definition:	Evaluation of professionals that have left the investment team.

Score:	*5 out of 5*
Commentary:	*The firm lost one junior analyst in 3/08, Julie Crelle. She decided to leave the industry completely. A reference check with her verified that she did not leave for cause and was a junior analyst who functioned more as support for Jamie. The firm has hired several people in the last few years to stay ahead of asset growth.*

Variable:	Team (Grade 1)
Definition:	Integration of the investment team. Team dynamic. Appropriate growth plan in place.
Score:	*4 out of 5*
Commentary:	*The team appears to work well together and from my personal observations as well as those from multiple references, Ted and Jaime have created an open environment where analysts can learn and grow. The firm has hired both investment and operational staff to stay ahead of growth. Given the level of position and sector concentration, they are adequately staffed at this time. They do have some room should assets increase to their stated max capacity of $500 million.*

Variable:	Transparency (Grade 1)
Definition:	Level and frequency of portfolio information provided to investors. Independent source?
Score:	*4 out of 5*
Commentary:	*FCM does not provide full monthly portfolio transparency, but they do provide detailed summary statistics (top five longs/shorts, gross and net exposure, net sector exposure). In addition, they are open to discussing and showing us all portfolio positions during any in-house visits. Last, they have agreed to provide us periodic access to summary-level reports prepared by their administrator as verification of assets and exposures.*

Variable:	Attribution (Grade 2)
Definition:	Does the attribution of performance match the story and stated style? Is it spread out or chunky?
Score:	*4 out of 5*
Commentary:	*We performed detailed attribution analysis of FCM's returns and found them to be in line with the firm's strategy and style. The attribution indicated that the performance can be volatile at times, but they have demonstrated returns that can be noncorrelated. Attribution highlights that they have made money on both sides of the book.*

Variable:	Capacity (Grade 2)
Definition:	How close are assets to stated capacity? Determine effectiveness of formula to determine capacity.
Score:	*4 out of 5*
Commentary:	*The fund currently has $300 million in assets vs. a capacity of $500 million. We have conducted analysis of the liquidity of recent portfolios (both the long and short books). The results indicate that FCM can manage roughly $700 million. This will provide a buffer between the asset level in which they will close vs. the fund's "true" capacity. All equal, the liquidity will be impacted above $700 million and we will need to monitor this closely.*

Variable:	Consistency (Grade 2)
Definition:	How consistent has the investment process been? If changes have been made, have they been additive?
Score:	*5 out of 5*
Commentary:	*The process has been remarkably consistent since the fund's inception. In fact, the process is not that much different from when they managed a fund at GCH (more focused by sector and position at FCH).*

Variable:	Drawdown Potential (Grade 2)
Definition:	Qualitative assessment of worst potential drawdown.
Score:	*2 out of 5*
Commentary:	*FCM manages the fund with a long bias. While they did successfully navigate a difficult market environment in 2008, we cannot assume that they would be able to time the market so well in the future. As a result, we can assume that the fund can fall nearly as much as the overall small-cap market in a worst-case scenario (if they are leveraged long and experience poor stock selection).*

Variable:	Systems (Grade 2)
Definition:	Proprietary and third-party systems. How manually intensive vs. automated.
Score:	*1 out of 5*
Commentary:	*Research systems are 100% Microsoft Excel based and manually intensive. The COO, Bill Hobson, indicated that they would likely automate some of the functions in the next 12 months (we should keep an eye on this development). Their trading system was provided by the prime broker and is industry standard.*

TABLE 12.1 Scoring Model—Investment Variables

Investment Variables			Score							Scaled
Grade	Variable	Description	0	1	2	3	4	5		Score
1	Edge	Qualitative assessment of the hedge fund's edge—process, systems, people or some combination? Level of conviction?				3				9
1	Experience/Pedigree	Number of years in the industry; number of years in specific role. Quality of past experience.					4			12
1	Process	Efficient and effective use of people and systems.					4			12
1	Professional turnover	Evaluation of professionals that have left the investment team.						5		15
1	Team	Integration of the investment team. Team dynamic. Appropriate growth plan in place.					4			12
1	Transparency	Level and frequency of portfolio information provided to investors. Independent source?					4			12
2	Attribution	Does the attribution of performance match the story and stated style? Is it spread out or chunky?						5		10
2	Capacity	How close are assets to stated capacity? Determine effectivness of formula to determine capacity.					4			8
2	Consistency	How consistent has the investment process been? If changes have been made, have they been additive?						5		10
2	Drawdown potential	Qualitative assessment of worst potential drawdown.			2					4
2	Systems	Proprietary and third party systems. How manually intensive vs automated.		1						2
		Total Investment Score								106 76%

TABLE 12.2 Scoring Model—Operational Variables

Operational Variables			Score							Scaled
Grade	Variable	Description	0	1	2	3	4	5		Score
1	Administration	Independent? Quality of firm? Length of service?						5		15
1	Audit	Independent? Quality of firm? Length of service?						5		15
1	BCP/DR	Process and procedures in place. Testing and review? Past issues?					4			12
1	BOD	Quality and independence of board members? Powers and authority. Past issues?						5		15
1	Business	Level of overall business risk. Growth plan in place?					4			12
1	Controls	Proper controls in place: trading, cash movement, separation of duties. Independent checks? Shadow processes?				3				9
1	Experience/Pedigree	Number of years in the industry; number of years in specific role. Quality past experience.					4			12
1	Internal investment	Amount of internal investment (as a percentage of liquid net worth). Decreases?						5		15
1	Liquidity match	Does investor liquidity match underlying position liquidity?					4			12
1	Pricing/Valuation	Formal written pricing and valuation policies. Independent pricing and valuation.						5		15
1	Professional turnover	Evaluation of professionals that have left the operations team.						5		15
1	Audit results	Verification that historical audits are unqualified and consistent with firm/fund strategy. Independent receipt. Audit timing.						5		15
2	Compliance	Process and procedures in place. Separation from investment function? Testing and review? Past issues?					4			8
2	Fees	Base, performance, penalties, subscription/redemption fees, fund expenses.					4			8
2	Liquidity	Investor liquidity.					4			8
2	Regulatory	Registered with local authorities? Any past issues? Review of documents (ADV).	0							0
		Total Operations Score								186 85%

TABLE 12.3 Scoring Model—Risk Variables

Risk Variables			Score							Scaled
Tier	Variable	Description	0	1	2	3	4	5		Score
1	Experience/Pedigree	Number of years in the industry; number of years in specific role. Quality past experience. Separation of duties?			2					6
1	Leverage	Amount and use of leverage.					4			12
1	Limits	Analysis of risk limits in place. Appropriate to strategy? Consistently applied? Applied to exposures and hedging activity.			2					6
1	Power	Is risk manager (team) independent? What authority/power do they have (i.e., can they take off risk)?	0							0
1	Process	Efficient and effective use of people and systems.				3				9
1	Systems	Proprietary and third party systems. How manually intensive vs. automated?				3				9
2	Concentration	Position, sector, industry, theme, geography, trade. Analysis of current portfolio.		1						2
2	Professional turnover	Evaluation of professionals that have left the risk team.						5		10
2	Quantitative	Analysis of quantitatively derived risk assessment (VaR, stress testing, scenario analysis, factor analysis, etc.).				3				6
								Total Risk Score		60 50%

TABLE 12.4 Scoring Model—Performance Variables

Performance Variables			Score						Scaled
Tier	Variable	Description	0	1	2	3	4	5	Score
3	Absolute	Historical annualized performance.					4		4
3	Relative to indices	Historical annualized performance relative to appropriate indices.						5	5
3	Relative to peer group	Historical annualized performance relative to appropriate peer group.						5	5
3	Volatility	Historical standard deviation; downside deviation. Sharpe ratio.						5	5
3	Drawdown	Largest historical drawdown. Sortino ratio.						5	5
3	Correlation	Historical correlation and Beta to market and peer group.					4		4
							Total Performance Score		28 93%

In Table 12.1, we can see that there are 11 variables (six with a grade 1 and five with a grade 2) in the investment section. The total scaled score (grade multiplied by the score for each variable) is 106 points out of a possible 140 points. This results in a percentage score of 76 percent (106/140).

Operational Variables

Variable:	Administration (Grade 1)
Definition:	Independent? Quality of firm? Length of service?
Score:	*5 out of 5*
Commentary:	*Top-tier administrator that provides full, completely independent NAV calculation. The relationship has been in place since the fund's inception.*

Variable:	Audit (Grade 1)
Definition:	Independent? Quality of firm? Length of service?
Score:	*5 out of 5*
Commentary:	*Top-tier auditor. The relationship has been in place since the fund's inception.*

Variable:	Business Continuity Plan (BCP)/Disaster Recovery (DR) (Grade 1)
Definition:	Process and procedures in place. Testing and review? Past issues?
Score:	*4 out of 5*
Commentary:	*FCM has had a written policy in place for each since 2009. They employed a third-party consulting firm to create and implement the procedures. The consulting firm is relatively new to the industry but they have a seasoned technology professional in charge of the FCM account. FCM could operate outside of their current offices (at Ted Acoff's home) within 24 hours if need be. Bill Hobson is in charge of the process.*

Variable:	Board of Directors (Grade 1)
Definition:	Quality and independence of board members? Powers and authority. Past issues?
Score:	*5 out of 5*
Commentary:	*FCM has a six-person board (three are independent). The three independent board members are all experienced in different areas within the hedge fund industry (legal, audit, risk) so that they can bring their expertise to the board and help maintain best practices. The BOD must vote and approve all major aspects of the fund's non-portfolio management activities.*

Variable:	Business (Grade 1)
Definition:	Level of overall business risk. Growth plan in place?

Score:	*4 out of 5*
Commentary:	*The fund has grown nicely over the last three years. They have a fairly diversified client mix (by number of clients as well as type of clients). The three partners have hired good people to support and help the business to grow. The fund has experienced strong performance and it appears that they may receive a consistent inflow of new capital over the next 6–12 months. We estimate that FCM is well above breakeven and, given recent asset raising trends, are in a good position in the immediate future.*
Variable:	Controls (Grade 1)
Definition:	Proper controls in place: trading, cash movement, separation of duties. Independent checks? Shadow processes?
Score:	*3 out of 5*
Commentary:	*Multiple signatures required for cash movements in excess of $10K (including one person from the investment side, COO, and the administrator). The CFO and her assistant provide daily reconciliations of all trades (but they work from the same trade system that the trader does). They reconcile this to the administrator and prime broker daily.*
Variable:	Experience/Pedigree (Grade 1)
Definition:	Number of years in the industry; number of years in specific role. Quality of past experience.
Score:	*4 out of 5*
Commentary:	*Bill Hobson, COO, has been in the hedge fund space for 14 years and had been with an audit firm for five years prior to that (outside of the hedge fund industry). Jennifer Cassell, CFO, worked as an auditor at a big four accounting firm before joining FCM in 2009. Aaron is fresh out of school.*
Variable:	Internal Investment (Grade 1)
Definition:	Amount of internal investment (as a percentage of liquid net worth). Decreases?
Score:	*5 out of 5*
Commentary:	*Each of the three partners has virtually all of their liquid net worth invested in the hedge fund. Jennifer (CFO) and Jacob (trader) have smaller amounts invested in the fund (both become investors in 2010). The other members of the team plan on investing a share of their 2011 bonuses in the hedge fund (but that has not yet occurred).*

Variable:	Liquidity Match (Grade 1)
Definition:	Does investor liquidity match underlying position liquidity?
Score:	*4 out of 5*
Commentary:	*FCM invests mostly in small-cap names and has in the past invested in some less liquid microcap names. While our analysis of the current portfolio indicates that the liquidity of the underlying portfolio does match investor liquidity (quarterly with 90 days' notice), we should be cognizant that liquidity can decrease in stressful times. Our analysis of the portfolio during the stressful 2008 period indicated that liquidity was poor, but that they would have been able to liquidate the book (with a minimal haircut in pricing) if they had redemptions (which they did not). The biggest question will come as assets approach and reach capacity—this must be monitored.*

Variable:	Pricing/Valuation (Grade 1)
Definition:	Formal written pricing and valuation policies. Independent pricing and valuation.
Score:	*5 out of 5*
Commentary:	*Exchange-traded securities that are fully independently priced and valued by the administrator. In our discussions with the administrator, they have never had any issues in pricing and have not had any challenges from FCM in the past.*

Variable:	Professional Turnover (Grade 1)
Definition:	Evaluation of professionals that have left the operations team.
Score:	*5 out of 5*
Commentary:	*No departures since launching the firm/fund. In fact, they have hired two dedicated people—CFO in 2009 and admin assistant in 2011.*

Variable:	Audit Results (Grade 1)
Definition:	Verification that historical audits are unqualified and consistent with firm/fund strategy. Independent receipt. Audit timing.
Score:	*5 out of 5*
Commentary:	*No audit done for 2006 (only 1 month stub period—accounted for in the 2007 audit). The audits are all unqualified and consistent with the fund strategy and information communicated by the firm.*

Variable:	Compliance (Grade 2)
Definition:	Process and procedures in place. Separation from investment function? Testing and review? Past issues?
Score:	*4 out of 5*
Commentary:	*No personal trading allowed at FCM. They recently hired a third-party compliance firm (Sep-11). It had been handled internally by Bill Hobson previously. The firm they are using is new to the business and, while they seem to have their act together, we will need to get comfortable with them to increase the score.*

Variable:	Fees (Grade 2)
Definition:	Base, performance, penalties, subscription/redemption fees, fund expenses.
Score:	*4 out of 5*
Commentary:	*1.5% management fee and 20% performance fee. The management fee falls to 1% for investors willing to lock up capital for one year. No additional fees. Expenses are industry standard.*

Variable:	Liquidity (Grade 2)
Definition:	Investor liquidity.
Score:	*4 out of 5*
Commentary:	*Quarterly with 90 days' notice is industry standard. One-year hard lock for investors in the 1% management fee share class.*

Variable:	Regulatory (Grade 2)
Definition:	Registered with local authorities? Any past issues? Review of documents (ADV).
Score:	*0 out of 5*
Commentary:	*Not registered with the SEC at this time.*

In Table 12.2, we can see that there are 16 variables (12 with a grade 1 and four with a grade 2) in the operational section. The total scaled score (grade multiplied by the score for each variable) is 186 points out of a possible 220 points. This results in a percentage score of 85 percent (186/220).

Risk Variables

Variable:	Experience/Pedigree (Grade 1)
Definition:	Number of years in the industry; number of years in specific role. Quality of past experience. Separation of duties?
Score:	*2 out of 5*

Commentary:	*Bill Hobson, COO, is the risk manager (since 2009). He has no formal experience as a risk manager and relies upon the internal systems created and maintained by the investment group to monitor activity in real time. He also uses risk systems and reporting provided by the prime broker and reviews trade reconciliations shadowed by his team (Jennifer and Aaron).*

Variable:	Leverage (Grade 1)
Definition:	Amount and use of leverage.
Score:	*4 out of 5*
Commentary:	*Fund's gross exposure typically in the 140% to 190% range. The OM states that leverage can go as high as 250% gross, but the manager has never exceeded 200%. Leverage is provided by the prime broker. FCM's leverage is in line with other equity long/short funds in its peer group. When the market declined in 2008, FCM took down leverage as opportunities on the long side of the book became less attractive.*

Variable:	Limits (Grade 1)
Definition:	Analysis of risk limits in place. Appropriate to strategy? Consistently applied? Applied to exposures and hedging activity.
Score:	*2 out of 5*
Commentary:	*The fund has position limits for both longs (10%) and shorts (5%). There are no sector or industry limits (this may lead to additional volatility at times). FCM employs a soft stop for short positions (20% loss) and does not have any stops in place for long positions. Their stock ranking model has done a good job of assisting them in weighting individual stocks and reducing exposure at opportune times.*

Variable:	Power (Grade 1)
Definition:	Is risk manager (team) independent? What authority/ power do they have (i.e., can they take off risk)?
Score:	*0 out of 5*
Commentary:	*The risk manager does not have any authority to reduce risk. Bill Hobson, COO, can only suggest to the PM and trader that they take off positions if he finds any issues.*

Variable:	Process (Grade 1)
Definition:	Efficient and effective use of people and systems.
Score:	*3 out of 5*

Commentary:	*Risk manager can review portfolio in real time (internal portfolio system—Excel based) and can use the prime broker's risk system to review portfolio risks (T + 1).*
Variable:	Systems (Grade 1)
Definition:	Proprietary and third-party systems. How manually intensive vs. automated?
Score:	*3 out of 5*
Commentary:	*Internal system is Microsoft Excel based (with real-time price feeds from Bloomberg). They also use the prime broker's risk system and reporting, which is sufficient for their needs (and industry standard).*
Variable:	Concentration (Grade 2)
Definition:	Position, sector, industry, theme, geography, trade. Analysis of current portfolio.
Score:	*1 out of 5*
Commentary:	*Highly concentrated by sector (more than 75% in technology and services). Largest long position in portfolio currently is 7%; largest short position is 3.2%.*
Variable:	Professional Turnover (Grade 2)
Definition:	Evaluation of professionals that have left the risk team.
Score:	*5 out of 5*
Commentary:	*No turnover (Bill Hobson is the only person who tracks risk separately from the investment group).*
Variable:	Quantitative (Grade 2)
Definition:	Analysis of quantitatively derived risk assessment (VaR, stress testing, scenario analysis, factor analysis, etc.).
Score:	*3 out of 5*
Commentary:	*Latest VaR analysis (provided by the prime broker) indicates a VaR of −3% for one day (95% confidence) and −10% for one month (95% confidence). Factor analysis indicates that the fund is driven by market and size factors (which makes sense) and stress testing indicates strong relative performance in both up and down market events*

In Table 12.3, we can see that there are nine variables (six with a grade 1 and three with a grade 2) in the risk section. The total scaled score (grade multiplied by the score for each variable) is 60 points out of a possible 120 points. This results in a percentage score of 50 percent (60/120).

Performance Variables

Variable:	Absolute Performance (Grade 3)
Definition:	Historical annualized performance.
Score:	*4 out of 5*
Commentary:	*Strong performance (+8.2% over the five years from Dec-06 to Nov-11). No down calendar years over that time frame.*

Variable:	Relative Performance—Indexes (Grade 3)
Definition:	Historical annualized performance relative to appropriate indexes.
Score:	*5 out of 5*
Commentary:	*Significant outperformance relative to long only (Russell 2000) and long/short (HFRI Equity Hedge). FCM +8.2% since inception vs. −1.5% for the Russell 2000 and 1.0% for the HFRI Equity Hedge.*

Variable:	Relative Performance—Peers (Grade 3)
Definition:	Historical annualized performance relative to appropriate peer group.
Score:	*5 out of 5*
Commentary:	*FCM has performed consistently in the first quartile among its peer group in most periods.*

Variable:	Volatility (Grade 3)
Definition:	Historical standard deviation; downside deviation. Sharpe ratio.
Score:	*5 out of 5*
Commentary:	*FCM exhibited one of the lowest levels of total volatility (7.7% annualized standard deviation) since its inception relative to the peer group. Sharpe ratio was among the highest in the peer group (high return and low volatility combined). Other quantitative measures of volatility are at or near the top of the peer group.*

Variable:	Drawdown (Grade 3)
Definition:	Largest historical drawdown. Sortino ratio.
Score:	*5 out of 5*
Commentary:	*One of the best maximum drawdown returns among the equity long/short peer group (−11.5% vs. an average drawdown in the group of −24.5%). FCM's recovery (8 months) was among the quickest in the peer group. Sortino ratio (0% MAR) since inception was the highest in the peer group (2.05)*

Variable: Correlation (Grade 3)
Definition: Historical correlation and beta to market and peer group.
Score: *4 out of 5*
Commentary: *FCM is correlated to other long/short funds, but at 0.38*
                  its correlation is among the lowest in the group. FCM's
                  beta to the Russell 2000 was 0.12 (among the lowest in
                  the peer group).

In Table 12.4, we can see that there are six variables (all grade 3) in the performance section. The total scaled score (grade multiplied by the score for each variable) is 28 points out of a possible 30 points. This results in a percentage score of 93 percent (28/30).

PUTTING IT ALL TOGETHER

Now that we have reviewed a summary of the model's four sections, we can put them together to calculate a total model score for the hedge fund. Table 12.5 lists the scores for each component as well as the combined score (which is simply based on the total points scored divided by the maximum potential points). FCM's total score was 380 out of a possible 510 points (assuming a perfect score of 5 for each variable). This translates to a 75 percentage score overall.

Now that we have calculated the total model score for FCM, we can compare the component and total score to other hedge funds in our portfolio or to others that we are currently reviewing. Table 12.6 compares FCM's scores to those of the other four hedge funds that we identified earlier in the book. FCM's total score is the highest in the group, but it does lag in two of the categories. When ranked by operations variables, FCM ranks second behind fund 1. When ranked by risk, FCM ranks in fourth place out of five

TABLE 12.5 Scoring Model—Total Score

Category	Points Scored	Possible Maximum	Percentage Grade
Investment	106	140	76
Operations	186	220	85
Risk	60	120	50
Performance	28	30	93
Total Score	380	510	75%

TABLE 12.6   Scoring Model—FCM vs. Peers

	Percent Grade				
Category	FCM	Fund 1	Fund 2	Fund 3	Fund 4
Investment	76	70	65	74	55
Operations	85	88	68	75	75
Risk	50	40	55	60	62
Performance	93	45	50	88	50
Total Score	75	69	63	72	65

(behind funds 4, 3, and 2). When we compare these scores to all of the other long/short equity funds in our portfolio and that we have reviewed over time, we can then put the total as well as the component scores in better perspective. In the absence of this broad comparison, it is clear that FCM's risk score is a laggard.

Once we score a given hedge fund in the model, we can update the score on a regular basis (monthly or quarterly) so that we can track the component and total scores over time. Figure 12.1 focuses on FCM's component scores over the previous two years (quarterly updates). It indicates that the manager's score has increased over the time reviewed, with the modest increases in the overall score coming from the investment and operations categories (risk and performance-related categories stayed roughly the same over the period).

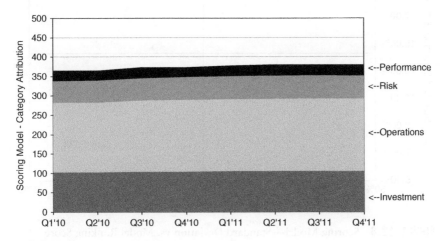

FIGURE 12.1   Scoring Model—FCM's Historical Scores

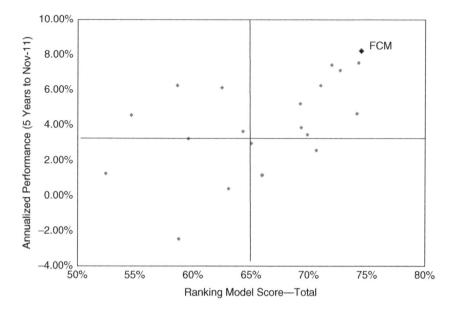

FIGURE 12.2 Scoring Model—Return vs. Model Ranking Score Graph

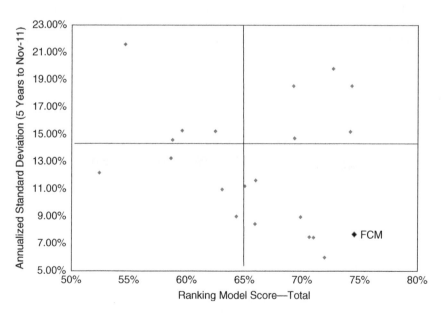

FIGURE 12.3 Scoring Model—Standard Deviation vs. Model Ranking Score Graph

Last, we can combine the hedge fund model scores with any number of other statistics. Figure 12.2 graphs annualized performance for the five years ended Nov-11 and the total hedge fund manager's latest scores from the scoring model. This universe of names includes the full equity long/short peer universe. It gives us the ability to measure FCM's performance vs. model ranking and also gives us the ability to spot trends. FCM appears in the upper right-hand corner of the chart, which translates to strong performance and a high model score. Figure 12.3 compares the peer universe's annualized standard deviation to the same total hedge fund model ranking score. Once again, FCM compares favorably (it has one of the lowest annualized standard deviation figures in the group), putting it in the lower right-hand corner of the chart).

About the Author

FRANK J. TRAVERS, CFA

Frank has over two decades of experience analyzing traditional long-only, private equity, and hedge fund strategies. He is currently a portfolio manager at Larch Lane Advisors. Previously he was the Director of Research at First Peninsula Capital and a Portfolio Manager at Pine Street Advisors and CIC Group. Additionally, he held positions as the Director of Due Diligence at CIBC World Markets, Associate Director of International Equity Research at Evaluation Associates, and Senior Analyst positions at Morgan Stanley Asset Management and RCB Trust. Frank is also the author of *Investment Manager Analysis: A Comprehensive Guide to Portfolio Selection, Monitoring and Optimization*. He received his BS in Finance from St. John's University and his MBA from Fordham University.

Index

Absolute return measures
  histogram, 146
  information ratio, 148–149
  MAR and Calmar ratios,
    149–150
  Omega ratio, 153–154
  Sharpe ratio, 147–148
  Sortino ratio, 152–153
  Sterling ratio, 150–152
Absolute returns, 7
Absolute risk measure, 154–164
  downside deviation, 156
  drawdown analysis, 161–163
  gain/loss ratio, 163–164
  kurtosis, 159–161
  kurtosis calculation interpretation,
    160–161
  semideviation, 157
  skewness, 157–159
  skewness calculation interpretation,
    158–159
  standard deviation, 154–155
Accounting firms, 64. See also
  Auditor(s)
Action plan, 140–143, 171, 196
Active activism, 38
Activist strategies, 37–38
Administration services, 307
Administrator services, 307
Administrators
  auditors, 275–276
  custodian, 280
  information technology, 278–279
  insurance, 280
  legal, 279–280
  primary administrative services,
    271–275

prime brokers/brokerages, 276–277
  trade life cycle, 280
Advance preparation, 208
Affiliated broker-dealers, 261
Allocations to hedge funds
  capital use efficiency, 51–52
  dispersion, 49–50
  diversification correlation, 45–49
  down market protection, 50
  return enhancement, 43–45
Allocators, 63
Alpha, 164, 165
Alpha investing, 7
Alternative Investment Management
  Association (AIMA), 80
Analysis. See also Portfolio analysis;
    Quantitative analysis
  2007, 186
  2008, 186–187
  2009, 187–188
  2010, 188–189
  2011, 189
  attribution, 174–186
  drawdown, 161–163
  factor decomposition, 330–333
  historical portfolio, 206–209
  legal, 59
  liquidity, 202–205, 296–297
  long portfolio sector, 209–211
  operational, 59
  peer, 358
  peer group, 168–171
  of performance, 173–174
  risk measures, 313, 314
  sector analysis, 194–196
  13F historical portfolio, 211, 212
  trade, 213–215

Analysis (*Continued*)
  up/down scenario, 329
  VaR, 317, 318, 319, 320, 321
Anti-money laundering (AML) policy,
  92
Apportioning, 358
Asset liquidity risks, 310
Assets under management (AUM),
  299–300
Attribution, 358
Attribution analysis
  about, 174–180
  analysis, 180–186
Audit firms, 274–275
Auditor(s), 64, 98–99, 275–276
Average long exposure, 180

Back checking, 89, 101
Background checks, 352–353
Barclay Hedge, 26
Barometers, 7
Base (management) fees, 295
Basis risks, 310
Bayou Group, 260
Bayou Securities, 260
Benjamin Graham Joint Account, 16
Beta, 164–165
Beta breakout, 202
Board of directors, 290–291
Body language, 222
Bottom up shop, 227, 233, 234
Bottom-up investing, 247
Buffet, Warren, 14
Business continuity, 92, 284–285
Business risks, 310

Calmar ratio, 150
Capco paper, 264
Capco Research, 263
Capital introduction, 63
Capital Market Risk Advisers (CMRA),
  313
Capital use efficiency, 51–52
Case Study Bayou Fund, 259–261
Cash management and controls,
  282–283

Cash procedures, 306
Cell phone use, 122
CFO experience, 270
Checks and balances, 252
Clawback provisions, 296
Client concentration risks, 310
Client relationship management
  (CRM), 278
Code of ethics, 287–288
"Coming of Age: Global Hedge Fund
  Surve 2011" (Ernst &Young),
  264, 265
Commodities trading advisor (CTA),
  40–42, 45, 49
Commodity risks, 310
Company information, 81–82
Compliance, 90–91, 308
Compliance manual, 287
Conditional value at risk (CVaR), 316,
  318
Consistency test, 219
Consultants, 227
Contracting references, 343–346
Contrarian investing, 5
Convertible bond arbitrage, 34–36
Convertible bonds, 35
Conviction value, 245, 251
Cooperman, Leon, 260
Correlation, 165, 166–167
Correlation risks, 310
Correlation table, 47, 75
Correlation(s), 245, 246, 251
  diversification, 45–49
  five year, 48
  long-term average, 48
Counterparty risks, 310
Credit risks, 311
Currency risks, 311
Custodial services, 276–277
Custodian, 98, 280

Data collection, initial, 80–105
  13 F analysis, 116–118
  about, 77
  data collection, 78–80

due diligence questionnaire (DDQ), 80

further analysis, 108–116

hedge fund journal, 119

other materials, 106–107

past performance, 77–78

research, 107

Data overview, 99–100

Data series, 6

Database and data analysis companies, 62–63

Database screening process, 68

Database search, 67

Databases, 60

Days to cover ratio, 200

Days to liquidate position, 204

Decile distribution, 168

Defined risk, 309–310

Derivatives risks, 311

Directional strategies, 40–42

Directors and officer liability (D&A), 280

Disaster recovery, 285–286

Disaster recovery/business continuity, 307

Dispersion, 49–50

Distressed strategies, 39–40

Diversification, 105

Diversification correlation, 45–49

Diversified Macro, 49

Documents to request, 267, 269

Dojima Rice Exchange, 4

Dollar-neutral investing, 7

Dollar-neutral portfolio, 36–37

Down market protection, 50

Downside deviation, 156

Downside risks, 311

Drawdown analysis, 161–163

Due diligence, negative results, 262–263

Due diligence process
 about, 57
 areas of focus, 57–60
 components of, 218
 databases, 60
 elements of, 58

fund terms, 59

initial thoughts, 70–75

manager sourcing, 60

performance-based fields, 62

process flowchart, 61

qualitative fields, 62

quantitative analysis, 59

regression-based fields, 62

service providers, 63–67

summary, 67–69

time/work distribution, 218

Due diligence questionnaire (DDQ), 80

Due diligence questionnaire (DDQ) sample, 81–100
 anti-money laundering (AML) policy, 92
 auditor, 98–99
 business continuity, 92
 company information, 81–82
 compliance, 90–91
 custodian, 98
 data overview, 99–100
 diversification, 105
 execution and trading, 89–90
 fees, 93
 fund administration, 95–96
 fund assets, 99–100
 fund capacity, 100
 fund directors, 95
 fund information/details, 92–93
 fund performance, 101
 historical redemptions, 100
 insurance, 92
 internal investment, 101
 investment and portfolio risk leverage, 105
 investment research, 89
 investment strategy, 102–104
 investors, 101
 legal, 91, 99
 liquidity, 94, 105
 miscellaneous, 101–102
 operational risk, 87–88
 operational risk for outsourced functions, 88–89
 organization, 82–85

Due diligence questionnaire (DDQ)
  sample (*Continued*)
  outsourced controls, 105
  ownership, 82
  portfolio construction, 104–105
  prime brokers/brokerages, 97–98
  references, 85
  risk management, 86–87
  template, 81
  third-party marketers, 99
  track record, 85–86
  valuation, 96
Due diligence team, 223

Earnings growth last 12 months
  (12 month EG), 198–199
Edge (advantage), 221–222, 248
Employees biography, 342–343
Equity market neutral strategy, 36
Equity-oriented strategies, 32–34
Ernst &Young, 264
Errors and omissions (E&O), 280
Evader references, 347
Event driven, 37–40
Event-driven strategies, 37
Excess skewness, 159
Execution and trading, 89–90
Exposure, gross, 238
Exposure and attribution report,
  175–177
Exposure-based risk, 314
Exposure-management hedging, 30

Facebook, 343
Factor decomposition analysis,
  330–333
Failure to meet minimum standards,
  262–263
Falsified pedigree, 261
Fat-tailed curve, 160
Fee options, 71
Fee schedule, 16
Fees, 30, 93
  other, 296
Fictional Capital Management,
  80–105

Fictional Capital Management (FCM),
  78
Fictional Capital Management (FCM)
  vs. historical portfolio analysis, 209
Fictional onsite interviews
  interview transcript, 229–248
  meeting notes, 246–249
Fidelity Trade Fund, 18
Financial analysis, 59
Financial exposure chart, 114
Firm overview, 81
Fixed income arbitrage, 36
Focus areas
  financial analysis, 59
  fund terms, 58–59
  legal analysis, 59
  operational analysis, 59
  portfolio analysis, 59
  qualitative analysis, 59
  quantitative analysis, 58
  references and background checks, 60
  risk analysis, 59
  sourcing and screening, 57
Fortune magazine, 17
*The Fountain of Gold, The Three
  Monkey Record of Money*
  (Homma), 5
Fraud, 260–261, 291, 311, 312, 334
Fund administration, 95–96
Fund assets, 99–100
Fund capacity, 100
Fund comparisons, 70–71
Fund directors, 95
Fund Five, 78
Fund information/details, 92–93
Fund performance, 101
Fund terms, 58–59
Fundamental analysis, 189–193
Fund-level gate, 298
Funds dispersion, 261
Further analysis, 108–116

Gain/loss ratio, 163–164
Gates, 298
General partner liability, 280
Geography risks, 311

Global macro management, 40–41
Google, 66–67, 345
Google alert, 342–343
Google Alerts, 66
Google Search, 66, 341
Graham, Benjamin, 14–17, 19
Graham-Newman Corporation, 16
Grahar Corporation, 15
Graphical depiction of hedge fund risks, 312–314
Gross exposure, 20, 170, 238
Groupthink, 220
Guggenheim Exploration Company, 14–15
Gut feelings, 223

Hard lockups, 297, 327
"Hard Times Come to Hedge Funds" (Loomis), 2
Harris, Lou, 15–16
Hedge fund
  candidates, 69
  database and data analysis companies, 62–63
  failures, 263
  journal, 118, 119
  liquidity of, 299
  operational issues, 263
Hedge fund asset class
  allocations to hedge funds, 43–52
  definition, 29–31
  hedge fund size and age performance impact, 52–54
  strategies, 32–43
  structure, 31–32
Hedge fund history
  about, 3
  academic work, 5–14
  innovator, 17–26
  inventors of, 4
  legend regarding, 14–17
  samurai connection, 4–5
Hedge fund information, 65–66
Hedge Fund Research, Inc., 44
Hedge fund scoring model, 358–374
  investment variables, 360–367

list of markets, 358–359
operational variables, 367–370
performance variables, 373–374
Hedge fund scoring model and decision making
  about, 357–358
  hedge fund scoring model, 358–374
  putting it all together, 374–377
Hedge funds
  asset growth, 24
  industry life-cycle, 25
  numbers of, 24
  pros and cons of investing in, 44
  strategy composition, 26
"The Hedge Funds on Paper" (Larsen), 13
"Hedge Principle" (Karsten), 12
Hedgefund.net, 273
HFRI Equity Hedge Index, 45, 149, 161, 166, 180
HFRI Equity Hedge Indexes, 108, 149
HFRI Hedge Fund Composite Index, 44, 45, 50, 51
HFRI Macro Index, 49
HFRI Systematic, 49
High water mark, 295
High-yield strategies, 39–40
Histogram, 146
Historical assets under management, 115
Historical portfolio analysis, 206–209
Historical redemptions, 100
Honma, Munehisa, 4–5
Hurdle rate, 296

Illiquid investments, 298
Incentive performance fees, 295–296
Independent administrator, 271
Independent auditors, 260
Independent board of directors, 260
Independent oversight, 291
Industry-specific indicators, 6
Information ratio, 148–149
Information request, 78–80
Information technology, 278–279
Initial call on meeting, 121–122

Initial thoughts
   correlation table, 75
   fund comparisons, 70–71
   risk/return charts, 72
   rolling correlation chart, 73
   UpDown cumulative performance
     comparisons, 74
Innovations, 14
Insurance, 92, 280
The Intelligent Investor (Graham), 14
Interest rates risks, 311
Internal capital, 299
Internal investment, 101
Internal policies. *See* Policy
Internal pricing and valuation
   committee, 289
Internet and social media, 341–343
Interview, initial
   basic tips, 122–123
   initial call on meeting, 121–122
   interview transcript, 124–139
   meeting notes, 139–143
   phone interviews, 122–139
Interview questions, 331–333
Interview transcript, 124–139,
   229–248
Interview with operational staff,
   301–308
   administration services, 307
   cash procedures, 306
   compliance, 308
   disaster recovery/business continuity,
     307
   pricing and valuation, 306–307
   trading, 305–306
Interviews, onsite
   about, 217–219
   fictional, 228–257
   meeting notes, 224, 226–228
   with more than one person at a time,
     222–2133
   note taking, 224–225
   one-on-one meetings, 219–222
   onsite meeting strategies, 219
   perspectives, 223–224
   question list, 226–227

Investigative firms, 352
Investment and portfolio risk leverage,
   105
Investment books, 5
Investment research, 89
Investment strategy, 102–104
Investment variables, 360–367
Investor communication, 261
Investors, 101
iPad, 225
Israel, Samuel, III, 259, 260, 261

Japanese candle chart patterns, 5
Jones, Alfred Winslow, 2, 19–21
   dollar-neutral portfolio, 36–37
   innovations, 23
"The Jones Nobody Keeps Up With"
   (Loomis), 17

Karsten, Karl, 5–8, 10–13, 19, 36–37
Karsten Statistical Laboratory, 5
Key pension risks, 311
Key-person clause, 83
Kurtosis, 52, 159–161
Kurtosis calculation interpretation,
   160–161

Lagging indicators, 7
Leading indicators, 7
Legal, 91, 99, 279–280
Legal analysis, 59
Leptokurtic curve, 160
Leverage, 10, 30, 227
Leverage risks, 311
Liability insurance, 280
"Life, Liberty and Property" (Jones), 19
LinkedIn, 342–343
Liquidation environment, 327
Liquidity
   analysis of, 296–297, 301, 327
   current status, 105
   guidelines, 240
   of hedge fund, 299
   management, 94
   measure of, 87
   mismatch risks, 311

monitoring, 133
redemption, 104
stated vs. projected, 204
Liquidity analysis, 202–205, 296–297
Liquidity profile, 226
Liquidity provisions, 30
Lockout period, 297
Lockups, 297
Long and short books
  analysis of, 206
  attribution, 181–185
  difference between, 20, 190
  exposure to, 174, 196, 210
  historical performance, 180–189
  liquidity and, 206, 362
  mismatch, 207, 210
  portfolio returns, 178
Long attribution, 178, 179, 180
Long based strategies, 32–33
Long portfolio attribution, 180
Long portfolio market capitalization,
  historical, 211–213
Long portfolio sector analysis,
  historical, 209–211
Long return, 170
Loomis, Carol, 3, 17–18
Low correlation, 31

Macro, 45
Macro call, 127–128
Macro environment, 234, 235–236
Macro hedge fund, 270
Manager sourcing, 60
MAR and Calmar ratios, 149–150
MAR ratio, 150
Marino, Daniel, 259, 260, 261
Market cap breakdown, 142
Market cap breakout, 196–197
Market capitalization, 196–197
Market capitalization exposure, 211
Market indicators, 6
Market risks, 311
Market sectors, 8
Markets list, 358–359
Marquez, James, 260
Mean excess loss, 316

Media, 64, 66
Media sources, 65–66
Meeting notes
  action plan, 140–143
  follow-up list, 256–257
  individuals, 249–256
  key points/questions, 139–140
  location, 249
  manager interview, 139–143
  on position and themes, 215
  usefulness of, 224–225, 246–249
Meltdown, 324
Meltdown scenario, 326
Meltdown security, 325, 326
Meltup, 324
Meltup scenario, 328
Merger arbitrage, 38
Microcaps, 197
Minimum acceptable return (MAR),
  149, 153, 156
Modeling, 129
  methods, 7
  risks, 311
  scores, 374
  variable weighting, 359–360
Modigliani, Franco, 147
Modigliani, Leah, 147
Monthly letters and quarterly reports,
  293
Monthly/quarterly letters, 106
Motors, market sector, 9
Multiple manger concept, 20
Multiple yellow dogs, 263
Multiple-person meetings, 222–223
Multiprime model, 277
Multi-strategy, 42

NASD, 260
Negative reference, 346
Negative skewness, 158
Net asset valuation (NAV), 271
Net exposure, 20, 170
Newman, Jerry, 16
Nondisclosure agreement (NDA), 139,
  240
Normal distribution, 160

Normalizing, 193
Note taking, 224–225
Note-Taking HD app, 225
Notional exposure, 174

Observations, 323–327
Offlist reference, 340–341
Oils, market sector, 9
Omega Advisors, 261
Omega ratio, 153–154
One-day stress test, 323
One-day VaR analysis, 317, 318, 319, 320
One-month VaR analysis, 320, 321
One-on-one meetings, 219–222
Onlist reference, 340–341
Onsite meeting strategies, 219
Onsite meetings
  general questions, 221
  number of attendees, 220
  sequence of, 220–221
  work prior to, 217
Operational analysis, 59
Operational categories, 5 P's, 268
Operational documents, 271
Operational due diligence (OpDD), 256, 259–308
  case study Bayou Fund, 259–261
  categorization, 267–300
  definition, 261–263
  importance of, 263–269
  interview with operational staff, 301–308
  operational issues, 266–267
  tips, 300–301
Operational due diligence (OpDD), categorization of
  board of directors, 290–291
  code of ethics, 287–288
  compliance manual, 287
  documents to request, 267, 269
  people, 269–271
  personal trading, 292
  policy, 286–294
  process, 281–286
  product, 294–300

providers, 271–280
transparency and reporting, 292–294
valuation policy, 288–290
Operational risk, 87–88, 311, 314
  for outsourced functions, 88–89
Operational variables, 367–370
Operations group, 281
Opinions, 312
Opportunistic mandates, 30
Organization, 82–85
Outlier positions, 228
Outsourced controls, 105
Overshadowing, 220
Ownership, 82

Paper portfolio
  annual performance, 11
  monthly performance, 10
  weekly performance, 11
Partners, 349
Passive activism, rumor-trage, 39
Past performance, 77–78, 359
P/E ratio, 207
P/E to growth (PEG) ratio, 207
Peer analysis, 358
Peer group analysis, 168–171
Peer group comparison, 205–206
PEG ratio (P/E to growth), 207
People, 269–271
Percentile ranking, 168, 170
Performance, 292–293
Performance analysis, goals of, 173–174
Performance based risk, 314
Performance comparisons, 46
  monthly chart, 109–111
Performance fee, 16
Performance measures, 146
Performance variables, 373–374
Performance-based fields, 62
Personal reference types, 346–348
Personal trading, 292
Perspectives, 223–224
Pertrac, 52
P/FC ratio, 207
P/FCF distribution, 198

Phone interviews, 122–139
Plinius the Elder, 309
Policy, 286–294
Politicians' references, 347
Portfolio analysis, 59
    about, 173–174
    advance preparation, 208
    attribution analysis, 174–189
    beta breakout, 202
    earnings growth last 12 months (12 month EG), 198–199
    evaluating portfolio data, 193–215
    fundamental analysis, 189–193
    historical portfolio analysis, 206–209
    liquidity analysis, 202–205
    long portfolio market capitalization, historical, 211–213
    long portfolio sector analysis, historical, 209–211
    market cap breakout, 196–197
    peer group comparison, 205–206
    price/earnings (P/E) breakout, 197–198
    price/free cash flow (P/FCF) breakout, 198
    return on equity (ROE) breakout, 200–201
    short ratio breakout, 200
    trade analysis, 213–215
Portfolio concentrations, 194
Portfolio construction, 104–105
Portfolio data evaluation, 193–215
Portfolio liquidity, 202, 213, 250
Portfolio management system, internal, 334
Portfolio managers, 20
Portfolio stress tests, 322
Portfolio theories, 247
Portfolio transparency, 189
Portfolio value at risk (VaR), 317
Position concentration risks, 311
Position level transparency, 217
Position-based factor decomposition, 330
Position-level information, 256–257

Position-level transparency, 138–139, 190
Positive skewness, 158
Predicted fund return, 164
Price discovery, 4
Price/earnings (P/E) breakout, 197–198
Price/earnings (P/E) ratio, 207
Price/free cash flow (P/FCF) breakout, 198
Pricing and valuation, 306–307
Pricing risks, 312
Primary administrative services, 272–275
Prime brokers/brokerages, 63–64, 97–98, 276–277, 334
Pro forma analysis, 114
Pro forma calculation, 115
Problematic references
    personal reference types, 346–348
    questions to ask, 348–349
    references to check, 349–350
Process
    business continuity, 284–285
    cash management and controls, 282–283
    disaster recovery, 285–286
    shadow reconciliation, 283–284
    trade life cycle, 281
Process flowchart, 61
Product
    about, 294–295
    assets under management (AUM), 299–300
    base (management) fees, 295
    gates, 298
    incentive performance fees, 295–296
    lockups, 297
    other fees, 296
    side pockets, 298–299
    subscriptions/redemptions, 296–297
Projected days to liquidate, 203
Providers
    administrators, 271–275
    custodian, 280
    information technology, 278–279
    insurance, 280

Providers (*Continued*)
  legal, 279–280
  prime brokers/brokerages, 276–277
Public filings, 190

Qualitative analysis, 59
Qualitative assessments, 312
Qualitative fields, 62
Quantitative analysis
  about, 145–146
  absolute return measures, 146–154
  absolute risk measure, 154–164
  peer group analysis, 168–171
  performance measures, 146
  regression-based strategies,
    164–168
  screening statistics, 58
Quantitative hedge funds, 293
Quantitative review, 171
Quartile distribution, 168, 169, 170
Question list, 226–227
Questions to ask, 348–349

Rails, market sector, 8
Red flags, 263, 265
Redemption, 296, 298, 300
Reference and background checks
  about, 339–340
  background checks, 352–353
  basic due diligence, 60
  contracting references, 343–346
  internet and social media, 341–343
  problematic references, 346–349
  reference call summary, 353–355
  reference checker selection, 344–346
  references, onlist and offlist, 340–341
Reference call summary, 353–355
Reference checks, 256
Reference list, 143
Reference questioner, 345–346
Reference scorecard, 351
References
  contact information, 85
  evader, 347
  negative, 347–348
  onlist and offlist, 340–341

politicians, 347
stonewaller, 346
References to check, 349–350
Regression-based fields, 62
Regression-based strategies
  alpha, 165
  beta, 164–165
  correlation, 166–167
  Treynor ratio, 167–168
  T-stat, 165–166
Regulatory issues and litigation, 260
Regulatory risks, 312
Relative value, 34–37
Relative value trade, 15
Relative velocity, 21
Reputation risks, 312
Research, 107
Return enhancement, 43–45
Return objective, 30
Return on equity (ROE) breakout,
  200–201
Reversion to the mean, 5
Richmond Fairfield Associates, 260
Risk aggregators, 294
Risk analysis, 59
Risk assessment, 256
Risk due diligence
  about, 309–312, 314–315
  factor decomposition analysis,
    330–333
  graphical depiction of hedge fund
    risks, 312–314
  risk concerns, 313
  risk manager interview, 333–337
  value at risk (Var), 316–322
Risk governance survey, 315
Risk management, 86–87, 265
Risk management policy, 336
Risk manager, 136–137, 335
Risk manager interview, 333–337
Risk measures, 154–164, 314
Risk measures analysis, 313, 314
Risk reports, 294, 335
Risk survey, 312
Risk/return charts, 71, 72
Risk/return graph, 44

ROE distribution, 201
Rolling correlation chart, 71, 73
Rolling lockup, 297
Russell 2000 Index, 80, 147, 155, 159, 166, 180, 324, 325, 329

S&P 500 Index (S&P 500), 50, 70, 71, 108, 146, 147, 149, 180
Scaled weight, 181
Scientific Forecasting (Karsten), 5
Scoring model
   comparison with peers, 375
   historical scores, 375
   investment variables, 363, 364, 365, 366
   return vs. model ranking, 376
   return vs. model ranking score, 376
"Secret sauce," 293
Sector analysis, 194–196
Sector attribution, 195
Sector breakdown, 142
Sector breakout
   about, 193
   action plan, 196
   sector analysis, 194–196
   sector breakout, 193–196
Sector concentration, 231–232, 251
Securities and Exchange Commission (SEC), 116
Security Analysis (Graham), 14
Sell discipline, 242, 244
Sell-side research, 89
Semideviation, 157
Service providers
   auditors/accounting firms, 64
   Google, 66–67
   media, 64, 65, 66
   prime brokers/brokerages, 63–64
   software vendors/IT firms, 64
Shadow (phantom) equity, 131
Shadow reconciliation, 283–284
Sharpe, William, 21
Sharpe ratio, 70, 71, 147–148
Short attribution, 179
Short based strategies, 33–34

Short book. *See also* Long and short books
   analysis of, 174
   elements of, 134
   employment of, 239
   historical exposures, 188
   portfolio attribution, 180, 186, 187, 188
   return approximation, 179
   as separate portfolio, 251
   turnover, 127
   use of, 32
Short portfolio attribution, 180
Short ratio, 207
Short ratio breakout, 200
Short ratio distribution, 200
Shorting vs. swap agreements, 206–207
Side pockets, 298–299
Skewness, 52, 157–159
Skewness calculation interpretation, 158–159
Skin in the game, 30, 301
Small caps, 202
Soft dollars, 90, 287
Soft lock, 70, 71
Soft lockups, 297
Software. *See* Information Technology
Software vendors/IT firms, 64
Sortino, Frank, 152
Sortino ratio, 152–153
Sourcing and screening, 57
Standard deviation, 154–155
Stated vs. projected liquidity, 204
Steels, market sector, 9
Sterling ratio, 150–152
Stock outliers, 327–329
Stock ranking model, 249, 250
Stock ranking system, 244–245
Stonewaller references, 346
Stop loss, 226, 243
Stop-loss limits, 86
Stop-loss policy, 242
Stores, market sector, 9
Strategies
   directional strategies, 40–42
   equity-oriented strategies, 32–34

Strategies (*Continued*)
  event driven, 37–40
  multi-strategy, 42
  relative value, 34–37
Stress test(s), 240, 312, 332, 338, 372
Stress tests and scenario
  about, 322–323
  observations, 323–327
  stock outliers, 327–329
Subscriptions/redemptions, 296–297
Systematic (CTA) Index, 49

Tail risks, 312
Tail VaR, 316
Tassin, Algernon, 15
Temporary reports, 273
Thin-tailed curve, 160
Third-party marketers, 99
13F analysis, 116–118, 226
13F filings, 141, 190
13F historical portfolio analysis, 211,
  212
13F long portfolio, 192
13F portfolio, 112, 117, 198, 200, 201,
  203, 204, 317, 318, 319, 320, 321,
  323, 325, 326, 328, 329, 330
13F reports, 208, 210
13F weight, 181
Tips, 300–301
Top-down factors, 252
Track record, 85–86
Tracking, 358
Trade analysis, 213–215
Trade life cycle, 280, 281
Trading, 305–306
Trading group, 281
Transparency, 30–31, 299
  and reporting, 292–294
  risks, 312

Treynor ratio, 167–168
T-stat, 165–166
Twitter, 343
"2Q 2011 HFFN Hedge Fund
  Administration Survey"
  (Hedgefund.net), 273
Types of risks, 310–312

"Understanding and Mitigating
  Operational Risk in Hedge Fund
  Investments" (Capco Research),
  263
Up/down chart, 113
Up/down cumulative performance
  comparisons, 74
Up/down ratio, 329
Up/down scenario analysis, 329
U.S. Securities and Exchange
  Commission (SEC), 190
Utilities market sector, 8

Valuation(s), 96, 246
  policy, 288–290
Value at risk (Var)
  about, 316
  additional information, 318–322
  percentage, 318
  problems with, 316–318
Value investing, 14
VaR analysis
  one-day, 317, 318, 319, 320
  one-month, 320, 321
Variable equity long/short strategies,
  32
Variable list, 359–360
Velocity calculations, 21

Wavering hedge fund, 290
Websites, 64, 66, 190–193, 343

Printed and bound by CPI Group (UK) Ltd, Croydon, CR0 4YY

23/04/2025

14661008-0004